THE NEW MIDDLE AGES

BONNIE WHEELER, *Series Editor*

The New Middle Ages is a series dedicated to pluridisciplinary studies of medieval cultures, with particular emphasis on recuperating women's history and on feminist and gender analyses. This peer-reviewed series includes both scholarly monographs and essay collections.

PUBLISHED BY PALGRAVE:

Women in the Medieval Islamic World: Power, Patronage, and Piety
edited by Gavin R. G. Hambly

The Ethics of Nature in the Middle Ages: On Boccaccio's Poetaphysics
by Gregory B. Stone

Presence and Presentation: Women in the Chinese Literati Tradition
edited by Sherry J. Mou

The Lost Love Letters of Heloise and Abelard: Perceptions of Dialogue in Twelfth-Century France
by Constant J. Mews

Understanding Scholastic Thought with Foucault
by Philipp W. Rosemann

For Her Good Estate: The Life of Elizabeth de Burgh
by Frances A. Underhill

Constructions of Widowhood and Virginity in the Middle Ages
edited by Cindy L. Carlson and Angela Jane Weisl

Motherhood and Mothering in Anglo-Saxon England
by Mary Dockray-Miller

Listening to Heloise: The Voice of a Twelfth-Century Woman
edited by Bonnie Wheeler

The Postcolonial Middle Ages
edited by Jeffrey Jerome Cohen

Chaucer's Pardoner *and Gender Theory: Bodies of Discourse*
by Robert S. Sturges

Crossing the Bridge: Comparative Essays on Medieval European and Heian Japanese Women Writers
edited by Barbara Stevenson and Cynthia Ho

Engaging Words: The Culture of Reading in the Later Middle Ages
by Laurel Amtower

Robes and Honor: The Medieval World of Investiture
edited by Stewart Gordon

Representing Rape in Medieval and Early Modern Literature
edited by Elizabeth Robertson and Christine M. Rose

Same Sex Love and Desire among Women in the Middle Ages
edited by Francesca Canadé Sautman and Pamela Sheingorn

Sight and Embodiment in the Middle Ages: Ocular Desires
by Suzannah Biernoff

Listen, Daughter: The Speculum Virginum *and the Formation of Religious Women in the Middle Ages*
edited by Constant J. Mews

Science, the Singular, and the Question of Theology
by Richard A. Lee Jr.

Gender in Debate from the Early Middle Ages to the Renaissance
edited by Thelma S. Fenster and Clare A. Lees

Malory's Morte D'Arthur*: Remaking Arthurian Tradition*
by Catherine Batt

The Vernacular Spirit: Essays on Medieval Religious Literature
edited by Renate Blumenfeld-Kosinski, Duncan Robertson, and Nancy Warren

Popular Piety and Art in the Late Middle Ages: Image Worship and Idolatry in England 1350–1500
by Kathleen Kamerick

Absent Narratives, Manuscript Textuality, and Literary Structure in Late Medieval England
by Elizabeth Scala

Creating Community with Food and Drink in Merovingian Gaul
by Bonnie Effros

Representations of Early Byzantine Empresses: Image and Empire
by Anne McClanan

Encountering Medieval Textiles and Dress: Objects, Texts, Images
edited by Désirée G. Koslin and Janet Snyder

Eleanor of Aquitaine: Lord and Lady
edited by Bonnie Wheeler and John Carmi Parsons

Isabel La Católica, Queen of Castile: Critical Essays
edited by David A. Boruchoff

Homoeroticism and Chivalry: Discourses of Male Same-Sex Desire in the Fourteenth Century
by Richard E. Zeikowitz

Portraits of Medieval Women: Family, Marriage, and Politics in England 1225–1350
by Linda E. Mitchell

Eloquent Virgins: From Thecla to Joan of Arc
by Maud Burnett McInerney

The Persistence of Medievalism: Narrative Adventures in Contemporary Culture
by Angela Jane Weisl

Capetian Women
edited by Kathleen D. Nolan

Joan of Arc and Spirituality
edited by Ann W. Astell and Bonnie Wheeler

The Texture of Society: Medieval Women in the Southern Low Countries
edited by Ellen E. Kittell and Mary A. Suydam

Charlemagne's Mustache: And Other Cultural Clusters of a Dark Age
by Paul Edward Dutton

Troubled Vision: Gender, Sexuality, and Sight in Medieval Text and Image
edited by Emma Campbell and Robert Mills

Queering Medieval Genres
by Tison Pugh

Sacred Place in Early Medieval Neoplatonism
by L. Michael Harrington

The Middle Ages at Work
edited by Kellie Robertson and Michael Uebel

Chaucer's Jobs
by David R. Carlson

Medievalism and Orientalism: Three Essays on Literature, Architecture and Cultural Identity
by John M. Ganim

Queer Love in the Middle Ages
by Anna Klosowska

Performing Women in the Middle Ages: Sex, Gender, and the Iberian Lyric
by Denise K. Filios

Necessary Conjunctions: The Social Self in Medieval England
by David Gary Shaw

Visual Culture and the German Middle Ages
edited by Kathryn Starkey and Horst Wenzel

Medieval Paradigms: Essays in Honor of Jeremy duQuesnay Adams, Volumes 1 and 2
edited by Stephanie Hayes-Healy

False Fables and Exemplary Truth in Later Middle English Literature
by Elizabeth Allen

Ecstatic Transformation: On the Uses of Alterity in the Middle Ages
by Michael Uebel

Sacred and Secular in Medieval and Early Modern Cultures: New Essays
edited by Lawrence Besserman

Tolkien's Modern Middle Ages
edited by Jane Chance and Alfred K. Siewers

Representing Righteous Heathens in Late Medieval England
by Frank Grady

Byzantine Dress: Representations of Secular Dress in Eighth- to Twelfth-Century Painting
by Jennifer L. Ball

The Laborer's Two Bodies: Labor and the "Work" of the Text in Medieval Britain, 1350–1500
by Kellie Robertson

The Dogaressa of Venice, 1250–1500: Wife and Icon
by Holly S. Hurlburt

Logic, Theology, and Poetry in Boethius, Abelard, and Alan of Lille: Words in the Absence of Things
by Eileen C. Sweeney

The Theology of Work: Peter Damian and the Medieval Religious Renewal Movement
by Patricia Ranft

On the Purification of Women: Churching in Northern France, 1100–1500
by Paula M. Rieder

Writers of the Reign of Henry II: Twelve Essays
edited by Ruth Kennedy and Simon Meecham-Jones

Lonesome Words: The Vocal Poetics of the Old English Lament and the African-American Blues Song
by M. G. McGeachy

Performing Piety: Musical Culture in Medieval English Nunneries
by Anne Bagnell Yardley

The Flight from Desire: Augustine and Ovid to Chaucer
by Robert R. Edwards

Mindful Spirit in Late Medieval Literature: Essays in Honor of Elizabeth D. Kirk
edited by Bonnie Wheeler

Medieval Fabrications: Dress, Textiles, Clothwork, and Other Cultural Imaginings
edited by E. Jane Burns

Was the Bayeux Tapestry Made in France? The Case for St. Florent of Saumur
by George Beech

Women, Power, and Religious Patronage in the Middle Ages
by Erin L. Jordan

Hybridity, Identity, and Monstrosity in Medieval Britain: On Difficult Middles
by Jeffrey Jerome Cohen

Medieval Go-betweens and Chaucer's Pandarus
by Gretchen Mieszkowski

The Surgeon in Medieval English Literature
by Jeremy J. Citrome

Temporal Circumstances: Form and History in the Canterbury Tales
by Lee Patterson

Erotic Discourse and Early English Religious Writing
by Lara Farina

Odd Bodies and Visible Ends in Medieval Literature
by Sachi Shimomura

On Farting: Language and Laughter in the Middle Ages
by Valerie Allen

Women and Medieval Epic: Gender, Genre, and the Limits of Epic Masculinity
edited by Sara S. Poor and Jana K. Schulman

Race, Class, and Gender in "Medieval" Cinema
edited by Lynn T. Ramey and Tison Pugh

Allegory and Sexual Ethics in the High Middle Ages
by Noah D. Guynn

England and Iberia in the Middle Ages, 12th–15th Century: Cultural, Literary, and Political Exchanges
edited by María Bullón-Fernández

The Medieval Chastity Belt: A Myth-Making Process
by Albrecht Classen

Claustrophilia: The Erotics of Enclosure in Medieval Literature
by Cary Howie

Cannibalism in High Medieval English Literature
by Heather Blurton

The Drama of Masculinity and Medieval English Guild Culture
by Christina M. Fitzgerald

Chaucer's Visions of Manhood
by Holly A. Crocker

The Literary Subversions of Medieval Women
by Jane Chance

Manmade Marvels in Medieval Culture and Literature
by Scott Lightsey

American Chaucers
by Candace Barrington

Representing Others in Medieval Iberian Literature
by Michelle M. Hamilton

Paradigms and Methods in Early Medieval Studies
edited by Celia Chazelle and Felice Lifshitz

The King and the Whore: King Roderick and La Cava
by Elizabeth Drayson

Langland's Early Modern Identities
by Sarah A. Kelen

Cultural Studies of the Modern Middle Ages
edited by Eileen A. Joy, Myra J. Seaman, Kimberly K. Bell, and Mary K. Ramsey

Hildegard of Bingen's Unknown Language: An Edition, Translation, and Discussion
by Sarah L. Higley

Medieval Romance and the Construction of Heterosexuality
by Louise M. Sylvester

Communal Discord, Child Abduction, and Rape in the Later Middle Ages
by Jeremy Goldberg

Lydgate Matters: Poetry and Material Culture in the Fifteenth Century
edited by Lisa H. Cooper and Andrea Denny-Brown

Sexuality and Its Queer Discontents in Middle English Literature
by Tison Pugh

Sex, Scandal, and Sermon in Fourteenth-Century Spain: Juan Ruiz's Libro de Buen Amor
by Louise M. Haywood

The Erotics of Consolation: Desire and Distance in the Late Middle Ages
edited by Catherine E. Léglu and Stephen J. Milner

Battlefronts Real and Imagined: War, Border, and Identity in the Chinese Middle Period
edited by Don J. Wyatt

Wisdom and Her Lovers in Medieval and Early Modern Hispanic Literature
by Emily C. Francomano

Power, Piety, and Patronage in Late Medieval Queenship: Maria de Luna
by Nuria Silleras-Fernandez

In the Light of Medieval Spain: Islam, the West, and the Relevance of the Past
edited by Simon R. Doubleday and David Coleman, foreword by Giles Tremlett

Chaucerian Aesthetics
by Peggy A. Knapp

Memory, Images, and the English Corpus Christi Drama
by Theodore K. Lerud

Cultural Diversity in the British Middle Ages: Archipelago, Island, England
edited by Jeffrey Jerome Cohen

Excrement in the Late Middle Ages: Sacred Filth and Chaucer's Fecopoetics
by Susan Signe Morrison

Authority and Subjugation in Writing of Medieval Wales
edited by Ruth Kennedy and Simon Meecham-Jones

The Medieval Poetics of the Reliquary: Enshrinement, Inscription, Performance
by Seeta Chaganti

The Legend of Charlemagne in the Middle Ages: Power, Faith, and Crusade
edited by Matthew Gabriele and Jace Stuckey

The Poems of Oswald von Wolkenstein: An English Translation of the Complete Works (1376/77–1445)
by Albrecht Classen

Women and Experience in Later Medieval Writing: Reading the Book of Life
edited by Anneke B. Mulder-Bakker and Liz Herbert McAvoy

Ethics and Eventfulness in Middle English Literature: Singular Fortunes
by J. Allan Mitchell

Maintenance, Meed, and Marriage in Medieval English Literature
by Kathleen E. Kennedy

The Post-Historical Middle Ages
edited by Elizabeth Scala and Sylvia Federico

Constructing Chaucer: Author and Autofiction in the Critical Tradition
by Geoffrey W. Gust

Queens in Stone and Silver: The Creation of a Visual Imagery of Queenship in Capetian France
by Kathleen Nolan

Finding Saint Francis in Literature and Art
edited by Cynthia Ho, Beth A. Mulvaney, and John K. Downey

Strange Beauty: Ecocritical Approaches to Early Medieval Landscape
by Alfred K. Siewers

Berenguela of Castile (1180–1246) and Political Women in the High Middle Ages
by Miriam Shadis

Julian of Norwich's Legacy: Medieval Mysticism and Post-Medieval Reception
edited by Sarah Salih and Denise N. Baker

Medievalism, Multilingualism, and Chaucer
by Mary Catherine Davidson

The Letters of Heloise and Abelard: A Translation of Their Complete Correspondence and Related Writings
translated and edited by Mary Martin McLaughlin with Bonnie Wheeler

Women and Wealth in Late Medieval Europe
edited by Theresa Earenfight

Visual Power and Fame in René d'Anjou, Geoffrey Chaucer, and the Black Prince
by SunHee Kim Gertz

Geoffrey Chaucer Hath a Blog: Medieval Studies and New Media
by Brantley L. Bryant

Margaret Paston's Piety
by Joel T. Rosenthal

Gender and Power in Medieval Exegesis
by Theresa Tinkle

Antimercantilism in Late Medieval English Literature
by Roger A. Ladd

Magnificence and the Sublime in Medieval Aesthetics: Art, Architecture, Literature, Music
edited by C. Stephen Jaeger

Medieval and Early Modern Devotional Objects in Global Perspective: Translations of the Sacred
edited by Elizabeth Robertson and Jennifer Jahner

Late Medieval Jewish Identities: Iberia and Beyond
edited by Carmen Caballero-Navas and Esperanza Alfonso

Outlawry in Medieval Literature
by Timothy S. Jones

Women and Disability in Medieval Literature
by Tory Vandeventer Pearman

The Lesbian Premodern
edited by Noreen Giffney, Michelle M. Sauer, and Diane Watt

Crafting Jewishness in Medieval England: Legally Absent, Virtually Present
by Miriamne Ara Krummel

Street Scenes: Late Medieval Acting and Performance
by Sharon Aronson-Lehavi

Women and Economic Activities in Late Medieval Ghent
by Shennan Hutton

Palimpsests and the Literary Imagination of Medieval England: Collected Essays
edited by Leo Carruthers, Raeleen Chai-Elsholz, and Tatjana Silec

Divine Ventriloquism in Medieval English Literature: Power, Anxiety, Subversion
by Mary Hayes

Vernacular and Latin Literary Discourses of the Muslim Other in Medieval Germany
by Jerold C. Frakes

Fairies in Medieval Romance
by James Wade

Reason and Imagination in Chaucer, the Perle-*poet, and the* Cloud-*author: Seeing from the Center*
by Linda Tarte Holley

The Inner Life of Women in Medieval Romance Literature: Grief, Guilt, and Hypocrisy
edited by Jeff Rider and Jamie Friedman

Language as the Site of Revolt in Medieval and Early Modern England: Speaking as a Woman
by M. C. Bodden

Ecofeminist Subjectivities: Chaucer's Talking Birds
by Lesley Kordecki

Contextualizing the Muslim Other in Medieval Christian Discourse
edited by Jerold C. Frakes

Ekphrastic Medieval Visions: A New Discussion in Interarts Theory
by Claire Barbetti

The [European] Other in Medieval Arabic Literature and Culture: Ninth–Twelfth Century AD
by Nizar F. Hermes

Reading Memory and Identity in the Texts of Medieval European Holy Women
edited by Margaret Cotter-Lynch and Brad Herzog

Market Power: Lordship, Society, and Economy in Medieval Catalonia (1276–1313)
by Gregory B. Milton

Marriage, Property, and Women's Narratives
by Sally A. Livingston

The Medieval Python: The Purposive and Provocative Work of Terry Jones
edited by R. F. Yeager and Toshiyuki Takamiya

Heloise and the Paraclete: A Twelfth-Century Quest (forthcoming)
by Mary Martin McLaughlin

THE MEDIEVAL PYTHON

THE PURPOSIVE AND PROVOCATIVE WORK OF TERRY JONES

Edited by

R. F. Yeager and Toshiyuki Takamiya

Hi Kevin
Best Medieval Wishes
Terry Jones

palgrave
macmillan

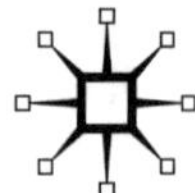

THE MEDIEVAL PYTHON

First published in 2012 by
PALGRAVE MACMILLAN®
in the United States—a division of St. Martin's Press LLC,
175 Fifth Avenue, New York, NY 10010.

Where this book is distributed in the UK, Europe and the rest of the world, this is by Palgrave Macmillan, a division of Macmillan Publishers Limited, registered in England, company number 785998, of Houndmills, Basingstoke, Hampshire RG21 6XS.

Palgrave Macmillan is the global academic imprint of the above companies and has companies and representatives throughout the world.

ISBN: 978–0–230–11267–4

Library of Congress Cataloging-in-Publication Data

The Medieval Python : the purposive and provocative work of Terry Jones / [edited] by R.F. Yeager and Toshiyuki Takamiya.
pages cm—(The new Middle Ages)
ISBN 978–0–230–11267–4 (hardback)
1. Jones, Terry, 1942—Knowledge and learning. 2. English literature—Middle English, 1100–1500—History and criticism. 3. Medievalists. 4. Literature, Medieval—Appreciation—England. 5. Civilization, Medieval—Study and teaching. I. Jones, Terry, 1942– II. Yeager, Robert F. III. Takamiya, Toshiyuki. IV. Jones, Terry, 1942– honouree.

PR251.M36 2012
820.9'001—dc23 2011049318

A catalogue record of the book is available from the British Library.

Design by Newgen Imaging Systems (P) Ltd., Chennai, India.

First edition: May 2012

10 9 8 7 6 5 4 3 2 1

Printed in the United States of America.

CONTENTS

ACKNOWLEDGMENTS

As anyone knows who has done it, producing a Festschrift, more than other kinds of books, relies upon the assistance of many. The efforts of contributors whose essays are named in the table of contents is obvious. To bring this volume into the hands of Terry Jones, however, there have been some indispensable "without whoms," as the phrase goes; their aid along the way the editors wish to acknowledge fully and gratefully here. Such thanks go to all those at St. Edmund Hall, particularly Gillian Powell, for her continuing, cheerful (and clandestine!) support of this project, and also to Candice McCourt and Gillman & Soame Photographers, generally, for their help and very kind permission to reproduce the excerpt from the S. E. H. matriculation photo from 1961 that accompanies the essay by V. A. Kolve. Thanks as well to Helen Richards for formatting assistance, and to Justin McCoy for preparing the "Works Cited" section. Our foremost indebtedness—and it is very great indeed—goes to Kate Baumann, whose technical expertise, perseverance, and devotion to excellence can hardly be praised enough.

Photo courtesy Anna Söderström.

INTRODUCTION

This is a book for Terry Jones, from some of his friends and admirers. Over the years, Terry has acquired quite a few of both, of course, and has enjoyed more than a few toasts and accolades honoring his work as a Python, a script writer, an actor and a film director, a television personality, an author of books for children—and of outspoken books and *Guardian* columns for their parents, attacking bigotry and injustice. (Some very serious people urged him to run for parliament once, and he nearly took them up on it. Pity he didn't, in some ways.)

But this book is different from all of that, except in its serious attempt to honor Terry. Here we celebrate the "Medieval Python," the Terry Jones whose name has been cropping up for more than 30 years in bibliographies and in footnotes in monographs and essays in scholarly journals (many written by contributors herein), the products not of journalists nor publicists nor outraged right-wingnuts but of serious students of the later Middle Ages, spread out across the full spectrum of sophistication and expertise. Had Terry turned out to be the teacher at university he once imagined he might become (pity he didn't, in some ways!), very likely a book of this sort would have fallen his way already, comfortably fitted into the hoary academic genre of Festschrift: a German invention of the nineteenth century, presented to a lofty *éminence grise* by his highest-achieving students when the *Überprofessor* had puffed his pipe in his book-lined office for the final time. The idea was, apparently, immortality—generations of acolytes keeping dust off the Great Man's *weltanschauung* by churning out scholarship of their own owing everything to his.

Well, all right for the Germans. But: that's not very much like Terry, is it? Why would an homage to Terry Jones, medievalist, veer far afield from the life of the man, as lived? To know Terry at all, even so much as to brush elbows with him in the underground, is to come away charged by his profound respect for the independent voice. E. Talbot Donaldson, a kindred contrarian, renowned medievalist, and one who happily would have contributed to this book, were he alive today, used to invoke "a man named Smith" whenever someone started a sentence with "In the Middle Ages people thought . . . ." "Hearing that," Donaldson would remark, "'Smith' (it could have been Jones!), would immediately have risen up in the back of the room and shouted loudly, 'No! I didn't!'"

Which is why, in fact, in a certain sense, this book is a kind of "*un*-Festschrift." No acolytes. (No students.) No institutional colleagues duty-bound to lionize one of their own. Not everyone appearing herein agrees with everyone else, and some indeed continue in print the vibrant controversy Terry's work—in every medium—has always intentionally generated. Much of that controversy many contributors have carried on in extended conversation, sometimes for years, face-to-face with Terry over pints of "real British beer," or pursued into the wee hours at his famously hospitable table, followed by a cab ride home, gift of the host's shilling. Thus Nigel Saul takes occasion here to differ politely with Terry's staunch defense of Richard II as "a much maligned ruler... obstructed by a gaggle of obscurantist barons, deposed by a slippery usurper and with his reputation besmirched by Lancastrian propaganda" (for the record: a view shared by several others herein).[1] Saul argues here, however, that "it is Richard's tyranny alone that explains his removal from the throne by his cousin in 1399."[2] Chris Given-Wilson too takes aim—though more obliquely—at Terry's peacemaker king (and, by way of it, propounds a reevaluation of Richard's early antagonist, Richard Fitzalan, Earl of Arundel), in an assessment of "the anger of King Richard II."[3] And Derek Pearsall also sets out to right the record of medieval monks and friars, as (mis)represented by "a long line of satirists in the estates-satire tradition, Gower and Chaucer [and Terry Jones] among them."[4]

Nonetheless, not everyone lines up here to argue with Terry, of course. Michael Bennett, for one, controverts his fellow historians Given-Wilson and Saul by reading the evidence for and against Richard II's hot temper somewhat differently. The king, Bennett avers, "had a sense of humor" and could play roles: "as Terry Jones has shown, Richard could do 'stern' like the best of kings."[5] Looking not at Richard, nor at the chroniclers, but rather at a contemporary witness of another order, Peter Nicholson revisits his own important early work on the manuscripts of John Gower's *Confessio Amantis,* provoked, he notes, by Terry's suspicions about the timing and causes of revisions in the all-important Oxford, Bodleian Library, MS Fairfax 3 (Macaulay's manuscript F). Nicholson's new conclusion is that the alterations, more than being merely scribal, suggest instead that "the poet had a more active part than we realized, to the point that the line between composition and copying becomes blurred, and 'collaboration' may be more appropriate than 'supervision'."[6] The poet's direct involvement with the changes in MS Fairfax 3 has major significance for Gower studies—and lends substantial support to Terry's grim assessment of the high degree of corruption in the historical record effected by Lancastrian "spin." Similarly, John Bowers finds himself emboldened by Terry's iconoclastic spirit, from the publication of *Chaucer's Knight* (1980) to "the redating of *An ABC* from the beginning of [Chaucer's] career to the end" in the collaboratively authored *Who Murdered Chaucer? A Medieval Mystery* (2003), to suggest a new chronology for Geoffrey Chaucer's *House of Fame* and *Legend of Good Women.*[7] W. Mark Ormrod too, in presenting one instance of rapacious "Needy Knights" taking advantage of "Wealthy Widows," credits *Chaucer's Knight* as "an important moment in the study of later medieval knighthood [that] sent something of a shockwave through the academy and produced significant reassessments of the motives, values, and social mores of the knightly class in the era of the Hundred Years' War"—including his own essay, presented here.[8] William A. Quinn, delving into the nature and extent of Chaucer's pacifism (which he terms "silly," in the Middle English sense of "spiritually favored, blessed, holy, virtuous") as suggested by Terry's less-than-chivalric Knight and other moments in the *Canterbury Tales*, uncovers in his essay, "Moral Chaucer and Philosophical Jones," a kinship of eirenic spirit that extends throughout the sundry works of Chaucer, Gower—and Terry Jones, invariably outspoken in his condemnation of the senselessness and futility of wars.[9] David Wallace offers a snapshot of a Chaucer similarly disenchanted, post-capture and ransom, in his careful reexamination of "Chaucer, Langland, and the Hundred Years' War."[10] And in "Gower in Winter: Last Poems," R. F. Yeager takes yet another (small) page from Terry's playbook by interrogating the broad critical acceptance, prima facie, of Gower's complaints about his age, blindness, and decrepitude, to conclude that indeed they may have been (among other things) Gower's canny device to escape making more Lancastrian propaganda after 1404–05. If true, the change of heart by Chaucer's friend would reinforce Terry's dark opinion of Henry IV's rule, even as it contradicts his view of Gower's character.[11]

But not everyone writing here has Terry's work to reinterpret the literary-historical record so directly in focus. Martha Driver and Richard Firth Green both consider his achievements as medievalist-cum-filmmaker. Nevertheless, in these essays too, the contrarian Terry is alive and well. Driver, noting that "Jones's work might be said to promote the underbelly of the idealized past, forcing viewers to question medieval stereotypes," presents a thorough, energetic, and penetrating paean to the value for teachers in the classroom of Terry's work for big screen and television.[12] Green takes a famous interlude with the limb-losing Black Knight from *Monty Python and the Holy Grail* as a starting point for revealing an entire subgenre, heretofore unheralded: "that of the bellicose amputee" who "fought upon his stumpes."[13] Green's essay thus opens a potentially rich new line of inquiry for future investigative reporters, set to plumb such provocative depths as "How much did Terry know while writing the Black Knight scene about Thomas Hood's poem 'Faithless Nellie Gray' (published 1826)—and when did he know it?"

Green's interest in the reach of literatures more modern into Terry's medieval scholarship, and vice versa, appears as well in the contributions of John J. Thompson and Toshiyuki Takamiya. Both choose as their subjects postmedieval works. Taking up a prayer roll once the property of the young Prince Henry VIII-yet-to-be, Thompson reviews and refutes a variety of claims about how, and by whom, the roll might have been used, citing as his procedural spark Terry's reclamations of "real human lives ordered by and caught up in the social hierarchies of their age."[14] Takamiya centers on another little-known but important text, the *Microcosmus* of Peter Heylyn (yet another Jonesian figure!): "a most prolific controversialist in the seventeenth century."[15] Takamiya's careful reading of Heylyn's magnum opus reveals among the cosmographer's diverse literary sources Malory's *Morte d'Arthur* and—more intriguing, perhaps—Heylyn's recollections of his viewing of a performance of *Macbeth*. And following an even more independent trajectory, Priscilla Martin elects to create her *own* postmedieval piece of fiction. Her short story, "Jack and John, the Plowman's Tale," locates its roots in Chaucer and William Langland, and draws inspiration from the medieval imaginary that proliferates in Terry's fictions for children.[16]

Unusual to find fiction in a Festschrift, of course (the Germans wouldn't have borne it); but then, this is an *Un*festschrift, intended to honor a most unusual man. Originary glimpses of Jones-in-progress (the *Un*festschrift as bildungsroman?) are lent by V. A. Kolve and Michael Palin. Kolve, professor emeritus, former president of the New Chaucer Society and the Medieval Academy of America (Terry has an essay in *his* Festschrift too....), contributes "a memory piece... about Oxford as it was half a century ago when Terry Jones came up to read English Language and Literature at St. Edmund Hall" in 1961–62.[17] Then a Junior Research Fellow and tutor to first-years, Kolve "think[s] back on Oxford as it was in those days—the good, bad, and indifferent of it—for whatever light it may throw upon the person Terry would become."[18] Picking up the thread in those days, Palin, F. O. J. [Friend-of-Jones] for life, follows "The Complete Mediaevalist" from Oxford to Edinburgh to London and beyond. Perhaps it is Palin who justly deserves the final—albeit introductory—word: "When I went down to... Terry's house in south London... I couldn't help noticing that his mediaeval library, far from being set to one side after the completion of *Holy Grail*, was expanding by the day. Even as he bent to the task of directing a comedic version of a ritual stoning in first-century Judea, a part of Terry was still as fascinated by Chaucer as it had been when we first met at Oxford fifteen years earlier.... A year later Terry was winning plaudits for directing one of the world's funniest films. A little more than a year after that Terry's book *Chaucer's Knight* was being described by the London *Observer* newspaper as 'a brilliant work of literary and historical detection.' Now that sort of thing doesn't happen to many comedy directors."[19]

To which all of us contributing here most heartily agree, while adding "Nor vice versa, either." Pity it doesn't, really.

Notes

1. Saul, 39.
2. Saul, 52.
3. Given-Wilson, 27.
4. Pearsall, 59.
5. Bennett, 131.
6. Nicholson, 84.
7. Bowers, 105.
8. Ormrod, 137.
9. Quinn, 176.
10. Wallace, 195.
11. Yeager, 87
12. Driver, 151.
13. Green, 181, 182.
14. Thompson, 216.
15. Takamiya, 229.
16. Martin, 207.
17. Kolve, 13.
18. Kolve, 14.
19. Palin, 58.

CHAPTER 1

THE MEDIEVAL WORKS OF TERRY JONES

Sanae Ikeda

This selected bibliography lists Terry Jones's works on medieval topics through 2011. The items are classified in two sections: films and documentary TV programs that he directed, wrote, and/or in which he performed; and his scholarly books and articles, and books for children. Works on non-medieval subjects are excluded.

The following abbreviations are used:

A article published in a book or in a periodical
B published book
C children's book, audiobook for children
D documentary TV program, and its companion book
F film, and its screenplay
O other categories
V video recording
TJ Terry Jones

I. Films and Documentary TV programs

1974

(F) *Monty Python and the Holy Grail.* Directed by TJ and Terry Gilliam. Written and presented by Graham Chapman, John Cleese, Eric Idle, Terry Gilliam, TJ, and Michael Palin. Screenplay TJ. Produced by Mark Forstater, John Goldstone, and Michael White. EMI Films; Sony Pictures Entertainment, 1974. Nominated as the "Best Dramatic Presentation" of The Hugo Awards in 1976.

(V) VHS. Monty Python Pictures, 1974; DVD. 1998; special ed. Burbank, CA: Columbia TriStar Home Entertainment, 2001.

1986

(F) *Labyrinth*. Dir. Jim Henson. Written by Dennis Lee and Jim Henson. Perf. David Bowie, Jennifer Connelly, and Toby Froud. Screenplay TJ. Prod. Eric Rattray, David Lazer, and George Lucas. TriStar Pictures. 1986.
(V) DVD. Culver City, CA: Columbia TriStar Home Video, 1986; 1999; anniversary ed. Sony Pictures Home Entertainment. 2007.

1989

(F) *Erik the Viking*. Written and Dir. by TJ. Perf. Tim Robbins, TJ, John Cleese, and Mickey Rooney. Prod. John C. Goldstone. Orion Pictures. 1989.
(V) VHS. New York: Orion Home Video, 1989; DVD. Twentieth Century Fox Home Entertainment, 2007.

1995

(D) *The Crusades*. Dir. Alan Ereira and David Wallace. Written by Alan Ereira and TJ.

Perf. TJ. 4 episodes. BBC Entertainment. 1995.
Episode 1. Pilgrims in Arms
Episode 2. Jerusalem
Episode 3. Jihad
Episode 4. Destruction

(V) VHS. 1995; DVD. New York: A. & E. Home Video, 2001.

1997

(C) *Sir Gawain and the Green Knight*. Translated by J. R. R. Tolkien. Read by TJ.
Children's audiobook. 2 sound cassettes. London: HarperCollins Audiobooks, 1997.

(C) *Pearl and Sir Orfeo*. Translated by J. R. R. Tolkien. Read by TJ. Children's audiobook.
2 sound cassettes. London: HarperCollins Audiobooks, 1997.

1998

(D) *Ancient Inventions*. Dir. Daniel Percival and Phil Grabsky. Written by TJ and Daniel Percival
Percival. Perf. TJ. Prod. David Souden, and Amanda Wilkie. 3 episodes. BBC. 1998.

Episode 1. City Life
Episode 2. Sex and Love
Episode 3. War and Conflict

(V) VHS. Bethesda, MD: Discovery Channel Video, 1998; DVD. [New York]: Discovery Communications, 2008. Videodisc. [Brighton, England]: Seven Art Productions, 2009.

2002–03

(D) *The Surprising History of Egypt* (released in USA in 2002); or, *The Hidden History of Egypt* (UK in 2003). Dir. Phil Grabsky. Written by TJ and Alan Ereira. DiscoveryChannel.
(V) DVD. Discovery Channel Video. 2003.
(D) *The Surprising History of Rome* (released in USA in 2002); or, *The Hidden History of Rome* (UK in 2003). Dir. Phil Grabsky. Written by Phil Grabsky, TJ, and Alan Ereira. Perf. TJ. Prod. Jack E. Smith, and Phil Grabsky. Discovery Channel.
(V) VHS. 2002. Videodisc. Bethesda, MD: Discovery Channel, 2003.
(D) *The Surprising History of Sex and Love.* Dir. Alan Ereira and Phil Grabsky. Discovery Channel. 2002.
(V) DVD. Seventh Art Productions, 2009.

2004

(D) *Terry Jones' Medieval Lives.* Dir. Nigel Miller. Written and presented by TJ. Prod. Paul Bradshaw and Nigel Miller. 8 episodes. BBC Two. 2004. The Episode *The Peasant* nominated for "Outstanding Writing for Nonfiction Programming" at the 2004 Emmy Awards.

Episode 1. The Knight
Episode 2. The Monk
Episode 3. The King
Episode 4. The Damsel
Episode 5. The Philosopher
Episode 6. The Minstrel
Episode 7. The Outlaw
Episode 8. The Peasant

(V) DVD. [London]: BBC Video; BBC Worldwide America, Warner Home Video, 2008.

2005

(D) *The Story of 1.* Dir. Nick Murphy. Perf. TJ. BBC. 2005.
(V) DVD. [Alexandria, VA]: PBS Home Video. 2005, 2006.

2006

(D)*Terry Jones' Barbarians*. Written by TJ, Alan Ereira, and David McNab. Perf. TJ.

Prod. David McNab. 4 episodes. BBC Two. 2006.
Episode 1. The Primitive Celts
Episode 2. The Savage Goths
Episode 3. The Brainy Barbarians
Episode 4. The End of the World

(V) DVD. Port Washington, NY: Koch Entertainment, 2006, 2007, 2008.

2008

(D) *Terry Jones' Great Map Mystery*. Dir. Alan Ereira. Written by Alan Ereira. Perf. TJ.

4 episodes. BBC Two Wales. 2008.
Episode 1. The Road to Aberystwyth
Episode 2. The Road to St. David's
Episode 3. St. David's to Holywell
Episode 4. Chester to Holyhead

(V) DVD. [Pyrmont, N.S.W.]: Roadshow Entertainment, 2010.

2009

(V) *Chaucer and "The Canterbury Tales."* Perf. TJ. DVD. Artsmagic, 2009.

II. Articles, Books, Reviews, and Books for Children

1972

(A) "Attention to Detail: The Workbooks of Ronald Welch." *Children's Literature in Education* 3, no. 2 (1972): 30–37.

1977

(F) Chapman, Graham, John Cleese, Terry Gilliam, Eric Idle, TJ, and Michael Palin. *Monty Python and the Holy Grail* (Book). London: Methuen, 1977.

1980

(B) *Chaucer's Knight: The Portrait of a Medieval Mercenary*. London: Weidenfeld and Nicolson; Baton Rouge: Louisiana State University Press, 1980. Second revised edition. London: Methuen, 1985. With new introduction, 1994.

1981

(C) *Fairy Tales.* Illustrated by Michael Foreman. London: Pavilion, 1981; New York: Schocken, 1982.

1983

(C) *The Saga of Erik the Viking.* Illustrated by Michael Foreman. London: Pavilion; New York: Schocken, 1983.

1985

(A) "Fings Ain't What They Used to Be: A Return to Victorian Values." *Listener.* July 11.

(C) *Nicobobinus.* Illustrated by Michael Foreman. London: Pavilion, 1985.

1986

(C) Froud, Brian, and TJ. *The Goblins of the Labyrinth.* Illuminated by Brian Froud. London: Pavilion, 1986.

1988

(C) *The Curse of the Vampire's Socks and Other Doggerel.* Illustrated by Michael Foreman. London: Pavilion, 1988.

1989

(O) Review of *Fantasy and Reason: Children's Literature in the Eighteenth Century,* by Geoffrey Summerfield. London: Methuen, 1984. *Children's Literature in Education* 20, no. 2 (1989): 129–30.

(F) *Erik the Viking: The Book of the Film of the Book.* London: Methuen Drama, 1989; New York: Applause Theatre Book, 1990.

1992

(C) *Fantastic Stories.* Illustrated by Michael Foreman. London: Pavilion; New York: Viking, 1992.

(C) *The Dragon on the Roof.* Illustrated by Michael Foreman. Penguin Children's 60s. London: Penguin, 1992.

1993

(C) *The Beast with a Thousand Teeth.* Illustrated by Michael Foreman. London: Pavilion; New York: Bedrick, 1993.

(C) *A Fish of the World.* Illustrated by Michael Foreman. London: Pavilion, 1993.

1994

- (D) TJ, and Alan Ereira. *The Crusades*. London: BBC Books, 1994; New York: Facts on File, 1995.
- (C) *Lady Cottington's Pressed Fairy Book*. Illustrated by Brian Froud. London: Pavilion; Atlanta: Turner, 1994.
- (C) *The Sea Tiger*. Illustrated by Michael Foreman. New York: Bedrick, 1994.
- (C) *The Fly-By-Night*. Illustrated by Michael Foreman. New York: Bedrick, 1994.
- (C) "The Tinderbox." In *The Oxford Treasury of Children's Stories*, compiled by Michael Harrison and Christopher Stuart-Clark. Oxford: Oxford University Press, 1994.

1996

- (C) TJ, and Brian Froud. *The Goblin Companion: A Field Guide to Goblins*. London: Pavilion; Atlanta: Turner, 1996. (Reissued in abridged form as *The Goblins of the Labyrinth* [1986])
- (C) TJ, and Brian Froud. *Strange Stains and Mysterious Smells: Quentin Cottington's Journal of Faery Research*. New York: Simon & Schuster, 1996.

1997

- (C) *The Knight and the Squire*. Illustrated by Michael Foreman. London: Pavilion, 1997.
- (C) *The Sea Tiger*. Illustrated by Michael Foreman. London: Puffin, 1997.
- (C) *Fairy Tales and Fantastic Stories*. A special fifteenth anniversary edition of TJ's short stories for children. London: Pavilion, 1997.

2000

- (A) "The Monk's Tale." *Studies in the Age of Chaucer* 22 (2000): 387–97.
- (C) *The Lady and the Squire*. Illustrated by Michael Foreman. London: Pavilion, 2000.

2001

- (A) "The Image of Chaucer's Knight." In *Speaking Images: Essays in Honor of V. A. Kolve*, edited by Robert F. Yeager and Charlotte C. Morse. 205–36. Asheville, NC: Pegasus Press, 2001.

2002

- (F) Chapman, Graham, John Cleese, Terry Gilliam, Eric Idle, TJ, and Michael Palin.

Monty Python and the Holy Grail: Screenplay. London: Methuen, 2002.

(C) TJ, and Nanette Newman. *Bedtime Stories*. Illustrated by Michael Foreman. London: Pavilion Children's Books, 2002.

2003

(B) TJ, Robert Yeager, Terry Dolan, Alan Fletcher, and Juliette Dor. *Who Murdered Chaucer?: A Medieval Mystery*. London: Methuen, 2003; New York: St. Martin's Press, 2004.

2004

(D) TJ, and Alan Ereira. *Terry Jones' Medieval Lives*. London: BBC Books, 2004.

2006

(D) TJ, and Alan Ereira. *Terry Jones' Barbarians: An Alternative Roman History*. London: BBC Books, 2006.

2008

(A) "Was Richard II a Tyrant? Richard's Use of the Books of Rules for Princes." *Fourteenth Century England* 5 (2008): 130–60.

2008

(A) "Richard II: Royal Villain or Victim of 'Spin'?" *Times of London*, 4 October.

2011

(C) *The Amazing Terry Jones Presents for the Very First Time His Incredible Animal Tales*. Illustrated by Michael Foreman. London: Pavilion Children's Books, 2011.

(C) *The Amazing Terry Jones Presents His Unbelievable Adventures and Fantastic Stories*. Illustrated by Michael Foreman. London: Pavilion Children's Books, 2011.

CHAPTER 2

YOUNG JONES AT OXFORD, 1961–62

V. A. Kolve

My title, I confess, claims too much. What follows is not an essay in biography, carefully researched, but a memory piece about Oxford as it was half a century ago when Terry Jones first came up to "read English" at St. Edmund Hall—a three-year course of study leading to an Honours BA in English Language and Literature. I'd earned the same degree a few years earlier as an undergraduate at Jesus College (1955–57), in two years rather than three because I already had an American BA. When Terry arrived in 1961, I was a fifth-year candidate for the D. Phil., working feverishly hard to finish a doctoral thesis on medieval drama. But I was also beginning my fourth year at the Hall, supported by a Junior Research Fellowship. I earned extra money (and valuable experience) by tutoring its first-year men reading English, usually ten in all, preparing them for the "preliminary" exams they would take at the end of their second term and introducing them to fourteenth-century literature in the term after that. I returned to the States—doctoral degree in hand, and with a job awaiting me at Stanford—at the end of that academic year.

So Terry and I had just one year of Oxford in common—his first, my last—too brief a time (and for me too harried) to form a friendship or even a deep acquaintance. That would come later. But university life changed slowly in those days, and as a six-year veteran of the place—in all three ranks, undergraduate, graduate student and young don—I knew both the university and the college reasonably well. Though "Teddy Hall" (as it's popularly called) is now one of the largest Oxford colleges, with some 400 undergraduates, 220 graduate students, and 40-plus Tutorial Fellows, it was small and intimate at the turn of the '60s. It had just over 200 students (virtually all undergraduate) and a Governing Body of Fellows, 15 in all, who lunched together Monday through Friday, and dined with the Principal more formally in Hall at least two or three nights a week. Those of us who "lived in" "dined in" more often.

Figure 1 "Fresher" Terry Jones. By special permission Gillman and Soame Photographers.

But Terry and I had other connections as well, since two of the three men who would tutor him in the years that followed ('62–'64) were among my closest friends. Reggie (R. E.) Alton, who regularly taught for Jesus as well as St. Edmund Hall, had been my tutor too, and Graham Midgley had been one of my examiners in the "Schools" (the 27 hours of final exams that determine the class of your Honours degree). So although Terry's Oxford and mine were not coterminous, like circles in a Venn diagram there was significant overlap between them. The editors of this volume have invited me to think back on that experience—the good, bad, and indifferent of it—for whatever light it may throw upon the person, both public and private, that Terry has become. That Oxford shaped the ways we thought about ourselves, doubted ourselves, and affirmed ourselves goes without saying. An intense self-fashioning was the goal of those privileged early years.

By way of introduction, I would like to share with you a few of the bawdy jests, the startling demolitions, the irreverent take on things that made Terry's weekly essays so memorable. How better to account for the protean comedy of the Python TV circus? the *Holy Grail* and *Life of Brian*? the skeptical eye Terry cast on the *Crusades*, the *Barbarians*, and certain archetypal *Medieval Lives*? Or more to the present point, how better to explain Terry's provocative books on *Chaucer's Knight* and the politics of Chaucer's death? But alas! I have no such memories to share. If Terry ever favored our tutorials with flashes of comparable wit and humor, those flashes, like François Villon's "snows of yesteryear," have left no trace behind. But perhaps I've simply forgotten: Terry has said his earliest attack on the "chivalry" of Chaucer's Knight was mounted in an essay for me. [1]

So I begin instead with an awkward acknowledgment. In 2001, at a three-day symposium marking my retirement from the University of California, Los Angeles (UCLA), Terry not only contributed to *Speaking Images*, the volume of essays presented to me on that occasion, a dazzling piece linking Sir John Hawkwood, the English mercenary, to the Ellesmere portrait of Chaucer's Knight, but at the farewell banquet gave the wittiest speech of the evening. Affecting puzzlement and regret, he began by recalling tutorials he'd had with me 40 years before—and couldn't remember a single word I'd said! : On this equally festive occasion, *50* years after our tutorials together, I find myself at a similar loss: I can't remember anything he said either. But perhaps neither of us should be overly embarrassed. Education is a mysterious process, not a drop box for deliveries made from the outside.

In any case, as readers of medieval romance know well, the youth of a hero is often obscure; his full colors aren't on show early on. So it should come as no surprise that my memories of Terry in his first year are not of a precocious Python-in-the-making, fond of pratfalls, saucy remarks, washerwoman drag, and screeching at the top of his lungs. I remember instead a rather intense young man, darkly handsome in a Welsh sort of way, who took his studies seriously and for much of that first year expected to go into teaching as a career. By means none of us could have guessed at then, it's clear he's accomplished that too.

But first a few facts about our hero's early life. Though born in Wales in 1942 to a bank-clerk father and a homemaker mother, he never saw his father, who was serving in the Royal Air Force, until after the war. The happiness of Terry's childhood in Colwyn Bay, four years of being raised by a doting mother and grandmother, came to an abrupt end when his father returned and moved the family to Surrey. Though Terry experienced the move as a rupture, a loss of Eden, it did in time facilitate his entry into the Royal Grammar School, Guildford, a day school founded in 1509 to educate "poor men's sons in the town," and chartered in 1552 as "the Free Grammar School of King Edward VI." It did not, however, always focus on that mission—entrance became highly selective—and has not always remained tuition free; its fees today are substantial. But from 1944 to 1977, including Terry's time there, it was fully funded by the state.

He did well there, serving as Captain of Boxing, Captain of Rugby, and "Head Boy" all in his final year. A multitalented lad, young Jones, ready for Oxford at the age of nineteen. Or better, as he "thinks he thought" then, ready for Cambridge. He'd applied to the College of Gonville and Caius because he was mad for poetry, and "modern poetry" could be studied there. (Not so at Oxford, not for many years to come.) But when Gonville and Caius put him on its waiting list (one of his A-level exams had been disappointing; he'd misread the instructions), he accepted the offer of a place at St. Edmund Hall, his alternative choice. Gonville and Caius, as it happened, sent him an acceptance just a week later, but Terry stayed with the choice he'd already made, a decision he looks back upon gratefully: "If I'd gone to Cambridge I'd never have joined the Footlights (too organized for me) and so I'd never have done any revue or comedy. Also I wouldn't have met either Mike Palin or Geoffrey Chaucer—and without those two meetings the rest of my life would have been quite different."[2]

Many things about the Oxford undergraduate experience remain to this day unchanged. But I find myself thinking instead of L. P. Hartley's *The Go-between*, a novel of love, loss, and betrayal set in the year 1900, which opens with these words: "The past is a foreign country; they do things differently there."[3] With that as my pretext, let me revisit in memory the Oxford that would receive Terry Jones, train him, and help him find his first footing, not solely as an actor/writer/director but as the grandly talented reviser of the medieval past he would soon become.

⋆ ⋆ ⋆

I start with Oxford itself, these days numbering 160,000 people and said to be visited by more than nine million tourists annually. We had visitors too, of course, and businessmen and strangers all going about their affairs—it had been the county seat since the early years of the tenth century. But in 1961, it was no more than a bustling university town populated by dons who lived there year-round, by students in residence just three terms a year, and by its townsfolk, many of them associated with the university in one way or another. There was industry nearby—MG sports cars were being manufactured at Abingdon, six miles away, along with Morris Minors (now Morris Minis) in the suburb of Cowley. But industry of that sort never much invaded or affected Oxford itself. At its historic center stood the university, a magnificent, unsystematic cluster of colleges and churches, parks and meadows, with two rivers running through it, the Cherwell and the Thames (locally called the Isis).

St. Edmund Hall, Terry's new home, didn't become a "college" until 1957. Since 1571, it had been technically an adjunct of Queen's College, just across the lane. But in fact, "halls" of its kind were among the oldest of Oxford's academic institutions—predating the colleges—with an effective history going back to 1167 when Henry II banned English students from further study at the University of Paris. Drawn to Oxford by eminent teachers who had settled there, they rented rooms in private houses, at the mercy of landlords and their own youthful high spirits, until required (for the sake of order and propriety, as well as their own protection) to live in approved residential halls. These too were privately owned but under the supervision of a Principal (generally a recent Bachelor of Arts, not yet a teaching Master). There are records from one time or another of more than 120 of such halls, most of them quite small. Over time, most of them failed financially or were absorbed into newly endowed "colleges" (originally small monastic institutions for graduates), the earliest of which was University College, founded in 1249, followed by Balliol in 1263, and Merton in

1264. But St. Edmund Hall somehow survived all this, the only one of its kind to do so. It was named after St. Edmund of Abingdon, a pious man and a devoted scholar who had studied at the University of Paris, would teach at Oxford, and much later become Archbishop of Canterbury. (His *Speculum Ecclesiae*, a guide to the preliminary stages of mysticism, comes down to us in Anglo-Norman as well and in fourteenth-century English.) Though St. Edmund was not the Hall's founder, records suggest he lived and taught in a house on its present site as a Regent Master of Arts in the late 1190s. It is certain he built at his own expense the Lady Chapel of St. Peter-in-the-East, adjacent to the Hall, so that he might hear Mass every morning before his lectures. The college proudly retained the name *Aula Sancti Edmundi* (first noted in records of 1317–18) even after being fully chartered. Its "old members" are known as Aularians.

Oxford's colleges and churches have never been less than impressive—thrilling even—to anyone seeing them for the first time, and they function very well. But in the '50s and early '60s they didn't in fact look good. The building stone, dove-grey or honey-colored, that so pleases students and visitors today was not only veiled by centuries of soot and dirt but eroded by acid rain. The look was monumental, to be sure, but also rather shabby, just this side of grim. Little money was available for repair. It wasn't until the late '60s that a university-wide program of cleaning and restoring the stonework began—a long and painstaking process. Deeply ingrained wartime behaviors meanwhile prevailed: Don't complain; Do without; Muddle through; Settle for whatever comes down.

Food rationing, for instance, begun in 1939, did not fully end until 1954—a year before I came up—leaving English kitchens depressed and defeated for a long time to come. At Oxford, we ate in splendid dining halls, waited on by college servants. But the food itself was beyond terrible. Dinner often began with a bowl of "brown Windsor soup," based on mystery ingredients, followed by a plate of brussels sprouts or watery cabbage boiled for hours, and accompanied by a thin piece of meat cooked nearly as long. Only when everything had reached the same shade of grey was it deemed ready to be served. Tasteless food served in scanty portions kept us slim—obesity was never a college problem—but we ate in cheap Indian restaurants as often our money allowed (not often), or at workers' cafes in the covered market between Jesus and the High Street when things got really bleak.

On a happier note: though three years of such food at Jesus just about did me in, my four years at "high table" in Teddy Hall could not have been more different. High table had a chef of its own—an accomplished chef—who prepared for us three- or four-course dinners accompanied by good wines (the reds put down long before) brought up from the college cellar. Afterwards, at least two or three nights a week, we would adjourn to the Old Library—a beautiful seventeenth-century room, long and narrow, oak-paneled and candle-lit, lined with ancient leather-bound books—for port to be passed and fruit and nuts to follow. It was all very gracious and really quite lovely, though it does seem terribly unjust, now that I think of it, that Terry should have been among those dining at one of the tables perpendicular to ours, on a floor a few inches lower than our own! (The humiliation! the shame!) But privilege of this sort made a huge difference to my last years at Oxford—several more years than originally intended—and Terry, I dare say, has more than caught up with me since. Our good friend has known food and wine at some very high tables ....

I pretend to this faux shame to make a serious point. Though it may seem strange, I don't remember feeling resentment as an undergraduate toward the "higher" provision on "high table" at Jesus, nor did I ever sense student resentment over its equivalent at Teddy Hall. Whatever one might think about "low table" food, dining at the long tables below had pleasures of its own, including the ceremonial. You filed in early, awaiting the arrival of the dons, who would enter in procession from the Old Library shortly after the seven o'clock chapel bell, engaged in casual conversation and wearing their MA gowns just as you wore yours. A senior scholar would intone the college grace in Latin, followed by a murmured general "Amen," after which everyone would take his seat and low-table talk (as in an Anglo-Saxon epic) would soon fill the high-raftered hall with noise. The dreadful food would be served, accompanied (if you wished) by pints of ale ordered up from the college buttery and drunk from silver tankards donated to the college centuries before. Lively conversation was conducted according to certain rules. You were not supposed to talk about your work, or politics, or romantic affairs: those subjects were expressly forbidden. And you were not to sit "above your station" at table. Scholars (those awarded a college scholarship) sat at its head, followed by exhibitioners (those awarded a college "exhibition," less valuable than a scholarship), followed by commoners (whose "commons," i.e., board and room, were paid for out of state grants) at the far end below. Most of us were commoners. If you broke these rules, penalties followed, usually involving the downing of a large "sconce" of beer (two-and-a-half pints), all at one go, or a round of beer at your expense for everyone at your end of the table.

But the deepest reason we didn't resent (or even much think to envy) the ceremonial airs and powers and privileges afforded the dons was that we never doubted that Oxford existed for us. The dons were there for our sake. However fleeting, our situation seemed as privileged as theirs. As one veteran Fellow sadly remarked: year after year students remain the same age; only the dons grow old. But even that is changed these days: Oxford has become a major research university, frequently ranked among the top half-dozen in the world. Boasting more than 9,000 graduate students (out of some 21,000 in all), it is nothing like as youthful or carefree or homogeneous as it used to be, and it is far more professionally focused. Fifty years ago it still conceived its chief business to be the education of undergraduates, most of them in the humanities, as a broadly useful preparation for whatever career might later come their way. That's what Oxford knew how to do, and it did it well. Most of the dons who taught us, even the most eminent, lacked graduate degrees. (The local MA doesn't count. It confers senior membership in the university, nothing more.) Oxford of that time was largely an undergraduate institution.

An even bigger change distinguishing Oxford's present from its past derives from the fact that the colleges today are no longer segregated by sex and that women now attend the university in numbers equal to men. Though the five "women's colleges" (as they used to be called) were founded in the 1890s, it was not until 1920 that women were granted full membership in the university and allowed to take degrees. Limitations on their number were nervously imposed in 1927, and not formally rescinded until 1957. Indeed, it was only in 1959, just two years before Terry came up, that their colleges were granted full collegiate status. True integration had to wait until 1974 when five men's colleges, acting together, broke their charters and offered admission to women on an equal basis. All the rest eventually followed, though the women's colleges were initially reluctant to do so. They found it hard to give up their separate-but-equal status, so recent and hard-won, and admit men. St. Hilda's, the last to fall in line, did so only three years ago (in 2008). In today's Oxford, men and women live on the same floors, called "staircases," take meals together in hall, buy drinks in the same college buttery, and are tutored by male and female Fellows of the same college—all unthinkable in Terry's day or mine.

As a result, "college life" as we knew it was segregated male or female, lived out in walled buildings arranged around beautifully kept lawns, and sealed off from the world every night by heavy gates that closed at ten or ten-thirty. You might entertain in your rooms a member of the opposite sex (usually over tea or sherry, and usually by prior invitation) but never in hall as your guest for dinner and never in the Junior Common Room, a site strictly reserved for young men at their ease. "University life," in contrast, brought the two sexes together for a vast range of club meetings, for beer and conversation in college-adjacent pubs, for films and plays and concerts, or in the long evenings of summer term for boating on the river, with punts skillfully maneuvered by men and women alike. But even on this level, men so far outnumbered women that a great deal of social life was centered on groups of men together. That had compensatory rewards: since there was not a lot of dating, deep and lasting masculine friendships could be made. But of course it was frustrating as well.

This unbalanced demographic worked to the advantage of young secretaries and nurses in the town, though romantic relationships of that kind, some of which would lead to happy marriages, were almost never part of the "college experience" as such. Even such adventures, extramural by definition, were constrained by the need to get back to college before the gate closed. Third-year men who "lived out" (i.e., in lodgings) might aspire to a bit more freedom, but Oxford landladies tended to keep a close watch on who came and went and for how long they stayed. It allowed them to maintain, in their own minds at least, a high moral tone.

The Oxford experience, in short, was shot through with rules and customs so old-fashioned and absurd as to seem Edwardian, even Victorian, in nature. If asked, most of us would have agreed this was part of its charm—an aspect of what made undergraduate Oxford a "time and space apart." Yet those time-honored traditions could seem infantilizing too— especially, I think, for men who came up after the war and before 1961, a period in which all able-bodied Englishmen aged 17 to 21 were required to spend two years in the armed forces. The most able among them were commissioned as officers and given positions of responsibility and command. When members of this "officer class" went on to university, as most of them did, they came up as men aged 20 or 21 with some experience in the world, not as boys fresh out of school. Because Terry's year was the first since the war not to be called up for National Service, he and his classmates had to make their way among second- and third-year men in many ways more sophisticated than themselves. But in fact everyone, whatever his age or life experience, chafed at some of the measures imposed on those *in statu pupillari*.

At Jesus in the '50s, for example, everyone was still initially assigned a "moral tutor"—in my case the college Chaplain, a shy and awkward man not much experienced in the ways of the world. Since I'd lost my faith at the age of 17, felt I was doing just fine without it, and rather bristled at any contrary assumption, I found this arrangement more than a little embarrassing. (Evidence, perhaps, I wasn't as sophisticated and mature as I liked to believe.) Most moral tutors had the grace (and diffidence) not to take their job very seriously, but the mere fact they were assigned to us seemed as weirdly anachronistic as the fact that two Proctors, senior officers of the university, walked the streets at night to ensure no undergraduate was engaged in risky or unseemly behavior, or might be found outside his college after the gates had been closed. They moved together through the town wearing mortarboards and black academic gowns, grave in demeanor, followed by two sturdy men (generally known as "bull dogs") in black suits, with bowler hats on their heads. The latter were a form of university police, sworn in as special constables, with the power to enforce university discipline within four miles of any university building. They were a curious sight.

That college gates were shut by ten-thirty every night would have been intolerable—were it not for the fact there was always a secret way or two to "climb in." At Jesus you had to surmount a stone wall eight or nine feet high topped with revolving sets of long iron spikes. The trick was to find a chained-up bicycle somewhere nearby, prop it against the wall, climb onto its seat, grab hold of an upright bar, and pull yourself over the spikes, straddling them carefully before jumping first onto the roof of a bicycle shed and then down to the pavement below. If by ill chance you fell, attracting the attention of the Junior Dean making his nocturnal rounds (this once happened to me), he would duly record your name and the time, invite you to call on him in his rooms at nine-thirty in the morning, and bid you a formal goodnight. The following day, after being fined a certain number of shillings, you would thank him and take your leave, silently fuming at rules that treated you like a delinquent boy! But we all played our parts—the Junior Dean fully as much as those who stayed out late—and carried on without further fuss; so long as the forms were observed, no one minded very much.

There was of course a *legitimate* way to enter late: you could knock on the gate, disturb the night porter, have your name taken, and be assessed a fine in the morning. But climbing in, so long as you succeeded, cost nothing and threatened your self-image less. Teddy Hall, in fact, had two "secret" ways to do so, well-known to everyone (including, of course, the Dean). The first took you through a set of undergraduate rooms fronting on the graveyard of St. Peter-in-the-East, adjacent to the Hall. You had first to climb the stone wall of the graveyard, not all that difficult a task, then make your way to a window that the undergraduate in residence, as a courtesy, always left unlocked. (He really had no choice.) The other way, more awkwardly public, was through a window on High Street (the major thoroughfare of the town), giving onto a set of undergraduate rooms just behind. Though my own rooms as a Fellow opened onto this same corridor, I chose not to hear its muffled after-hours traffic—even as Acting Junior Dean, whenever the Dean was away. My occasional tenure in that office, I like to think, was characterized by a vast tolerance, perhaps even by a degree of laxity. It seemed the Oxford thing to do.

I've been reminiscing here about creature comforts, which in the end do not matter much, and minor affronts to one's precarious youthful dignity, which matter even less, however vexing at the time. More seriously peculiar was the construction of the syllabus itself, never called by that name, but determined by the 27 hours of comprehensive exams administered at the end of the third year. Those nine exams (each three hours long, morning and afternoon for four-and-a-half days) tested your stamina both physically and mentally. The first four (twelve hours in all) examined you on language and literature up to 1475 (*Beowulf* through *Morte d'Arthur*); a fifth tested your knowledge of William Shakespeare; a sixth posed questions on Edmund Spenser and John Milton; the seventh and eighth looked at the seventeenth and eighteenth centuries, culminating in the romantic period of the early nineteenth. The ninth exam, in the History of the Language, was also heavily weighted toward the medieval. These formidable exams determined the structure and range of all the formal teaching on offer, not only in college tutorials but in the university-wide lectures arranged for us each term, never obligatory and seldom attended for long. That this "syllabus" (unnamed) seemed willful and arbitrary and desperately behind the times goes without saying: all that Anglo-Saxon, so much medieval, no Victorian, no modern, no American, and no options whatsoever—except for two versions of the degree more forbiddingly philological still. Nor could one choose in the American way to "minor" in a complementary subject like History or French or Psychology. Officially, for three years, one "read English" only—English literature to 1824, ending with Lord Byron's satiric epic *Don Juan*. That was that, and that was all. Like Terry, I'd come to Oxford chiefly interested in modern poetry, but by the time I took those exams I was thinking of myself as a medievalist. Something like that must have happened to Terry too.

The syllabus, in short, was philological, insular, and absurdly abrupt in its decision to end English Literature with the romantic poets. Yet it was also well focused, historically coherent, and too vast and rich (as one soon discovered) to be mastered in just three years. More important still, it did not discount or disparage what it found no room to include. Only within its formal bounds did literature stop with Lord Byron. Everything after was left for us to discover, as part of an ongoing tradition still vibrant and alive. It was an extracurricular pursuit—and we pursued it passionately, in poetry clubs and college literary societies, in the production of plays and operas, in private reading during the "vacs" and endless conversation with friends during term.

At the invitation of some group or other, virtually every major writer in England came to read his or her work aloud—as did many others on the verge of such renown. Chief among them was W. H. Auden, Oxford Professor of Poetry for three years, who chose to be in residence each spring. He could be found most mornings at eleven o'clock, notably untidy in carpet slippers and rumpled clothing, taking coffee upstairs in the Cadena Café, and making himself available, in a pleasantly grumpy sort of way, to anyone who wanted to talk. (Not everyone dared.) We heard his predecessor, C. Day Lewis, as well, and his successor, Robert Graves. Edith Sitwell read *Façade* to us in her mannered way through a megaphone from behind a painted screen; Anne Ridler, Philip Larkin, and Louis MacNiece read and talked to us too. Even the "Beats"—Alan Ginsberg and Gregory Corso—visited for three days in 1958, bringing with them in a small suitcase the first copies of *Howl* and *Gasoline* that England had ever seen. At once gentle and ferocious, they caused a fabulous uproar. (It was the one year I lived outside college; they stayed with me.) Alan first read *Howl* aloud to my college literary society, the Henry Vaughan, a thrilling evening that ended sooner than expected after Gregory asked the dignified, white-haired Principal of Jesus, "Man, don't you just want to fuck the stars?" Alan read *Howl* again, two nights later, at a meeting of the Oxford Poetry Society in a room at New College, this time to faint applause and general riot. Shoes were thrown. Gregory enjoyed comparable success with a poem of just two lines: "In the Mexican zoo / They have ordinary American cows."

So it didn't much matter—it seemed no limitation—that the syllabus, like a bus whose motor suddenly failed, stopped short at Lord Byron. We read the Victorian poets and novelists because we wanted to, and the moderns, especially William Butler Yeats and T. S. Eliot, Dylan Thomas, E. M. Forster, Samuel Beckett, and the early Iris Murdoch (still a philosophy don at St. Anne's) because they spoke to us urgently as well. Fully as important, we had writers among us, friends our own age, who were publishing books of poetry, novels, and personal memoirs: Dom Moraes, Quentin Stevenson and Peter Levi, SJ, among the poets; Julian Mitchell, David Caute, and Reynolds Price among the novelists; Ved Mehta among those already mining the story of their own lives. London noticed us as well: Oxford theater (Oxford University Dramatic Society [OUDS] and Experimental Theatre Club [ETC], along with the Eights-Week revues) got reviewed in the national papers; John Lehmann, who edited *The London Magazine*, visited Oxford often, as did Stephen Spender, who edited *Encounter.* Eliot, then poetry editor at Faber and Faber, invited Dom Moraes, the prize-winning young Indian poet then in his first year at Jesus, to lunch with him in London. Cambridge writing too was part of our Oxford world: F. R. Leavis, among others, came to lecture, and we read new poems by Sylvia Plath in copies of the Cambridge *Varsity* that turned up weekly in college Junior Common Rooms. Mary McCarthy visited Lincoln College and talked with a small, invited audience. Yevgeny Yevtushenko, briefly allowed to leave Russia, read his "Babi Yar" (1961) to a packed house in the Taylorian—an impassioned poem that dared to criticize the Stalinist whitewash of the Nazi murder of more than thirty thousand Jews of Kiev in 1941, as a part of his nation's continuing anti-Semitism. Tall, blond, and heroically intense, Yevtushenko (who spoke no English) recited the Russian text in a booming voice and prophetic style—waving his fist and stamping his feet in time with the meter—like no poet or poetry any of us had ever heard, seen, or imagined. All this was as real to us as anything on the syllabus, maybe even more so. We weren't just reading literature for a degree, we were charting courses of our own. The goal was to become an educated person.

And here is the secret that made it all possible: the tutorial system, as it was then, left us so much time and freedom to do other things. None of us had ever been so much in control of our lives. Because council grants fully funded the costs of a higher education (board, room, and tuition), gainful employment could be strictly forbidden during term and strongly discouraged during the vacations. Our studies were demanding, of course; the implicit competition among ourselves intense; and the prospect of final exams, when we could bring ourselves to think about them, quite terrifying. But mostly we didn't admit to such concerns, certainly not to others, and seldom to ourselves. The year-and-a-half between "Prelims" and the run-up to "Schools" seemed particularly free of care. As the formidable Helen Gardner (later Professor Dame Helen Gardener) wrote to my Rhodes Scholar contemporary, the budding novelist Reynolds Price, at the end of our first year (she was supervising him for the degree of B. Litt.):

> *Dear Mr. Price,*
>
> *When do you propose to get to work?*
>
> *Yours sincerely,*
> *Helen Gardner*[4]

At one time or another our tutors no doubt asked that question (ever so tactfully) about us all. The spacious world between first exams and "Schools" was so very rich with other opportunities.

The way we worked went something like this. We used a substantial part of every vacation (at home or abroad) to get a head start on the books to be read the next term. At Oxford itself we dedicated our mornings to work, sometimes making room for a lecture or two. Between tea at four o'clock and dinner at seven, we usually found time to do a little more, and on the night before a tutorial we would spend five or six hours writing an essay on a topic assigned the week before.

The hours between lunch and tea (one to four o'clock) were kept almost scrupulously free for other things—for rowing on the river, for instance, or for rugby, soccer, or cricket on playing fields just outside the city center. With Oxford so overwhelmingly gendered male, intramural sports were an important part of college life. Teddy Hall absolutely excelled in sports, sometimes to the detriment of its academic reputation. But it had a great track record in the arts as well, especially in the theater, and for those not athletically committed, the afternoons were given up to music, long walks in the parks, reading outside the "syllabus," and for many, including our own Terry Jones, the mounting of plays (both obscure and well known) and original theatrical revues. It was all in student hands: there was no professional coaching in sports, no Department of Drama for those who wanted to act, direct, or design. And nobody would have had it any other way.

Unless you were woefully ill-prepared—which no one dared to be often or for long—tutorials themselves were anything but ordeals. You would be received with respect and courtesy in a spacious sitting room, book-lined and comfortably furnished; black academic gowns, worn by tutor and student alike, imposed a pleasant formality; and for the space of an hour, you could count on his attention being fully focused on you—or on you and your partner, if you were being taught in pairs. You would read your essay aloud, uninterrupted, as your tutor listened and then at length replied. If he chose to smoke—as most everyone did in those days—you'd be invited to do so too. Good manners required no less. Someone long ago described an Oxford education as "being smoked at for three years"—and in the old days there was some truth in that. Nothing like a long drag on a cigarette to gain some thinking time, whenever a quick need arose. And if your tutorial was set for six o'clock, the last of the day, you might be offered a glass of sherry as discussion of your essay got seriously underway. The chapel bell at seven o'clock, summoning the college to dinner, would formally bring it to a close.

I recently came upon Sir James Darling's account of an undergraduate tutorial in the '20s:

> I read to him my ten-page essay on something and he smoked and, I think, listened. I finished. "Thank you very much, Mr. Darling," he said. "That is very good." The decency of gentlemanly politeness having been satisfied he would go on. "But why have you omitted to mention this and this and that?," thereby, if one had sufficient sense to see it, completely destroying the validity of one's argument.[5]
>
> Not every tutorial proceeded in so mannered a fashion or to so devastating an end, but there is truth in this anecdote concerning the manner in which most tutorials were conducted. Within the walls of that room and for that privileged hour you were treated like a serious young person—a young gentleman even—in a context that left you no place to hide. This rather formal manner of teaching—the irreducible core of Oxford as a "time and space apart"—raised the stakes, put you on your best behavior and made you eager to do well. In the course of three years you learned more than you realized, and not just about your subject.

St. Edmund Hall was unusual at that time in having no less than three dons teaching English; in most colleges two sufficed. Graham Midgley, the college Dean, a gravely humorous Yorkshireman who was also an ordained priest, edited the poems of Daniel Defoe, wrote the life of an eighteenth-century clergyman/buffoon known as Orator Henley, and completed a history of eighteenth-century Oxford (a time of scandalous laxity). Students savored his classes on "Minor Poets of the Eighteenth Century" and its sequel "Eighteenth-Century Poets More Minor Still," for they were as witty as they were insightful. Reggie Alton, a decorated war hero, enthusiastic county cricketer, and risk-taking Bursar of the Hall during the period of its greatest growth, was a generalist (as were most dons back then) and published almost nothing. But he was a caring tutor and all-around good guy, an expert in Elizabethan handwriting, a major authority on nineteenth-century English watercolor painting, and for many years edited *The Review of English Studies* with great distinction. Bruce Mitchell, who taught

Anglo-Saxon literature and the history of the language, was the most dedicated scholar of the three. In 1985, he published a two-volume (two-thousand-page) study of *Old English Syntax*, 25 years in the making, that remains the definitive work on the subject. The university awarded him an honorary doctorate, the D. Litt., virtually upon publication. A "down-under" Australian fond of jokes against the English, he was a demanding tutor who cared for his students as a papa bear might care for his cubs, roughing them up a bit every now and then to get them ready for the real world out there. It was in tutorials with Bruce that Terry-the-Medieval-Python-to-be gained the linguistic competence that his alter ego Terry-the-Medieval-Scholar would need—and for nearly 50 years now a vast and grateful public (professional medievalists most certainly included) has been the richer for both.

For more than 30 years, Graham, Reggie, and Bruce made up a powerful "English trifecta" at the Hall, deeply loved by their students and respected by their colleagues. It was my good fortune from 1958 to 1962 to be a fourth member of that group—and my privilege in the last of those years to teach for a while the young Terry Jones.

Notes

1. Robert F. Yeager, and Charlotte C. Morse, eds. *Speaking Images: Essays in Honor of V. A. Kolve* (Asheville, NC: Pegasus Press, 2001), 205.
2. Graham Chapman, et al., *The Pythons' Autobiography by the Pythons* (London: Orion, 2003), 49.
3. L. P. Hartley, *The Go-between* (London: Hamish Hamilton, 1953), 1.
4. Reynolds Price, *Ardent Spirits: Leaving Home, Coming Back* (New York: Scribner's, 2003), 130.
5. Sir James Darling, "Tutorial," *American Oxonian* 97 (2010): 328.

CHAPTER 3

THE EARL OF ARUNDEL, THE WAR WITH FRANCE, AND THE ANGER OF KING RICHARD II

Chris Given-Wilson

On January 25, 1386, according to a brief chronicle written at the Hospitaller priory at Clerkenwell in London, "there was a disagreement (*dissencio*) between the king of England and the earl of Arundel, as a result of which the said lord king struck him with his fist and knocked him to the ground."[1] This was probably the first time that Richard II had physically assaulted one of the great men of his realm, but it was not the first time he had tried to do so: about a year before this, while being rowed across the Thames in his barge, the king had passed the Archbishop of Canterbury, William Courtenay, coming the other way, and had quarreled so violently with him that, according to the Westminster Chronicler,

> the King drew his sword and would have run the Archbishop through on the spot if he had not been stoutly resisted by the Earl of Buckingham, Sir John Devereux and Sir Thomas Trivet, with whom he was so angry that in their fear they jumped from his barge into the Archbishop's boat.[2]

The Earl of Arundel was, however, the only person whom Richard II is known to have actually assaulted, and he did so not once but twice. In August 1394, at the funeral of Queen Anne in St. Paul's Cathedral, the king once again proved unable to restrain himself. As the St. Albans Chronicler, Thomas Walsingham, described it, Richard

> was displeased with the Earl of Arundel for some trivial reason hardly to be considered, so taking his attendant's cane he struck the Earl violently upon the head with such force that he collapsed and his blood flowed profusely over the pavement. The King would have liked to kill him in the church if he had been permitted. This act was perpetrated at the beginning of the funeral office. He was obliged to delay the funeral while the priests of the church hastened to the solemn service

> of reconciliation. It was nightfall before the funeral ended. The result was that everything was in a turmoil, the whole atmosphere confused. The reason for the King's anger was that the Earl was not present at the procession and carrying of the Queen's body when it was taken from the church of St Paul's to Westminster. And when he arrived late, he was first of everybody to ask permission to withdraw because of certain matters which were causing him concern.[3]

Richard II's loathing for the Earl of Arundel is well known, and it ended badly for the earl, who was convicted of treason and beheaded on Tower Hill on September 21, 1397. That the relationship between king and earl was a profoundly unsettling factor in the politics of the reign is generally recognized, but these outbursts also raise different issues. What was it (other than their personalities) that drove the two men apart? And what were the acceptable limits of royal anger in the late Middle Ages? It is with these questions that this chapter is concerned.

The Earl of Arundel and the French War

Born in 1346, Richard Fitzalan, Earl of Arundel, succeeded to his earldom at his father's death in January 1376. His father (also called Richard) had been the wealthiest magnate in England, a man noted for his consistent loyalty and record of service to Edward III, and it appeared during the early years of Richard II's reign that the son would follow in his father's footsteps. He was a member of the Continual Councils of 1377 and 1378 and of the reform commission set up in the parliament of 1380, and in November 1381 he and Michael de la Pole were appointed to remain in the royal household "to counsel and govern the king's person."[4] Within another couple of years, however, it was clear that Arundel and the young king had fallen out. At the Salisbury parliament of 1384, the earl's intemperate speech claiming that England was going to the dogs prompted the king, according to the Westminster Chronicler, to burn with such anger (*excanduit*) that, turning to the earl in fury and with a snarling face (*in furorem ac torvo vultu*), he told him that he was lying in his teeth and could go to the devil.[5] Any chance of repairing the breach probably evaporated with the king's first physical assault on the earl in January 1386, and by the time of the political crisis of 1387–88, Arundel and his ally the Duke of Gloucester had clearly emerged as the most hawkish of the Appellant coalition that humiliated the king, temporarily deprived him of power, and sent eight of his friends and associates to the gallows. There is probably much truth in the contemporary allegation that had they not been restrained by the more moderate Appellants, they would have deposed Richard there and then.[6] In the January 1394 parliament, Arundel launched another verbal assault on the king, accusing him of overfamiliarity with John of Gaunt and of favoring Gaunt's personal ambitions abroad to the detriment of English foreign interests.[7] Seven months later came the incident at Queen Anne's funeral, following which Arundel was sent to the Tower of London for a week to cool his heels, and within another three years he had been arrested and charged with treason.[8] Generally speaking, historians have not been kind to Arundel, describing him as rash, violent, bad-tempered and ruthless. This is probably true, but it does not provide a wholly satisfactory explanation as to *why* he acted as and when he did.

The first point worth making is that the timing of Arundel's quarrels with the king was not random. Richard's preference for making peace with France, which was supported from 1383 onward by his chancellor Michael de la Pole, and then during the 1390s by John of Gaunt, is well documented.[9] Arundel's preference, which was shared by the Duke of Gloucester, the Earl of Warwick, and by certain other magnates, was not necessarily for a continuation of the war at all costs, but it was certainly not for making peace on the terms proposed by Richard and his supporters. Twice during the reign, the king and his supporters went so far as to draw up draft peace treaties with the French that they then presented to parliament for ratification. The parliaments in question were those of April 1384 at Salisbury and January 1394 at Westminster, the same two parliaments that witnessed Arundel's outbursts. In 1394, we know from the official record that what he complained about was the proposal to grant Aquitaine in fee to John of Gaunt, the most fundamental and controversial aspect of the draft treaty.[10] His speech in April 1384 was recorded by the Westminster Chronicler only in general terms, but once again it was almost certainly the draft treaty that mainly concerned him.[11] On both occasions, it is worth noting, although Arundel suffered personal humiliation for his pains, his point of view carried the day, for both draft treaties were rejected by parliament.

The *dissencio* between the king and the earl in late January 1386 very probably arose from a similar cause, for this occurred during the visit to England of the deeply unpopular Leo, King of Armenia, an exile from his kingdom who was touring the courts of Western Europe trying to encourage kings and nobles to help him regain his throne. Having just spent several months in Paris, he arrived in England around Christmas 1385 bearing a set of proposals from Charles VI and hoping to act as peace broker between the two monarchs. Although Richard II was seduced by his charms, many of the English nobles took against him and wanted nothing to do with his proposals, believing him to be a French stooge and, in Walsingham's view, a charlatan (*illusor*).[12] One measure of his unpopularity is the fact that when Richard II granted Leo £1,000 a year from the English exchequer on February 3, 1386, he felt obliged to conclude the grant with the anathema, "The curse of God, St Edward and the king on any who contravene this grant!"[13] This was just ten days after the king had punched Arundel, and it seems probable that the two events were related. Yet once again Arundel ended up on the right side, for shortly after this Leo was sent back to France with his peace mission aborted, and when he sought leave to return to England a few months later, he was refused a safe conduct.

Thus if Arundel's aim was to prevent the making of peace with France on terms that he considered unacceptable, his well-publicized quarrels with the king were neither as ill-judged nor as ineffectual as they are sometimes thought to have been. This, however, was not his only aim, for he clearly held a particular view as to how the war should best be conducted, namely, by destroying French and Castilian galleys and the ports from which they operated in order to protect the English coastline and to keep the Channel and the North Sea safe for English shipping. It was probably his position as the greatest landholder in Sussex (the county most vulnerable to cross-Channel raids) that led him to this view—a view that his father, who twice acted as one of Edward III's admirals in the 1340s, seems to have shared. At the time of the elder Richard's death in January 1376, an Anglo-French truce was in place, but within just a few days of its expiration in June 1377 the French launched a series of attacks on the Sussex coast. As the local magnate and Commissioner of Array, Arundel was blamed for failing to organize any resistance, and he determined to make amends.[14] A few weeks after Richard II's coronation, he thus had himself appointed as admiral of the southern and western fleet, and in the following spring he and the Earl of Salisbury led a raid on Harfleur in Normandy, the port from which the French force had sailed the previous summer. Three months later, he and John of Gaunt led another English attack on Saint-Malo, also a haven for French raiders, though this ended in failure when Arundel's lack of vigilance is said to have allowed the French defenders to destroy a mine that the English were constructing.[15] In July 1380, the French raided Sussex once again, burning and looting Winchelsea, and once again Arundel was criticized for failing to defend the coast: Walsingham accused him of "belittling the honor of his earldom and the nobility of English knighthood."[16]

Arundel's involvement in the Anglo-French war during the early years of Richard II's reign thus proved to be a rather humbling experience, but if, as his later actions suggest, he was keen to atone for his failures, he was for the moment given little opportunity to do so. By 1380, he had been replaced as admiral in the south, and over the next few years his ability to influence English foreign policy steadily dwindled. Instead, John of Gaunt's ambitions in Iberia and the ostensible opportunities presented by the revolt of Ghent against French rule meant that it was the so-called "way of Flanders" or "way of Spain" that dominated English strategic thinking, while the king himself and his ministers were increasingly inclined towards making peace. When Arundel offered to go to the assistance of the Bishop of Norwich's floundering "crusade" to Flanders in the summer of 1383, and even to meet some of the cost of the expedition himself, he was informed that his services were not required.[17] Yet to judge from the ceaseless pleas and complaints of the commons in the parliaments of 1380–86 about the government's failure to provide for the safeguard of the sea, there was widespread anger at the way in which resources were being misspent, and both Arundel and the commons would soon be proved right, for by 1386, years of neglect of England's navy had allowed the French to assemble a fleet of over one thousand ships in Flanders with which to launch a full-scale invasion of England.[18]

The great invasion scare of 1386, which fortunately for England failed to materialize due to bad weather, caused widespread panic and was one of the main causes of political disquiet during the Wonderful Parliament that met in October of that year. It also signaled an important shift in English foreign policy. On December 10, 1386, two weeks after the parliament ended, Arundel, a member of the Commission of Government that had taken power from the king, was appointed as Admiral of England, that is, admiral of both the northern and southern fleets. This was the first time that both admiralties had been held by one man in wartime.[19] He also made sure that he had the financial resources to do the job properly, as a result of which the fleet that sailed out from Margate under his command in March 1387 was manned by 2,500 properly trained soldiers—"men of valor," in Walsingham's words, rather than the "cobblers and tailors" who, he claimed, were usually impressed into naval duty.[20] This policy was resoundingly successful, for on March 24, Arundel's fleet destroyed the Franco-Flemish wine convoy, capturing between fifty and a hundred ships and four thousand or more tuns of wine, which were taken back to England and sold off cheaply, greatly enhancing the earl's popularity.[21] Arundel's victory crippled French naval power and put paid, at a stroke, to the threat of invasion.[22] Given that just six months earlier England had been in real danger of being invaded for the first time in nearly two centuries, this was no mean achievement, but the king showed little inclination to acknowledge it, and when Arundel and his second-in-command, Thomas Mowbray, the Earl Marshal, arrived at court expecting congratulations, Richard and his friends simply sneered that it was "only merchants" whom they had defeated. Arundel tried to repeat his success in the summer of 1388, and Walsingham credited him with destroying some eighty French ships and burning a number of ports in Poitou and Brittany, but his expedition does not seem to have won him the same acclaim as his victory in 1387, and in May 1389, when Richard II resumed power, he immediately dismissed Arundel from both the admiralty and the captaincy of Brest.[23]

After 1389, Arundel withdrew from government, spending more time on his estates in the northwest, avoiding the court except when required to attend, and taking little part in either military or diplomatic initiatives. He did not accompany Richard to Ireland in 1394, and he was never appointed to an embassy—although the latter is perhaps not surprising, since diplomatic tact does not seem to have been his forte. Nor did he receive any patronage to speak of from the king during the 1390s—but then Arundel, as Richard II well knew, had no need of royal patronage. It was not just his irascible nature that made Richard fear Arundel, it was his wealth too, and the independence of action that it allowed him.[24] His father, the richest man in England, had bequeathed lands worth some £4,500 a year to him, as well as over £50,000 in hard cash, most of which was still stored in chests at his castle of Holt in the Welsh March at the time of his forfeiture in 1397.[25] Like Henry of Bolingbroke, who had his father Gaunt's resources to draw on, Arundel could afford to stand aloof from the court, and he could afford to oppose the king. Yet Arundel's wealth was also something that the king resented, and with good reason. His father had been willing to lend his money to the crown in time of need: between 1338 and 1375 he loaned over £70,000 to Edward III, mainly in order to finance military campaigns, including one enormous loan of £20,000 in the summer of 1374. Arundel the son, on the other hand, advanced virtually nothing to Richard II, just three small loans amounting in total to less than £2,000, and this at a time of dire financial need for the crown. To Richard II, Arundel's niggardliness must have smacked of a lack of patriotism. To Arundel, convinced as he was that resources were being squandered by a corrupt and incompetent administration, it doubtless appeared as prudence, especially in the early to mid-1380s when the government's credit was so low that he would have been entitled to wonder both how and when he was likely to be repaid. In fact, as already noted, he *was* prepared to put up his own money for the war if he felt that the cause was justified, and it is worth noting that Walsingham was fulsome in praise of the earl's generosity and public-spiritedness in 1387.[26]

If Arundel's failure to make his enormous resources available to the crown in the form of short-term loans was almost certainly yet another bone of contention between him and the king, he also probably saw it as a way of trying to achieve something more positive, that is, the steering of foreign policy in directions that he regarded as more likely to provide security both for his own lands and tenants and for England. Sometimes depicted as almost irrationally cantankerous and embittered, he had in fact a clear idea of what he thought ought (and ought not) to be done, but unfortunately for him it was all too personal, the mutual hatred between him and the king became irreparable, and in the end even his former allies turned against him. "You, Henry earl of Derby, you are lying through your teeth!" he raged at Bolingbroke at his trial in September 1397, when Bolingbroke accused him of plotting to depose the king ten years earlier, thus echoing the words that Richard II had hurled at Arundel himself in 1384. Little good it did him. Led out from Westminster to Tower Hill for his beheading, followed by a crowd that, in the words of the monk of Evesham, "mourned him as much as they dared," he remained defiant to the end. According to Walsingham, "he no more shrank or changed color than if he were going to a banquet," while the chronicler Adam Usk was convinced that following his decapitation he had been admitted forthwith to the company of the saints. Within hours of his death, miracles began to be reported at his tomb, and ten days later Richard II ordered his body to be exhumed in order to check that his head had not reattached itself to his trunk, which, according to Walsingham, was his recurring nightmare. Having satisfied himself on that score, the king had his body reinterred in an unmarked grave as a precaution against popular veneration.[27]

The Anger of Richard II

All this suggests that, rash and tactless as he surely was, the causes that Arundel stood for were things that other people believed in too. Whether he displayed anger towards the king, or just a sort of cold impudence, is not clear from the sources, but there is no doubt that Richard II displayed anger towards him. This was not necessarily a bad thing. Although classed as one of the seven deadly sins, anger was a long-established and very useful weapon in the armory of rulers. When Richard wrote to the Earl of Warwick in October 1382 telling him that he was "moved to anger" at the earl's attempts to lay claim to the manor of Bishopston (Glamorgan), he was acting in a traditional and perfectly acceptable fashion for a king.[28] This was what has been described as "bureaucratized" or "officialized" anger, a quasi-procedural way for a king to signal displeasure without the necessity to resort to legal procedure, to act instantly with the threat of worse to come if the offender chose not to comply, and to exclude men from the king's patronage or presence until he had been appeased. In more serious cases, it effectively put a man outside the king's (if not, technically, the law's) protection, and let other men, including the offender's enemies, know that that was the case. It could be used against communities as well as individuals, as witness King John's treatment of the Cistercians.[29] Anger might also reap further benefits for a king: it might need to be remitted, usually by payment of a fine, or it might precede a royal pardon, thus permitting the king to exercise *clementia,* mercy. Anger of this sort was quite different from Richard II's rage against the Earl of Arundel: controlled, formalized, and negotiable, it was calibrated in accordance with the degree of the offense and measurable both in its intensity and its duration.

Between these two poles the expression of anger covered a wide spectrum. It has been pointed out on a number of occasions that an understanding of the uses of royal and noble anger in the Middle Ages depends as much upon a reading of the way it is represented in contemporary sources as upon an analysis of the (apparent) facts of any given case.[30] A particularly instructive case in this regard, because based upon the testimony of the king himself as recorded in his chronicle, is that of the Aragonese King James I's negotiations with the *Cortes* (Estates) at Barcelona in 1264.[31] James had summoned the Estates in the hope of securing a subsidy to campaign against the Moors, but when he put his request to the barons, a number of them declared that first the king should deal with their complaints. When a second request only met with the same reply, James became angry: "Why answer me so ill and so basely! I will depart from you, as much displeased as any lord ever was with his people," and so saying he walked out. Some of the members tried to follow him, begging him not to be angry, but rather than listening to them James raised the stakes by refusing to eat and threatening to leave Barcelona.[32] Eventually, though only after much pleading, he agreed to hear some of the lords, who begged him to remain, for "on no account would they let me leave in anger with them." In the end a compromise was agreed: James received his subsidy ("although they maintained I had no right to it"), in return for which the king agreed to deal with the complaints of the lords.

The tone in which James recounted the successful outcome to this show of petulance has a touch of triumphalism about it, and with good reason: as he doubtless understood, it was never easy for those against whom a display of royal anger was directed to know quite how deep the king's feelings ran. What we read about here has more to do with the way in which the king wanted his subjects to think that he was feeling than with the way that he necessarily felt. Richard II's anger was, on occasions, portrayed similarly, at least in official documents. In February 1397, according to the Roll of parliament, word reached the king that the commons had sponsored a bill criticizing the cost of the royal household. This, he declared, was a matter that touched his regality, and he took "great offence and affront" at their presumption. The commons were consequently ordered to produce the author of the bill, which they did, whereupon the unfortunate culprit, the clerk Thomas Haxey, was promptly sentenced to death as a traitor. Whether Richard really intended to execute Haxey is doubtful, for just four days later he was pardoned, but only after a groveling apology from the commons and an elaborate display of humility by the Archbishop of Canterbury and all the other prelates, thus permitting the king to exercise his "royal pity" and "most abundant grace" as well as to secure an admission from the parliament that "the royal estate and regality of the king should be for ever saved and kept from blemish."[33] This was a measured and effective display of anger from the king: the imposition of the death sentence was clearly intended to indicate the depth of Richard's feelings, and it rapidly achieved the desired result. If a threat that subsequently needs to be carried out can be seen to some extent as a threat that has failed, then this was a threat that achieved its objective.

The representation of anger as "good" or "bad" naturally depended in part upon the point of view of the source, but it could be presented, or explained, in a number of different ways. One, obviously, was the degree of justification, or provocation. God, or gods, frequently displayed righteous anger, and their wrath was not to be questioned, but mortals, even kings, came under closer scrutiny. Walsingham's description of the scene at Queen Anne's funeral in 1394 makes it clear ("for some trivial reason hardly to be considered") that he held Richard II to blame for this deeply embarrassing incident. Anger might also be judged by its consequences: "Sing, O goddess, the anger of Achilles son of Peleus, that brought countless ills upon the Achaeans," begins *The Iliad.* An "enormous source of dangerous energy," anger was all too capable of instigating an appalling cycle of vengeance and feud.[34] Another way in which anger might be weighed was by its effect upon the person who displayed it. Loss of self-control was rarely something to be admired: medieval authors such as John of Salisbury and Geoffrey of Vinsauf believed that although anger might be feigned, it should never be truly felt, for anger that was truly felt diminished self-control and induced irrationality. The association between loss of temper and loss of reason was common in both classical and medieval philosophical texts, and was taken up by chroniclers.[35] The catastrophic defeat of the French army at Crécy in 1346 was explained by Froissart at least in part by King Philip VI's anger: coming within sight of the English forces, "his blood boiled, for he hated them. Nothing could now stop him from giving battle," and so he ordered his vanguard to attack despite the fact that they were exhausted after a long march. The sack of Limoges in 1370, perhaps the greatest stain on the character of Edward the Black Prince, occurred, said Froissart, because he was "so inflamed with anger that he would not listen" to pleas for mercy, so that men, women and children were massacred indiscriminately.[36] Whether it was actually the case that either Philip VI or the Black Prince had acted in a "blind rage" is impossible to know (and how likely is it, one might ask, that Froissart would have known?), but this was how the chronicler, whose chief concern was with the lessons to be learned from these events, chose to present it. On the other hand, the ability to use anger to inspire bravery or righteous indignation in others was clearly a quality to be admired. A contemporary poet unstinting in his praise of Henry V reported that when the king was at peace with himself he had the eyes of a dove, but when roused to anger he had those of a lion, and it is quite clear that this was not intended as a criticism of the king.[37]

Richard II, however (like his father, the Black Prince, perhaps) clearly had what would nowadays be described as an "anger management problem." The author of the *Vita Ricardi Secundi* said that he often displayed anger towards his servants, and one of the charges laid against him in the *Record and Process* was that when his lords or justices offered him advice, they were "so often sharply and violently rebuked and reproved by the king that they dared not speak the truth."[38] Henry III had a problem with anger too, and one of the scenes chosen to decorate the walls of the king's Painted Chamber at Westminster, *The Triumph of Debonerete or Meekness over Anger,* was probably intended to remind the king to "eschew violent anger and respond to provocation and frustration in courtly but firm style." This was not simply because Henry's anger caused him significant political difficulties (especially in his relations with great nobles such as Simon de Montfort and Roger Bigod), but also because displays of intemperate rage were becoming less acceptable in the courtly society of the later middle ages.[39] Violent anger of the sort that led to an uncontrollable physiological reaction was coming to be associated with brutishness, a lack of refinement or *courtoisie.* There may too have been a sense that as the bureaucratic and judicial procedures available to a ruler developed in complexity and scope, his right to rule "by his passions more than by his kingship" was also becoming less acceptable.[40]

The most extreme manifestation of a loss of self-control was physical violence. It was far from uncommon for medieval kings to be accused of cruelty—Rufus, King John, Edward II, and indeed many others—but the stern, even brutal punishment of an enemy or the premeditated requital of an insult or injury was not the same thing as an involuntary paroxysm of physical fury.[41] It is very rare to find examples of kings punching or striking anyone, let alone members of the aristocracy, and it is very difficult to believe that Richard II's contemporaries thought better of him for hitting the Earl of Arundel.[42] On the other hand, it is difficult not to think that, *pace* Walsingham, Richard was entitled to feel provoked by Arundel's rudeness. Was the latter deliberate? Quite possibly, but even so there must have been many who thought that the king should have learned by now to control himself. His outbursts in 1385 and 1386 could (just) be put down to youthful immaturity, but still to be lashing out at the age of 27 was to invite precisely those taunts about "perpetual youth" that Richard seems never to have quite managed to shake off.[43] Richard simply did not have the political (or perhaps the emotional) subtlety to enable him to deal with difficult men such as Arundel. Yet, while it is clear that Arundel's sharply pointed criticisms of the king sprang from genuine disagreements over policy and the advocacy of an alternative strategy for fighting the war, his behavior might well have tested the patience of even the most forbearing of monarchs. Indeed it is not inconceivable that, knowing his man, he was deliberately trying to provoke Richard into losing his temper, although this was a dangerous game to play.

Like Edward II and Thomas of Lancaster, Richard II and Arundel allowed their political differences to become submerged beneath a tide of personal hostility, with profound and disastrous consequences not just for them but for many others who became caught up in their quarrel. Like Thomas of Lancaster, Arundel ended his life on the gallows but subsequently achieved the status of popular saint.[44] Like Edward II, Richard II ended his life in prison, deposed, murdered, and subsequently discredited. Richard, like many and perhaps all medieval kings, used anger as a deliberate weapon: instructing his clerks to inform a recalcitrant subject of his "feelings" was simple, acceptable, effective, and required no public dissimulation, but when it came to publicly voicing his anger, he seems to have found it difficult at times to establish the requisite balance between threat and dissimulation. Richard, in other words, was not just an angry young man. He seems to have been a rather poor actor.

Notes

1. This previously unnoticed incident is recorded in Dublin, Trinity College Library MS 500, fol. 3v: "Memorandum quod die Iovis in festo conversionis sancti Pauli anno domino millesimo ccc'mo [octogesimo] quinto erat dissencio inter regem Angl' et comitem Aroundell ita quod idem dominus rex ipsum verberavit cum pugnore et ipsum prostravit ad terram." The chronicle covers the months from October 1385 to May 1386. A number of entries relating to the Hospitaller Priory at Clerkenwell suggest that it was written there.
2. Leonard C. Hector and B. F. Harvey, eds., *The Westminster Chronicle 1381–1394* (Oxford: Clarendon Press, 1982), 116–17. This incident occurred in March 1385.
3. Thomas Walsingham, *The St. Albans Chronicle I, 1376–1394*, ed. John Taylor, Wendy R. Childs, and Leslie Watkiss (Oxford: Clarendon Press, 2003), 960–62.
4. Chris Given-Wilson, "Wealth and Credit, Public and Private: The Earls of Arundel, 1306–1397," *English Historical Review* 106 (1991): 1–26; Chris Given-Wilson, "Richard (II) Fitzalan, Third Earl of Arundel and Eighth Earl of Surrey," *Oxford Dictionary of National Biography On-line* (Oxford: Oxford University Press, 2004–2011).
5. *Westminster Chronicle*, 68. The king's outburst was followed by complete silence until the Duke of Lancaster made a skillful speech mitigating Richard's *furor.*
6. Nigel Saul, *Richard II* (London: Yale University Press, 1997), 186–89.
7. *The Parliament Rolls of Medieval England 1275–1504 [PROME], 7 (Richard II 1385–1397)*, ed. Chris Given-Wilson (Woodbridge, Suff.: The Boydell Press, 2005), 258–59; Walsingham, *St. Albans Chronicle*, 956.
8. *Calendar of the Patent Rolls Preserved in the Public Record Office (CPR), Richard II 1392–1396* (London: His Majesty's Stationery Office, 1903), 307.
9. The most detailed discussion is in John Joseph Norman Palmer, *England, France and Christendom 1377–1399* (London: Routledge and Kegan Paul, 1972), 44–64, 142–50.
10. *PROME*, 7 (*Richard II 1385–1397*), 259–60.
11. Jonathan Sumption, *Divided Houses: The Hundred Years War III* (London: Faber and Faber, 2009), 523–24.
12. Walsingham, *St. Albans Chronicle*, 784–85, 804–805; *Westminster Chronicle*, 154–60.
13. *CPR, Richard II 1385–1389*, 110.
14. Walsingham, *St. Albans Chronicle*, 164–66.
15. Walsingham, *St. Albans Chronicle*, 228, 234; Sumption, *Divided Houses*, 323–27.
16. Walsingham, *St. Albans Chronicle*, 374; Nicholas A. M. Rodger, *The Safeguard of the Sea: A Naval History of Britain I, 660–1649* (London: Harper Collins, 1993), 505–06.
17. *Westminster Chronicle*, 40.
18. Every parliament between 1380 and 1386 witnessed pleas (and some promises) to devote greater resources to the safekeeping of the seas and coasts around England: see *PROME*, 6 (*Richard II 1377–1384)*, ed. Geoffrey Martin and Chris

Given-Wilson, 188, 192, 200, 217, 221, 274, 291, 293, 313, 327–8, 345, 350, 384; and 7 (*Richard II 1385*–1397), 24, 26, 51. For the inadequacy of the government's naval activity and the decline of the royal fleet in the early 1380s, see James Sherborne, "The English Navy: Shipping and Manpower, 1369–1389," in *War, Politics and Culture in Fourteenth-Century England*, ed. Anthony Tuck (London: Hambledon Press, 1994), 29–39, especially 32, 35, 38; and Rodger, *Safeguard of the Sea*, 112–14.

19. Rodger, *Safeguard of the Sea*, 505.
20. Walsingham, *St. Albans Chronicle*, 808–14.
21. Adrian R. Bell, "Medieval Chroniclers as War Correspondents during the Hundred Years War: The Earl of Arundel's Naval Campaign of 1387," *Fourteenth Century England* 6 (2010): 171–84.
22. Saul, *Richard II*, 169, states that it "dealt a mortal blow to French naval strength and delivered the realm from the threat of invasion for the remainder of the king's reign"; according to Anthony Tuck, *Richard II and the English Nobility* (London: Edward Arnold, 1973), 114, Arundel's campaign was "the most successful of the past decade."
23. Walsingham, *St. Albans Chronicle*, 852–54; George H. Martin, ed., *Knighton's Chronicle 1337–1396* (Oxford: Clarendon Press, 1995), 528–29.
24. And fear him Richard most certainly did: it was Arundel whom the king attempted to arrest at his castle of Reigate in early November 1387, thus sparking the Appellant rising, and it was Arundel's retinue which he forbade the Londoners to supply with weapons or victuals a few days later: *Westminster Chronicle*, 208–209; Walsingham, *St. Albans Chronicle*, 828–30.
25. For the Fitzalans' loans, see Given-Wilson, "Wealth and Credit, Public and Private," 22–26.
26. *Westminster Chronicle*, 40; Walsingham, *St. Albans Chronicle*, 812.
27. For these accounts of Arundel's execution, see Henry Thomas Riley, ed., *Johannis de Trokelowe Chronica et Annales* (London: Rolls Series, 1866), 216–19; Chris Given-Wilson, ed., *Chronicles of the Revolution 1397–1400* (Manchester: Manchester University Press, 1993), 59–60; Chris Given-Wilson, ed., *The Chronicle of Adam Usk 1377–1421* (Oxford: Clarendon Press, 1997), 28–31.
28. *Calendar of the Close Rolls Preserved in the Public Record Office (CCR) Richard II 1381–1385* (London: His Majesty's Stationery Office, 1920), 163 (see also 35, 335). For just a few (of many) examples of Edward III being "moved to anger," see *CCR Edward III 1369–1374*, 41, 124, 249, 265, 402, 439, 490.
29. I am very grateful to Professor Bill Millar for his many helpful comments on an earlier draft of this section of my paper. The classic, and seminal, discussion of royal anger is that of John Edward Austin Jolliffe, *Angevin Kingship* (London: Adam and Charles Black, 1955), chapter 4 ("*Ira et Malevolentia*"), 87–109 (for King John and the Cistercians, see 101–02). For "bureaucratized" and "officialized" royal anger, see Stephen D. White, "The Politics of Anger." In *Anger's Past: The Social Uses of an Emotion in the Middle Ages*, ed. Barbara H. Rosenwein (Ithaca, NY: Cornell University Press, 1998), 127–52, at 146.
30. Barbara Rosenwein, "Introduction," in *Anger's Past*, 1–6.
31. John Forster and Pascual de Gayangos, eds., *The Chronicle of James I of Aragon* (London, 1883; consulted via Library of Iberian Sources Online), 503–07.
32. The text at this point reads "e quan nos estauem aixi que no voliem menjar"—literally, "and when we were thus that we did not wish to eat."
33. *PROME*, 7 (*Richard II 1385–1397*), 313–18; Terry Jones, "Was Richard II a Tyrant? Richard's Use of the Books of Rules for Princes," *Fourteenth Century England* 5 (2008): 130–60, at 147–48.

34. *The Iliad, Book 1,* l. i (Internet Classics archive: http://classics.mit.edu/Homer/iliad.html); Albrecht Classen, "Anger and Anger Management in the Middle Ages: Mental Historical Perspective," *Mediaevistik* 19 (2006): 21–50, at 49.
35. Classen, "Anger and Anger Management," 27–31; Lindsay Diggelmann, "Hewing the Ancient Elm: Anger, Arboricide, and Medieval Kingship," *Journal of Medieval and Early Modern Studies* 40, no. 2 (2010): 249–71, at 263; William V. Harris, *Restraining Rage: The Ideology of Anger Control in Classical Antiquity* (Cambridge, MA: Harvard University Press, 2001), 404.
36. Froissart, *Chronicles*, ed. Geoffrey Brereton (London: Penguin Books, 1968), 88, 178.
37. *Memorials of Henry V King of England,* ed. Charles Augustus Cole (London: Rolls Series, 1858), 66 (lines 77–78): "Clare lucentes oculi, subrufe patentes / Pace columbine, sed in ira sunt leonine."
38. George B. Stow, ed., *Historia Vitae et Regni Ricardi Secundi* (Philadelphia: University of Pennsylvania Press, 1977), 166 (*in domesticos multum iram attendens*); *Chronicles of the Revolution,* 179.
39. Paul Hyams, "What Did Henry III of England Think in Bed and in French about Kingship and Anger?" in *Anger's Past,* 92–126, at 120–24.
40. Jolliffe, *Angevin Kingship,* 87.
41. This is not to say that one or the other is "better" or "worse," but merely that they are different.
42. According to Matthew Paris, Henry III came close to it in 1258 when, irate with Philip Lovel, his former treasurer, for abusing his position, he "seized him roughly by the arm," stripped him of office, and banished him from court (Harry Rothwell, ed., *English Historical Documents III 1189–1327* (London: Eyre and Spottiswoode, 1975), 134, 137, 143). Edward I's exasperation with the future Edward II went a step further: furious with his son for asking that the county of Ponthieu be granted to Piers Gaveston, he seized the Prince's hair with both his hands and pulled out all of it that he could before throwing him out of the room. Then, calling his nobles to his presence, he decided, with their advice, to exile Gaveston from the realm in perpetuity (Harry Rothwell, ed., *The Chronicle of Walter of Guisborough* [London: Camden Series 89, 1957] 382–83). The way that Paris and Guisborough described these incidents suggests that in both cases they considered the King's anger to be justified.
43. Christopher Fletcher, "Manhood and Politics in the Reign of Richard II," *Past and Present* 189 (2005): 3–39, at 5–6, 36–38.
44. John Theilmann, "Political Canonization and Political Symbolism in Medieval England," *Journal of British Studies* 29 (1990): 241–66.

CHAPTER 4

TERRY JONES'S RICHARD II

Nigel Saul

For Terry Jones, Richard II is a much maligned ruler. Obstructed by a gaggle of obscurantist barons, deposed by a slippery usurper, and with his reputation besmirched by Lancastrian propaganda, Richard, in Terry's view, is deserving of better in the eyes of posterity. Far from the self-centered, vengeful monarch portrayed in the textbooks, Richard, for Terry, was actually a wise and beneficent ruler who sought the good of his people. In his final years, when he ruled without baronial constraint, he conducted what Terry calls "a bold experiment in ideal kingship."[1] Its aim was to shield the king's humbler subjects from the policy of aggressive war with France that suited only the warmongering baronage. After 1399, however, when Henry IV seized the crown from his cousin, history was rewritten to blacken the former king's name. Our assessment of Richard's kingship, Terry argues, should be based not on the hostile Lancastrian accounts but on sources that date from the king's own lifetime. In particular, we should try to judge Richard's achievement in the light of contemporary expectations of kingship for the common good. Viewed in this light, Richard can be seen for what he was—an exponent of the ideas in the "mirrors for princes" literature, a monarch who triumphed over faction, ruling in the common interest. Such in outline are Terry's arguments, first articulated in *Who Murdered Chaucer?* in 2003 and developed five years later in his essay "Was Richard II a Tyrant?"[2] It is a case that Terry argues with great passion and learning. But how far does it actually convince?

Terry's arguments draw extensively on the "mirror for princes" literature—that is to say, on the treatises, written chiefly by administrators, expounding the duties of kingship and offering guidance to rulers on how to govern. Terry's argument is that in the later years of his reign, Richard sought to put into practice many of the maxims offered by these writers. The most widely read "mirrors"—those of Giles of Rome and Marsilius of Padua—as Terry rightly argues, took as their starting point Aristotle's treatise, the *Politics*. A key idea of Aristotle's was the distinction between kingship and tyranny: "among monarchical forms of government the type which looks to the common interest is called kingship . . . [while] tyranny is a government by a single person directed to the interests of that person."[3] The distinction between the two forms of government was picked up and reiterated in the thirteenth century by St. Thomas Aquinas in his reconciliation of Aristotle's ideas with Christian political thinking. St. Thomas wrote, "if a community of free men is ordered by a ruler in such a way as to secure the common good, such rule will be right and just. . . . If, however, the government is directed . . . towards the private good of the ruler . . . such a ruler is called a tyrant . . . if just government belongs to one man alone, he is properly called a king."[4] Toward the end of the thirteenth century, this distinction was again reiterated in one of the most influential of all medieval interpretations of Aristotle, Giles of Rome's *De Regimine Principum*. Terry cites John Trevisa's English version of the original Latin: "a kyng taketh heede to ye comyne profit and a tyrand to his owne profit." As he points out, Giles's text circulated widely in fourteenth-century England, in both Latin and French and by the beginning of the next century in English too.[5]

Terry argues that in the eyes of contemporaries the key issue was not so much the simple matter of how much power a king wielded but how he used it. He writes: "If [the king] ruled in the interests of his people, he was a rightful ruler. If he ruled in his own interests, however, he was a tyrant."[6] The essence of Terry's revisionist case is that Richard in exercising his kingly powers most certainly did rule in his subjects' interests. Heedful of the common good, he argues, Richard brought peace to his subjects, and in the fourteenth century "peace meant peace both inside the realm and outside."[7] In the 1390s, Richard not only asserted strong government within the realm, quashing those who opposed him, but he also sought reconciliation with England's traditional enemies, the French. Both policies, Terry maintains, were well received by his subjects. "A strong central monarchy was seen as the only way to control the . . . barons," who might otherwise tear the country apart, while external peace was justifiable "in terms of the economy, the tax burden on ordinary people, and the devastation" of France.[8] There were dangers for the king in this choice of priorities, which differed sharply from those associated with England's chivalric monarchy. Terry writes, "[I]t laid the monarchy open to easy charges of weakness and cowardice, from those magnates and men-at-arms who still saw the war with France as their greatest opportunity for gain and glory."[9] "These men formed a pretty formidable opposition," he continues; they were the hawks of their day. The ordinary people may not have liked them, but they could draw on great reserves of power and they were ruthless. In 1399, they showed no hesitation in deposing Richard when it suited them. Within months of his accession Henry IV began systematically rewriting the history of his predecessor's reign, to the lasting detriment of his reputation.

An obvious objection to this radical new interpretation that Terry has proposed is that it looks at fourteenth-century English politics through the distorting lens of twenty-first century assumptions. Whereas today we would all agree that the waging of external war is both morally wrong and illegal under international law, in the Middle Ages it was upheld provided the cause in which it was fought was just. Thus in the fourteenth century the English king's claim to the French crown enjoyed the warm support of his subjects, because it bore a resemblance to the case of a landowner who had been unjustly disseised of his inheritance. In the eyes of the parliamentary Commons, the interests of the king's subjects were bound up in their ruler's claim, meaning that, if he were to renounce it, they would suffer disherison too. In the Commons' opinion, what was involved in the war against France was a matter not merely of political expediency but of honor. True peace could only be found through the medium of a due settlement of their king's claims. It was in these essentially legal terms that the English political class viewed the king's war aims, an interpretation that saw them as defensive rather than aggressive in intent. While it is hardly the way in which we would approach such matters today, it is important to recognize that this was the outlook espoused by people at the time. If, as Terry enjoins us, we make the effort to judge Richard's kingship in terms meaningful to his contemporaries, it is equally important that he does the same in respect of matters important to the king's critics.

Terry's arguments can be countered, however, not only on the grounds of method, but on the ground on which he himself argues: namely that Richard, in establishing unfettered royal authority, offered government for the common good. It is worth noting that in the key statement of Richard's political aims, Bishop Stafford's opening speech to the St. Lambert's day parliament of 1397, the common good is never once mentioned. Throughout the speech, the emphasis is placed on obedience. Addressing the estates, Bishop Stafford said that for good government three things were required: the king should have the power to govern, the laws by which he ought to govern should be kept and justly executed, and the king's subjects should be duly obedient to him and his laws. The overall tenor of the address was strongly authoritarian. Nor is the common good mentioned in any of the letters that Richard sent to various foreign rulers following his arrest of the former Appellants. In these documents, too, the emphasis is highly authoritarian, emphasizing the king's vengeance on his former enemies. Writing to the Byzantine emperor, Manuel Paleologus, in 1398, Richard condemned the "wantonness and rebellion" of his enemies among the magnates, which, he said, had led him to stretch forth his arm, tread on the offenders' necks, and grind them down not only to the bark but to the root, so bringing to his subjects a peace that, with God's blessing, would last forever.[10] This was a letter in which Richard presented his action in strongly Biblical terms, using Old Testament language to describe Old Testament-style justice and emphasizing his subjects' duty of submission to the king as sovereign ruler.

Against this background, it is worth noting that in the 1390s Richard developed a new doctrine of taxation, which stressed the subject's obligation to sustain and support the king. Traditionally rulers had sought public taxation in the name of the common good, which was identified with defending the realm in time of necessity. Richard, however, faced with meeting the peacetime costs of government, abandoned this doctrine and sought grants of taxation in time of truce. In the preamble to the first peacetime grant made in 1393, no mention was made of the common good; the emphasis was placed on upholding the crown, honoring the king, and expressing gratitude for the king's government:

> In reverence of God, and for the good and tranquillity of the realm, and because of the great trust which the commons have in our lord king and in his royal majesty, and for the great charity and affection which the king has for his crown and for his said commons, to discharge them by good governance about his person, as far as he can, from any impositions or tallages in time to come, and to maintain and sustain them in his just laws, both rich and poor; the said commons, of their good grace and free will, by the assent of the lords spiritual and temporal, have granted.... [There follows the grant of indirect taxes]
>
> And also the commons have granted to our lord king by the assent aforesaid for the defence of the realm, and for the costs and charges of the king, and to honour the person of the king, be there truce, peace or sufferance of war.... [There follows the grant of direct taxation.][11]

The king had resort to novel doctrines of taxation again at the end of the parliament of 1397–98, when another substantial grant of taxes was made. On this occasion too, no appeal was made to the common good, for the realm was still at peace (or, to be precise, enjoying a truce). Two grants were conceded, one of direct taxation—a subsidy and a half on moveable property—and the other of indirect taxation: an unprecedented award of the wool and leather subsidies for life. The first grant was made on similar terms to that of 1393: namely, the Commons recognized the great charity and wholehearted love that the king had for his subjects.[12] The indirect grant, however, was made in return for the concession by the king of a general pardon. So, far from being an expression of a shared concern for the common good, the tax was actually made the occasion for a display of the king's mercy and might. Richard's conception of kingship in his last years was one in which his subjects were allowed no part. The state was identified solely with his own regality. What Richard offered was a vision of kingship that stressed the power of the prerogative and emphasized the submissiveness of the subject. The obedience that Richard exacted was manifested in Speaker Bushy's "ascribing not human but divine honor to the king" and in the abject submission and adulation of the Londoners on his entry to their city in August 1392.

To turn from Richard's statements to his actions in the last years of his reign is again to seek in vain for evidence of his concern for the common good. So, far from bringing "peace" and unity to his realm, Richard appears to have brought only faction and discord. The magnates whose downfall Richard procured in 1398 were men whose local followings were underpinned in many cases by carefully nurtured traditions of family service. When Richard removed these magnates from the scene and replaced them with members of his new courtier nobility, he was unleashing tensions that unsettled local society and undermined public order. At least one of the fallen nobles, Richard, Earl of Arundel, became the focus of a posthumous cult. According to Thomas Walsingham, pilgrims flocked to his burial place in London and there were reports of miracles there.[13] In the localities where the former Appellants had held sway, the maintenance of peace was dependent on a careful balancing of power between rival interest groups that Richard's precipitate actions upset. Retainer was now set against retainer, royalist against localist, insider against outsider.

The working out of these tensions can be illustrated well from events in Gloucestershire at the end of the reign. Gloucestershire was a single-faction society, with political life dominated by one resident baronial family—the Berkeleys of Berkeley Castle.[14] For much of Richard's reign, Thomas IV, Lord Berkeley (1353–1417) had brokered the flow of royal patronage and favor to the local gentry, and Berkeley family power was reflected in the presence of many Berkeley retainers in local office. Toward the end of the 1390s, however, the Berkeleys' ascendancy was challenged by the rise of another lord with interests in the county, a close ally of Richard's, Thomas, Lord Despenser, whom Richard raised to the earldom of Gloucester. In the wake of Lord Despenser's sudden ascent, the Berkeleys found themselves sidelined in Gloucestershire politics, and in the later years of the reign it was Despenser retainers who held the main offices in the county. By 1398 the growth of factionalism in the county was spilling over into violence. Shortly before Easter that year a series of attacks was made on the property of Sir Andrew Hake, a curialist and a newcomer to the county, who had married the widow Blanche, Lady Bradeston, herself a lady favored at court. Around Easter a group of malefactors led by Richard Panter and John Crok gathered at Winterbourne, ransacked Hake's property, and drove off his tenants. The malefactors almost certainly acted with Berkeley's tacit approval if not directly on his instructions. The true nature of Berkeley's feelings about the state of Gloucestershire politics became apparent in the following year, when he welcomed Henry of Lancaster to his castle and brokered the deal between the Duke and Richard's lieutenant, York.

In neighboring Warwickshire another established local magnate found himself under pressure from the courtier party, none other than the former Appellant Thomas Beauchamp, Earl of Warwick.[15] In the autumn of 1387, Richard had alienated the earl when he had poached one of his bachelor knights, Sir John Russell of Strensham (Worcs.), receiving him into the royal household—an action to which the earl responded by cutting off the knight's retaining fee. The pressure on the earl intensified in the 1390s, when Richard began systematically undermining his influence in Warwickshire and Worcestershire, the counties where he held greatest sway. In Worcestershire the king backed Russell in his bitter dispute with Sir Nicholas Lyllyng, Warwick's steward and one of his most senior retainers. In the parliament of 1393, Russell was to claim that his own steward had been murdered by a group of Warwick's men and that Lyllyng had done nothing to bring the malefactors to justice—Lyllyng, indeed, going on to deny him entry to his manor house at Dormston. Lyllyng, who was one of Worcestershire's two Members of Parliament (MPs), was impeached and imprisoned, an outcome that Russell was able to achieve even though not actually an MP himself. Equally suggestive of Richard's manipulation of local society was his support for his notorious councilor, Sir William Bagot. Bagot was a newcomer to Warwickshire society and resided at Baginton, near the royal patrimonial city of Coventry. His arrival on the scene constituted a threat to the interests of the Beauchamp earls, whose chief seat was just a few miles to the south at Warwick. In 1391 and 1392, the earl was present at sessions at which a group of malefactors almost certainly associated with Bagot were indicted, accused of murder. In 1396 an attempt was made to indict Bagot himself, but he arrived at the sessions with a gang of armed men, one of whom assaulted a Warwick retainer before the justices. In 1396, when an attempt was made to bring Bagot to book in King's Bench for his involvement in rioting in Coventry, he was initially granted bail, and when his case was finally heard in 1397, he was acquitted. So extensive was Bagot's influence in Warwickshire that he was elected an MP for Warwickshire on no fewer than ten consecutive occasions between 1388 and 1397. When the hapless Warwick and his two fellow Appellants were arrested in July 1397, Bagot gained his reward in grants from the fallen men's estates. His ascent affords the most spectacular example of Richard's manipulation of local society to promote a favorite's interests. Richard's interventions in Warwickshire were not a response to any evidence of growing tensions in county life; rather, they were actually the cause of such tensions. Instead of working with the grain of local society, the king worked against it. He was not promoting the common good; he was undermining it.

In the northwest, a phenomenon equally unsettling in its effects on local society was Richard's elevation of his Cheshire retinue, which encouraged the Cheshiremen to lord it over their neighbors. Richard's creation of a large bodyguard recruited from Cheshire was a characteristic of the last years of his reign. Until 1397, he had taken into his service men from almost every county of England. From the beginning of the "tyranny," however, the great majority of those he retained came from the northwest, the majority from his principality of Chester. At the heart of the retinue was his famous bodyguard of Cheshire archers, some 300 strong, which was divided into seven "watches." In addition to this, there was a reserve bodyguard of over 100 archers retained for life, and a further 197 who were retained during pleasure. The total cost of retaining these men came to a colossal £5,000. The Cheshiremen rapidly acquired a reputation for arrogance and rapine. When the king visited Canterbury in April 1399, the city fathers bought their favor by wining and dining them at a cost of £3 0s 8d.[16] According to Adam Usk, "wherever the king went, they stood guard over him, armed as if for war, committing adulteries, murders and countless other crimes."[17] Writers commented on the familiar tone they adopted with the king. According to the Kenilworth Chronicler, the watch leaders said to Richard, "Dycun, slep sicury quile we wake, and dreed nouzt quile we lyve sestow."[18] Richard showed such favor to the Cheshiremen that, in Usk's words, "[H]e would not listen to anyone who complained about them, indeed regarding such people with loathing."[19] The Cheshiremen took advantage of their privileged standing with the king to cause havoc among their neighbors in Shropshire and Staffordshire. In the wake of Richard's downfall, the people of these counties presented petitions to Henry IV to seek redress against them.

Contemporary evidence that all was not well in Richard's realm is found in the Oxfordshire rising of 1398, which hints at the tensions lying under the surface of ordinary life.[20] According to the testimony of the Oxfordshire indictment juries, on the night of Palm Sunday a group of insurgents led by John Milford, a weaver from Cogges, rose in rebellion and plotted the death of the king and the destruction of the magnates. When numbering some two hundred, they met at Cokethorpe and elected as their leader one Gilbert Vaughan, to whom as a symbol of authority they gave a pair of gilt spurs. The rebels then marched to Yelford and Bampton, the main local town, gathering supporters as they went. At Bampton, one Henry Roper, another leader, rallied them, crying, "Arise all men and go with us, or else truly and by God ye shall be dead." William Barbour and one or two others who resisted were beaten and threatened with death. Roper was then chosen by the rebels as their main leader, and he headed off to Gloucestershire, allegedly to seek out and punish the king and the magnates and destroy the laws of England. His fate was to be arrested by the local gentry and committed for trial at Oxford. For a few weeks around Easter the government was seriously worried by events. In May the treasurer, Guy Mone, Bishop of St. Davids, wrote with relief to the king saying that the worst was over and order was now restored. Quite possibly there was unease in other parts of the country. The Dieulacres Chronicler, a writer sympathetic to Richard, admitted that in the wake of the king's fiscal exactions "evil rumours began to spread because of the harsh bondage to which the whole community was being subjected."[21]

When the evidence from the localities is examined, it is difficult to find much support for the view that Richard's rule from 1397 was concerned to promote the common good. So, far from acting "with the best interest of his subjects at heart," as Terry maintains, Richard's governance produced only faction and feud.[22] Richard's interventions in local government were concerned primarily to strengthen his power and advance the interests of his dependents. For a year, beginning in May 1389, he had worked in association with the parliamentary Commons to promote their twin aims of better order and peace commissions free of magnate influence.[23] In the autumn of 1390, however, he abandoned this policy in favor of the creation of a great magnate-style affinity of his own, its members identified by the badge of the White Hart. Thereafter it was through the agency of his favored dependants—and, later, of his newly promoted courtier magnates—that he sought to achieve his aim of a stronger, more autocratic style of regal government.

Further evidence of Richard's tyrannical rule in the final years of his reign is found in the deposition articles brought against him in parliament in September 1399. Terry would immediately maintain that the articles are valueless because they form part of the smokescreen of propaganda designed by the king's detractors to discredit him and procure his removal. To deny their value, however, is to risk the loss of much evidential wheat amidst the admittedly extensive propagandist chaff. While some of the charges are either inaccurate or exaggerated, many others can be confirmed from independent record evidence from the reign. Where this is the case, it is fair to say that Richard stands condemned by his own actions.

A well-known instance is afforded by the charge in article 8, that Richard manipulated parliament. According to this article, at Shrewsbury in 1398 the king secured the appointment of a standing committee, ostensibly to deal with outstanding petitions, but in practice to deal with other matters "at the will of the king, in derogation of the estate of parliament" and establishing an unfortunate precedent. To give this committee "a certain color and authority," the king caused the parliament rolls "to be deleted and changed."[24] As J. G. Edwards showed long ago, the charge laid out in this article is substantially correct. Richard arranged for the record of the parliament of 1397–98 to be altered so that the powers of the standing committee established at Shrewsbury were enlarged beyond those originally approved. Three full copies of the parliament roll were written, two of them for all practical purposes duplicates, but the third, from which the printed version of the roll was taken, different. The two broadly similar versions stop with a record of events of March 19, 1398, and give the committee quite narrowly defined powers, whereas the third copy adds an account of business transacted on March 18, 1399, and gives the committee somewhat broader powers. The third copy is made without any interlineations or additions, and is written throughout in the same hand. Edwards concluded that this third copy cannot be an original roll, the other two rolls constituting the authentic record of the parliament; accordingly, it must have been written up later, probably soon after March 18, 1399, when for some reason Richard wanted the committee's powers extended. Edwards identified the motive behind Richard's manipulation of the record in his yearning for the condemnation of two minor associates of the Appellants of ten years before. These were Sir Robert Plessington, a former chief baron of the Exchequer, who had acted on Gloucester's behalf, and Henry Bowet, a clerk who assisted Hereford in his petition to be allowed to receive inheritances by attorney. Both men are recorded as having been hauled before the king and adjudged traitors by assent of the committee. The charge levied in article 8 is shown to be substantially correct.

Three articles in the indictment related to Richard's manipulation of the office of sheriff. According to articles 13 and 18, Richard selected as sheriffs men "who were his familiars or who he knew would be entirely amenable to his will," keeping them in office for more than one year contrary to statute. In article 20 it was further alleged that he required the sheriffs to swear a special oath to obey all royal mandates, including orders under his signet seal, and to arrest and imprison anyone speaking in public or in private to the discredit or slander of the king.

On the evidence of their affiliations there can be little doubt that the majority of the sheriffs appointed in the last years of Richard's reign were royalist in their sympathies. At least 11 of the 27 sheriffs who were appointed in November 1397 had connections with the household or royal affinity. These were John Worship (Beds.), John Golafre (Berks.), Andrew Newport (Cambs.), John Colshull (Cornwall), Thomas Clanvow (Heref.), Henry Retford (Lincs.), John Mulsho (Northants.), Adam Peshale (Salop), William Walsall (Staffs.), Richard Mawarden (Wilts.), and John de Eynsford (Warks.). In counties for which no trusty royal retainer could be found a retainer of a courtier magnate was named. Thus in Gloucestershire John Brouning, a retainer of Thomas Despenser, Earl of Gloucester, was appointed; in Norfolk and Suffolk William Rees, a retainer of the Earl Marshal; and in Rutland Thomas Oudeby, an associate of William, Lord Zouche.[25] Simultaneously Richard filled the lesser offices and commissions, such as those of the bench, according to similar principles: household men were appointed where they were available, and retainers of courtier lords where they were not. On the Herefordshire peace commission, for example, a body with a total membership of ten, there were two courtier magnates, two justices and three knights with connections with the household. By the end of 1397, the government of the shires had been almost wholly assimilated to the structures and political imperatives of the courtier-led regime.

It can equally be shown that there was substance in the charge that Richard kept his hand-picked officers in post for longer than the statutory one year. Slightly under a half of the sheriffs appointed in the summer and autumn of 1397 were kept in office when their terms expired in the following year. Those reappointed appear to have been principally men who had ties with the king or with magnates who were close to him. Richard's policy was in direct contravention of the statute of 1371, which prescribed annual rotation of sheriffs, and represented the first sustained breach of its terms by the crown.[26]

A number of charges in the articles referred to "financial tyranny," the king's interference with the property of his subjects. Article 14 alleged that Richard borrowed money from the men of the realm whom he provided with letters patent guaranteeing repayment by a certain date, but, in spite of this, the loans were not repaid within the agreed term, whereby the creditors were aggrieved. Caroline Barron has shown that the article refers to the so-called "forced loans" that were advanced to the king in the late summer of 1397.[27] The loans were not actually "forced" in the sense of being exacted under duress. Rather, they fall into the category of no-profitable obligatory lending to the Crown in a time of "necessity," for which a right of refusal was allowed if proof could be afforded of insufficient security, poverty, or illness. In the receipt rolls of the exchequer for 1397 and early 1398, some 220 lenders are recorded as having lent to the king sums amounting to just over £22,000. In respect of no fewer than 194 of these individuals, letters patent were issued guaranteeing repayment by Easter 1398. Yet, as Barron has again shown, only eight of these lenders are recorded as ever having been repaid. The allegation made in the article can be shown to be substantially correct.

The same can be said of the charges in articles 6 and 7 relating to the king's demand for fines for pardon. Richard was accused, first, of having made those who had risen against him in 1387–88 sue for pardon in spite of his promise that they should not have to do so, and, second, of making those who had already bought letters of pardon pay again before they could obtain security from such letters. The charge made in the article originated in Richard's decision to exempt "fifty persons whom it will please the king to name" from the general pardon that was announced by the Chancellor in the parliament of September 1397. Following the announcement, hundreds of people who felt insecure as a result of their involvement in the Appellant uprising of a decade before came forward to sue out such pardons. No fewer than 596 did so between October 1397 and September 1398, and two supplementary pardon rolls had to be created to record their names. Although little indication is found in the receipt rolls of the levying of fines for these pardons, there can be no doubt that fines were in fact charged. According to an undated council minute, the money obtained from the fines was to be placed in a special bag kept by the treasurer and, if the individual failed to agree with the council, he was to be imprisoned.[28] It was evidently conciliar policy that the fines for pardon were to be accounted for in such a way as to avoid normal Exchequer procedures. Communities as well as individuals were affected by the king's demands. A fine of no less than £2,000 was raised from the men of Essex and Hertfordshire under color of a pardon for their treasonable conduct before October 1397.

The third aspect of Richard's financial misgovernment alleged in the articles was the use of "blank charters." According to article 21, the king, to secure money, forced the people of 17 counties to submit themselves as traitors by letters under their seals, by virtue of which he obtained great sums of money, and, although the letters were returned to those who had sealed them, the king then made proctors, acting for individuals in the counties, seal similar letters. As Barron has shown, the documents referred to in this clause were so-called not because they were blank but because communities submitted to the king carte blanche, admitting guilt for treasons and other evil doings and acknowledging their need for the king's grace.[29] The earliest such charter, preserved in the letter book of Christ Church, Canterbury, and dated 1396, contains a submission to the king by the monks in the most abject terms and an acknowledgement of such by the king. Individual blank charters were superseded by proctors' letters in the late summer of 1398. The draft of a proctor's letter of submission survives in the formulary book in All Souls College, Oxford, and may be the prototype drawn up in chancery and sent out to counties and communities for their use.[30] Although the chroniclers were to mention sums of as much as £1,000 being paid to the king by communities when they submitted, there is no firm evidence that money was handed over. It is possible that, as with the fines for pardon, sums were received and accounted for by the council, but on the whole it is likely that the king's motive in exacting the letters was to satisfy his craving for security rather than actually to extract money.

Another set of articles related to the apparatus of oath-taking by which Richard sought to secure and uphold his regime. In article 20 Richard was accused of requiring the sheriffs to swear a novel and unaccustomed oath committing them to obey all writs sent to them and to arrest all those who spoke ill of the king, while in article 21 he was alleged to have demanded general oaths from his subjects that were hateful to them. Again, the two charges made in these articles can be shown to be substantially correct on the basis of contemporary evidence. As a letter under the signet shows, in 1398 at least one sheriff, Adam Peshale, appointed to Shropshire, was required to take a "new oath" (*nouvelle serement*) administered to him by a clerk sent by the king.[31] While no evidence survives for other counties, what was considered fitting for the sheriff in Shropshire is likely to have been considered fitting for the sheriffs of other counties. It can likewise be demonstrated that the king exacted "general oaths" from various city and county communities. It seems that the purpose of these pledges was to secure acceptance of the enactments of the Revenge parliament and of the judgments that had followed it. In October 1398, the newly elected mayor of London, Drew Barentyn, swore an oath on behalf of the citizens of London that included a pledge to uphold the acts of that parliament but also the judgments and ordinances made at Coventry. In the *Liber Albus*—the letter book—of Worcester Cathedral there survives the text of a similar oath administered by the sheriff of Worcester to the people of his bailiwick.

The various oppressions condemned in the deposition articles constituted tyranny in the ancient Greek sense of an illegitimate interference with the property of the subject. Thus, when Walsingham wrote in his account of 1397 that Richard began to "tyrannise" his people, his use of the word *tyranny* was technically justified. The deposition articles made a case for Richard acting as a tyrant in another sense too. They maintained that the king placed himself above the law, acting as a source of law. In article 16 it was alleged that he showed no interest in upholding the rightful laws of the realm but preferred to act according to his own arbitrary will, saying to the justices that the laws were in his mouth or, at other times, that they were in his breast. A more specific charge relating to his interest in civil procedures was made in article 27, which alleged that he used the Court of Chivalry as an instrument of oppression. Richard is said to have had people who maligned or dishonored his person arrested, imprisoned, and hauled before the court, where they were not allowed to enter any response other than that they were not guilty, nor to defend themselves other than by their bodies.

As Anthony Tuck has shown, there is very likely some substance in the charge made in this clause. In 1398 substantial new powers were granted to the constable and marshal of the court, the Dukes of Aumerle and Surrey. On March 15, the Dukes were authorized to arrest all traitors found within the realm, these persons to be punished on conviction "at discretion according to their deserts." Later, on September 10, Aumerle was empowered to hear cases involving the king—presumably slander and disparagement—and to deal with them in his court. At least one case brought under this order has come to light. This was an accusation made in December 1398 by William Scrope and members of the council that John Dyne, Richard French, and William Pilkington had been heard slandering the king. The three were ordered to appear in the Court of Chivalry before the constable and the marshal, but they denied the Court any jurisdiction in the matter, and the case was still being heard in 1399 when Richard was deposed and the case abandoned. In clause 39 of Magna Carta, in 1215 the principle had been laid down that "no free man should be arrested or in any way destroyed... unless by lawful judgement of his peers or by the law of the land." The powers granted by the king to Aumerle and Surrey to take alleged traitors and punish them according to their discretion were in contradiction with the fundamental principles laid down in the Charter.

It is thus apparent from supporting record evidence that the charges levied against Richard in the deposition articles cannot be dismissed simply as Lancastrian propaganda. The charges may be Lancastrian-compiled, but they are not entirely Lancastrian fabrication. Richard emerges from the sources as a ruler unforgiving to his enemies, obsessed with his own security, concerned for his own interests above the common good, and determined to secure the obedience of his subjects by a regime of bonds and oaths. Richard's powerful monarchical government, which Terry views with such approval, was purchased at the price of the fear and insecurity of his subjects. It can hardly be denied, as Terry maintains, that after 1399 Henry IV systematically blackened Richard's reputation. New and insecure regimes are often given to discrediting the governments they have displaced. The version of Ricardian history written in the early 1400s, however, was not altogether a tissue of invention. It had a solid enough grounding in the evidence that Richard himself provided by his actions. Richard's regime collapsed with remarkable suddenness in the wake of Henry's landing at Ravenspur in June 1399. If Richard had been pursuing policies as popular with his subjects, as Terry maintains, he would surely have attracted greater support than he did. Even allowing for his absence in Ireland and for the delays that attended his return, the lack of support for him is remarkable.

Terry's enthusiasm for Richard's kingship, however, is not based solely on his evaluation of his actions as king; it is, to some extent, the natural complement of his intense dislike for the magnates, or the barons, as he calls them. Terry's argument here is that Richard's interests and those of his senior barons were irreconcilably opposed. For Terry, Richard II's strong, centralizing monarchy was a force for good, bringing peace and order in its wake, whereas the barons were a malign influence, concerned more for their own interests than the well-being of the people. Terry sees the mutual opposition of the interests of king and barons most tellingly illustrated by the arguments about foreign policy. For Terry, Richard's espousal of peace with France brought his subjects relief from taxation and the king himself more money to spend on the arts, while the hawks—notably Gloucester, Warwick and Arundel—hankered after war so that they could ravage the French countryside and line their own pockets. Terry sees the policy differences between Richard and his baronial critics reproduced in differences in lifestyle. Richard was drawn to the new civilian court culture of the period, whereas the barons subscribed to an older, more militaristic set of values. Richard shunned baronial company as far as he could, favoring the company of administrator knights such as Bushy, Bagot, and Green, whom the barons snobbishly looked down on.[32]

We can agree with Terry that there was a vigorous debate in the English governing elite in the late fourteenth century about foreign policy and, in particular, about policy toward France. At the same time, however, it should be emphasized that by the 1390s the differences of view between the two sides were narrower and less sharply defined than Terry maintains. In the 1380s there had been long-running debates in council about whether to send a royally led expedition against the French and their allies or, instead, to concentrate on England's coastal defenses. In 1387, the parliamentary-sponsored "continual council" renewed hostilities, sending an expedition to sea under the Earl of Arundel, and this aggressive stance had been maintained by the Appellants. The failure of Arundel's second expedition at sea in 1388, however, coupled with the sheer difficulty of securing parliamentary consent to taxation led to the abandonment of this policy, and in late 1388 the Appellants' own envoys began negotiating for a truce. In 1389 a three-year break in hostilities was agreed, and in 1392 negotiations were opened for a final settlement of the war. To this background of growing rapprochement with the French, the one-time hawks on foreign policy began to lose the hold on public opinion that they had had. According to the Westminster Chronicler, John of Gaunt, the king's uncle, and the chief architect of a negotiated peace, had completely marginalized his brother Gloucester by the time the draft treaty was submitted to parliament.[33] The debates on foreign policy in the 1390s were concerned not so much with the choice between war and peace as with the precise terms on which peace with the French could be secured. Richard was prepared to assent to a treaty in which the principle of liege homage for Aquitaine was conceded, whereas his critics among the nobility and parliamentary Commons were opposed. After 1394 those who advocated outright renewal of hostilities were both numerically insignificant and politically irrelevant. For the most part, the military class was content to seek chivalric fulfillment in international tourneying and crusading against the enemies of Christendom on the Baltic or in the East.

If the differences between king and barons on foreign policy were less acute than Terry supposes, on domestic issues there was hardly any dissent at all. In the last quarter of the century the matter of greatest concern to the political class was the maintenance of the social order in the face of the growing assertiveness of the lower classes. The Great Revolt of 1381 had surprised and shocked those in authority, and in its wake there was much debate about how best to respond. For a while, the parliamentary Commons—the gentry and the richer townsmen—urged reform, in particular an end to corruption in government, while the courtiers and household officials preferred to emphasize the subject's obligation of obedience.[34] In the years immediately after 1381 there was a small number of issues, notably the administration of justice, on which the Commons managed to wring concessions from ministers. Increasingly, however, the argument went in favor of those who emphasized submission and obedience. A consensus emerged that the lower orders had to be kept in their subordinate place in the hierarchy. A key factor favoring authoritarianism was the perceived connection between heresy and revolt, making it necessary for all to support the established powers of Church and Crown.

From the mid-1380s the need for obedience and the consolidation of the social order were themes repeatedly stressed by ministers, whether of courtier background or Appellant-leaning. In 1383, Chancellor de la Pole, a curialist, reflecting on the causes of the Revolt, had stressed that obedience to the king was "the sole foundation of all peace and quiet in the realm."[35] In 1395, Archbishop Arundel, one-time chancellor to the Appellants, declared that subjects had a general obligation "to honour, cherish and obey the king, and to employ all their power in his service."[36] In 1397, Bishop Stafford, promoted Chancellor in Arundel's place, declared in the Revenge parliament that in a well-governed realm "every subject should be duly obedient to the king and his laws."[37] The preoccupation with obedience, a recurrent theme in the political discourse of the reign, was not so much an obsession of Richard's or of those who advised him as a concern of the entire political class. Some of the most repressive measures of the reign were taken by Richard's critics, the Appellants, among them the Statute of Laborers, passed in the Cambridge parliament of 1388, and the order for the seizure of heretical writings, issued by the Appellant council. The series of conservative initiatives passed in the middle and later years of Richard's reign expressed the views of a united, landowning elite. In the tough new labor legislation, the limits on the movement of laborers, the suppression of illicit meetings, and the curbs on the spread of ideas, the elite expressed their commitment to deployment of the apparatus of the state to bear down on the challenge from below.

The differences between Richard and his opponents were thus much narrower than might at first be supposed. The differences did not actually center on matters of belief in the sense of policy, for both sides were of essentially the same outlook; rather, they related to Richard's manipulation of the powers vested in him as king. Richard's critics considered his rule capricious, authoritarian, and divisive. Instead of "peace," they saw only faction and discord; instead of a concern for the common good, they detected only the pursuit of a selfish royal will. Richard's manipulative rule posed a threat to a constitution in which the king exercised his powers in accordance with and under the law. It is hard to picture Richard in his years of majority making any sustained attempt to realize the maxims offered by the authors of the "mirrors for princes" texts. We may applaud Terry for his achievement in making us think anew about Richard's exercise of his kingship in those last years when the trammels of restraint were removed. Terry's work, as always, is pungent, stimulating, and original. Along with Paul Strohm and George Stow, he has performed a service in demonstrating the extent of the Lancastrian rewriting of history after 1399.[38] In the end, however, the traditional view of Richard's kingship is probably to be preferred to Terry's provocative revisionism. The fact of Richard's tyranny can be demonstrated without recourse to what G. O. Sayles once called the "smokescreen" of Lancastrian propaganda.[39] Moreover, it is Richard's tyranny alone that explains his removal from the throne by his cousin Henry in September 1399. As John of Salisbury had observed back in the twelfth century, it is the fate of tyrants to be deposed.

Notes

1. Terry Jones, "Was Richard II a Tyrant? Richard's Use of the Books of Rules for Princes," in *Fourteenth Century England, V*, ed. Nigel Saul (Woodbridge, Suff.: Boydell and Brewer, 2008), 130–60 (at 160).
2. Terry Jones, et al., *Who Murdered Chaucer? A Medieval Mystery* (London: Methven, 2005); Jones, "Was Richard II a Tyrant?"
3. Jones, "Was Richard II a Tyrant?," quoting Aristotle, *Politics*, trans. E. Barker, revised R.F. Stalley (Oxford: Oxford UP, 1995), vol. 7, 100–01.
4. R. W. Dyson, ed. *St Thomas Aquinas: Political Writings De Regimine Principum*, ch. 4 (Cambridge: Cambridge University Press, 2002), 9.
5. Jones, "Was Richard II a Tyrant?," 130–32.
6. Jones, et al., *Who Murdered Chaucer?*, 51.
7. Jones, "Was Richard II a Tyrant?," 135.
8. Jones, et al., *Who Murdered Chaucer?*, 50; idem, "Was Richard II a Tyrant?," 135.
9. Jones, "Was Richard II a Tyrant?," 135.
10. *English Historical Documents, IV: 1327–1485*, ed. A. R. Myers (London, 1969).

11. Chris Given-Wilson, ed., "Richard II: Parliament of January 1393, Text and Translation," in *The Parliament Rolls of Medieval England*, ed. Chris Given-Wilson et al. (Leicester: Scholarly Digital Editions, 2005) item 5. http://www.sd-editions.com/PROME (December 19, 2010); *Rotuli Parliamentorum* (6 vols., London, 1767–77), 3: 301.
12. "Richard II: Parliament of September 1397, Text and Translation," in *The Parliament Rolls of Medieval England*, ed. Given-Wilson et al., item 3. http://www.sd-editions.com/PROME (January 4, 2011).
13. *Annales Ricardi Secundi et Henrici Quarti*, in J. de Trokelowe *et* Anon., *Chronica et Annales*, ed. Henry Riley (London: Rolls Series, 1866), 219.
14. For this paragraph, see Nigel Saul, *Richard II* (New Haven, CT: Yale University Press, 1997), 442–43, and the sources there cited.
15. For discussion of Warwickshire, see Alison Gundy, "The Earl of Warwick and the Royal Affinity," in *Revolution and Consumption in Late Medieval England*, ed. M. E. Hicks (Woodbridge, Suff.: Boydell and Brewer, 2001), 57–70.
16. Saul, *Richard II*, 394n.
17. *The Chronicle of Adam Usk, 1377–1421*, ed. Chris Given-Wilson (Oxford: Oxford University Press, 1997), 48–49.
18. Maud Violet Clarke, *Fourteenth Century Studies*, ed. Lucy Sutherland and May McKisack (Oxford: Clarendon, 1968), 98.
19. *Chronicle of Adam Usk*, 48–49.
20. *Oxfordshire Sessions of the Peace in the Reign of Richard II*, ed. E.G. Kimball (Oxfordshire Record Soc., 53, 1983), 82–85.
21. *Chronicles of the Revolution, 1397–1400*, ed. Chris Given-Wilson (Manchester: Manchester University Press, 1993), 98. My translation varies slightly from Given-Wilson's.
22. Jones, "Was Richard II a Tyrant?," 153.
23. Robin Storey, "Liveries and Commissions of the Peace, 1388–90," in *The Reign of Richard II*, ed. Robin Du Boulay and Caroline Barron (London, 1971), 131–52.
24. J. G. Edwards, "The Parliamentary Committee of 1398," in *Historical Studies of the English Parliament*, ed. E. B. Fryde and E. Miller (Cambridge: Cambridge University Press, 1970), 317-29.
25. Saul, *Richard II*, 383–84.
26. For the legislation, see Nigel Saul, *Knights and Esquires: the Gloucestershire Gentry in the Fourteenth Century* (Oxford: Oxford University Press, 1981), 110.
27. Caroline Barron, "The Tyranny of Richard II," *Bulletin of the Institute of Historical Research*, 41 (1968): 1–18, at 2–6. *PROME*, Parliament of 1397/January 1398, m. 13.
28. Barron, "Tyranny," 8.
29. Barron, "Tyranny," 11–12.
30. *Anglo-Norman Letters and Petitions*, ed. M. D. Legge (Anglo-Norman Text Society, 3, 1941), 11–13.
31. Barron, "Tyranny," 14.
32. Jones, et al., *Who Murdered Chaucer?*, 15–16, 53–54.
33. *The Westminster Chronicle, 1381–1394*, ed. L. C. Hector and B. F. Harvey (Oxford: Clarendon Press, 1982), 518.
34. Anthony Tuck, "Nobles, Commons and the Great Revolt of 1381," in *The English Rising of 1381*, ed. R. H. Hilton and T. H. Aston (Cambridge, UK: Cambridge University Press, 1984), 194–212.
35. *The Peasants' Revolt of 1381*, 2nd ed., ed. R. Barrie Dobson (London: Macmillan, 1983), 362–63.

36. "Richard II: Parliament of January 1395, Text and Translation," in *The Parliament Rolls of Medieval England*, ed. Given-Wilson et al., item 5. http://www.sd-editions.com/PROME (January 4, 2011).
37. Chris Given-Wilson (ed.), "Richard II: Parliament of September 1397, Text and Translation," in *The Parliament Rolls of Medieval England*, ed. C. Given-Wilson et al., item 13. http://www.sd-editions.com/PROME (January 4, 2011).
38. Jones, "Was Richard II a Tyrant?," 154–59; idem, "Richard II: Royal Villain or Victim of Spin?," *The Times of London*, October 4, 2008; Paul Strohm, *England's Empty Throne. Usurpation and the Language of Legitimation, 1399–1422* (New Haven, CT: Yale University Press, 1998); George Stow, "Richard II in the *Continuatio Eulogii*: Yet Another Alleged Historical Incident?," in *Fourteenth Century England, V*, ed. Saul, 116–29.
39. G. O. Sayles, "The Deposition of Richard II: Three Lancastrian Narratives," *Bulletin of the Institute of Historical Research* 54 (1981): 257-70, at 257.

CHAPTER 5

TERRY JONES: THE COMPLETE MEDIEVALIST

Michael Palin

First of all Terry is very bright. He has a grasp of arguments that is way beyond mine, and in this brief tribute I apologize if I misrepresent him or fail to explain to his satisfaction what exactly it is that I am trying to say.

Any objective judgment of the man founders almost immediately on a personal friendship that goes back nearly fifty years, to 1963, when I first met Terry at Oxford University. He smoked in those days (but never with much conviction), wrote poetry, and was a highly regarded actor (excellent in Bertolt Brecht's *Good Woman of Szechuan* at the Oxford Playhouse). He was also a dab hand at graphic design. Terry introduced me to the wonders of Letraset, and designed some of the most striking modern covers for the University's *Isis* magazine. He was also funny, both as a writer and performer, and particularly fond of Indian food. In August 1964, I was offered the chance to join Terry and three others in the cast of The Oxford Revue at the Edinburgh Festival. The show was exhaustingly good fun and also very successful, with full houses every night, and one extra performance, I remember, at one o'clock in the morning. I am not sure if it was the same for Terry, but for me that three-week stint at Edinburgh changed the course of my life, by making me aware, for the first time, that such talent as I had for writing and performing comedy could possibly, just possibly, be something that might one day earn me a living. Of course, I could not breathe a word of this to my parents. My father was dead set against either me or my sister becoming in any way involved in theater, which he saw as the slippery slope toward penury and general depravity. When I left Oxford in 1965, it was Terry, who had left a year earlier, who reached out a helping hand to help me pursue my hazy dream of somehow entering the entertainment business. Terry heaved me on board as cowriter of a project that he had persuaded a genial, drily witty English impresario by the name of Willie Donaldson, to back.

It was to be called "The Love Show" and combined two of Terry's great interests: sex and history. At Oxford Terry and I had appeared in a theatrical documentary about capital punishment (not abolished in the UK until 1969). "The Love Show" was to deliver a similar sort of theatrical polemic, only the subject this time was attitudes to sex through the ages. Flush with my first-ever paycheck (fifty pounds, handed over to me in a London pub), I set to work in my new role as Terry's cowriter (a prolific partnership that lasted until the end of Monty Python seventeen years later).

Terry, a sometimes volatile mix of the passionate Welshman and the deeply warm, considerate, and funny Welshman, was taking "The Love Show" very seriously, and I realized early on that this was something more than an extension of the comedy sketches we had been involved in writing and performing at Oxford. Terry had access to naughty, restricted books in the British Library, and more often than not my bedtime reading was the Kinsey Report or the work of Masters and Johnson. Perceived injustice, or any hint of establishment hypocrisy, got Terry very angry, and he was deeply committed to exposing, in an entertaining way, what he saw as a world of sexual cant and hypocrisy stretching back through history. I was more concerned with earning another fifty pounds.

Despite, or more probably because of, these different perspectives, we got on rather well together. I made him laugh. He made me think. Above all he gave me confidence in my material, and though "The Love Show" was never produced, it cemented our writing partnership. We made the first steps along the road to becoming professional scriptwriters when we were asked to contribute to a new British Broadcasting Corporation (BBC) series called *The Frost Report*, with David Frost and, among the cast, a new young star from Cambridge called John Cleese.

In his basement flat near Lambeth Walk, just round the corner from the Archbishop of Canterbury's Palace, Terry and I labored to create pages of jokes for each weekly show, for which we were paid tiny amounts. Slowly but surely the acceptance rate of our material crept up until, in a good week, it would be almost 10 percent of our total output. After, and often during work, we would listen reverentially to the latest Beatles LP. Terry was particularly enamored of the more wistful McCartneyesque numbers like "Penny Lane." We talked about history a lot. I am not exactly sure, though, when the medievalist in Terry fully emerged. He had read English at St. Edmund Hall in Oxford and was, from the first time I met him, a huge fan of Geoffrey Chaucer, which he took great pleasure in reciting in the original Middle English. Over a pint or three of beer Terry would wax eloquent about his other favorite writers. One was Henry George, the nineteenth-century American who argued that everything found in nature belongs equally to all humanity and advocated a land value tax whose proceeds would be shared by all.

His other hero at the time was Ivan Illich, and Terry found a sympathetic voice in books like *Deschooling Society,* which made the case for taking knowledge out of the hands of élites, and *Tools for Conviviality,* which did the same for the medical and other self-sustaining establishments. Illich's mistrust of machines, which only a few understood, in favor of tools that everybody could use, may have resurfaced many years later in Terry's opera *Evil Machines,* premiered in Lisbon in 2008. Terry remained doggedly anticorporate and anti-big government. He believed that the Industrial Revolution had had the damaging effect of stripping the common man of control and participation in what he produced, resulting in an exploitation of the individual that contrasted unfavorably with the rights and duties of the feudal system. I remember at the time that we had mild fun thinking up new names for English pubs. So instead of the "Fox and Duck" and "The Rose and Crown," we'd have "The Bone of Contention" or "The Hidden Agenda." If Terry had had a pub of his own at the time, he would probably have called it "The Myth of Progress."

During the first few years of our professional relationship we wrote jokes, fairly indiscriminately, for anyone who would buy them. For Terry, two enthusiasms were emerging. One was his love of film and the other an increasing interest in medieval history. These two strands came together in 1973 when the Pythons decided to try and make a film of their own. It would be directed by Terry Jones and Terry Gilliam and would be set in a period whose comic potential Terry and I had already begun to explore: the Arthurian legend.

Terry and I came up with script material that was often inspired by Terry's political and historical views. In the "Constitutional Peasants" scene, a mud gatherer is not at all impressed with King Arthur's credentials:

> "Oh very nice. King eh! And how d'you get that? By exploiting the workers! By hanging on to outdated imperialistic dogma which perpetuates the social and economic differences in our society."

Later, on learning that Arthur is a king, the mud gatherer's wife joins in, "Oooh! I didn't know we had a king. I thought we were an autonomous collective." Terry played the part of the Old Woman with more than a hint of the Wife of Bath.

Terry enjoyed reconstructing the Middle Ages, and it showed his ability to be very funny and very serious about something at the same time. Terry's intellect and my instinct could at best produce comedy that was funny and meant something. Though audiences might find it hard to believe, an awful lot of reading went into the *Holy Grail,* and Terry's shelves were stacked with books about the Arthurian legend.

Terry's fascination with the fine detail of the Middle Ages showed in the design and direction of the film, in which he collaborated with Terry Gilliam. I seem to remember that all three of us were impressed by the Italian director Pier Paolo Pasolini's rich medieval imagery.

Terry and I had always been advocates of filming comedy on location rather than in the studio, and in the case of *Monty Python and the Holy Grail,* there were not only comic but also sound economic reasons for this preference. With only peanuts to spend creating an historical epic, the two Terrys realized that we could use the dramatic and impressive landscape of Scotland for free. There was a setback when the Scottish Heritage Department refused to let us use any of the buildings under their stewardship, citing our script as being "incompatible with the dignity of the fabric of the buildings." When you consider the number of bodies boiled in oil and heads stuck on pikestaffs over the ages, objecting to a bit of French taunting from the battlements seems almost pathetic.

Terry Jones refused to be disheartened, and finally the directors settled on Doune Castle, near Stirling, which was privately owned. It turned out to be a wise choice for us and for the family who owned the Castle, who have reaped the benefits of *Grail* tourism, with crowds of Japanese coming to have their photo taken where the wooden rabbit was dropped and to buy coconut shells to knock together and pretend to be horses.

It needed a feeling for history to make the film work as well as it did, and Terry and Terry Gilliam had that in abundance. So stunning and spectacular is the landscape and so authentic the props and costumes that people are astonished when they hear that the entire movie cost less than £230,000. Around $300,000.

The need for authenticity and historical accuracy that made *Monty Python and the Holy Grail* more than just a comedy underlay Terry's preparations for the next Python film, *Monty Python's Life of Brian,* of which he was the sole director. When I went down to write material for *Brian* at Terry's house in south London, I might well find him deep in some book about Messiah fever in the Roman provinces, but I could not help noticing that his medieval library, far from being set to one side after the completion of the *Holy Grail,* was expanding by the day. Even as he bent to the task of directing a comedic version of a ritual stoning in first-century Judea, a part of Terry was still as fascinated by Chaucer as it had been when we first met at Oxford 15 years earlier.

A year later Terry was winning plaudits for directing one of the world's funniest films. A little more than a year after that Terry's book *Chaucer's Knight* was being described by the *Observer* newspaper as "a brilliant work of literary and historical detection."

Now, that sort of thing does not happen to many comedy directors!

Terry has proved that making people laugh and making people think are not incompatible. He is a scholar, a teacher, and a respected academic. He is also, thank goodness, a very silly person.

London, May 2011.

CHAPTER 6

MEDIEVAL MONKS AND FRIARS: DIFFERING LITERARY PERCEPTIONS

Derek Pearsall

One of the targets of Terry Jones's comic-satirical "history" programs for television was the medieval church. There was much fun to be got out of its corruption and hypocrisy and ridiculousness, and also that delightful whiff of scandalous outrage that these things should have gone on and been *allowed* and, it was hinted, should have been kept from us by stuffy academic historians. It was, with a nod to the popular press and a baseline assumption of the public's ignorance, a kind of exposé. It was never thus, of course, neither in real-life history nor in "history," but in satirizing the medieval church, especially the orders of monks and friars, Terry joined a long line of satirists in the estates-satire tradition, John Gower and Geoffrey Chaucer among them. In this essay I want to look again at this tradition, with an eye to another possible view of the story. Maybe medieval monks and friars were not always, or even ordinarily, fat, greedy, lecherous, and hypocritical, or at least did not yield themselves up so readily to ridicule as such. The problem is that, whatever I manage to say, it will not be nearly as much fun as the Terry Jones vision of history, for which, still, we thank him.

The twelfth century witnessed a profound spiritual revival in the church, partly as a result of the institutional reforms of Pope Gregory VII, partly because of the more settled state of Europe, unthreatened now by either Vikings or Muslims. The revival was widespread through the church, beginning with the monastic reforms of the early twelfth century and the establishment of the Cistercian order of white monks in 1115, and reaching its climax in the foundation of the orders of friars in the early thirteenth century.

The Cistercians came to England in 1128 and by 1152 had founded over 40 houses, mostly in the north and west and most famously at Rievaulx, Fountains, and Tintern. There were other new orders, both of monks and canons (who differed in not leading a fully enclosed life), but the Cistercians outdid them in both numbers and in the quality of their spirituality, inspired above all by St. Bernard of Clairvaux. The ambition was to return to a kind of apostolic simplicity of life, renouncing all possession and ostentation (St. Bernard was both fascinated and appalled by the riotous beauty of Romanesque carving), embracing austerity, and devoting their days to the performance of the divine office, to private prayer, reading, and study, and to manual work in the fields, which they shared with large numbers of lay brothers or *conversi*. They settled in remote places and built simple, unadorned churches. The purity of early Cistercian life was such as to encourage the great modern historian of monastic England, *parti pris* though he may have been, to rise to an unusual eloquence:

> For a brief space they gave, as fully and as unhesitatingly as can be given here below, an answer to the question: "Good master, what shall I do that I may possess eternal life?" Bernard of Clairvaux, William of Rievaulx needed to answer no more than: "Enter here: live as we do: this do, and thou shalt live."[1]

The spirit of Cistercianism remained strong for some decades, longer than is usual with such movements, partly because of Bernard's own strict organization and his supervision of the rule through visitation by himself or his appointees. But success brought failure, as the Cistercian houses drew in great wealth and endowments from the nobles of Stephen's reign. Everyone who could afford it wanted to be remembered and buried in such spectacularly holy places, and with wealth came expansion of the estates, more elaborate rebuilding of the churches, more work for *conversi,* careers for estate administrators. Greed began do its work, and envy that had been silenced by the reputation of blameless virtue found vent. The *Speculum ecclesiae* of Walter Map reserved its venom almost exclusively for the Cistercians:

> When Gerald [of Wales] related to him a sad story of two white monks becoming Jews, Map remarked that it was strange that, having decided to change their lives for the better, they had not made the conversion complete by becoming Christians.[2]

Elsewhere, in the satirical *De nugis curialium* (Courtiers' trifles), Map refers to the Cistercian practice of seeking remote sites for their houses:

> Their rule requires that they should dwell in a solitude; if, therefore, they cannot find one, they make it for themselves.[3]

The estates of northern Cistercian houses often incorporated the sites of former villages that were cleared by the monks.

The Benedictines, or black monks, formerly the only order of monks in England and still by far the largest and most wealthy, reacted cautiously to the new wave of enthusiasm (though Matthew Paris, the monk-historian of St. Albans, was denouncing the Cistercians for their greed and luxuriousness as early as

1244), and there was some tightening up of their regulatory organization. But high spirituality did not sit easily with the maintenance of large estates and with an important role in public affairs (many black abbots were ex officio members of the upper house of Parliament). Henry of Blois is an early and brilliant example of the monastic administrator. He was the nephew of Henry I, who brought him over from Cluny in 1126 and installed him as abbot at Glastonbury with the intention of having him restore that ancient and potentially wealthy abbey from centuries of decay. He made his name and his fortune there, and later, as bishop of Winchester, he proved a valuable advisor and administrator to his brother, King Stephen. Learned, appreciative of the arts, highly educated, a letter-writer of genius, he was not what we think of as a "monk." As Dom David Knowles says, he was like a modern-day businessman who, having made his millions and proved his competence as an administrator in the private sector, is recruited to government service.[4]

A century and a half later, Henry of Eastry was a different kind of administrator, but just as successful and representative. Under his priorate (1285–1331), the Benedictine abbey of Christ Church, Canterbury, with its extensive estates amid some of the richest agricultural land in England, became a major producer of grain for the market (comparable to the Cistercians producing wool for the market on their vast sheep ranches or latifundia in the north). Henry himself is described as "stiff, dry and masterful, a great high farmer and superbly able man of business."[5] He was not a man renowned for his devotion, but during his priorate the revenue of the abbey rose from £2050 to £2450 per annum. That is how success was measured. Thomas de la Mare, a little later, was abbot of St. Albans for nearly 50 years (1349–96). He made his reputation as a tireless litigant for the primacy of his abbey among all other black abbeys, and otherwise devoted himself to the rebuilding, renewing, and refurbishment of the church and the acquisition of expensive vestments and vessels. Yet he was not a man of personal display or acquisitiveness.

Let us leave that image of the monk as "man of business" to stand for a while and turn to the friars.

Pope Innocent III gave approval to St. Francis's first rule in 1210, and from the first the order was inspired by the direct example of Francis. There was to be a complete renunciation of worldly possessions, and a life modeled on that of Christ, wandering homeless and moneyless among the poor. The Franciscans came to England in 1224, and by 1240 they had 40 settlements, all in towns and cities, where they begged for their food and lived in the simplest dwellings. Their zeal in the pursuit of Francis's ideal accepted no compromise: when William of Nottingham, the English provincial in the 1240s, found the walls of the friars' dormitory at Shrewsbury had been built of stone, he had them pulled down and replaced with clay.[6] The Dominicans meanwhile had arrived in England in 1221, and spread hardly less rapidly. From the first they thrived by efficient organization rather than passionate example, and dedicated themselves to preaching and to education. They formed the backbone of the rapidly expanding universities at Paris and Oxford. For Dominicans, preaching was paramount, along with the development of the edifice of Truth (most notably by St. Thomas Aquinas) and the extirpation of error: the pursuit of heresy was their special calling.

The enormous initial success of the friars, especially the Franciscans, was their undoing, and they soon came under attack, especially from William of St. Amour in his *De periculis novissimorum temporum* (On the dangers of the final days) (1256), where the friars are associated with the heretics condemned in the epistle of Timothy because they undermine the whole church. Their popularity aroused the fierce resentment of the secular clergy, who saw them trespassing on their preserves. The seculars resented the rights assumed by the friars to preach, to hear confession and administer the sacrament, and to receive burial dues the parish clergy thought rightly theirs. The most serious accusation was that they offered easy confession and mild penance and made off with the relieved sinner's grateful offerings. No one does it better than Chaucer's Friar:

> Ful swetely herde he confessioun,
> And plesaunt was his absolucioun.
> He was an esy man to yeve penaunce,
> Ther as he wiste to have a good pitaunce.[7]

This struck at the church's whole apparatus of moral regulation through confession and penance, for the friars had no necessary continuing relation with the people to whom they ministered and no power, even if they wished, of securing the performance of the promises of penance made to them. The practice was the more insidious for giving equal satisfaction to both giver and recipient, the only losers being the parish clergy and, presumably, the poor parishioner's immortal soul.

The hostility toward the friars of the parish clergy and the bishops (the "possessioners" in the debate with the "mendicants") was fierce, and the backing given to them by a succession of mendicant popes in the thirteenth century did not help to make the friars any more popular. Nor did the profession of poverty fit well with an increasing ostentation of life, and the ideal of poverty itself became a matter of intense debate. How poor is poor? Was Christ poor? Did poverty mean renunciation of legal dominion over property, or did it mean material hardship? A split in the Franciscan order pitted the proponents of absolute poverty (the "Spirituals") against those who thought that not-quite-so-poor would suffice. A decisive moment came with the papal bull *Super cathedram* of 1311, which finally gave official sanction to the friars' rights to confession and burial. The way was clear for the torrent of antifraternal satire and abuse in the fourteenth century. Richard FitzRalph, archbishop of Armagh, was the most famously vehement in his condemnation of the friars, in his English preaching in London in 1356–57 and in his *Defensio curatorum,* translated into English by John Trevisa, in which he inveighed against the friars for usurping the jurisdiction and rights of parish priests. Yet in all this it should be remembered that the orders were differently reprehensible, and that professional antifraternalism did not speak equally to all nor for everyone. It means something that late fourteenth-century and fifteenth-century kings chose friars as their confessors, as did John of Gaunt (the poet Richard Maidstone)—even though the friars they chose were of the order of Carmelites, long respected for their piety.

William Langland's *Piers Plowman* gives the most vivid representation of antifraternal attitudes in the later part of the century.[8] His poem focuses insistently upon the friars as the chief agent of corruption within the church. They pervert the office of confession and the sacrament of penance to their own ends and in effect sell absolution for money. They are merchants on the spiritual exchange market and the heralds of impending apocalypse:

> Mony of thise maistres of mendenant freres
> Here moneye and marchandise marchen togyderes.
> Ac sith charite hath be chapman and chief to shryue lordes
> Mony ferlyes han falle in a fewe yeres,
> And but holi chirche and charite choppe adoun suche shryuars
> The moste meschief on molde mounteth vp faste.[9]

Characteristically, Langland gives animation to the commonplaces of antifraternal satire by incorporating friars into the action. An accommodating friar oozes forward when the maiden Meed goes to confession, promising in advance that whatever she has done he can absolve her for a small consideration:

> "Thow lewed men and lered men haued layn by the bothe,
> And Falshede yfonde the al this fourty wyntur,
> Y shal assoyle the mysulue for a seem of whete."[10]

He promises in return for her generosity to have her name inscribed in the grand new window that is being installed in his friary church, and have the brothers sing for her "as for a sustre of oure ordre."[11] These "confraternities" were another way in which the friars wormed their way into the confidence and purses of the well-to-do, and guaranteed them, living and dead, the benefit of the convent's prayers in return for their regular "subscriptions" or offerings. The cozy and profitable relationship of the slimily hypocritical friar of Chaucer's "Summoner's Tale" with citizen Thomas—and his wife—is guaranteed by their letters of fraternity.[12] Nothing in Langland equals the brilliance of Chaucer's narrative of a friar "in action."

Langland also attacks the friars' "glosing" of the gospels, that is, the twisting of the interpretation of scripture to their own ends: "Glosynge is a glorious thyng, certeyn," says the Summoner's friar.[13] Again, like Chaucer, Langland shows them in action, first the two friars (friars traveled in pairs so that they could act as "chaperones" for each other) whom the dreamer meets when he is first searching for Dowel. "Look no further," they say, "he dwells with us,"[14] answering the dreamer's reasonable enough demur with a cunningly devised scriptural parable. The fat doctor at the feast of Patience is another such doctrinal expert. At the end of the poem, Langland dramatizes the penetration of the church, the house of Unity, by a wheedling friar who promises easy confession and penance to those who have been wounded in the battle against the besieging Sins. Contrition's "plasters" of penance have been too sore and biting, says the friar,

And goeth gropeth Contricion and gaf hym a plaster
Of a pryue payement and "Y shal preye for yow
And for hem that ye aren holde to al my lyf-tyme
And make of yow *memoria* in masse and in matynes
Of freres of oure fraternite for a litel suluer." [15]

The friar is called "Sire Penetrans-domos," alluding to the name given to the friars by William of St. Amour, who takes it from the prophecy of impending apocalypse made in the epistle of Timothy.[16] Among those whose presence will be perilous in the last days, he says, "are those who *insinuate themselves into households,* and subdue to their purposes weak and foolish women."[17] The Summoner's friar indulges in a mildly flirtatious version of such seduction with Thomas's wife.

One is struck, perhaps puzzled, by the almost obsessive nature of Langland's preoccupation with the friars. He returns to them again and again, begins his poem with them and ends with them. They are everywhere, just as Chaucer's Wife of Bath imagined them swarming through the world in place of the fairies and incubi of old. Langland too speaks of their numberlessness: though they are "lymytours," there is no limit to them. All others—soldiers in the army, monks in the cloister—have a certain number:

Of lewed and of lered the lawe wol and asketh
A certeyne for a certeyne—saue oenliche of freres.[18]

One reason for this perception is that friars were always conspicuously out and about, unlike monks. Whatever they did, good or bad, was done in public: they seemed to be ubiquitous.

But it may be that Langland's obsession with the friars, even as he echoes familiar complaints against them, has to do with a deep attachment to their original ideals, and a painful awareness that they have failed in their vocation. Like most antifraternal writers, he speaks nostalgically of the days of Francis and Dominic, when true charity was to be found among friars.[19] Once the spearhead of the church's mission to save, they have succumbed to worldliness and betrayed the hopes they first stimulated. They remain nevertheless powerful in Langland's imagination, for bad or for good. It is they who bring the church to near destruction at the end of the poem, but it is remarkable that in the very last lines, as Conscience turns wearily from the waste and chaos all around and goes again in search of Piers Plowman, it is the friars that preoccupy him. His quest will be that "freres had a fyndynge that for nede flateren."[20] Such is the potential of the friars that the world will be saved if they can be guaranteed a living and do not have to perjure themselves by begging. A disillusioned admirer of the friars, Langland reminds us of the promise they once and still held out. They were the great preachers of their day, and pioneers in the adaptation of the vernacular to religious lyric and other literature of penance, homiletic instruction, and devotion. All were ordained priests (unlike monks), many had spent time in the universities, and some had degrees (and liked to be called "maister"), where monks could be quite ignorant. They brought a whiff of a different world of learning and cosmopolitan sophistication into the ordinary streets of towns and villages. Langland did not want to see them as a lost cause.

Langland's view of the monks is very different. Monks were cloistered for the most part and would come into only occasional contact with people outside. A monk or two might be seen at the gate of the abbey at the daily distribution of alms to the poor, and the great and rich on their travels would at least see the four-star quarters assigned to them by abbots always aware of the need to cultivate the powerful. There may have been suspicion and resentment aroused by the wealth and power of the larger abbeys and the influence they exerted in public affairs, but for most people monks were a world apart. It is, for us, difficult to see the point of monks. They farmed their estates, protected their endowments, magnified their churches, and wrote vast chronicles in Latin and, later, English. Many individual monks no doubt led holy lives, but the dedication of their orders was to the preservation and enhancement of their institutional wealth, power, and privileges. But their contribution to the community was real enough, albeit invisible. It was understood that monks acted as witnesses to the faith and made intercession through prayer for all Christians. It was good to know that there were whole orders of men and women somewhere out there praying to God for everyone else and performing daily, forever, the Opus Dei. Above all, out of sight, they had the great advantage of not being friars.

Monks make no appearance in the Confession of the Sins in *Piers Plowman,* except in the confession of Wrath, where it is specifically nuns who are subject to fits of unseemly anger. Monks are exempted:

> Amonges monkes Y myhte be, ac mony tyme Y spare,
> For there aren many felle frekes myne aferes to aspye,
> That is, priour and suppriour and oure *pater abbas*. . . .
> Y haue no luste, lef me, to longe amonges monkes.[21]

Langland has some warnings to monks of the fate that awaits them if they do not keep their rule, but otherwise he sees their life, and that of scholars, as paradise:

> For yf heuene be on this erthe or eny ese to the soule
> Hit is in cloystre or in scole, by many skilles Y fynde.[22]

Langland has perhaps some happy memories of his own days in the cloister school at Malvern abbey or briefly at college, but it is distance that gives enchantment to the view. *The Land of Cokaygne,* a poem that survives unique in a multilingual Franciscan miscellany from Kildare in Ireland (British Library MS Harley 913), describes an abbey that is a real "paradise on earth," where the walls are built of puddings and pies and the geese fly up ready roasted from the spit crying "Gees, al hote, al hot!"[23] The monks' adventures with the local nuns are touched with gentle erotic fantasy. As for the earthly paradise, the point about Cokaygne is that it is *better:*

> What is þer in Paradis
> Bot grasse and flure and grene ris [leafy twig]?

Whether Langland would have found this comic parody funny or not, Chaucer would certainly have appreciated it, for it disarms criticism in a manner that he himself perfected.

Of course, Langland, as well as his idealization of the cloistered life, has a memorably disenchanted picture of a monk, too:

> Ac mony day, men telleth, bothe monkes and chanons
> Haen ryde out of aray, here reule euele yholde,
> Ledares of louedays and londes ypurchaced
> And pryked aboute on palfrayes fram places to maneres,
> An hep of houndes at here ers as he a lord were.[24]

This monk, however, condemned for his worldliness, his love of hunting, his entanglement in worldly affairs, his lordliness, is an "outrydere." Such monks were licensed to go abroad to attend to the abbey's affairs and to supervise the workers at distant abbey farms ("granges"), and they had many opportunities to fall into worldly ways. Like William Clowne, the hunting abbot of Leicester (1345–78), they could argue that they had to have fine horses to make a good impression on the local lords with whom they would often be negotiating land deals.

It is no accident that Chaucer's Monk is also an "outrydere." It is this that gives him license for all his apparently un-monk-like ways—his hunting and his fine horses, his fondness for good food and fine clothes, his inclination to be a "modern" monk and to welcome a relaxation of the monastic rule:

> What sholde he studie and make hymselven wood,
> Upon a book in cloystre alwey to poure,
> Or swynken with his handes, and laboure,
> As Austyn bit? How shal the world be served?
> Lat Austyn have his swynk to hym reserved![25]

Given that he is nothing like the conventional idea of a monk, he is yet not an unattractive figure. This may have something to do with Chaucer's opinion of monks, but more to do with his technique of withdrawing from the moral positions that estates-satire usually takes up. It is as if we were relishing him as a "character," not judging him as a representative type of misbehavior. Moral judgment is suspended as we take aesthetic pleasure in the character's vitality, as Jill Mann has shown in rich detail.[26] What for Langland is a moral challenge is for Chaucer an artistic challenge: how to represent these creatures as human. Chaucer's irony in such a case is given no purchase by the implication of shared agreement with the reader on what is to be morally approved, as in the line, "A manly man, to been an abbot able."[27] What is it to be "manly"? Is to be "manly" a good thing or a bad thing for a prospective abbot? The answers escape us. Even the monk of the "Shipman's Tale," who significantly is also one of those licensed by his abbot "out for to ryde / To seen hire graunges and hir bernes wyde," evades moral censure despite his immorality.[28] He is easygoing, and his acceptance of the wife's offer is not due to the pent-up lasciviousness that satire conventionally associated with monks, but an amiable readiness to oblige the lady. It is unfortunate that to oblige the lady he has to disoblige her husband, but it is hard to bear the monk ill will.

The Friar of the General Prologue is another character who forces us to reexamine how we make moral judgments. Again, he is in many ways an attractive "character," vigorous, physically a fine man, genial, gregarious, a "good fellow." But the inherently exploitative nature of his profession, the fact that there are *victims,* makes a total suspension of moral judgment impossible. His fault is not that he cultivates secular patrons and is familiar in their houses, one of the traditional accusations of antifraternal satire, but that he shuns the poor, the lepers, the beggars:

> It is nat honest; it may nat avaunce,
> For to deelen with no swich poraille,
> But al with riche and selleres of vitaille.[29]

This "poraille," these "lazars" and "beggesteres," are those very poor, we remember, to whose welfare and salvation his order is dedicated.

Monks have no such victims, and they are in danger of getting off lightly because writers get only a glimpse of them. The rest lies hidden behind the monastery wall, except for the reports of visitations. Some of the larger abbeys were exempt from episcopal visitation, and fought hard to preserve this exemption, but others, large and small, were subject to inspection by the diocesan bishop. The records of the visitations are often of infractions of the rule that are reassuringly humdrum: avoiding services, not saying the office properly, drinking after compline (very common—monks too enjoyed a nightcap), wandering beyond the abbey's confines. Occasionally, the records make alarming reading, but of course there were old scores to be settled and scandalous exaggerations to be enjoyed, and in any case not much was ever done to make radical improvements. As the fifteenth century progressed, and Henry V's attempt to reform the black monks ended abruptly with his sudden death, the visitation records begin to show how monasteries are changing. There continue to be the usual routine criticisms, but the reports also begin to show a new pattern. There are now complaints that point to increasing secularization: monks frequenting taverns, bringing visitors, even women, back to the monastery, accepting private gifts and money, and taking excessive advantage of the concessions allowed to obedientiaries, that is, those appointed to some monastic office, who might amount to half the total of monks. These concessions included the provision of private apartments, even private altars, and exemption from many offices. We can well believe that John

Lydgate, monk of Bury St. Edmunds, disciple of Chaucer, renowned poet and translator, itinerant in the royal service, was granted a private room in which to keep his books and pen his long poems. He seems to have got away with receiving £3.6s.8d (five marks) from abbot Whethamstede of St. Albans for writing a verse life of St. Alban, but when Humphrey of Gloucester secured a pension for him for the writing of the *Fall of Princes,* the poet had difficulty collecting it until a compromise was devised by which the money (£7.13s.4d per annum) was paid jointly to him and to the lay treasurer of the abbey, John Baret of Bury.[30] Lydgate, late in life (he was 70), went to considerable exertions to secure this payment: he had become a "man of business." This, long anticipated, was the future for monks. When the Dissolution came, many accepted their pensions quite contentedly.

Lydgate's own perception of monks and friars, given his profession, is of peculiar interest, and it finds expression in the *Danse Macabre,* as the different estates of society are summoned by Death. The satiric portraits of the fat and luxury-loving Abbot and the richly dressed Abbess are predictable, but Death's summons to the ordinary Monk (in his "blake abite," like Lydgate) merely reminds him that his life is transitory and he must now make his reckoning. His answer is sober enough:

> I had levere in the cloystre be
> Atte my boke and studie my service.[31]

The claustral ideal, however, is made uncompromisingly explicit in the answer of the Carthusian monk, member of an order that had seized the spiritual initiative in England in the early fifteenth century. For him the coming of death is a mere physical confirmation of a spiritual choice already made:

> Unto the world I was dede long agon
> Be my ordre and my professioun.[32]

This is the true meaning of Langland's "heaven on earth" topos: the life of the monk, since he is dead to the world, is an adumbration of life in heaven hereafter. As to the "frere menoure," it is to Lydgate's credit he makes the same sober response as the black monk.

Literary attitudes toward monks and friars continue to develop in the fifteenth century, sometimes in unexpected ways. There was of course much reiteration of the old complaints against the friars, which had become shriller in Wycliffite writing and in the popular sermons associated with the Lollards. *Mum and the Sothsegger,* a poem on contemporary affairs of about 1402, influenced by Lollardy, has an especially lengthy attack on the friars (lines 392–520). *Pierce the Ploughmans Crede,* a fiercely Lollard poem in the *Piers Plowman* tradition, tells of a poor man who goes about looking for someone to teach him his Creed.[33] He meets in turn friars of all four orders, who spend most of their time abusing each other; they pay little attention to the poor man's request, but instead offer him absolution on the spot and tell him that learning his Creed is less important than giving them offerings to help pay for their lavish churches. Another work with strong Lollard sympathies is the alliterative prose *Jack Upland*, which bundles all the charges against the friars together, serious and frivolous, and shoots them off indiscriminately, like a blunderbuss.[34] Friars, says the eponymous author, with something of Wycliff's restraint, are "þe fellist folk þat euer Anticrist foond" (line 69).

Marcol and Solomon, a sprawling satirical poem in the Langlandian tradition, has as its main theme the need for a reconciliation between the possessioners and the mendicants. It is by John Audelay, who was chaplain to the Lestrange family before retiring to live as a pensioner in the house of Austin canons at Haughmond in Shropshire. His unusually favorable view of the friars may owe something to what was described above as a kind of "subtext" in Langland. He includes some of the familiar criticism of their covetousness and neglect of their rule, but he says, most unexpectedly (he is not a friar, nor amongst friars), that the realm would be in ruin if it were not for the example they set to secular priests by their life and teaching: they are chosen by God to be "clene kalender, the sekelers on to see."[35] Unlike Langland, Audelay deplores the idea of providing friars with a regular income (a "fyndynge"). They should beg, but not from the poor; if rich people would give to them freely, there would be no need to beg (lines 456–57)—which, to be sure, is what Langland often implies as a solution to begging in general. For the monks, who are addressed at length, there is a mixture of admiration and exhortation, as in Langland. They are praised for keeping their vows of stability and abstinence, for performing the office faithfully, for singing in tune, for charity to the poor, for holding all things in common, and for their office of intercession for all. Audelay perhaps felt he should be extra polite to his hosts, who were after all a kind of monk.

Some pieces of writing give us, so to speak, an "accidental" portrait of monks and friars, not targeted at or directly concerned with either, and, for that reason perhaps, the more trustworthy as a record of contemporary attitudes. The "poore old hoor man" who listens patiently to Hoccleve's money worries in the dialogue preceding the *Regiment of Princes* and calms him down meantime with gently unexceptionable advice, goes off at the end to mass at the Carmelite friary.[36] This, in a way, reflects well on the order, as does, possibly, the fact that it supplied many royal confessors during this period, including friar John Maidstone, confessor to John of Gaunt. Friars come out well too in *The Book of Margery Kempe.*[37] A "holy ankyr" at the Dominican friary in Lynn was her first spiritual director, a man of great sanctity, whose death she lamented pointedly to Christ: "rewe on me, for þu hast takyn awey þe ankyr fro me."[38] There are also good words for the holiness of the Carmelite master, Alan of Lynn, for William Southfield, Carmelite of Norwich, and for an unnamed grey friar, also at Norwich. If she was not on the best of terms with a certain celebrated preacher friar, who had to dismiss her because she was making so much noise in the church with her yowling and roaring, it is hardly the man's fault. Monks are less sympathetically portrayed. They eat and drink well, laugh and carouse, and, though amiable enough, do not like their peace disturbed by this annoying woman. When she lectured to the Cistercians at Hailes abbey, they welcomed her but swore many "gret othys and horrible" in her presence—which they may have thought fairly normal behavior.[39] At Christ Church, Canterbury, an old monk, who had been formerly in secular life treasurer to Queen Joanna, asked her what she could say of God. She told him a story from scripture; his response was to censure her and wish her closed in a house of stone so that no one might ever hear her speak again. This gave her the perfect opening for her favorite retort to her detractors: I am grateful to suffer abuse, she said, since it offers me pain and penance without my having to seek it out.[40]

In the Robin Hood plays and poems, another source of "accidental" insight, the monks we meet are again outriders. In "Robin Hood and the Monk," the mean and crafty monk seems to spend all his time on the road and at times behaves almost like the sheriff's agent. Another monk, in the long *Gest of Robyn Hode*, is cellarer of St. Mary's in York, riding out to check on reeves who have been cheating on their accounts, for all the world like someone sent down from business headquarters—indeed, many of these monastic officials were being replaced by lay functionaries in the fifteenth century.[41] "Friar Tuck" descends from a renegade outlaw who took the name "Frere Tuk" in 1417 and later had his name attached to the jovial buffoon who tips Robin Hood off his back as he carries him across the stream. He contributed to a popular reputation friars had as likeable rogues.

The *Paston Letters* give us a vivid image of one particular friar, and how closely he had become integrated into secular society. The Franciscan doctor John Brackley was a preacher in great demand, full of vituperation and personal animosities, and a vehement partisan of the Pastons in their many disputes with their neighbors. In the early 1460s, until his death in 1466, he was in constant correspondence with Sir John Paston I, to whom he acted as confessor, and whom he addresses in his letters as "worschipful and most interely bitrustid mayster and specyal frend."[42] Often he wrote from London, where he sometimes preached at St. Paul's, with on-the-spot reports of developments in Paston's suits. He is a lively and often violently opinionated correspondent, and his letters, sometimes in English, sometimes in Latin, are among the best in the collection. The full significance of his relationship with Paston is perhaps suggested by the fact that he was one of the executors of Sir John Fastolf's will in 1459, the provisions of which were a constant cause of contention. John Paston III reported to his father in 1467 (letter 327) that Brackley on his deathbed twice swore the truth of his testimony that the will presented in court by John Paston I was truly Fastolf's will (I. 535). This was faithful service indeed.

Other literary evidence, where the author is a committed party, has to be treated cautiously. "Miracles of Our Lady" often tell us of monks who are saved by the Virgin from the consequences of a not-very-heinous sin, and elsewhere all kinds of people are saved by the Virgin's intervention—immoral women, scribes, children, merchants, even cities. Friars very rarely figure. But then, they wrote most of these things.[43] Similarly with the late-thirteenth-century poem in Bodleian MS Digby 2, "I will become a friar"—"No more ne willi wiked be.... Frer menur I wil me make / and lecherie I wille asake"—which would be more convincing as a tribute to the order if the whole manuscript were not a Franciscan miscellany.[44]

The writers that we have been discussing dealt in perceptions of reality, not facts, and their perceptions were influenced by convention and prejudice and served particular cultural needs. Their views may have been more or less related to what monks and friar were "really" like. But being wary of these possibilities makes one more alert, and there are some tentative conclusions one might draw. The first is that friars, despite the continuous assault waged upon them from the earliest years of their inception, and especially upon the Franciscans, by their professional rivals and enemies, the seculars, retained considerable support among the writers discussed here. Those who perhaps were among the most likely to feel grateful, the poor, are of course silent, but in both Langland and Audelay, and more unselfconsciously elsewhere, one can see an admiration for their ideals and the Christian practice they sustained that had survived the campaigns against them as well as the real evidence of their greed and corruption. Later, friars had a looser popular reputation as men of the people and "good fellows." Monks receive less attention. Because they were cloistered for the most part, and would come into only occasional contact with people outside, their faults were not generally visible, any more than their virtues. When monks did emerge into the public sphere, it was for reasons that made their faults only too obvious. Monks were granted none of the popular reputation that somehow accrued to the friars. Later, when it has all ceased to matter, William Shakespeare uses friars as well-intentioned and obliging agents for sorting out marital and related problems, like their medieval forebears: so with the unlucky Friar Laurence in *Romeo and Juliet,* the deus ex machina friar in *All's Well*, and the Duke-cum-friar of *Measure for Measure.* Monks rate barely a mention.

Notes

1. Dom David Knowles, *The Monastic Order in England 940–1216* (1940; 2nd ed., Cambridge: Cambridge University Press, 1963), 220.
2. Quoted thus in translation by Knowles, *The Monastic Order in England*, 675.
3. Quoted thus in translation by Knowles, *The Monastic Order in England*, 676.
4. Knowles, *The Monastic Order in England*, 290.
5. Knowles, *The Religious Orders in England*, 3 vols, Vol. I, 1216–1340 (1948; 2nd ed., Cambridge: Cambridge University Press, 1963), 51.
6. Knowles, *The Religious Orders in England*, 1: 141.
7. *Canterbury Tales*, Prologue, I. 221–24. Chaucer is cited from *The Riverside Chaucer*, 3rd ed., ed. Larry D. Benson (Boston: Houghton Mifflin,1987).
8. An excellent general survey is given by Penn R. Szittya, *The Antifraternal Tradition in Medieval Literature* (Princeton, NJ: Princeton University Press, 1986).
9. *Piers Plowman*, Prologue, 60–65. Quotations are from *Piers Plowman: A New Annotated Edition of the C-Text*, ed. Derek Pearsall (Exeter: University of Exeter Press, 2008).
10. *Piers Plowman*, C III. 40–42.
11. *Piers Plowman*, C III. 54.
12. Chaucer, *Canterbury Tales*, "Summoner's Tale," III. 1942–47.
13. "Summoner's Tale," *Canterbury Tales*, III. 1793.

14. *Piers Plowman*, C X. 18–19.
15. *Piers*, C XXII. 340, 363–67. [*gropeth*: "searches the wound of"].
16. See Wendy Scase, *Piers Plowman and the New Anticlericalism* (Cambridge: Cambridge University Press, 1989), 32–39, 113–17. William St. Amour anticipates Langland in associating the friars with imminent apocalypse.
17. 2 Tim. 3: 6 (my italics)
18. *Piers Plowman*, C XXII. 266–67.
19. *Piers Plowman*, C XVI. 356, C XXII. 252.
20. *Piers Plowman*, C XXII. 383.
21. *Piers Plowman*, C VI. 151–53, 158.
22. *Piers Plowman*, C V. 168–79, 152–53.
23. See Jack A.W.Bennett and Geoffrey V.Smithers , ed., *Early Middle English Verse and Prose* (Oxford: Clarendon Press, 1966), 142.
24. *Piers Plowman*, C V. 156–60.
25. *Canterbury Tales*, General Prologue, I. 184–88.
26. Jill Mann, *Chaucer and Medieval Estates Satire* (Cambridge: Cambridge University Press, 1973), 17–37.
27. *Canterbury Tales*, General Prologue, I. 167.
28. *Canterbury Tales*, "Shipman's Tale," VII. 65–66.
29. *Canterbury Tales*, General Prologue, I. 246–48.
30. See Derek Pearsall, *John Lydgate (1371–1449): A Bio-bibliography*, English Literary Studies, Monograph Series No. 71 (Victoria, BC: University of Victoria, 1997), 35, 37.
31. Florence Warren and Beatrice White, ed., *The Dance of Death*, EETS, o.s. 181 (1931), lines 385–86.
32. Warren and White, *Dance of Death*, 353–54.
33. Walter W. Skeat, ed., *Pierce the Ploughmans Crede*, EETS, o.s. 30 (1867).
34. See V.J. Scattergood, *Politics and Poetry in the Fifteenth Century* (London: Blandford Press, 1971), 239–45, with quotation from Peter L. Heyworth, ed., *Jack Upland, Friar Daw's Reply and Upland's Rejoinder* (London: Oxford University Press, 1968).
35. *Marcol and Solomon*, line 410 (see also 599), quoted from *The Poems of John Audelay*, ed. Ella Keats Whiting, EETS, o.s. 184 (1931). In this edition, the poem (10–46) has only a Latin rubric for the title, *De concordia inter rectores fratres et rectores ecclesie*. "Marcol and Solomon" is the title given in the more recent edition by Susanna Fein, *John the Blind Audelay: Poems and Carols*, Medieval Institute Publications: TEAMS, Middle English Texts Series (Kalamazoo: Western Michigan University, 2009). "Marcol" (usually "Marcolf") is a familiar character in didactic debate poetry.
36. Thomas Hoccleve, *The Regiment of Princes*, ed. Charles Blyth, Medieval Institute Publications: TEAMS, Middle English Texts Series (Kalamazoo: Western Michigan University, 1999), lines 122, 2007.
37. Sanford Brown Meech and Hope Emily Allen, ed., *The Book of Margery Kempe*, EETS, o.s. 212 (1940).
38. Meech and Allen, *Book of Margery Kempe*, 142.
39. Meech and Allen, *Book of Margery Kempe*, 110.
40. Meech and Allen, *Book of Margery Kempe*, 27–28.
41. For these two pieces, see R. B. Dobson and J. Taylor, *Rymes of Robyn Hood: An Introduction to the English Outlaw* (Book Club Associates, 1976), 113–22, 208–214; cf. also 158–64. For Friar Tuck's name, see 41.

42. Norman Davis, ed., *The Paston Letters*, 2 vols (Oxford: Clarendon Press, 1976), 2: 221.
43. Peter Whiteford, ed., *The Myracles of Oure Lady* (from Wynkyn de Worde's print), Middle English Texts, 23 (Heidelberg: Carl Winter, 1990), 134–38.
44. Carleton Brown, ed., *English Lyrics of the Thirteenth Century* (Oxford: Clarendon Press, 1932), 126.

CHAPTER 7

GOWER'S MANUSCRIPT OF THE *CONFESSIO AMANTIS*

Peter Nicholson

One of the greatest contributions that Terry Jones has made to medieval studies has been to compel us to return to questions that we thought were already decided and to reexamine the evidence for our conclusions. In an essay published in 1987 in which I made an effort to minimize John Gower's role in the production of the manuscript copies of his work, I pointed out that the Fairfax manuscript of the *Confessio Amantis* contains several additions to the text that appear to be intended to move a large decorated initial into the first line of the next column.[1] There was a paradox there that I dismissed rather than resolved, but Terry's inquiries about the way in which Fairfax was revised have made me revisit the question of its origin and arrive, finally, at a somewhat different answer than I did before.

The early fifteenth-century manuscripts of the *Confessio Amantis* display a remarkable uniformity, not just in the high quality of their text but also in such things as the placement of the illustrations, the use of decorative initials, and the organization of the Latin apparatus that must, as Derek Pearsall claims, derive from the authority exercised by exemplars that had been carefully prepared from the poet.[2] Two of the earliest of these manuscripts, Oxford, Bodleian Library, Fairfax 3 (Macaulay's manuscript *F*) and Oxford, Bodleian Library, Bodley 902 (Macaulay's *A*), both because of their remarkable resemblance to one another and also because of some differences in the ways in which the scribes responded to difficulties that they faced, may provide us with a closer and more precise idea of what Gower's prototype manuscript looked like and of the ways in which the poet prepared his manuscript for copying.[3]

Fairfax is the best known of the manuscripts of the *Confessio* because G. C. Macaulay chose it for his edition of the poem, and all modern citations from the *Confessio*, including the line numbering, are based upon this copy. The original portion is one of the earliest surviving manuscripts of the poem, perhaps dating to the last years of the fourteenth century. In its revised form, Fairfax belongs to what Macaulay called the "third recension": it now contains the later versions of the opening and closing to the poem; it does not have any of the additional passages and rearrangements in Books 5, 6, and 7 that distinguish the "second" recension, but it does have some shorter additions in the Prologue and Book 1 (which we will examine more closely) that distinguish it from both the "second" recension and the "first."[4] Macaulay judged Fairfax to be the best representative of Gower's final intention for his poem. Whether or not this assessment is correct, Fairfax certainly reveals its closeness to the poet. The text is very carefully prepared and corrected. This is one of two manuscripts that M. L. Samuels and Jeremy Smith identify, on the basis of the orthography, as "as good as autograph copies" of the poem.[5] And whoever owned it continued to have access to the latest revisions of the poem after the manuscript was produced, for it is the only one of the surviving copies actually to have been altered to include the revised opening and closing. Bodley 902, slightly later in date, is a manuscript of the "first" recension, containing the original opening and closing and none of the additional passages that characterize recensions "two" and "three." It is remarkably similar to Fairfax in appearance, adhering to the forty-six-line format of all of the best of the early copies of the poem. It is uniformly decorated throughout, indicating that it was planned and executed as a single project, but it is the work of three separate scribes, the first of whom copied the first two gatherings (fols. 2–16, containing Prol.144–1.1704), the second the next eight (fols. 17–80, 1.1705–4.3596), and the third the remainder of the poem (fols. 81–184, 4.3597-end).[6]

It is the work of the second scribe that draws our attention first. Not just textually but also orthographically, his work is nearly identical to that of the corresponding pages of *F*, and he is the only one of the three scribes of *A* whose orthography Smith identifies, like that of *F*, as "Gowerian."[7] And even more remarkably, his work lines up precisely column for column with *F* from fol. 21r (fol. 22r in *F*) through to the end of his stint on fol. 80v (*F* fol. 81v). Given the advantages to the scribe, not just in having all his formatting choices made in advance but also simply the greater convenience of moving his eye back and forth to the same spot in both exemplar and copy, it is surprising that this type of matching did not occur more often.[8] Once the 46-line format was abandoned, of course, any hope of column-to-column correspondence was lost. But even among the manuscripts that retain the 46 lines, different decisions on the size and number of illustrations or the choice to incorporate some or all of the Latin marginalia into the column of English text made it impossible even to consider adhering to the layout of the exemplar. There are two other instances of column-for-column copying among the surviving *Confessio* manuscripts: Geneva, Fondation Bodmer, MS 178 (formerly Keswick Hall, Macaulay's *K*) matches the layout of *F*, and Cambridge, University Library, MS Mm.2.21 (Macaulay's *M*) matches that of *A*, but in both cases there is evidence that these manuscripts were derived directly from *F* and *A*, perhaps by way of one or more intermediaries. They must be the subject of a different essay. In distinction to these, the second scribe of *A* was not copying from *F*, for he omits the three added passages in

Book 1 of *F* that fell within his stint, nor is *F* (the earlier manuscript) copied from *A*. Both must be derived from a common exemplar—perhaps by way of intermediary copies in each case, though the degree of consistency in text and orthography argues against it—which each scribe has copied very faithfully. And that prototype exemplar, to the extent that we can reconstruct it, brings us one step closer to Gower's own manuscript of the poem.

While in arrangement and text the corresponding pages of these two copies are as nearly identical as it is possible for two manuscripts to be, there are some small differences in the decorative scheme that were apparently left to the discretion of whoever planned and organized their production. *A* is the more deluxe of the two, providing more elaborate borders for the pages on which new books begin, for instance, and decorated paraphs at the beginning of each passage of Latin in the margins, but it uses a somewhat simpler scheme for the hierarchy of initials.[9] The initials themselves are not merely a decorative device: as a way of organizing and subdividing the poem, they also provide a visual key to its structure, and the degree of consistency that does exist between *A* and *F* indicates that the scheme must originate with Gower.[10] The first grade in the hierarchy is represented by the one-line decorated initials that occur at the rate of roughly two to three per page. These are used to mark the opening line of a Latin epigram; to mark a switch of subject, either within a long speech or within a tale (the equivalent of a paragraph break); to mark the switch of speaker, especially within the dialogue between Genius and Amans, where they have much the same function as quotation marks;[11] and to mark the beginning of some of the shorter exempla, which Gower evidently felt did not rise to the level of "tale."[12] Larger initials are used at the beginnings of tales and in the opening lines of major new sections of the text, typically the discussion of another of the subtypes of the sin, which are also marked by the insertion of the Latin epigrams. Here is where *A* and *F* differ slightly: this portion of *A* uses three-line initials for both tales and sections, while *F* uses a three-line initial for most tales and a four-line initial for most sections. The determiner seems to have been the presence of the epigram, for the two tales in Book 1 that are exceptionally preceded by epigrams ("Nebuchadnezzar's Punishment," at 1. 2785, and "The Three Questions," at 1.3067) also get a four-line initial.[13] This scheme is maintained with great consistency except in the longer discursive sections in Book 5 and Book 7, where it required some adaptation, including the introduction of two-line initials in both manuscripts.

The arrangements at the beginning of a book were a little different from those at the beginning of a tale or section. The "boundary" appears to have been formed by the "Explicit... Incipit..." that occurs at each book division. In two of the three instances in which a new book begins in the section of the poem that we are considering (and also at the beginning of Book 1, within the stint of the first scribe of *A*), the explicit and incipit occur, either on two separate lines or in larger script (with abbreviations) on a single line, at the very bottom of a column, and the opening epigram of the book is placed at the top of the next. It thus appears that the first line of the epigram, rather than the first line of the English text, was regarded as the true beginning of the book, though the large decorated initial, up to eight lines in height and with customary decoration, appears at the beginning of the English text, six to eight lines below the top of the column.

The fact that two of the three books in this section, and three out of the first four books in the poem, begin on the first line of the column in both manuscripts is itself remarkable. We might have to attribute it to coincidence were it not for another fact, that a disproportionate number of tales and sections also begin at the very top of the page in this section of the poem, again in both copies. Of the 58 initials of more than a single line in height that mark the larger divisions, fourteen, or very nearly a quarter, occur in the first line of the column. All new tales and all new sections begin with the first line of a couplet (that is, with an odd-numbered line), and there are thus 23 positions in a 46-line column in which such an initial might occur. Were these 58 initials distributed evenly, there would be on average about 2.5 in each position. The actual distribution is shown on the table in the note.[14] Some variation, of course, is to be expected by chance. Thus it is not surprising that there should be no initials in lines 11 and 19 and as many as six in lines 9 and 39. But only at lines 3 and 5 and at lines 41, 43, and 45 do we find an absence of initials in consecutive positions. The much higher than expected number in line 1 is accompanied by a complete absence of initials in the three positions that precede and the two that follow.

The result is another device, in addition to the very use of initials, to give visual form to the poem's structure: a new column can mark the beginning of a new section of the text. Such a concern with the arrangement of the text is not unknown elsewhere. Pearsall cites two other copies of the *Confessio*—Oxford, Magdalen College, MS lat. 213 (Macaulay's *Magd*) and London, British Library, MS Add. 12043 (Macaulay's *Ad*)—in which the scribes can be found arranging to place the opening initial of a book on the top line of a column, either by leaving a blank space in the text, or using larger than normal script, or even omitting some of the Latin.[15] But in *A* and *F* the concern embraces not just the boundaries between books but also the smaller divisions in the text, and these copies employ no merely scribal rearrangements: there is no white space, for every line in the preceding column in each case is filled; there are no omissions; and there is never any more or less than 46 lines per column. Now this attempt to align the major divisions with the column arrangement is not obsessive. The Latin epigram at the beginning of Book 2, to take the most notable exception, begins on the sixth line on the page, after the last four lines of Book 1 and the two-line explicit-incipit (*A* fol. 27v, *F* fol. 28v). The six-line shortening that would have been required to bring this opening in line with those of Books 1, 3, and 4 is greater than we observe in the other instances, but it would certainly not have been impossible if someone were so determined. Nonetheless, the concern for the arrangement is real, and unless we attribute the manipulation of the text to a nameless scribe, who had other far easier devices to utilize and whose copying, at least of *F*, was evidently subject to someone's scrupulous correction, then we have to believe that the accommodations stem from the poet.[16] The only satisfactory explanation of what we find here is that the 46-line column goes back not to Gower's first scribal editor but to the poet himself, and that Gower wrote with an eye to the arrangement and appearance of the poem on the page. More specifically, it appears that whenever he had the opportunity either to lengthen the text by as many as six lines or to shorten it by as many as four in order to place the beginning of a new tale or a new section in the first line of a column, then he did.

The significance of the pattern of distribution of initials in this section of both *A* and *F* receives some confirmation when we compare the work of the second scribe in *A* to that of the third, who copied the portion of the book that begins on fol. 81. This scribe, whether simply to save space, as Macaulay suggests, or to segregate the Latin and the English, chose to write the epigrams and the explicit-incipits together with the other Latin apparatus in the margins.[17] The result is to throw off whatever plans for arrangement there might have been in the exemplar, and the placement of the initials is left entirely to chance. Distributed evenly, the 120 initials of more than a single line in this section would occur on average at a rate of about five in each position. We find only four in line 1. There are four in line 3, four in line 5, and at the bottom of the page, six in line 41, ten in line 43, and six in line 45, all positions that are left vacant in the preceding section. One of the results is illustrated on one of the pages reproduced by Pearsall.[18] The initial at 7.3215 on fol. 154v falls on line 45 (something that we infer would never have occurred in the prototype), and since it should be three lines high, it extends above and below the space that was left for it by the scribe. A similarly random distribution of initials occurs throughout the poem in the manuscripts that abandon the 46-line column and in those that keep it but adopt the opposite arrangement of moving the Latin marginalia into the column of English text. We find less correspondence of arrangement to structure, and initials occur in positions that are deliberately avoided in the most finished portions of the text in *A* and *F*.

F too, however, gives less evidence of a careful fitting of the text to the page in the final section of the poem than it does on fols. 22–81, and it indicates that Gower's own exemplar was not necessarily left in as neatly organized a condition throughout. The scribe adheres to the same format: 46 lines per column, no white space, and epigrams in the text column, but the results are not quite as neat. Books 5, 6, and 8 all begin in mid-column. Book 7 begins at the top (fol. 139r), but not in a way that conforms to the pattern in the earlier section, for the column actually begins with the first line of the English text and both the explicit-incipit and the opening epigram are at the foot of 138v. Of the 116 initials of more than a single line,[19] sixteen occur in line 1, or 14 percent of the total, more than in any other position but not as high a proportion as in fols. 22–81, and we also find two at line 3, five at line 5, and one each at lines 43 and 45, the positions earlier left vacant. The initials that give the most persuasive evidence of intentional design rather than mere coincidence are those that occur in the same position in close proximity to one another. Thus on fols. 111–16, four of the five large initials occur on line 1; on fols. 128r-129r, two of the three; and two of the three again on fols. 132v-133r. On fols. 146r-148r, three successive initials fall on line 5 (the last two of these preceded by four lines of Latin verse that head the column), and it appears that both the discussion of the Fifteen Stars (7.1281–1506) and that of Rhetoric (7.1507–1640) were originally written in a precise number of columns. There are three other instances in which a sequence of initials falls on the same line but not at the top of a column. On fols. 116v-118r, three successive initials fall on line 35; on fols. 154v-156r, three of six initials fall on line 25; and on fols. 181v-185r, three successive initials fall on line 9. (There are no similar sequences in fols. 22–81.) And finally, the second large initial in Book 5 (at 5.455) falls on line 27, the same line as the initial Latin verse of Book 5, which would be line 1 if Book 5 began as three of the four earlier books do. The evidence here is not quite as compelling, but if it suggests that these portions of the poem were composed to fit the 46-line format, it also indicates that the scribe had before him an exemplar that was much less finished than that of the preceding section of the poem, perhaps in separate sections rather than a single continuous version. It may be no coincidence in this regard that this is the part of the poem that Gower evidently continued to tinker with, as indicated by the additional passages and the rearrangements—which actually occur in at least two different combinations—that characterize what Macaulay labeled "recension two."[20]

Some similar problems arise in the first section of the poem (fols. 1–20 in *A*, fols. 2–21 in *F*), which also appears to have been left to some degree in a less finished form than the second section, and where too we may not be able to determine precisely what the exemplar looked like. But we are able to observe very closely how the scribes handled the arrangement of the text, because each was faced with precisely the same challenge, and they handled it in two very different ways. The challenge was that the text of this portion as Gower left it evidently did not fit precisely into columns, but it was necessary to find some way of making it line up so that they could begin copying column for column the more finished second portion of the exemplar. In order to meet this goal, each scribe had to fill up a total of 76 lines before 1.2372, from which point they are aligned with each other and also, we presume, with their common exemplar. To make their different efforts even more intriguing, their two texts converge and then fall out of alignment again three separate times before finally lining up at 1.2372, and each of the three points of convergence is marked by a large initial in the first line of a column.

It is obviously going to be necessary to trace these arrangements in some detail in order to make all of this clear. The two copies must have started out aligned, with the beginning of the Prologue at the top of the first page. Unfortunately the first leaves of both manuscripts are lost. In *A* there is a substitute leaf in a much later hand, evidently copied from Berthelette.[21] The second leaf begins with Prol. 144, an even-numbered line, already an oddity. The original first leaf, with space for 184 lines (four columns of 46) must have included the preceding 143 lines of English text plus the 18 lines for two Latin epigrams, for a total of 161. The remaining 23 lines would have been enough for a miniature, an incipit, and maybe a little white space as well. Columns continue to break in mid-couplet up to fol. 3v, at the bottom of the second column of which the scribe has inserted a one-line Latin gloss from the margin: "De statu plebis ut dicunt secundum accidencium mutabilia" (Concerning the fickleness of the people, as they say, according to the condition of events), immediately after the Latin epigram that follows Prol. 498, filling up the space so that the large initial N of Prol. 499 stands at the top of the next column, on fol. 4r.

F too lacks its original first page, which was replaced shortly after the manuscript was produced by another so that the original dedication to Richard II could be removed and replaced with another passage of exactly the same length. The layout of the original cannot have been very different from that of the present leaf. It begins with a miniature that occupies18 lines of the first column of text. The six-line opening epigram is next, followed by an incipit and a single blank line, and then 146 lines of English text and 12 more lines of Latin fill up all of the remaining space on recto and verso. The second leaf (now numbered fol. 3) thus starts with Prol. 147. Having gotten three more lines onto the first leaf than in *A*, the scribe has to fill up four lines instead of one in order to get the initial at Prol. 499 into place at the top of the column, which he does by supplying the four lines of English text that now appear in Macaulay's edition as Prol. 495–98.

There are no further adjustments in *A* in the Prologue. The next point at which the two manuscripts converge is at the beginning of Book 1, which again occurs at the top of a column. The remaining text of the Prologue is too short to fill up all of the intervening space, however, and the *A* scribe simply leaves six blank lines at the bottom of the first column of fol. 7r following the explicit and incipit that mark the boundary between the Prologue and Book 1. The *F* scribe, experiencing a greater *horror vacui* than the scribe of *A*, is not yet done. In order to get the beginning of Book 1 into the proper place and to fill up the entire space, he adds the six-line passage at Prol. 579–84 on fol. 5r. He chose this place because it also achieves a second desirable effect, of moving the next initial, the T of Prol. 585 that marks the beginning of the account of Nebuchadnezzar's dream, into position on the first line of fol. 5v.

But while the two manuscripts are thus in alignment with the opening of Book 1, they immediately fall out of alignment again because the *F* scribe chooses to begin with the second miniature, at the top of the second column of fol. 8r. The *A* scribe places the miniature after 1.202, the more usual position in later copies of the poem, on his fol. 8r.[22] *A*'s miniature is also smaller: *F*'s is 16 lines in height, while *A*'s is restricted to the twelve-line space that remained at the bottom of the column. Before finishing, however, each must fill up a total of 42 lines. *A* is still 30 lines short, and the scribe resorts again to moving some of the marginalia into the text. He leaves the Latin summaries in the margin up through 1.480, but he then chooses three successive glosses on fols. 10r-11v to move into the text column, an eight-line gloss to "Ulysses and the Sirens" before 1.481, a 5-line gloss on Pride after the epigram that precedes 1.575; and a 12-line gloss to "Mundus and Paulina" before 1.761. Since the second of these occupies an odd number of lines, each of the columns on fols. 10v-12v ends in mid-couplet, a situation that is not remedied until the end of fol. 13r, where the scribe simply leaves a blank line at the bottom of the column, after 1.1076. He was obliged to do so because 1.1077, the first line of "The Trojan Horse," begins with an initial for which there was not sufficient room, which now stands at the top of fol. 13v. The scribe is still four lines short, and after copying the glosses in the margin on fols. 13v-14r, he makes his final adjustment on fol. 15r, inserting the 3-line gloss on "Murmur and Complaint" into the text column immediately after the epigram that precedes 1.1343, and then supplying "Exemplum super eodem" (apparently of his own invention) before 1.1407, the first line of the tale of Florent.

This is the last of the *A* scribe's additions. His text is presumably aligned with his exemplar from fol. 15v forward, and his own stint concludes at the end of fol. 16v. The *F* scribe gets started on his adjustments later than *A*, at just about the point where the *A* scribe is done, and as in the Prologue, he compensates not by inserting Latin text but by providing 26 new lines in English. Together with those in the Prologue, his additions are the passages that for Macaulay distinguish the recension "three" of the text from recensions "one" and "two." They occur on fol. 16r, where a four-line passage (1.1403–06 in Macaulay) replaces a two-line passage in *A*; on fol. 20v (1.2267–74, eight lines); on fol. 21r (1.2343–58, the 16-line conclusion to "Narcissus"); and on fol. 22r (1.2369–72, four lines). But the additions in *F* achieve more than just filling up the space needed to align with the next section of the exemplar. As in the Prologue, each is also written with an eye to the arrangement on the page. The two additional lines on fol. 16r result in the placement of the initial T of the first line of the tale of Florent (1.1407) at the top of the next column, and the four additional lines on fol. 20v move the initial T of the first line of "Narcissus" (1.2275) into line 1. The long addition at the end of "Narcissus" is a little different, for it results in the tale itself occupying precisely a single page, and the top of fol. 21v begins with Amans's response. On the next page, the last addition, of four lines, is all that is now required to line up the text with the exemplar, and *F* and *A* are also in alignment from that point on.

We have to presume, given the finished condition of the second section of the poem, which each scribe was able to copy so exactly, that at some point the underlying exemplar of the opening section of the poem must also have been in just as finished a state, and that the disturbances that made the scribes' intervention necessary must have happened afterwards. In that respect the opening differs from the final section, for which there does not ever seem to have been an exemplar in so finished a form. The decision to include the illustrations may account for some of the rearrangements in the opening: the fact that they differ both in size and location in *A* and *F* suggests that they were not part of the original plan. But it does not account for all, for in neither manuscript does the number of added lines together with the space left for the miniatures add up to a multiple of 46, the number that would be necessary to preserve the column arrangement if this were the only cause. There must have been other changes too, either additions or cancellations in the exemplar that are not detectable now because they have become incorporated into both copies.[23] It seems reasonable to suppose that Book 1 began at the top of a column in the exemplar, and the initial at Prol. 499 very likely headed a column as well. All that we can really be sure of, however, is that disruptions in the original plan required the scribes to make further adjustments, and while we can not be sure precisely what their exemplar looked like, we can observe their very different strategies.

The expedients that appear in *A* are those available to any scribe of this poem, and they did not require the assistance of the poet. While the *A* scribe works hard to align his text, he displays no aversion to leaving white space when necessary, and he shows no special interest in matching the arrangement of the poem to its structure: the one instance in which he manages to place an initial at the top of a column (at 1.1077) appears to have been the result of accident rather than design. The *F* scribe, on the other hand, not only fills up every line of the available space, he also works to align new sections of the poem with the first line of the column whenever possible, and he does so by supplying new lines of English text. And again, unless we believe that Gower had a scribe who not only chose to eschew the more obvious devices available to him and to his peers but was also skillful enough to compose verse that is indistinguishable from Gower's, then these passages must have been written by Gower himself, and for this purpose. Both the evident consciousness of the manuscript arrangement of the poem and the composition of text to a required length are consistent with Gower's later revisions of the poem, in which he replaced a passage of precisely 69 lines in the Prologue in order to remove the personal references to King Richard and another of precisely 30 lines in Book 8 in order to remove a reference to Geoffrey Chaucer. The passages we are looking at, of course, are shorter, and most serve a more practical end. They are most consistent with what we have inferred about the adjustments to length in the second section of the manuscript, and it appears that what we have in fols. 2–21 of *F* is a chance to observe the very process by which the poet brought about the accommodation of the layout to the structure that is evident in fols. 22–81.

If all this is true, then it appears that some portions, at least, of the *Confessio Amantis* were shaped quite literally by the amount of space that was available on the page. Whether this is a flattering or unflattering view of the poet I do not venture to determine, though I think that the answer should probably lie more in the results than in the procedure.[24] The shorter of the additions that Gower made could be dismissed as filler, and so too could some of the lines that he wrote to replace the canceled passages in the Prologue and Book 8, but he has also added the graceful description of the nymphs' reaction to Narcissus's death, which we would probably not want to do without. Whether for good or for bad, however, what the additions to the Prologue and Book 1 in *F* indicate is Gower's high degree of involvement, if not in the production of this manuscript, then in that of its immediate, identical exemplar, for precisely how many lines would be needed to place the initials at the top of a column would not have been known until the manuscript was being produced. And if he provided the additional lines, he must also have had a hand in the decisions that made these adjustments necessary, particularly the addition of the two miniatures, which in turn makes it all the more possible to think that other cancellations and additions that we cannot now detect might also have occurred.

It thus appears that Gower must have been more directly involved in the actual creation of the manuscripts of his works than I was willing to credit in my earlier essay, and some of Macaulay's suppositions about Gower's involvement with Fairfax—including his participation in its correction and updating—do not seem quite as farfetched to me now as they did before.[25] That conclusion, unfortunately, has no direct bearing on the date of the later revisions of *F*, which is where Terry's greatest interest lies, though it might lend some indirect support for his notion that Gower himself supervised the updating and revision of his key manuscripts, as Macaulay also believed. It gives greatest support to Derek Pearsall's supposition that Gower must have carefully supervised the exemplars from which the early manuscripts of his works derive. And while the scribes had their role, it appears that in one of the earliest and most important manuscripts, at least, the poet had a more active part than we realized, to the point that the line between composition and copying becomes blurred, and "collaboration" may be more appropriate than "supervision."

Notes

1. Peter Nicholson, "Poet and Scribe in the Manuscripts of Gower's *Confessio Amantis*," in *Manuscripts and Texts: Editorial Problems in Later Middle English Literature*, ed. Derek Pearsall (Cambridge, UK: D. S. Brewer, 1987), 134–35 [130–42].
2. Derek Pearsall, "The Organisation of the Latin Apparatus in Gower's *Confessio Amantis*: The Scribes and their Problems," in *The Medieval Book and a Modern Collector: Essays in Honour of Toshiyuki Takamiya*, ed. Takami Matsuda, Richard Linenthal, and John Scahill (Cambridge, UK: D. S. Brewer, 2004), 99–100 [99–112]; and "The Manuscripts and Illustrations of Gower's Works," in *A Companion to Gower*, ed. Siân Echard (Cambridge, UK: D. S. Brewer, 2004), 80–81 [73–97].
3. G. C. Macaulay, ed, *The English Works of John Gower*, 2 vols., EETS, e.s. 81–82 (London: Oxford University Press, 1900–01). For the description of the manuscripts see 1:cxxxviii-clxvii.
4. Macaulay's account of the different recensions is on 1:cxxvii-cxxxviii; his description of *F* on 1:clxii-clix.
5. Michael Samuels and Jeremy J. Smith, "The Language of Gower," in *The English of Chaucer and His Contemporaries*, ed. Jeremy J. Smith (Aberdeen, Scotland: Aberdeen University Press, 1988), 21 [13–22].
6. The first leaf has been removed and replaced; see below. The first scribe has been identified as "Scribe D," who participated in the copying of at least five other manuscripts of the *Confessio*. See A. I. Doyle and M. B. Parkes, "The Production of Copies of the *Canterbury Tales* and the *Confessio Amantis* in the early fifteenth century," in *Medieval Scribes, Manuscripts & Libraries: Essays presented to N.R. Ker*, ed. M.B. Parkes and Andrew G. Watson (London: Scolar Press, 1978), 174–82, 192–96 [163–203].
7. Jeremy J. Smith, "Spelling and Tradition in Fifteenth-Century Copies of Gower's *Confessio Amantis*," in *The English of Chaucer and his Contemporaries*, 110 [96–113].
8. Derek Pearsall has described well the challenges posed to the scribe by a text as complicated as the *Confessio*, especially when it was decided to move the marginal apparatus into the text column; "Organisation," 105–12. Those who remember what it was like to include footnotes at the bottom of the page in the Age of Typewriters will have some appreciation for the difficulties that the scribes faced.

9. On the grades of decoration, see Pearsall, "Organisation," 101–02; "Manuscripts," 98.
10. Pearsall, "Organisation," 101. What little variation there is between *A* and *F* could well be due to scribal inattention. Thus *A* omits one-line initials found in *F* at 1.3271, 2.1051, 3.574, 3.1312, 3.1362, 4.17, 4.1359, but includes one that *F* omits at 3.2235. There are also a few variations in the inclusion of speaker markers (see below).
11. When used in the frame narrative, the initials are supplemented, in these and most other early manuscripts, by speaker markers, typically identifying "Confessor" and "Amans," but these are often not necessary, and used within the tales, the initials also sometimes serve to make a "quod he" or "quod she" at the beginning of a speech unnecessary, e.g. at 4.1383, 1387, 1406. The initials occur only at the beginning of a line and thus are not used, where they could have been helpful, to mark a switch of speaker within a line, as at 2.455, 3.20, 3.2490.
12. So at 2.2451, 2.2459, 2.3085, 3.818, 3.2438, 3.2599, 4.234, 4.250, 4.1035, 4.1901, 4.1935, 4.1963, 4.2135, 4.2148, 4.2183.
13. The only other tale in the poem with its own epigram, "Apollonius of Tyre" at 8.271, also gets a four-line initial in *F*. But if that is the pattern, then there are "mistakes": "Tarquin and Aruns" also gets a four-line initial at 7.4593 (fol. 164r), though it has no epigram, and a three-line initial occurs following an epigram at 3.843 (fol. 52v).
14.

line no.	*initials*	*line no.*	*initials*	*line no.*	*initials*	*line no.*	*initials*
1	14	13	2	25	3	37	1
3	0	15	3	27	2	39	6
5	0	17	2	29	1	41	0
7	2	19	0	31	5	43	0
9	6	21	5	33	2	45	0
11	0	23	3	35	2		

15. Pearsall,"Organisation," 109–10.
16. Scribes were capable of providing text when called upon, but usually only to fill an obvious, much shorter gap, and usually with much less happy a result. See Macaulay's note on the "made up lines" in manuscripts of the "second" recension, 1:clv.
17. Macaulay, 1:cxxxviii.
18. Pearsall, "Organisation," 104.
19. Four fewer than in *A* because *F* uses only one-line initials at 7.3387, 7.4181, 7.4257, and 7.4757.
20. Macaulay gives a not very clear account of these, 1:cxxxiii-cxxxiv.
21. Macaulay, 1:cxxxix.
22. See the helpful table in Jeremy Griffiths, "*Confessio Amantis*: The Poem and Its Pictures," in *Gower's Confessio Amantis: Responses and Reassessments*, ed. Alastair Minnis (Cambridge, UK: D. S. Brewer, 1983), 177 [163–78].
23. I have suggested elsewhere that the abrupt transition at Prol. 513 might indicate either the insertion of the preceding passage or a cancellation within the passage that follows. *Love and Ethics in Gower's Confessio Amantis* (Ann Arbor: University of Michigan Press, 2005), 117–18.

24. The closest modern equivalent I can think of is Douglas Hofstadter's *Le Ton Beau de Marot* (New York: Basic Books, 1997), in which the author proudly describes how he has manipulated his text to fit his notions of how it should appear on the page (see p. xx). His effort is consistent with a pervasive self-absorption that makes this one of the most irritating books that I have ever tried to read. Somewhat ironically, on the day that I arrived in Oxford to complete the research for this essay, the *Guardian* ran an article about a scholar's discovery that, after a restoration to their presumed original form, "within a margin of error of 1 percent–2 percent, many of Plato's dialogues had line lengths based on round multiples of 1,200" and that these fell naturally into 12 even sections, indicating that "Plato was organizing his texts according to a 12-note musical scale, attributed to Pythagoras." ("Academic Crack's Plato's Code of the Power of 12," *The Guardian*, June 30, 2010, A7. The article refers to an essay by Jay Kennedy in the journal *Apeiron* that I have not seen.) It is not known what symbolic importance Gower might have attached to the number 46.
25. Macaulay, 1:cxxx, cxxxv.

CHAPTER 8

GOWER IN WINTER: LAST POEMS

R. F. Yeager

J'ai parlé jusqu'ici de la vieillesse comme si ce mot recouvrait une réalité bien définie. En vérité, quand il s'agit de notre espèce, il n'est pas facile de la cerner.[1]

Simone de Beauvoir
Preface to *La vieillesse*

On those many occasions (surely!) when we close our eyes and call up John Gower, the image that I wager we conjure most often is of an elderly, bearded man in a long robe. Depending upon our degree of familiarity with the realia of Gower scholarship, that robe might be blue and the beard medium-length, forked, and salt-and-pepper (as "he" appears, along with beehive hat and longbow, in London, British Library MS Cotton Tiberius A.iv, fol. 9^{v}); or, alternatively, the gown might be red and gold, and the beard shorter, a rounded Van Dyke, thick and lustrous black (as presently on his tomb effigy, in Southwark Cathedral);[2] or the gown is wholly red and the beard white, long, and unshaven from ear to scraggly end near mid-chest (Oxford, Bodleian Library MS Bodley 902, fol. 8^{r}). Or perhaps, if one is a true aficionado, Gower appears (as he does in a tiny miniature in London, British Library MS Additional 42131, fol. 209^{v}), naked from the collarbone up, bald on top but with shoulder-length, wavy white hair below, bushy white eyebrows and a white beard, grizzled and forked, that extends from earlobe to what would have been four or five inches below his chin if blown up to scale.

What most of these "Gowers," real and assumed, have in common is their representation of their subject as a graybeard, if not an aged man. A mental image based on the tomb effigy, of course, presents an alternative (an interesting one, since Gower undoubtedly oversaw its construction, and presumably its decoration),[3] and one might cite others: Oxford, Bodleian Library MS Fairfax 3, fol.8^{r} (perhaps the best-known *Confessio Amantis* manuscript, thanks to G. C. Macaulay, who chose it for his now-standard edition)[4] has, instead of a white-bearded gent, a smooth-cheeked young man in hooded robe kneeling before his confessor; Oxford, Bodleian Library MS Bodley 294, fol. 9r has another such youth in the same position, but in this case *sans* hood, to reveal a thick brown head of hair above bare cheeks. What, then, keeps the image before us of Gower as old?

A number of things, perhaps, some learned, some not. The miniatures of the kneeling youth in MSS Fairfax 3 and Bodley 294 are obviously not, we say knowledgeably, true portraits of the poet—they are of Amans, the eponymous chief character of the *Confessio Amantis*, and are drawn generically, according to contemporary illumination style.[5] Yet the aged, kneeling gentleman in MS Bodley 902 was as much intended to represent Amans, too—and, in the consistent format that Jeremy Griffiths has shown governed the placement of miniatures in the production of *Confessio* manuscripts, this image of the aged Amans occupies the same locus respectively as the youthful ones.[6] Arguably, it is as much determined by the poem's fiction as they. Why then do we "feel" its face to be more "Gower-like" than the young man's?

Perhaps, the answer might be, because we are so familiar with how the *Confessio* concludes, with Amans' forced recognition of his aged face in Venus's mirror, not long after he has given his name to be "John Gower" (VIII. 2321). Or it could be because the old Amans of MS Bodley 902 closely resembles the fork-bearded archer in BL MS Cotton Tiberius A.iv, a manuscript the making of which Gower is thought by some to have supervised.[7] But one might suggest, at the risk of being difficult, that Gower's involvement in the production of the Cotton Tiberius A.iv text and illumination, even were we certain of it, does not make the archer a portrait. It could, after all, be just a drawing of an archer with a salt-and-pepper beard that Gower particularly liked, or had to accept for want of a better. As men with beards, of course, both the aged Amans of MS Bodley 902 and the archer of Cotton Tiberius A.iv do at least resemble the tomb effigy, but—whether or not Gower oversaw its creation—fourteenth-century English stone carving of the sort on his tomb, like manuscript "portraits" of the period, is mostly generic.[8] An attempt by the carvers to copy Gower's effigy from life, except in the most general way (e.g., the figure has a beard) would have been extraordinary. On the other hand, it has been suggested that the balding, white-haired, and bearded face in BL MS Additional 42131 (the Duke of Bedford's Psalter-Hours) may have been drawn from memory, by a painter who conceivably could have known Gower alive.[9] But (not to be difficult again) the head appears in the psalter as part of the decorated "V" of the first word of Psalm 141, *Voce mea domine clamavi* (I cried with my voice to the Lord). This seems almost too apt a letter-placement for a Gower portrait (which it definitely is, for his name is inscribed below it), given Gower's appropriation of Isaiah 40:3, *Vox clamantis in deserto* (The voice of one crying in the wilderness), and his proclaimed identification with John the Baptist for the title and spirit of his own poem,[10] so much so, indeed, that if the Bedford illuminator were sufficiently well acquainted with Gower's work to make that connection, he (or she) might also have been familiar with the bearded archer drawing in BL MS Cotton Tiberius A.iv, which primarily contains the *Vox Clamantis*, or another manuscript like it. The Bedford illuminator could have transposed his own "Gower" image from that. Or, to knot it all up nicely, it has been suggested that the Bedford "portrait" was taken from still another *Confessio Amantis* manuscript that I have yet to mention—Cambridge, Pembroke College MS 307, fol. 9^r—which shows an aged Amans, bald on top but with long white hair below and a forked white beard, kneeling before the Confessor.[11]

The apparently futile circularity of such observations nevertheless makes a worthy point: it would seem that we are not alone in our envisioning of Gower exclusively as an old man. His illuminators, both those whom he might have influenced, either by explicit direction or as a live model, and many of those who came later, imagined him that way also.[12] Now, were we art historians, we would no doubt find these elderly miniatures unremarkable. Author portraits from life, we would say, were only beginning to take hold in England at the turn of the fifteenth century, the earlier custom having been to establish a representational figure identifiable by function, placement, or symbolic clue.[13] Once set, the stylized "portrait" was then replicated by succeeding painters, upon demand. No doubt this accounts in large part for the relative uniformity of the "Amans/Gower" figures in the manuscripts—and the pictures' influence perhaps explains why modern readers imagine Gower the way they do, as old.

But many of us are not art historians, and in the end neither explanation answers the question we have been pursuing. That is, to reframe it more precisely: why did Gower elect to put forward for posterity, visually and verbally, an image of himself as an elderly man?

For it is clear that the choice was Gower's. Griffiths has convincingly traced the presence of a controlling hand over the general content and placement of the illuminations in the best and earliest manuscripts. If Gower's involvement with the copying of his works is as extensive as we believe—and I for one agree that it must have been, especially over a handful of early manuscripts including BL Cotton Tiberius A.iv—then to one degree or another that hand was most likely Gower's. Moreover, as noted above, Gower decided to give Amans his own name in the *Confessio*, and designed the poem's denouement around the surprise—to the reader, at least—of the Lover's agedness.[14] I say "a surprise at least" because in the all-too-familiar tradition Gower was following, of the *Roman de la Rose* and the *dits amoreux*, there are no known examples in which the Lover is not a youth, except two—Guillaume de Machaut's *Voir dit* and Jean Froissart's *Joli buisson de Jonece*. Both, or either, of these no doubt provided precedent for what Gower did in the *Confessio*, but (it should be stressed) *only* because he *chose* one or both of these from a majority of quite different available models with predictably youthful protagonists.[15] Why pick them instead of the others?

Well, because Gower was himself old when he wrote the *Confessio*, is a common explanation. He was drawn, we say, to the *Voir dit* and *Joli buisson*, both written when Machaut and Froissart were also long (and somewhat long) in the tooth, as more honest exemplars for a poet of his years.[16] (*CA* VIII, 2412–20, sometimes interpreted as suggesting Amans/Gower's sexual impotence, would seem reinforcing.)[17] Yet unlike Gower, neither Machaut nor Froissart makes a secret of his age at any point, with the result that, despite certain superficial similarities, the *Confessio* ultimately is quite different in its effect from the *Voir dit* and the *Joli buisson*. C. S. Lewis took the revelation of Amans's age to be artful premeditation, calling it "Gower's master-stroke"—as doubtless it is.[18] But such a reading places great pressure on the comforting assumption of verisimilitude. Where is the rule recorded that a poet must put aside writing fiction and privilege brutal self-denigration if, after a certain age, he decides to write on love?

It is in this context—the proper understanding of the *Confessio*, Gower's most important poem—that the testimony of his lesser-known minor Latin poems may be particularly helpful. In the past, several have been occasionally set alongside the more familiar dedicatory epistle to Archbishop Thomas Arundel that prefaces Oxford, All Souls College MS 98, containing the *Vox Clamantis* and the *Cronica Tripertita*, to catalogue Gower's decrepitude.[19] In the epistle, written after 1400, Gower refers to himself as *senex et cecus* (prose, l. 1–2), *cecus* (verse, l. 17), defective of body and crippled with age ("Corpore defectus, quamuis michi curua senectus," verse, l. 19), with sight divided from his body ("diuisus meus est a corpore visus," verse l. 27), old, sick, and physically miserable ("Corpus et egrotum, vetus et miserabile totum," verse l. 29), and a blind man (*cecum*, verse, l. 32). The All Souls manuscript concludes with a short poem in distichs, known simply from its first words as "Quicquid homo scribat" (Whatever a man writes) under a prose heading, both in the same hand as the opening *epistola* to Arundel. In the heading and the poem, Gower says he can write no more; in the verses he explains further, twice over, that he is blind (*cecus*, ll. 4, 15). The little "Quicquid homo scribat" exists as well in two other distinct versions in four other manuscripts. In one, London, British Library Additional MS 59495 (sometimes called the Trentham manuscript), Gower says his blindness and cessation of writing came on in the first year of Henry IV (i.e., 1400–01); in the other three (Cotton Tiberius A.iv; London, British Library, Harley MS 6291; and Glasgow, University Library, Hunterian MS T.2.17), Gower claims his blindness occurred in the second year of Henry's reign (i.e., 1401–02).[20]

Although these dates for Gower's claims of blindness are worth noting—and we shall return to them later—heretofore not much has been made of them. Probably correctly, preference instead has been given to the evidence in aggregate, which is that Gower at the end of his life had lost his sight, and was feeling the ravages of age. It is there in the denouement of the *Confessio Amantis*, in the *epistola* to Arundel, and in "Quciquid homo scribat." But if we accept all of this, an interesting conundrum erupts, no matter how we date the different versions of "Quicquid." If we take the usually accepted date of 1386 for the completion of the *Confessio*, Gower was some 14 to 16 years younger when he wrote it than when he wrote the *epistola* to Arundel, and the versions of "Quicquid." When did Gower, in fact, grow old?

One way to answer that question—the most obvious way—is unfortunately denied us. Although his will states that Gower died in 1408, we have no equivalent document to indicate when he was born.[21] It is conventional to speak of 1330, but there is no hard proof: for all we know, Gower could have been younger than Geoffrey Chaucer, and born after 1340.[22] Our modern convention of Gower's earlier birth year may thus be itself a kind of imaginative back-formation, derived like the "portraits" in the manuscripts from the "fact"—or fiction—of Amans/Gower *senex* and the late Latin voice of the Arundel *epistola* and "Quicquid homo scribat," which, in one version or another, apparently closed a significant number of copies of the *Vox Clamantis* and *Cronica Tripertita*—and enjoyed, thus, a certain influential provenance among readers and illuminators.

But clearly a decade one way or another could make a great deal of difference. If Gower were born in 1340, instead of 1330, he would have been in his mid-forties when he finished the *Confessio*, and about sixty when he wrote the *epistola* and "Quicquid." While both ages may seem old at first glance, particularly given conventional assumptions about brief life expectancy in the Middle Ages, significant historical data exist to indicate that, especially for a man of his apparent socioeconomic status who was neither a soldier nor a plague victim, Gower had a statistical chance of surviving into his seventies or later.[23] Indeed, with the exception of Chaucer, whose days may have been cut unnaturally short, longevity runs strong amongst late medieval writers: Petrarch and (probably) Hoccleve each died at 70, Machaut at 72, Eustache Deschamps and Froissart at 68 and 67, respectively, and John Trevisa at 86. If Gower actually *were* born in 1330, then he was 78 when he died, and thus pretty much a poster child for the upper-right-hand quadrant for gerontological survivability.

So perhaps a better way of asking the question is, at what age might Gower have begun to *speak* of himself as old, and not be perceived to be making an incongruous joke? John Burrow has shown that, when describing the *cursus aetatis*, the late Middle Ages recognized

> four main traditions, each offering a different way of dividing life up into ages, whether three, four, six, or seven, not to speak of lesser traditions; and there was also, within each tradition, a good deal of variation in naming the ages and in defining their limits.[24]

As Burrow suggests, the full situation is complex far beyond what space can be allotted here (he himself has presented the case admirably in two-hundred-plus pages), but for our purposes several features common to the more important schema can be isolated usefully. In all, the first age or ages are associated with growth, physical energy, love, and folly. Wisdom, along with a turn toward civic and social responsibilities, including both politics and marriage, commences during some form of middle age (if the number of divisions in the model is three or four),[25] or in one or more periods of "old age" (in schema with six, seven, or more divisions),[26] as bodily vigor wanes and reason and experience take control over action.[27] In the final age or ages, decrepitude is reached, with a reversion to weakness, even helplessness, as in the first age of childhood and infancy.

Not every commentator taking up the question of age divisions attempted to provide numerical thresholds for the beginning and ending of each, nor were all the conclusions quite the same that they adopted when they did. Augustine, in *quaestio* 58 of his *De diversis quaestionibus octoginta tribus* (On eighty-three diverse questions), posited six ages—*infantia*, *pueritia*, *adolescentia*, *iuventus*, *gravitas*, and *senectus*—but left them unspecified as to years.[28] Isidore of Seville, however, adapted Augustine's divisions to the individual life, assigning the first seven years to *infantia*, the next seven to *pueritia*, then fourteen to *adolescentia*, the following twenty-two to *iuventus*, then twenty to *gravitas*, and the remainder to *senectus* and *senium*, the latter being the brief time immediately preceding death. Thus for Isidore, true old age—*senectus*—does not commence until 70.[29] Dante, in *Il convivio* (IV.xxii-xxiv), calculated a middle age of wise judgment developing for 20 years, between 25 to 45, and then slowly declining through *senettute* to *senio*, decrepitude, which (also) began after 70.[30] In this he agrees fairly closely with Aristotle, who noted in the *Rhetoric* that "the body is in its prime from thirty to thirty-five, and the mind about forty-nine."[31] Other writers, especially of medical treatises that used a hebdomadal schema of seven divisions attributed to Hippocrates, push the "middle" and "old" ages of wisdom forward to 56, and even to 70.[32]

So Gower could have called himself "old" at any time from his mid-forties to his mid-fifties—which is roughly his actual age when he was writing the *Confessio Amantis* in 1386, whether he was born in 1330 or 1340—and not raised many eyebrows. If he wrote the *epistola* to Arundel and "Quicquid homo scribat" in 1400–1402, he would have been in his early seventies or early sixties, respectively, depending on his birth year. What is intriguing about these speculations, of course, is that, in the *rationes aetatis* (systems of ages) familiar in the fourteenth century, only if Gower were *senior*—well over 70—would he have approached the category of decrepitude he claims for himself in the "Quicquid" versions and the Arundel *epistola*. Any younger than that and his "agedness," especially in the *Confessio*, would very likely have been intended, and understood, altogether differently from how we commonly assess it nowadays: not, in other words, as doddering incapacity and imminent senility, but rather as achieved sagacity, and hence as a "bully pulpit" from which to dispense learned admonishments, arrived at through maturation of the mental faculties, his perspectives earned and tested after surviving the world's snares. Inappropriate it might be to the antic passions of youth, but the "old age" that Gower attributes to Amans and "himself" is fully employable nonetheless in weightier enterprises, such as offering advice on governance to a 19-year-old monarch, as Richard II was in 1386. (Gower, of course, in the earliest version of the *Confessio*, ll. *24-*56, claims he was "charged" by Richard to write the poem.)[33]

The dual effect of such an understanding is to play down, of course, the framing fiction of love in the *Confessio*, and to configure Gower's poem as primarily political, as perhaps it is increasingly being read nowadays.[34] Equally, if we accept Amans/Gower's age as a device intended from the beginning to stake out a credible didactic ground—to tutor first Richard, then Henry of Lancaster and the extended nation together—the further result is to render more cohesive the events of the fictional confession with the cautionary, authorial address to the "real world" of the *Confessio*'s prologue and epilogue. As an "old man" (or, probably better put, as "one fully mature"), the "John Gower" who transforms out of the feckless Amans at the end of the *Confessio* gains thereby a substantial credibility as a truth-speaker. This is a *gravitas* much needed if the poem is to realize Gower's sweeping ambitions for it at court, as well as in poetry's courtly arena.

What may help explain the *Confessio Amantis*, however, is less effective when we turn to Gower's self-presentation in the *epistola* to Arundel and "Quicquid homo scribat." Here the apparently autobiographical elements are most degrading, to the degree that it seems impossible for Gower's claims of blindness, disease, and physical decay to be uncovered as deliberate devices. What could he possibly have gained, literarily or in any other way, from such self-descriptions, particularly if they weren't true?

Before attempting to answer the literary question, however, it may be helpful to inquire briefly after the latter. How badly off *was* Gower physically, in and around 1400? While of course there is no way to know exactly, there may nevertheless be clues left among his little-read late Latin minor poems. Ascribing accurate dates to many of these is problematic, but one, "Est amor," can be pegged with assurance to 1398, the year of his marriage to one Agnes Groundolf, a woman otherwise of almost complete mystery. "Est amor" (Love is) is a poem of two parts, the first of 15 lines in single rhyme containing a series of oxymora familiar from the Petrarchan school,[35] and ending in a pair of rather gnomic couplets apparently intended as instruction; the second section, of eight single-rhyme lines, is ruminative, and turns steadily more personal, to conclude with "hinc vetus annorum Gower sub spe meritorum / Ordine sponsorum tutus adhibo thorum" (Thus I, Gower, old in years, in hope of favor, / Safely approach the marriage bed in the order of husbands.")[36]

"Est amor" is intriguing for a number of reasons, not the least of which is its appearance in a slightly altered version in *Vox Clamantis* V.53 ff., where the oxymora are intended to dissuade knights from diverting their attentions toward women, away from their nobler duties as protectors of society. That Gower should recall them in "Est amor," and apply them to himself late in life, intimates a degree of inner turmoil seldom associated with our carefully fostered image of the old, moralist poet. It is a struggle borne out by a careful reading of "Est amor" itself, which strives to contain the self-destructive energies of amorous attraction, first by casting them as unreasonable contradictions, then by putting on a schoolmasterly voice (l. 18), "Instruat audita tibi leccio sic repetita" (Thus a lecture heard repeatedly may instruct you)—but who, should we say, is "you"? Then at last by adopting—essentially, even concedingly—the Pauline dictum that it is better to marry than to burn (ll. 24–25): "Hec est nuptorum carnis quasi regula morum, / Que saluandorum sacratur in orbe virorum" (For those married in the flesh this is like their rule of morality / Which makes it sacred in the world for those who are to be saved).[37]

If "Est amor" expresses a divided soul over the matters of love, it is not the only one among the minor Latin pieces to do so. "Ecce patet tensus" (Lo, the taut bow) is undatable from any internal real-world reference heretofore recognized. Usually, however, it is taken to be roughly contemporary with "Est amor." "Ecce patet tensus" is similarly anguished:

O human nature, irresistibly disposed
To that unlawful thing which it cannot shun!
O human nature, that contains two mixed contraries

But is not allowed to follow the deeds of both!
O human nature, which always has war within itself
Of body and soul, both seeking the same authority![38]

"Ecce patet tensus" ends with a plangent plea for release (ll. 35–36): "Nullus ab innato valet hoc euadere morbo, / Sit nisi quod sola gracia curet eum" (No one is strong enough to evade this inborn malady, / Unless grace provides the cure). Only one copy is known of "Ecce patet tensus," in BL Add. MS 59495 ("Trentham"), where it is followed by a missing leaf—a fact that led Macaulay, Gower's great nineteenth-century editor, to consider it incomplete, perhaps because it lacks the firm, moralizing resolution Macaulay had come to expect in Gower's work.[39]

But suppose it isn't incomplete? Had it been written by anyone other than Gower—or in a later century—might Macaulay have thought "Ecce patet tensus" finished? The poem does, after all, come to a perfectly plausible, though rather tortured, conclusion, not one we have grown used to imagining from Gower in his "dotage," but perhaps that says more about our image of Gower in later life than about the man as actually he was. He did marry, at about 58 or 68, depending on his birth year, the unknown Agnes Groundolf, although from her surname we can speculate with some assurance that she was a commoner, and probably of *Doche* descent (German-speaking Flemish). The customary explanation, both for the late marriage and the request granted by the Bishop of Winchester to permit the rites to take place in Gower's rooms, is that Gower was too infirm to venture out, and took Agnes as his nurse.[40] We have, however, no more evidence to support this than to suppose that Agnes was a prostitute to whom Gower took a fancy (not unlike Edward III did to Alice Perrers, upon whom he fathered as many as three children between 1369 and his death eight years later, when he was 65).[41] All that separated Gower's home of many years at the priory at St. Mary Overeys from Maiden Lane and the Bankside stews, chief providers for London, were the bishop's palace grounds. In 1390, *cynk Estufes de Bordell* were apparently thriving in St. Olave's parish, a stone's throw across the Southwark High Street from the priory gates, just east of London Bridge. Going to and from the city, whether by foot or boat, it would have been difficult to avoid traversing one or another such district.[42] Was it Agnes's background that initiated the request for a private wedding, a request the Bishop of Winchester might be likely to grant, since several of the Southwark brothels were his rental properties?[43] Is it significant that many of the prostitutes in Southwark were Flemish, as, seemingly, was Agnes?[44] Or, more to the point, perhaps: did Agnes need to have been a prostitute for Gower to—simply and naturally—fall in love with her? Gower would hardly have been the only moralist writer afflicted against his will by the *sagitta volans ardor amoris*—"the flying arrow [that is] the flame of love" that he describes in "Ecce patet tensus" (l. 2). In his *Secretum*, which he was still revising when he was 50, Petrarch gives voice to his own divided nature through the figures of "Augustinus" and "Franciscus," the latter maintaining throughout an inability to abjure his love of women.[45] This is precisely the question Isabella Yeager proposes, arguing, per Occam's Razor, that Gower and Agnes may have married just because they were in love.[46]

That Gower, who has been accused in the past of being Chaucer's model for the Man of Law, might actually turn out to be January, and a good deal livelier and more physically healthy in his last years than we commonly grant nowadays is not, however, the present purpose. There is no need to go that far to question plausibly our perhaps-too-easy assumption that Gower was as decrepit as he states in the Arundel *epistola*, or in "Quicquid homo scribat." (Indeed, the fact that he seems to have continued to revise "Quicquid" to suit various manuscripts suggests, perhaps, that he was less blind than he claims in that poem.) Rather, our purpose is to investigate Gower's professions of old age for signs of literariness, for evidence of device. I suggested above, in discussing the denouement of the *Confessio*, how the odd trick of turning Amans both suddenly old, and into the author himself, might direct and empower the poem's political lessons, especially if its audience, as initially conceived, were the youthful King Richard II.

To this end, it is worthwhile considering the following. In the Prologue to Book II of the *Vox Clamantis*, which Gower wrote sometime prior to 1381, he indirectly but effectively takes on the voice of an old man, in order, it appears, to justify his authority in speaking advice:

> In sene scire parum multum solet esse pudori
> Temporis amissi pre gravitate sui;
> Set modo siqua sapit docet aut proviso senectus,
> Vix tamen hec grata vox iuvenilis habet.
> Que scribent veteres, licet ex fervore studentes,
> Raro solent pueris dicta placere satis;
> Obloquioque suo quamvis tamen ora canina
> Latrent, non fugiam qui magis ista canam.
>
> (*VC* II.31–40)[47]

Still more telling is II. Pro. 53: "Est oculus cecus, aurisque manet quasi surda" (My eye is blind, and my ear is almost deaf). How are we to read this? If Gower were deaf and blind around 1380, he would have been 40 to 50 years old—hardly *senectus* by any authoritative standard—and he functioned remarkably well for nearly a quarter-century thereafter, completing, during that period, the bulk of his poetry. To this conundrum line 31, above—"In sene scire parum multum solet esse pudori"—may offer a clue. It is lifted directly from the *Aurora* of Peter Riga, in the centonic manner Gower pursued throughout the *Vox*.[48] Its presence suggests that by 1380 he had begun to adopt great age, attested to by its infirmities, as a purposive construct, a literary persona. Not insignificantly, about this time (i.e., ca. 1382–86) Gower received from Chaucer his most lasting epithet, in the dedication of *Troilus and Criseyde* to "moral Gower."[49] Superficially the two personas mesh quite well, each over time perhaps contributing to the other's mythology.

As to what might have suggested such a strategy to Gower, the choices are numerous. Most of the contemporary literature on age divisions includes the notion that wisdom ripens with age; the *topos* is common enough in books Gower knew.[50] Given, however, the sociopolitical use to which Gower sought to put the *Vox*, and subsequently the *Confessio Amantis* as an advice book for Richard II, Aristotle offers an especially attractive possibility. As he notes in the *Politics*:

> It cannot be disputed that rulers have to be superior to those who are ruled. It therefore becomes the duty of the lawgiver to consider how this is to be brought about.... Nature herself has provided one way to choose:... in respect of birth... she has divided into older and younger, the former being fit for ruling, the latter for being ruled.[51]

The distinction is natural, because "the young have strength, the older have practical wisdom" (*Pol.* VII.viii.1329a2). The end of "practical wisdom," Aristotle elaborates in the *Nichomachean Ethics*, is "to tell us what we ought to do, and what we ought not to do."[52] Hence "practical wisdom deals with what is just, noble, and good for man; and it is doing such things that characterize a man as good" (*NE* VI.xii.1143b), and further, "We attribute good sense, understanding, practical wisdom, and intelligence to the same persons, and... (we imply)... that they have a mature intelligence..." (*NE* VI.xi.1143a).

For Gower in the late 1370s, when he must have been beginning the *Vox Clamantis*, the appeal of such distinctions in the *Nichomachean Ethics* and the *Politics* could only have been strong. Above all, the *Vox* is a poem that endeavors to set out "what is just, noble and good for man," and polemically tells us "what we ought to do, and what we ought not to do" in a pointedly political sphere, as opposed to the broadly Christian one he cultivated in the *Mirour de l'Omme*. As such, the *Vox* represented a new beginning for Gower, a full-scale invasion of a territory into which, in the *Mirour*, he had only ventured with the guidance of the Virgin. To draw on Aristotle's mantle and seek protective authority in the guise of an aged wise man (who might also sound like John the Baptist, for good measure) makes, under the circumstances, very shrewd sense indeed.

But what possible reason could Gower have had to profess blindness and decrepitude in the *epistola* to Arundel, and in "Quicquid homo scribat," a poem found concluding the *Vox Clamantis* and *Cronica Tripertita* in most known manuscripts?

Well, let me end by suggesting one. Although we do not know when Gower presented a copy of the *Vox* and the *Cronica* to Arundel, it must have been after 1400 and the latter's restoration to the archbishopric of Canterbury by the usurping Henry IV. Likely, in fact, it came closer to 1402–03, or even 1404, in order to give Gower time to write the *Cronica*—which he could not have started before late 1399—and have the presentation manuscript prepared.[53] By that time, a good number of disturbing events had taken place, including the burning of the Lollard William Sawtre for heresy (finally rendered a capital offense in 1401 under the royal edict *De haeretico comburendo*, a decree long sought by Arundel), open rebellions against Lancastrian rule in several parts of the country, and the death of Chaucer, possibly by foul means.[54] Although Gower himself probably had Lancastrian roots, going well back, I think, to the early years of Gaunt's children, we have little way to know how these events would have affected him.[55] One thing we might surmise without fear of contradiction is that Gower recognized how parlous were the times around him—and how important it might be to stay on the right side of power, one indisputable center of which, particularly for a writer with at least some Ricardian court ties, was Arundel. Perhaps Gower, if he worried over it, felt that his writing the *Cronica* (doubtless at the behest, if not more likely the direct command, of Lancastrian interests), put him above concern.[56] It is inconceivable that such a polemic could have been other than heartfelt, the work of a partisan—at least at the time of its writing. However, must we assume therefore that *nothing* could have changed his view, as Lancastrian government pursued its ends—not even, perhaps, the executions and murders in those first years of so many he knew?[57]

It would be helpful, of course, to have something tangible attesting to such an altering state of mind, say, a bona fide letter from Gower's hand, of the kind sent by Petrarch to his brother Gherardo.[58] Short of this, however, we may have something like it in the brief Latin poem "Unanimes esse qui secula" (To be of one mind he who the ages). Also difficult to date with assurance, "Unanimes ess qui secula" is nonetheless a late work. We find it appended to manuscripts containing the *Vox* and the *Cronica*, and no doubt it went, in that way, to Arundel. Its simple plea to "love each other" (*Diligamus invicem*, l. 11) and rebuild the divided kingdom through Love is strikingly anti-Lancastrian (albeit not un-Gowerian), but it could easily emanate, not incongruously, from the pen of a deeply religious and reflective older man recently wed, who was beginning to think differently about the new state faction.

If so, Gower might have sought a way to avoid yet another request to glorify the court in verse—and more to the point, perhaps, also avoid any consequences such a refusal might incur.[59] A claim of age and blindness would certainly provide an escape, as well as—more remotely, but who could say?—precisely such a boost of authority as to make "Diligamus invicem," his final wish in "Unanimes esse," be taken seriously by those at court into whose hands it came.

Notes

1. Simone de Beauvoir, *La vieillesse* (Paris: Gallimard, 1970), p. 15. "Until now I have spoken about old age as if that term expressed a well-defined reality. In truth, in so far as it concerns our own species, old age isn't easy to define" (trans. mine).
2. In 1631, John Stow described the effigy's hair as brown, and its garment as purple: see *Annales, or, A General Chronicle of England* (1631), 326. Since then, however, the tomb has been moved, repaired and repainted many times, most recently, as I was informed by a Cathedral representative, by a group of school-age parishioners, using "available" paint.
3. On Gower's tomb, see John Hines, Nathalie Cohen, and Simon Roffey, "*Johannes Gower, Armiger, Poeta*: Records and Memorials of His Life and Death," in *A Companion to Gower*, ed. Siân Echard (Cambridge, UK: D. S. Brewer, 2004), 36–41.
4. G. C. Macaulay, ed., *The Complete Works of John Gower*, 4 vols. (Oxford: Clarendon Press, 1899–1902); vols. II-III reprt. as *The English Works of John Gower*, EETS, e.s. 81–82 (London, 1968). All quotations from Gower's writing are drawn from this edition.

5. On generic English manuscript portrayal in the late fourteenth century, see Sabrina Mitchell, *Medieval Manuscript Painting* (New York: Viking Press, 1964), esp. "The International Gothic Style," 33–41; Gervase Mathew, *The Court of Richard II* (New York: Norton, 1968), 38–52, and 204–05, nos. 14 and 15; J. J. G. Alexander, "Painting and Manuscript Illuminations for Royal Patrons in the Later Middle Ages," in V. J. Scattergood and J. W. Sherborne, eds., *English Court Culture in the Later Middle Ages* (London: Duckworth, 1983), 141–62. Also valuable are the views of Millard Meiss: see *French Painting in the Time of Jean de Berry*, 2 vols. (London: Phaidon, 2nd ed., 1969), ch. 4, "The Portraits of Jean de Berry," 2, 68–94, esp. 68. On MS Bodley 294, see particularly the discussion of Gareth M. Spriggs, "Unnoticed Bodleian Manuscripts, Illuminated by Herman Scheerre and His School," *Bodleian Library Record* 7 (1962–67), 193–203. Also helpful is Selby Whittingham, "The Chronology of the Portraits of Richard II," *Burlington Magazine* 113 (1971), 12–21, who points out (12) that "the attempt to date a portrait by reference to the apparent age of the person portrayed is fraught with hazards."
6. Jeremy Griffiths, "*Confessio Amantis*: The Poem and Its Pictures," in A. J. Minnis, ed., *Gower's Confessio Amantis: Responses and Reassessments* (Cambridge, UK: D. S. Brewer, 1983), 163–78. On the ordered placement of illuminations in *Confessio* manuscripts, see also Richard K. Emmerson, "Reading Gower in a Manuscript Culture: Latin and English in Illustrated Manuscripts of the *Confessio Amantis*," *Studies in the Age of Chaucer* 21 (1999), 143–86; Joel Fredell, "Reading the Dream Miniature in the *Confessio Amantis*," *Medievalia et Humanistica*, n.s. 22 (1995), 61–93; and Thomas J. Garbáty, "A Description of the Confession Miniatures for Gower's *Confessio Amantis*, with Special Reference to the Illustrator's Role as Reader and Critic," *Mediaevalia* 19 (1996), 319–43.
7. On Gower's involvement with MS Cotton Tiberius A.iv, see Derek Pearsall, "The Manuscripts and Illustrations of Gower's Work," in *Companion to Gower*, ed. Echard, 72–97, esp. 85–86.
8. Attempts at portraiture in English stone carving are rare in England before the middle of the fifteenth century; see *The Oxford History of Western Art*, ed. Martin Kemp (Oxford: Oxford University Press, 2000), 145; and Lawrence Stone, *Sculpture in Britain in the Middle Ages* (Harmondsworth: Penguin, 1955), 161, 178. Also useful is Derek Pearsall, "Chaucer's Tomb: The Politics of Reburial," *Medium Aevum* 64 (1995), 51–73. Vasari remarks that even in Italy, portraiture in sculpture began late in the fourteenth century: see "Orcagna" and "Jacopo dalla Quercia" in *The Lives of the Painters, Sculptor and Architects*, ed. William Gaunt, trans. A. B. Hinds, 4 vols. (New York: Dutton, 1963), I.149 and 210, respectively.
9. That is, the Bedford Psalter-Hours painter has been identified as the artist known as "The Master of the Great Cowchers," who was in London between 1406 and 1408; see Sylvia Wright, "The Author Portraits in the Bedford Psalter-Hours: Gower, Chaucer and Hoccleve," *British Library Journal* 18 (1992), 190–201.
10. *Vox Clamantis* II, Pro. l. 83. For "the voice of one crying in the wilderness," see also Matt. 3:3; Mark 1:3; Luke 3:4; John 1:23. Maria Wickert has pointed out that the title is intentionally both messianic and political; see *Studien zu Gower* (Cologne: University Press of Cologne, 1953), 65–67, and trans. Robert J. Meindl, *Studies in John Gower* (Washington, DC: University Press of America, 1981), 75–77.
11. Wright, "Author Portraits," 192.
12. E.g., the printer Thomas Berthelette, who calls Gower a "worthy olde writer" in the epistle to Henry VIII that fronts his edition; see *Jo. Gower de Confessione*

Amantis (London, 1532), aa.ii.v. Shakespeare refers to him as "ancient Gower" (*Pericles*, I.1.2).

13. See Mitchell, "International Style," *Medieval Manuscript Painting*, 29; Wright, "Author Portraits," 190; and Whittingham, "Chronology," passim, who finds a possible exception in the treatments of Richard II ca. 1390.
14. On the revelation of Amans's age as intentional surprise, see especially John Burrow, "The Portrayal of Amans in *Confessio Amantis*, in *Responses and Reassessments*, ed. Minnis, 5–24; for a different view, see Donald Scheuler, "The Age of the Lover in Gower's *Confessio Amantis*," *Medium Aevum* 36 (1967), 152–58.
15. The case for Gower's dependence on Machaut has been made forcefully and eloquently by Peter Nicholson, *Love and Ethics in Gower's Confessio Amantis* (Ann Arbor: University of Michigan Press, 2005).
16. Assuming that the *Voir Dit* is indeed autobiographical, Machaut was in his middle sixties when he wrote it, and so famous that neither his lady Peronelle nor his audience would not have known it; see the discussion of R. Barton Palmer, *Guillaume de Machaut: Le Livre dou Voir* Dit (The book of the true poem), ed. Palmer and trans. Daniel Leech-Wilkinson (New York: Garland Publishing, 1998), xi-lvii. Froissart completed the *Joli buisson* in 1373, at about age 35. See F. S. Shears, *Froissart: Chronicler and Poet* (London: Routledge, 1930), 205; and the edition of Anthime Fourrier, *Le joli Buisson de Jonece* (Geneva: Librarie Droz, 1975), 29.
17. Burrow, for one, reads the lines this way: see "Portrayal of Amans," *Responses and Reassessments*, 18. Amans/Gower's impotence may itself have literary precedent in Maximianus, whose confession of erotic excess and erectile dysfunction is a possible analogue seldom, if ever, mentioned in connection with the conclusion of the *Confessio*—an odd omission, perhaps, since as David Carlson remarks in private correspondence—"He was an elementary circular author, too, with the *Disticha Catonis*'—I am grateful to Carlson for calling this to my attention.
18. C. S. Lewis, *The Allegory of Love* (Oxford: Oxford University Press, 1930), 200.
19. The *epistola* is printed by Macaulay, *Complete Works*, IV, 1–2, and translated by Eric W. Stockton, *The Major Latin Works of John Gower* (Seattle: University of Washington Press, 1962), 47–48.
20. The versions are printed by Macaulay, *Complete Works*, IV, 365–66. The reference to Gower's blindness becomes vaguer as the versions of *Quicquid* progress. In the earliest, he says he went functionally blind in the first year of Henry IV, though it had been coming on for some time ("Henrici quarti primus regni fuit annus, / Quo michi defecit visus ad acta mea"); in (clearly) subsequent versions, including the one dated 2 Henry IV, Gower says only that he was blind when they were written, in decreasingly specific terms: "Henrici regis annus fuit ille secundus, / Scribere dum cesso, *sum quia cecus ego*"; the same phrase repeating even more vaguely in the latest version, "Quicquid homo scribat, finem natura ministrant / Que velut umbra fugit, nec fugiendo redit; / Illa michi finem posuit, quo scribere quicquam / Ulterius nequio, *sum quia cecus ego*" (italics mine).
21. Macaulay, ed., *Complete Works*, IV, xvii-xviii, translates Gower's will; for the Latin text, see Sir Harris Nicolas, "John Gower, the Poet," *Retrospective Review*, 2nd series, 2 (1828), 103–17 (104).
22. On the "traditional" assumption of Gower's birth year as 1330, see John H. Fisher, *John Gower, Moral Philosopher and Friend of Chaucer* (New York: New York University Press, 1964), 46. Of course, we have no birth record for Chaucer, either.

23. A good deal of this work has been done by David Herlihy using Italian data: see especially "The Generation in Medieval History," *Viator* 5 (1974), 347–64; "Veillir à Florence au Quattrocento," *Annales E.S.C.* XXIV, 1328–52, repr. as "Growing Old in the Quattrocento," in Peter N. Stearns, ed., *Old Age in Preindustrial Society* (New York: Holmes and Meier, 1982), 105–18; with Christiane Klapisch-Zuber, *Tuscans and Their Families: A Study of the Florentine Catasto of 1427* (New Haven, CT: Yale University Press, 1985), esp. ch. 3, "Population Movements, 1300–1550," 60–92; and "Age, Property and Career in Medieval Society," in *Aging and the Aged in Medieval Europe*, ed. Michael M. Sheehan, CSB, Papers in Mediaeval Studies 11 (Toronto: Pontifical Institute of Mediaeval Studies, 1990), 143–58. See further, in the same volume, Anne Gilmour-Bryson, "Age-Related Data from the Templar Trials," 129–42, and Joel T. Rosenthal, "Retirement and the Life-Cycle in Fifteenth-Century England," 173–88. Also useful is Rosenthal, "Medieval Longevity: and The Secular Peerage, 1350–1500," *Population Studies* 27 (1973), 287–325. Most of these studies focus primarily on males; see, for conditions affecting females differently, Vern Bullough and Cameron Campbell, "Female Longevity and Diet in the Middle Ages," *Speculum* 55 (1980), 317–25; and, from a slightly later period, Richard C. Trexler, "A Widows' Asylum of the Renaissance: The Orbatello of Florence," in *Old Age*, ed. Stearns, above, 119–50.
24. John A. Burrow, *The Ages of Man: A Study in Medieval Writing and Thought* (Oxford: Clarendon Press, 1986), 93.
25. So, for example, Dante in *Il convivio*, IV, xxiv, following Cicero, *De Senectute*, IV, xxiv.8, and Aristotle, *De Anima*, III.12.434ᵃ. Compare also Thomas Aquinas's commentary on the passage, Lectio XVII.§848.
26. E.g., in the many representations verbal and visual of the "Seven Ages of Man," which Burrow derives from Claudius Ptolemaeus; *Ages of Man*, 36–37; and further the richly illustrated study of Elizabeth Sears, *The Ages of Man: Medieval Interpretations of the Life Cycle* (Princeton, NJ: Princeton University Press, 1986), 38–79, 134–40 and their accompanying plates.
27. On the full range of age divisions, numbering from three to twelve and beyond, albeit with emphasis on a slightly later period, see Samuel C. Chew, *The Pilgrimage of Life* (New Haven, CT: Yale University Press, 1962), especially 153–73.
28. See the edition of Almut Mutzenbecher, Corpus Christianorum, Series Latina 44A (Turnhout: Brepols, 1975), 106–07. Instead of providing age thresholds for a single individual, Augustine defines the six ages eschatologically, e.g., *infantia* is the span from Adam to Noah, *pueritia* from Noah to Abraham, etc.
29. Isidore of Seville, *Etymologiarum sive originum*, ed. W. M. Lindsay, 2 vols. (Oxford: Clarendon Press, 1911), 2, XI.2, 1–9, esp. 6.
30. *Il convivio*, IV, xxiv, 5.
31. Aristotle, *Rhetoric*, II.14, 1390ᵇ; trans. W. Rhys Roberts (Oxford, 1924; rpt. New York: Random House, 1954), 126.
32. E.g., Papias, *Elementarium Doctrinae Rudimentum*; see Burrow's discussion, *Ages of Man*, 85. Isidore, *Etymologiarum* XI.2, 6, commences *senectus,* at seventy.
33. Gower's claim, that he wrote the *Confessio Amantis* at royal command after a meeting with Richard on the Thames, for long universally accepted, has nonetheless sparked controversy: e.g., see, among doubters, V. J. Scattergood, "Literary Culture at the Court of Richard II," in *English Court Culture*, ed. Scattergood and Sherborne, 29–43 (at 31), and Frank Grady, "Gower's Boat, Richard's Barge, and the True Story of the *Confessio Amantis*: Text and Gloss," *Texas Studies in Literature and Language* 44 (2002), 1–15; and for the defense, most recently, Joyce

Coleman, "'A bok for King Richardes sake': Royal Patronage, the *Confessio*, and the *Legend of Good Women*," in *John Gower: Essays at the Millennium*, ed. R. F. Yeager, (Kalamazoo, MI: Medieval Institute Press), 2007.

34. First to make this claim was George R. Coffman, in two seminal essays: "John Gower in His Most Significant Role," in *Elizabethan Studies and Other Essays in Honor of George F. Reynolds*, University of Colorado Studies, series B, II, 4 (Boulder, 1945), 52–6; and "John Gower, Mentor for Royalty: Richard II," *PMLA* 69 (1954), 953–64. More recently, see, e.g., Russell A. Peck, *Kingship and Common Profit in Gower's Confessio Amantis* (Carbondale and Edwardsville: Southern Illinois University Press, 1978) and his more recent "Governance in Gower" in *Companion to Gower*, ed. Echard, 215–38; Judith Ferster, "O Political Gower," in *Fictions of Advice: The Literature and Politics of Counsel in Late Medieval England* (Philadelphia: University of Pennsylvania Press, 1996), 108–36; María Bullón-Fernández, *Fathers and Daughters in Gower's Confessio Amantis: Authority, Family, State and Writing*, Publications of the John Gower Society 4 (Cambridge, UK: D. S. Brewer, 2000); Lynn Staley, "Gower, Richard II, and Henry of Derby, and the Business of Making Culture," *Speculum* 75:1 (2000), 68–96.

35. E.g., ll. 1–5: "Est amor in glosa pax bellica, lis pietosa, / Accio famosa, vaga sors, vis imperiosa, / Pugna quietosa, victoria perniciosa, / Regula visciosa, scola devia, lex capitosa, / Cura molestosa, gravis ars, virtus viciosa. . . ." (In the glossaries Love is a warlike peace, a dutiful strife, / Infamous invitation, wavering fate, unforceful force, / A peaceful fight, a ruinous victory, / A rule besmirched, an erroneous school, an irregular law, / A troublesome cure, a grievous art, a vicious virtue. . . ." My translation.)

36. For the full text, see Macaulay, ed., *Complete Works*, IV, 359. All translations are my own.

37. Cf. Paul, I Cor. 7:9.

38. "O natura viri, que naturatur eodem / Quod vitare nequit, nec licet illud agi! / O natura viri, duo que contraria mixta / Continet, amborum nec licet acta sequi! / O natura viri, que semper habet sibi bellum / Corporis ac anime, que sua iura petunt!" Macaulay, ed., *Complete Works*, IV, 358, ll. 25–30.

39. Macaulay, ed., *Complete Works*, IV, 418.

40. See Macaulay's discussion of Gower's marriage, and the Bishop's dispensation, *Complete Works*, 4:xvii; the full Latin text of the dispensation was published by W. H. Gunner, *Notes & Queries*, 1st series, 9 (1854), 487, and is reprinted by Fisher, *John Gower*, 336, n.68. On Gower's marriage to Agnes, Fisher remarks: "Such a marriage of convenience between an elderly invalid and his nurse would explain the permission to perform the wedding in Gower's lodgings," *John Gower*, 65. See also following note.

41. On Edward III's children with Alice Perrers, see Michael Prestwich, *The Three Edwards: War and State in England, 1272–1377*, 2nd ed. (London: Routledge, 2003), 253; *Dictonary of National Biography* XV, 898–900, where Alice is supplied with two daughters, one of whom is attributed to Edward, while no father is named for the other; and Michael Packe, *King Edward III*, ed. L. C. B. Seaman (London: Routledge & Kegan Paul, 1983), 286, who cites a son, John. Interestingly, "Hermentrude," *Notes and Queries*, 7th series 7 (1889), 449, asserts Dame Alice as Edward's "sick nurse," as she may well have been in the last months of his life, although (despite an assuredly remarkable bedside manner) what recommended her initially must not have been her medicinal skills. Eve Salisbury gives attention to Agnes's status in an important essay, "Promiscuous Contexts: Gower's Wife,

Prostitution, and the *Confessio Amantis*," in *John Gower: Manuscripts, Readers, Contexts*, ed. Malte Urban (Turnhout: Brepols, 2009), 219–40.

42. See Martha Carlin, *Medieval Southwark* (London: Hambledon Press, 1996), ch. 9, "The Stews and Prostitution," 209–29, and maps, 34–35.
43. Indeed, prostitutes were known in London at the end of the fourteenth century as "Winchester geese": see A. R. Myers, *London in the Age of Chaucer* (Norman, OK: University of Oklahoma Press, 1972), 11.
44. See, e.g., *The Anonimalle Chronicle, 1333 to 1381*, ed. V. H. Galbraith (Manchester: University of Manchester Press, 1927), 140; *Memorials of London and London Life in the XIIIth, XIVth, and XVth Centuries A.D. 1276–1419*, ed. H. T. Riley (London: HMSO,1868), 535. As Carlin, *Medieval Southwark*, 222, remarks, "evidently many [prostitutes] came from the Low Countries."
45. See, e.g., *Secretum* in *Prose*, ed. Guido Martellotti et al. (Milan-Naples: Ricciardi Editore, 1955), 176–77. Petrarch's contortions are pointedly examined by James D. Folts, Jr., "Senescence and Renascence: Petrarch's Thoughts on Growing Old," *Journal of Medieval and Renaissance Studies* 10 (1980), 207–37.
46. Isabella Neale Yeager, "Did Gower Love His Wife? And What Does It Have to Do with the Poetry?" *Poetica* [Japan] 73 (2010): 67–86.
47. "Knowing very little used to be a great disgrace for an old man, because of the magnitude of the time he had lost. But nowadays if old age is wise in any way or teaches what it has learned earlier, its voice hardly receives the welcome of a youth's. Even if they are fervent in their zeal, the words which old men write are, as a rule, acceptable to young men only quite rarely. Yet no matter how much the voices of the dogs may bark in objection, I shall not run away, but instead I shall sing out my words." Trans. Stockton, *Major Latin Works*, 97. Book 1 of the *Vox*, sometimes called the "Visio," describes the Rising of 1381, and is thought to have been appended to the original beginning of the poem, i.e., what is now Book II—hence the assumed pre-1381 dating of Books 2–7. On the chronology, see Wickert, *Studien*, 13–31.
48. See Paul E. Beichner, "Gower's Use of the *Aurora* in the *Vox Clamantis*," *Speculum* 30 (1955), 582–95. On Gower's centonic style, see my "Did Gower Write *Cento*?" in *John Gower: Recent Readings*, ed. Yeager (Kalamazoo, MI: Medieval Institute Press, 1988), 113–32.
49. *TC* V.1856; for the date of composition of *Troilus*, see Larry D. Benson, gen. ed., *Riverside Chaucer* (Boston: Houghton Mifflin, 1987), xxix.
50. See Ernst Robert Curtius's discussion of the topoi of age and wisdom in *European Literature and the Latin Middle Ages*, trans. Willard R. Trask (New York: Pantheon, 1953), 98–101, 170–71.
51. Aristotle, *The Politics*, VII.xiv.1332b32; trans. T. A. Sinclair, rev. Trevor J. Saunders (Harmondsworth: Penguin, 1981), 432. All quotations from *Politics* are from this volume.
52. Aristotle, *Nichomachean Ethics*, VI.x.1143a; trans. Martin Ostwald (Indianapolis, IN: Bobbs-Merrill, 1962), 164. All quotations from *Nichomachean Ethics* are from this volume. See also VI.xiii.1145a (trans. Ostwald, 172): "Virtue determines the end, and practical wisdom makes us do what is conducive to the end."
53. On the complex matter of dating Gower's Latin poetry, David R. Carlson's work is essential reading: see "Gower's Early Latin Poetry: Text-Genetic Hypotheses of an Epistola ad regem (ca. 1377–1380) from the Evidence of John Bale," *Mediaeval Studies* 65 (2003): 293–317; "The Invention of the Anglo-Latin Public Poetry (circa 1367–1402) and Its Prosody, esp. in John Gower," *Mittellateinisches Jahrbuch*

39 (2004): 389–406; "A Rhyme Distribution Chronology of John Gower's Latin Poetry," *Studies in Philology* 104 (2007): 15–55; "Gower on Henry IV's Rule: The Endings of the *Cronica Tripertita* and Its Texts," *Traditio* 62 (2007): 207–36; "English Poetry, July-October 1399, and Lancastrian Crime," *Studies in the Age of Chaucer* 29 (2007): 375–418.

54. For the possibility that Chaucer was killed for political reasons on the orders of Henry IV and Arundel, see Terry Jones, R. F. Yeager, Terry Dolan, Alan Fletcher, and Juliette D'Or, *Who Murdered Chaucer? A Medieval Mystery* (London: Methuen, 2003). On Sawtre, see Peter McNiven, *Heresy and Politics in the Reign of Henry IV: The Burning of John Badby* (Woodbridge, Suff.: Boydell & Brewer, 1987), esp. 79–92. On Arundel's extensive attempts to legalize executions, see Margaret Aston, *Thomas Arundel: A Study of Church Life in the Reign of Richard II* (Oxford: Clarendon Press, 1967), 320–25, and McNiven, 63–78.
55. On Gower's possible early involvement with Gaunt's household, see my "Gower's Lancastrian Affinity: The Iberian Connection," *Viator* 35 (2004), 483–515; and further Joyce Coleman, "The Flower, the Leaf, and Philippa of Lancaster," in *The Legend of Good Women: Context and Reception,* ed. Carolyn P. Collette (Cambridge: D. S. Brewer, 2006), 35–58, and Coleman, "Philippa of Lancaster, Queen of Portugal—and Patron of the Gower Translations?" in *England and Iberia in the Middle Ages, 12th-15th Century: Cultural, Literary, and Political Changes*, ed. María Bullón Fernández (New York: Palgrave Macmillan, 2007), 135–65.
56. That Gower served at the order of the regime is delineated by David R. Carlson, "The Parliamentary Source of Gower's *Cronica Tripertita* and Incommensurable Styles," in *John Gower, Trilingual Poet: Language, Translation and Tradition*, ed. Elisabeth Dutton, with John Hines and R. F. Yeager (Cambridge, UK: D. S. Brewer, 2010), 98–111.
57. For a description of Gower's (and Chaucer's) probable responses to the Lancastrian assumption of power, see my "Chaucer's 'To His Purse': Begging, or Begging Off?," *Viator* 36 (2005), 373–414.
58. From Carpi, September 25, 1348: see *Petrarca: Le Familiari*, ed. Vittorio Rossi and Umberto Bosco (Florence: Sansoni, 1933–42), X. 3; or XXII.10, to Francesco Nelli (from Milan, September 18, 1360), describing his turn away from secular to religious writing; or XXIII.19, on literary imagination, to Giovanni Boccaccio from Pavia, October 28, 1366.
59. After seizing power, Henry IV, perhaps influenced by observation of Gian Galeazzo Visconti during a visit to Milan, actively sought laudation and support from poets, including Christine de Pisan, undoubtedly Gower, and probably Chaucer as well—very likely to the latter's detriment. In the case of Christine, as she states in her *Vision*, Henry led her to believe that he held her son a hostage pending her coming to England to write for his court. See Sister Mary Towner, ed., *Lavision-Christine*, Catholic University of America Studies in Romance Languages and Literatures 6 (Washington DC: Catholic University of America, 1932), 166. For the full case, see my "Chaucer's 'To His Purse'," and Jones, Yeager, Dolan, Fletcher, and D'Or, *Who Murdered Chaucer?*, passim.

CHAPTER 9

THE NAUGHTY BITS: DATING CHAUCER'S *HOUSE OF FAME* AND *LEGEND OF GOOD WOMEN*

John M. Bowers

Terry Jones surprised his Monty Python fans by publishing *Chaucer's Knight: The Portrait of a Medieval Mercenary*, but continues to surprise Chaucer colleagues with challenges to the conventional thinking that is hard to swallow but difficult to resist. Like Terry's memorable movie character Mr. Creosote, readers of *Who Murdered Chaucer? A Medieval Mystery* find themselves gorged with so many tantalizing tidbits that I want to select just one—the redating of *An ABC* from the beginning of the poet's career to the end—as an appetizer for considering other rearrangements in the chronology.[1] Chaucer's dream poems *House of Fame* and *Legend of Good Women* have always been "naughty bits" difficult to fit into any tidy sequence of the poet's career.

The Chaucer chronologies have been described by Derek Pearsall as "a spider's web of hypothesis" and by Kathryn Lynch as a "house of cards" with foundations laid down a very long time ago.[2] By the end of the nineteenth century, Chaucer's career had emerged as the three orderly phases of French, Italian, and English proposed by Bernhard ten Brink and destined to reach into the twenty-first century.[3] Walter W. Skeat's six-volume *Complete Works* required a chronology of texts that he restated by his *Chaucer Canon*, always insisting upon its speculative nature: "The following list is arranged, *conjecturally*, in chronological order."[4] The italics are Skeat's own. He nonetheless created many pitfalls for later scholars by his enthusiasm for detecting literary echoes and treating them as hard evidence. For example, he identified references to the *Legend of Good Women* in the *Testament of Love* by Thomas Usk, executed in 1388, hence the *terminus ad quem* for Chaucer's work. Even when Ramona Bressie disproved this claim, Skeat's authority persisted.[5]

John S. P. Tatlock's *Development and Chronology of Chaucer's Works* pushed conjectures further by detecting more echoes from poems like John Gower's *Mirour de l'Omme*, often just as difficult to date, as well as the absence of echoes from works Chaucer ought to have known, like Giovanni Boccaccio's. Hunches turned into facts. Suppositions were reborn as certainties. Networks of inference were pursued as if air-tight logic. The questions of dates sparked skirmishes during the first half of the twentieth century by the leading authorities George Lyman Kittredge, Robert K. Root, John M. Manly, John L. Lowes, Howard R. Patch, and Kemp Malone, but overall George Kane's observation remains true today: "there has been no attempt of real scope on the subject since Tatlock's youthful work in 1907."[6]

When Kane warned against "agreed conclusions reached by the best kind of argument which editorial blandness and the veneer of print convey," he had been discussing the *Riverside Chaucer.*[7] On the face of things F. N. Robinson retained Skeat's open-mindedness when he wrote "the greater number of Chaucer's writings can be only arranged in a probable order," and he offered a "tentatively constructed" chronological table that largely repeated ten Brink's. Robinson retained the section "Canon and Chronology of Chaucer's Writings" verbatim in his second edition of 1957 despite the emergence of new, contradictory evidence.[8] For example, John Livingston Lowes had decided that the *Legend* cited Eustache Deschamps's *Lai de Franchise* dated 1385, and so Robinson's first edition relied upon this evidence for dating the F Prologue about 1386.[9] Years later Marian Lossing concluded Chaucer did *not* know the French poem at all,[10] and in his second edition, Robinson welcomed Lossing's correction as an opportunity to date the poem even earlier, to 1384.[11]

By the second half of the twentieth century, Robinson's edition itself had achieved canonic status. "To say anything against the notes would be to come out against God, home, and mother."[12] Larry Benson added new information in the third edition of 1987, but repeated almost exactly Robinson's chronological assignments.[13] And nobody much cared. Precise dating no longer mattered for New Criticism because the immediate historical context was excluded from close textual analysis. Nor did dates figure in the procedures of Exegetics based on an idealized notion of the Middle Ages as a vast monolithic historical period ca. 500–ca. 1500.[14] But in the last generation New Historicism, which investigates the interplay of texts and contemporary events, has required a far more reliable time frame for literary productions so that even relatively minor relocations of Chaucer's works carry major implications. When dated differently, his poems *mean* different things. *House of Fame* "means" something very different if composed in the late 1380s rather than the late 1370s[15] —as I shall be suggesting—and *Legend of Good Women* "means" something different if both the F and G versions of its Prologue belong to the middle 1390s instead of the middle 1380s.[16]

The *House of Fame*

Many will be surprised to learn that early Chaucer scholars agreed *House of Fame* postdated *Troilus* and immediately preceded the *Canterbury Tales.* The narrator's reference to spending his days bent over his reckonings (*HF* 652–58) indicated the poem belonged to his long period of service 1374–86 as Controller in the Port of London. Ten Brink and Skeat settled upon the fairly precise period 1383–84.[17] Tatlock put the dream poem after *Troilus* because the reference to Lollius (*HF* 1468) made no sense unless it followed Chaucer's Trojan epic in which the poet introduced this pseudoauthority (1.394; 5.1653).[18] Even Alastair Minnis suggested *House of Fame* just might have been composed after *Troilus*.[19]

Chaucer's catalogue of six authorities for the Trojan War—Homer, Dares, Dictys, Lollius, Guido delle Colonne, and *Engliysshe Gaufride* (*HF* 1464–72)—compounds the mystery of Lollius with the new historical witness "English Geoffrey." Skeat identified this figure as Geoffrey of Monmouth, and his gloss was accepted by Robinson in his 1933 edition and repeated by the most recent Riverside editor.[20] In the inaugural volume of *Speculum*, however, E. K. Rand suggested that Chaucer named himself as the English Geoffrey who had extended the fame of Troy in *Troilus*.[21] Already confident that *House of Fame* was written later than *Troilus*, Tatlock was glad to accept this view of the poet's self-naming in his final summation of Chaucer's literary achievement.[22]

David Wallace has pointed out that Chaucer repeatedly used the "sixth-of-six" formula from Dante's roster of great authors in the *Inferno* (4.100–02). Chaucer employs this topos first near the end of *Troilus* (5.1792) when he placed himself sixth in the similar lineup of the epic poets, and later more humorously when he places himself sixth among the General Prologue's scoundrels the Reeve, Miller, Summoner, Pardoner, Manciple, "and myself—ther were namo" (*CT* I, 542–44).[23] This recurrent practice of placing himself sixth among storytellers serves as further evidence that he pictured himself as the sixth and final supporter of Trojan memory in *House of Fame*.

It is surprising, then, to find Robinson succumbing to the principle of metrical determinism for placing the work prior to *Troilus*: "The use of the octosyllabic couplet would have been more natural at that time than later."[24] The fact that Gower composed his *Confessio Amantis* in octosyllabic couplets attests to the viability of this verse form into the 1390s when the two poets maintained close contact.[25] Helen Cooper's *Times Literary Supplement* (*TLS*) advocacy for a later dating "at the end of 1384 when *Troilus* was complete or almost complete" actually confirmed earlier claims by ten Brink and Tatlock.[26] Cooper points to "Engliysshe Gaufride" as part of Chaucer's double self-inscriptions beginning when the Eagle calls him "Geffrey" (*HF* 729). The Geffrey/Gaufridus distinction marks cultural as well as linguistic differences. When John Lydgate honored Chaucer's elevated status as historian of the Trojan War, he too used the Latinized form of "Noble Galfride, poete of Breteyne."[27] This metamorphosis of book 2's "Geffrey" into book 3's "Gaufride" makes perfect sense after Chaucer had finished *Troilus* and found himself in a position to consider his prospects for literary fame, as well as its liabilities. Often read as an *ars poetica* bespeaking mature reflection,[28] *House of Fame* in book 3 specifically confronts the force of tradition and fame's power to impose crushing burdens. Chaucer's nightmare of upholding a particular construction of literary history would become, in a sense, our own.

Ten Brink thought this dream vision was the comedy promised at the end of *Troilus* (5.1788) and its closing lines anticipated the *Canterbury Tales* with its shipmen, pardoners, and pilgrims jumbling true and false tidings (*HF* 2121–29).[29]

These generic pilgrims will shortly become the Shipman and Pardoner in the General Prologue where the noisy House of Rumour is converted into the boisterous Tabard Inn. By returning to the early view of Skeat and Tatlock, we have much to gain by repositioning *House of Fame* as a transitional work between *Troilus* and the *Canterbury Tales*, functioning as a theoretical prologue for the poetry that would occupy Chaucer during the final period of his career. "Chaucer uses the *House of Fame* not to switch allegiances from France to Italy but, instead, to make a declaration of literary independence."[30]

We can also begin gauging Chaucer's reaction to certain jolts and aftershocks in the political landscape. Court life in the middle 1380s had provided the young King Richard with a domestic honeymoon of sorts, and Chaucer wrote *Troilus* partly as a reflection of the king's adolescent self-absorption. The Wonderful Parliament of 1386, in which Chaucer sat as knight of the shire for Kent, sought to curb the king's excesses and control his choice of advisers.[31] In the Merciless Parliament of the next year, the Appellants secured condemnations for several of the king's favorites including some of Chaucer's friends and colleagues, as well as men with literary connections like Thomas Usk.[32]

Chaucer was most likely selected knight of the shire as a reliable "king's man" and therefore could have anticipated sharing the backlash of 1387–88 against Richard II. *House of Fame* dramatizes the anxiety that attends this degree of public visibility. The Eagle as symbol of royal authority transported him into a loud, turbulent assembly where he stood as a helpless witness to cruel reversals and savage judgments. One item perhaps gave him specific worry. Among the Commons petitions of 1386 was a request that controllers of customs should be removed on suspicion of financial misconduct. A week after payment of his fee in December 1386, Chaucer's replacement was named and his Aldgate residence was vacated. Pearsall thinks that Chaucer, always the survivor, had quietly decamped to Kent.[33] Nobody could have predicted what "man of great authority" might emerge from these wranglings. Yet Chaucer himself emerged successfully with appointment as Clerk of the King's Works in 1389. The later its date, the more deeply *House of Fame* meditates upon the capriciousness of men's fortunes.

More time also permitted responses to developments within the energetic community of vernacular poets elsewhere in London. Frank Grady wonders if the book the narrator was reading until his expression was totally dazed (*HF* 657–60) might have been *Piers Plowman* in the B-version read in the metropolis by the early 1380s. Chaucer's Aldgate residence was no more than a quarter mile from Langland's Cornhill address, and the later *House of Fame*, the more convincing Grady's argument sounds.[34] *Piers* would have reminded Chaucer of the dream vision's value as a genre so utterly conventional, so apparently divorced from reality, that it evaded a degree of responsibility for its contents. William Langland (if that was his name) also seems to have won security in the anonymity that Chaucer comes to request: "Sufficeth me, as I were ded, / That no wight have my name in honde" (*HF* 1876–77). Chaucer was too widely known as someone who profited from high-visibility appointments, but it is noteworthy that the 493 documents of *Chaucer Life-Records* never once mention him as a poet.

Following the visionary *House of Fame*, Chaucer returned to the contemporary scene in the *Canterbury Tales*, only at a safe remove. Just as the dreamer fled the harsh authority of the Palace of Fame, the poet turns his back on the Palace of Westminster. Wallace has written about London as the "absent city" because the General Prologue's action is displaced to Southwark.[35] The Tabard Inn's fellowship provides the raucous but ultimately productive hubbub fulfilling the poet's quest for "Tydynges other this or that / Of love or suche thynges glade" (*HF* 1888–89) as the subject matter for the *Canterbury Tales*—his very next title in this revised chronology.

The *Legend of Good Women*

And now for something completely different. Or is it?

Repositioning *House of Fame* to the mid-1380s as a transitional work between *Troilus* and the *Canterbury Tales* creates a problem for dating the work usually assigned to this slot. *Legend of Good Women* is reckoned an anomaly in Chaucer's career and an embarrassment for Chaucerian criticism. Pearsall calls it "the least noticed of Chaucer's longer poems,"[36] and Robert Burlin describes it more harshly as "a colossal blunder."[37] The courtly dream vision does not fit the discursive formation of a career that was supposed to have rejected the artificiality of French practices and moved steadily toward the homegrown realism of the *Tales*. Its incompleteness has been taken as Chaucer's admission of a failed experiment, and scholars have worked hard at dating it as early as possible, squeezing it between the completion of *Troilus* around 1386 and the start of the Canterbury collection around 1388.[38]

Ten Brink grouped the *Legend* along with the *Canterbury Tales* in the final third of the poet's career. Its decasyllabic couplets and list of Chaucer's prior works (F 414–41) required this later dating. Composition was supposed to have begun after February 1385 when Chaucer was relieved of his record-keeping duties as controller of customs. Appointment of a permanent deputy was thought to have resulted from Queen Anne's intercession, so Chaucer expressed his appreciation in a poem praising her in the guise of Queen Alceste. Skeat accepted ten Brink's dating and his reasons for it.[39] The case was undercut, however, by the discovery that Chaucer's exemption from keeping the ledger in his own hand came through the offices of Robert de Vere, Earl of Oxford, and not Queen Anne.[40] Ten Brink altered his opinion and dated the F Prologue much later, to 1393, just before Queen Anne's death.[41] As so often happened, once the speculative date had been fixed in the standard editions—first Skeat's and then Robinson's—it became immune to adjustments even when the original evidence was found faulty.

These conjectures were driven by Tatlock's strong presumption that Chaucer operated as a single-focused writer: "We can hardly believe that the *Legends* were continued after the *Canterbury Tales* were once under way."[42] Published a year after Tatlock's book, Eleanor Prescott Hammond's *Bibliographical Manual* sounded an altogether more skeptical note. As evidence for dating, she raised doubts about the one-way direction of Chaucer's metrical practices and the reliability of his changes in sources from French to Italian, assailing "the tacit assumption that a scale of Chaucer's work can be constructed in a sort of geometrical progression . . . or that, as in the Prologue to the *Legend*, he may have returned to French models long after those of Italy had become familiar to him."[43]

Chaucer was a master of multitasking. During the 1380s he engaged almost simultaneously on his *Boece, Troilus*, and *Palamon and Arcite* as well as his *St. Cecilie*. In 1391, when we imagine him concentrating upon the *Tales*, he diverted his attentions to write the *Treatise on the Astrolabe*, coinciding with Richard II's enthusiasm for astrology, as witnessed by his *Liber Judiciorum* in a manuscript also datable to 1391.[44] When external circumstances demanded, Chaucer was perfectly capable of undertaking more than one literary project at a time, a practice that probably explains why he left so many unfinished.

Robert K. Root thought that the *Legend* must then have been an ongoing project after work on the *Tales* was already far advanced.[45] Agreeing that the Man of Law's catalog of love martyrs attests to the provisional status of the *Legend*, Hammond accepted ten Brink's revised chronology and suggested some "outside pressure" that promped the F Prologue in the 1390s.[46] We are left to inquire what external occasions pressed Chaucer to undertake two versions of the *Legend* without completing either of them.

Paul Strohm's essay "Queens as Intercessors" explores the fourteenth-century role of the English queen in royal theatrics, "*petitionary* in the sense that it cast the queen as one seeking redress rather than one able to institute redress in her own right, and *intercessory* in that it limited its objectives to the modification of a previously determined male resolve."[47] Because Richard II was quick to fits of white-hot anger, Queen Anne was cast as a negotiator between her husband's wrath and the king's clemency. Her most public enactment of this role came during the 1392 royal entry into London, when she helped to resolve a quarrel between Richard and London's citizens over a large loan. This grand civic procession was described in the Latin panegyric *Concordia* by the Carmelite friar Richard Maidstone (d. 1396). The symbolic drama culminated in Westminster Hall where Queen Anne performed her function as mediatrix between the offended king and the penitent Londoners. Richard II makes a great show of submitting to his wife's intercession, his forgiveness contingent upon the people's better conduct, including the avoidance of heresy.[48]

This famous event of 1392 seems to provide evidence that the occasion for the original F Prologue to the *Legend* was part of the "outside pressure" that Hammond believed motivated the poem, and John Norton-Smith concluded that Queen Anne's intercession for the London people must have inspired Queen Alceste's intercession for the London poet.[49] Remember that ten Brink give his final nod to 1393. The *Legend* Prologue casts Chaucer in the role of an offender who provoked the God of Love by writing his *Troilus*. As Richard II accused Londoners of embracing "new doctrines," the God of Love indicts Chaucer of producing heretical writings—"That is an heresye ayeins my lawe" (F 330)—-allegedly in his *Romaunt of the Rose* but with a sinister allusion to Lollard heresies circulating at the time. Several of Chaucer's most important court connections, notably Sir Richard Stury and Sir Lewis Clifford, were destined to be branded as Lollard Knights.[50] In 1395, under circumstances like those described in the Prologue, King Richard compelled Stury to swear an oath abjuring heresy and warned him that any backsliding would be punished by execution.[51] Stury's connections with Chaucer and with court poetry generally are well-attested. He owned a manuscript of the *Roman de la Rose* and arranged the occasion in 1395 when Jean Froissart presented the king with a deluxe manuscript of his poetry.[52] Queen Alceste rescues the dreamer by counseling, as an act of penance, the writing of holy "legends" honoring women martyred for the sake of love, in one sense countering Lollard objections to the popular veneration of saints, but in another sense aligning him with these objections by lampooning the sacred genre.

In his account of the 1392 royal entry, Maidstone described the young king as "handsome as Troilus," a reference that makes sense only if his contemporary London readers recognized Chaucer's use of Richard as his model for his Trojan prince. Richard valued books even if we do not know how closely he read them.[53] Evidence that he did not feel flattered by the depiction of Troilus (his youthful alter ego) can be read in the *Legend* Prologue when the God of Love (his more mature alter ego) responds with such anger to Chaucer.[54] Though the explicit complaint is the portrayal of women in *Troilus*, the outburst camouflaged something more personal. The king was not amused. Even while avoiding further difficulties by writing the *Canterbury Tales* in private as a closet work—pace Terry Jones who imagines Archbishop Arundel leafing through the *Tales*[55]—Chaucer managed "damage control" after the unpleasant impact of *Troilus* at court.

The period 1392–94 offers itself as the most likely time for the F Prologue between the London entry, when Queen Anne performed the exemplary role as intercessor, and her sudden death at Sheen Palace. The G Prologue was revised after her 1394 death, as is known because it lacks lines commanding the work be delivered to her at Sheen (F 496–97). Richard was so distraught that he ordered destruction of the royal residence. Lowes was the first to emphasize a connection between the death of Queen Anne and the deleting of this reference from the Prologue,[56] and Tatlock agreed that F was originally written as commendation to Queen Anne and revised after her death, settling upon 1394–95 for the G Prologue.[57]

Widely considered as aberration on top of an aberration, this revision has been taken as proof that Chaucer conceived the work under royal duress, proceeded with fitful obstinacy, and finally left the collection incomplete when he felt no further pressure to continue. So vexing is the idea that Chaucer devoted his attentions to the *Legend* when he was supposed to be concentrating on the *Tales* that some critics have even argued the G Prologue might be the earlier of the two versions.[58] These contortions are motivated by the unstated and largely unexamined desire to create a neatly partitioned chronology, basically ten Brink's, which would safeguard the last dozen years of Chaucer's life as the exclusive preserve of the *Canterbury Tales*.

John Fisher restated the case for the G Prologue during 1395–97 along with Chaucer's second outside motivation—Richard II's marriage to Isabelle of France.[59] The king's rapprochement with France had proceeded throughout the last decade of his reign, and when he was suddenly a young widower in 1394, a lengthy truce was formalized by his marriage to Charles VI's seven-year-old daughter. Wallace explains how Chaucer managed the switch from one queen to the other in his *Legend*.[60] To suppress decades of the Francophobia, Richard II encouraged fraternization between the two sides, welcoming Frenchmen such as Froissart and Jean Creton into the royal household. This pro-French attitude during the 1390s clearly left Chaucer in the lurch since his entire career had been fashioned as an almost postcolonial assault upon the French tradition.[61] The king's official about-face induced a kind of literary schizophrenia that characterized the final decade of Chaucer's career, a "split poetic personality" most clearly symptomatized by what I believe to have been the simultaneous productions of the *Legend* and the *Canterbury Tales*.

In the context of a pro-French royal culture exemplified by the warm welcome granted to Froissart in 1395,[62] Chaucer undertook the writing and rewriting of his late dream vision. Paralleling the satire on relics in the *Canterbury Tales*, the dreamer's veneration of the daisy draws upon more recent French poems like Froissart's *Dit de la Marguerite*. When the narrator kneels before the daisy, the scene becomes a travesty of the genuflecting before French courtly icons made official at England's court in the 1390s.[63]

Concurrent projects have been dismissed for the reasons expressed by the latest *Riverside Chaucer*: "[T]he F Prologue was composed sometime in the period 1386 at the earliest to 1388 at the very latest, since the General Prologue to the *Tales* would surely have been mentioned, in Alceste's catalogue of the poet's writings, after that date" (p. 1060). Yet the G Prologue, almost certainly undertaken after 1394, continued to ignore the existence of the *Tales*. Lynch offers the perfect riposte to anyone objecting that the *Legend* Prologue fails to mention his late ongoing masterpiece: "Nobody has yet argued, as far as I am aware, that the absence of the *House of Fame* in the Man of Law's list implies that Chaucer had not yet written that poem."[64] Robert Payne wondered about this silence, "Why didn't Chaucer revise into it some indication, or even a mention, of the *Canterbury Tales*?"[65] The answer, I suggest, may be that the two works simply did not inhabit the same social space. What I term his literary schizophrenia meant splitting his career into the public and the private, the official and the closeted, the one designed for immediate courtly consumption and the other intended for a trusted coterie as well as a posthumous readership. That is, Chaucer imagined two prestige audiences for these two very different kinds of poetry: King Richard for the *Legend*, and literary posterity—us—for the *Canterbury Tales*.

While Chaucerians like imagining the *Legend*'s simple-looking narratives as belonging to the early 1380s, no external evidence prevents them from being late, perhaps very late, delivered separately as little command performances on the installment plan throughout the 1390s. Richard II's appreciation of classical tales may have been considerable, since he commissioned Gower's *Confessio* and even arranged to have himself eulogized as "Homer" on his tomb in

Westminster Abbey.[66] The Man of Law's extensive catalogue of the "Seintes Legende of Cupide" (*CT* II, 60–76) names eight ladies who do not appear in the final *Legend*, and Chaucer's Retraction designates this collection "The Book of the XXV Ladies" even though only nine female narratives survive. These anomalies suggest the fluidity and open-ended ambitions of a project ongoing during the 1390s, not shelved in the 1380s.

More likely the *Legend* was unfinished because the reign of Richard II was unfinished. His autocratic rule after 1397 lost him more and more adherents. This disappearance of supporters is eerily inscribed in the G revision.[67] Whereas in the earlier version the God of Love leaves the scene with a huge entourage, commending his twenty thousand virtuous ladies to the dreamer as subjects worthy for future books (F 559–64), the G Prologue omits these lines and thus deprives the God of Love of his vast retinue of loyal followers. Here the regal figure is granted no operatic exit, vanishing instead as the figment of a troubled sleep.

These omissions suggest that Chaucer, ever the shrewd observer, had foreseen the desertion of the monarch's supporters, especially in London. As a poem composed for and about Richard II's court, the *Legend* had no ready-made audience at the beginning of the new Lancastrian era. All its manuscripts are late, thought to derive from a single exemplar written about 1420.[68] The outcast status of the later G Prologue is suggested by the fact that it survives in only one copy also dated around 1420.

So who was reading the *Legend* besides Chaucer's friend Gower? Young Edward of Albemarle had become one of the rising stars of Richard's court following the purges by the Appellants in 1387–88.[69] While imprisoned during Henry IV's reign, Edward, now second duke of York, translated *Le Livre du chasse* by Gaston Phébus as his *Master of Game* with its reference to lines from the *Legend* Prologue: "ffor as Chaucer saiþ in this prologe of the xxv. good wymmen. Be wryteng haue men of ymages passed for writyng is þe keye of alle good remembraunce."[70] He names Chaucer, he cites the same title used in the Retraction, but he recollects vaguely as if by memory the original passage (G 25–26).[71] As one of the survivors of Richard's inner circle, York's specific knowledge of Chaucer's *Legend* provides our best testimony that this love vision had won attention at a court suddenly scattered and leaderless after 1399. Perhaps the 16 "missing" legends were lost as part of the general disruption of Richard II's court, and this loss was rendered permanent by Lancastrian efforts at destroying the relics of this royal culture.[72]

Now some will complain that I have been worrying far too much about dating Chaucer's dream vision poems—that is, taking far too much trouble, whether it is "Spam, eggs, sausage, and tomato" or "eggs, sausage, tomato, and Spam"—but still just plain old Spam whichever way we cut it. Michel Foucault's *What Is an Author?* explained how we invent a writer's career to support our interpretations of his works, and *Who Murdered Chaucer?* demonstrates how our poet's literary biography becomes newly invented by moving even a minor text like the *An ABC*. (This lyric's petitionary discourse apologizing for heresy, by the way, fits nicely with the later dating for the *Legend* Prologues.) Yet the stakes remain high for those of us who cherish poetry, storytelling, and even a good laugh.

More than a century ago John Livingston Lowes was focusing upon "what is vastly more important than mere dates—the course of Chaucer's artistic development"[73]—and today we wonder afresh about the poet's relations with his follow Englishmen, including his literary contemporaries as living colleagues and even lively rivals, not just inert sources. For example, traditional dating has Chaucer's God of Love from the *Legend* Prologue informing Sir John Clanvowe's God of Love in his *Boke of Cupid*.[74] But what if the direction of influence moved the other way?[75] And if the early F Prologue dates from 1392, the text has a completely different relationship with Gower's *Confessio* as the receiver of influence, not its donor, and we start reading the Man of Law's Introduction very differently, too, as a half-playful, half-serious exchange between London's two master-poets of the 1390s.[76]

And is not the best-possible understanding of the *Canterbury Tales* the Holy Grail that all Chaucerians are questing for?

Notes

1. Terry Jones, Robert Yeager, Terry Dolan, Alan Fletcher, and Juliette Dor, *Who Murdered Chaucer? A Medieval Mystery* (New York: St. Martin's Press, 2004), 337–43.
2. Derek Pearsall, *Life of Geoffrey Chaucer: A Critical Biography* (Oxford: Blackwell, 1992), 3, and Kathryn L. Lynch, "Dating Chaucer," *Chaucer Review* 42 (2007): 1–22 at 2.
3. Bernhard ten Brink, *Chaucer: Studien zur Geschichte seiner Entwicklung und zur Chronologie seiner Schriften* (Münster: Russell, 1870), became the basis for the English version *History of English Literature: Volume II: Wyclif, Chaucer, Earliest Drama, Renaissance*, trans. William Clarke Robinson (London: George Bell & Sons, 1893), 33–206.
4. Walter W. Skeat, *The Chaucer Canon* (Oxford: Clarendon, 1900), 154–55; see his *Complete Works of Geoffrey Chaucer*, 6 vols. (Oxford: Clarendon, 1894), 1:lxii-lxiii.
5. Ramona Bressie, "The Date of Thomas Usk's *Testament of Love*," *Modern Philology* 26 (1928): 17–29 at 19.
6. George Kane, "Outstanding Problems of Middle English Scholarship" (1977), rept. *Chaucer and Langland: Historical and Textual Approaches* (Berkeley: University of California Press, 1989), 228–41 at 235.
7. Kane, "Outstanding Problems," 235.
8. *The Poetical Works of Chaucer*, ed. F. N. Robinson (Boston: Houghton Mifflin, 1933), xxiv-xxv; *The Works of Geoffrey Chaucer*, ed. F. N. Robinson, 2nd ed. (Boston: Houghton Mifflin, 1957), xxviii-xxx.
9. *Poetical Works of Chaucer*, 952; John S. P. Tatlock, *The Development and Chronology of Chaucer's Works* (London: Chaucer Society, 2nd ser. 37, 1907), 22–23, 122, and 130–31. See A. J. Minnis with V. J. Scattergood and J. J. Smith, *Oxford Guides to Chaucer: The Shorter Poems* (Oxford: Clarendon, 1995), 327–28, on the persistence of this dating.
10. Marian Lossing, "The Prologue to the *Legend of Good Women* and the *Lai de Franchise*," *Studies in Philology* 39 (1942): 15–35.

11. *Works of Geoffrey Chaucer*, ed. Robinson, 839.
12. George F. Reinecke, "F. N. Robinson (1872–1967)," in *Editing Chaucer: The Great Tradition*, ed. Paul G. Ruggiers (Norman, OK: Pilgrim Books, 1984), 231–51 at 248.
13. *The Riverside Chaucer*, gen. ed. Larry D. Benson (Boston: Houghton Mifflin, 1987), xxvi–xxix.
14. Lee Patterson, *Negotiating the Past: The Historical Understanding of Medieval Literature* (Madison: University of Wisconsin Press, 1987), 3–39.
15. Larry D. Benson, "The 'Love-Tydynges' in Chaucer's *House of Fame*," in *Chaucer in the Eighties*, ed. Julian N. Wasserman and Robert J. Blanch (Syracuse, NY: Syracuse University Press, 1986), 3–22, offers a topical reading based on the speculative dating of 1379.
16. Kellie Robertson, "Laboring in the God of Love's Garden: Chaucer's Prologue to *The Legend of Good Women*," *Studies in the Age of Chaucer* 24 (2002): 115–47, explores the poem's social and political meaning if dated to the middle 1380s.
17. Eleanor Prescott Hammond, *Chaucer: A Bibliographical Manual* (New York: Macmillan, 1908), 376–77.
18. Tatlock, *Development and Chronology*, 37.
19. Minnis, *Oxford Guides to Chaucer*, 171.
20. *Complete Works*, ed. Skeat, 3:278; *Poetical Works*, ed. Robinson, 895; *Riverside Chaucer*, 365n and 988.
21. Edward Kennard Rand, "Chaucer in Error," *Speculum* 1 (1926): 222–25.
22. J. S. P. Tatlock, *The Mind and Art of Chaucer* (Syracuse, NY: Syracuse University Press, 1950), 64.
23. David Wallace, *Chaucerian Polity: Absolutist Lineages and Associational Forms in England and Italy* (Stanford, CA: Stanford University Press, 1997), 80–82.
24. *Poetical Works*, ed. Robinson, pp. 887–88. These remarks on dating are retained in the 1957 *Works*, 779.
25. John H. Fisher, *John Gower: Moral Philosopher and Friend of Chaucer* (London: Methuen, 1965), 33.
26. Helen Cooper, "Welcome to the House of Fame: 600 Years Dead: Chaucer's Deserved Reputation as 'the Father of English Poetry'," *TLS* 5091 (October 27, 2000): 3–4 at 4; see also "Chaucerian Representation," in *New Readings of Chaucer's Poetry*, ed. Robert G. Benson and Susan J. Ridyard, intro. Derek Brewer (Cambridge, UK: D. S. Brewer, 2003), 7–29.
27. *Lydgate's Troy Book*, ed. Henry Bergen, EETS, e.s. 97, 103, 106, 126, 1906–35, 279 (II, 4697).
28. Dorothy Everett, "Some Reflections on Chaucer's 'Art Poetical'" (1950), rpt. *Essays on Middle English Literature*, ed. Patricia Kean (Oxford: Clarendon, 1955), 149–74, and Laurence K. Shook, "*The House of Fame*," in *Companion to Chaucer Studies*, ed. Beryl Rowland (Oxford: Oxford University Press, 1968), 341–54.
29. Ten Brink, *History of English Literature*, 2:108.
30. Deanne Williams, "The Dream Visions," in *The Yale Companion to Chaucer*, ed. Seth Lerer (New Haven, CT: Yale University Press, 2006),147–78 at 156.
31. Pearsall, *Life of Geoffrey Chaucer*, 198–202.
32. Paul Strohm, "The Textual Vicissitudes of Usk's *Appeal*," in *Huchon's Arrow: The Social Imagination of Fourteenth-Century Texts* (Princeton, NJ: Princeton University Press, 1992), 145–60.
33. Pearsall, *Life of Geoffrey Chaucer*, 205.
34. Frank Grady, "Chaucer Reading Langland: *The House of Fame*," *Studies in the Age of Chaucer* 18 (1996): 3–23 at 4–9.

35. Wallace, "Absent City," in *Chaucerian Polity*, 156–81.
36. Pearsall, *Life of Geoffrey Chaucer*, 191.
37. Robert B. Burlin, *Chaucerian Fiction* (Princeton, NJ: Princeton University Press, 1977), 34.
38. For its dating 1386–88, see John Livingston Lowes, "The Prologue to the *Legend of Good Women* Considered in its Chronological Relations," *PMLA* 20 (1905): 749–864, and Robert W. Frank, Jr., "The Legend of the *Legend of Good Women*," *Chaucer Review* 1 (1966): 110–33.
39. Ten Brink, *Chaucer Studien*, 147–50; Skeat, ed., *Complete Works*, 3:xvi-xxi; and ten Brink, *History of English Literature*, 2: 108–16.
40. J. R. Hulbert, "Chaucer and the Earl of Oxford," *Modern Philology* 10 (1912/13): 433–37.
41. Hammond, *Bibliographical Manual*, 379–82 at 381.
42. Tatlock, *Development and Chronology*, 130.
43. Hammond, *Bibliographical Manual*, 70–71.
44. Linne R. Mooney, "Chaucer's Interest in Astronomy at the Court of Richard II," in *Chaucer in Perspective: Middle English Essays in Honour of Norman Blake*, ed. Geoffrey Lester (Sheffield: Sheffield Academic Press, 1999), 139–60.
45. Robert K. Root, "Chaucer's Legend of Medea," *PMLA* 24 (1909): 124–53.
46. Hammond, *Bibliographical Manual*, 260; see pp. 381–83 on the question of the two Prologues.
47. Strohm, "Queens as Intercessors," in *Hochon's Arrow*, 95–119 at 95.
48. Richard Maidstone, *Concordia (The Reconciliation of Richard II with London)*, ed. David R. Carlson, trans. A. G. Rigg (Kalamazoo, MI: TEAMS Medieval Institute Publications, 2003), 76–77 (lines 521–24).
49. John Norton-Smith, *Geoffrey Chaucer* (London: Routledge and Kegan Paul, 1974), 63.
50. K. B. McFarlane, *Lancastrian Kings and Lollard Knights* (Oxford: Clarendon, 1972), 139–232.
51. *Annales Ricardi Secundi et Henrici Quarti*, ed. Henry Thomas Riley (London: Rolls Series, 1866), 183.
52. V. J. Scattergood, "Literary Culture at the Court of Richard II," in *English Court Culture in the Later Middle Ages*, ed. V. J. Scattergood and J. W. Sherborne (London: Duckworth, 1983), 29–41.
53. Patricia J. Eberle, "Richard II and the Literary Arts," in *Richard II: The Art of Kingship*, ed. Anthony Goodman and James Gillespie (Oxford: Clarendon, 1999), 231–53.
54. John M. Bowers, "'Beautiful as Troilus': Richard II, Chaucer's Troilus, and Figures of (Un)Masculinity," in *Men and Masculinities in Chaucer's "Troilus and Criseyde"*, ed. Tison Pugh and Marcia Smith Marzec (Cambridge, UK: D. S. Brewer, 2008), 9–27.
55. Jones et al., "*The Canterbury Tales* as Death-Warrant," in *Who Murdered Chaucer?*, 183–227.
56. Lowes, "The Prologue to the *Legend of Good Women*," 780–81.
57. Tatlock, *Development and Chronology*, 102–20 and 122.
58. John Eadie, "The Author at Work: The Two Versions of the Prologue to the *Legend of Good Women*," *Neuphilologische Mitteilungen* 93 (1992): 135–43; see also Geoffrey Chaucer, *Dream Visions and Other Poems*, ed. Kathryn L. Lynch (New York: W. W. Norton, 2007), 118–19.
59. John H. Fisher, "The Revision of the Prologue to the *Legend of Good Women*: An Occasional Explanation," *South Atlantic Bulletin* 43 (1978): 75–84.

60. Wallace, "'If That Thou Live': Legends and Lives of Good Women," in *Chaucerian Polity,* 337–78.
61. John M. Bowers, "Chaucer after Retters: The Wartime Origins of English Literature," in *Inscribing the Hundred Years' War in French and English Cultures,* ed. Denise N. Baker (Albany, NY: State University of New York Press, 2000), 91–125, and "Chaucer after Smithfield: From Postcolonial Writer to Imperialist Author," in *The Postcolonial Middle Ages,* ed. Jeffrey Cohen (New York: St. Martin's Press, 2000), 53–66.
62. Froissart, *Chronicles,* ed. and trans., Geoffrey Brereton (London: Penguin, 1978), 408.
63. H. C. Goddard, "Chaucer's *Legend of Good Women,*" *Journal of English and Germanic Philology* 7 (1907): 87–129 and 8 (1909): 47–111.
64. Lynch, "Dating Chaucer," 6.
65. Robert O. Payne, "Making His Own Myth: The Prologue to Chaucer's *Legend of Good Women,*" *Chaucer Review* 9 (1975): 197–211 at 199.
66. Michael J. Bennett, "The Court of Richard II and the Promotion of Literature," in *Chaucer's England: Literature in Historical Context,* ed. Barbara Hanawalt (Minneapolis: University of Minnesota Press, 1992), 3–20 at 16; see also Lisa Kiser, *Telling Classical Tales: Chaucer and the "Legend of Good Women"* (Ithaca, NY: Cornell University Press, 1983).
67. Robert R. Edwards, "Ricardian Dreamwork: Chaucer, Cupid, and Loyal Lovers," in "*The Legend of Good Women*": *Context and Reception,* ed. Carolyn P. Collette (Cambridge, UK: D. S. Brewer, 2006), 59–82.
68. M. C. Seymour, *A Catalogue of Chaucer Manuscripts: Volume I, Works before "The Canterbury Tales"* (Aldershot: Scolar Press, 1995), 79–100 at 79; see 83 for Cambridge CUL Gg 4.27.
69. Nigel Saul, *Richard II* (New Haven, CT: Yale University Press, 1997), 245.
70. Edward, Second Duke of York, *The Master of Game,* ed. W. A. and F. Baillie-Grohman, intro. Theodore Roosevelt (London: Ballantyne, Hanson & Co., 1904), 3–4.
71. Julia Boffey and A. S. G. Edwards, "The *Legend of Good Women,*" in *The Cambridge Companion to Chaucer,* 2nd ed., Piero Boitani and Jill Mann (Cambridge: Cambridge University Press, 2003), 112–26 at 112–14.
72. See Jones et al., *Who Murdered Chaucer?,* 228–31 on the destruction of Richard's court culture and 329–30 on the missing installments of *LGW.*
73. Lowes, "The Prologue to the *Legend of Good Women,*" 864.
74. Lowes, "The Prologue to the *Legend of Good Women,*" 753. Dana M. Symons, *Chaucerian Dream Visions and Complaints* (Kalamazoo, MI: TEAMS Medieval Institute Publications, 2004), offers a new edition with old textual relationships, that is, Chaucer's *Legend* Prologue inspiring Clanvowe (35–36).
75. John M. Bowers, "Three Readings of *The Knight's Tale*: Sir John Clanvowe, Geoffrey Chaucer, and James I of Scotland," *Journal of Medieval and Early Modern Studies* 34 (2004): 279–307 at 279–87.
76. Aage Brusendorff, *The Chaucer Tradition* (Oxford: Clarendon Press, 1925), 142–43, concluded that the discrepancy between Man of Law's list of names and the extant *Legend* resulted from some jesting rivalry between Chaucer and Gower. See John M. Bowers, "Rival Poets: Gower's *Confessio* and Chaucer's *Legend of Good Women,*" in *John Gower, Trilingual Poet: Language, Translation, and Tradition,* ed. Elisabeth Dutton with John Hines and R. F. Yeager (Cambridge, UK: D. S. Brewer, 2010), 276–87.

CHAPTER 10

HONI SOIT QUI MAL Y PENSE: ADULTERY AND ANXIETIES ABOUT PATERNITY IN LATE MEDIEVAL ENGLAND

Michael Bennett

In May 1390, there were several notable passages of arms between English and Scottish knights in London.[1] They arose from challenges exchanged by knights during military action on the border in 1389. The duel between Lord Welles and Sir David Lindsay was well calculated to generate interest. In naming the place and the day, Welles proposed London Bridge, and Lindsay, enticed by the prospect of a victory in the English capital on an English red-letter day, proposed St. George's Day. The tournaments took some planning and were eagerly anticipated. As he approached the first anniversary of the beginning of his personal rule, Richard II was keen to present himself as a patron of chivalry.[2] According to Andrew of Wyntoun, a Scots chronicler, Richard and Queen Anne watched the duel on London Bridge from a "summer palace," presumably a temporary pavilion. During the contest Lindsay was able to appeal successfully to Richard's adjudication and, when he had Welles to the ground at his mercy, he chivalrously offered his adversary up to the service of the queen.[3] Another Scots chronicler, Walter Bower, focused his attention not on the duel itself but the celebrations afterwards. The centerpiece of his account is a humorous exchange between an English and Scots knight. Though the story has doubtless been honed in the retelling, there is little reason to doubt that it derived from the Scots who returned triumphant in 1390.[4] It still rates as a good joke. The exchange is worth relating, not least in an offering to Terry Jones, connoisseur of chivalry in the age of Chaucer, Ricardian loyalist, and comic genius.[5] It also prompts reflection on deep-seated anxieties, not least in a patrilineal society like Ricardian England: anxieties about female chastity and paternity.

According to Walter Bower, the English knights hosted a dinner for Lindsay and his companions after the tournament. Richard II himself was in attendance.

At the end of the meal, an English knight addressed Sir William Dalziel, one of the Scots, in a haughty manner. He acknowledged that there were spirited Scots but sought leave to explain the source of this noble spirit, challenging Dalziel to be bold enough to tell his compatriots in Scotland what he had learned from a truthful Englishman. The English knight then went on to say:

> It will not have escaped your recollection that not long ago your unhappy province was carved up and conquered by noble Englishmen. At that time there were perhaps among you some fair and desirable young ladies with whom some noble Englishmen of high birth and brave spirit had sexual relations and fathered young branches growing from noble roots. Such a man perhaps is this Sir David Lindsay of yours whose bravery in combat is explained by his surname Lindsay, since he takes his name and stock from our people. It is for this reason that he has conducted himself so robustly to the extent that hearing in mind his origin, his distinction should by rights be ascribed to his English blood.

After the Englishmen in the group had laughed heartily, Sir William Dalziel called for silence and said:

> This worthy knight has put together, with sufficient oratorical skill, words which are amiable and polished for eager ears. I say this to him by way of riposte, not denying that a large part of our land was lately carved up and occupied by the contrivance of the English, but thanks be to God it was not held by them for long. Also I acknowledge that then as now some fair and desirable women and young ladies have dwelt among us, and I also do not deny that gentlemen and magnates from England did then father on them some high-spirited and proud sons. But what are we to make of this? It is certain that while the English lords were staying in our kingdom, their various wives whom they had left at home, being delicate, cosseted, brought up for a life of leisure and having time on their hands for pleasure, being deprived for too long of marital sexual relations and not having the strength to contain themselves any more but desiring new sexual partners, invited into the closest intimacy cooks and churls, serfs and villeins, and sometimes friars and confessors. From these unions there emerged (unless I am mistaken) men neither suited to warfare nor efficient at fighting battles. We rejoice therefore that we have arisen from your stock and that we are born as gentlemen, while you from your stock have turned out degenerate.

Drawn by the hubbub, Richard heard the last part of the speech. He then asked the two knights to repeat their speeches before the entire company. According to Bower, he sharply rebuked the English knight and congratulated and rewarded Dalziel for his response. The records reveal that Richard did indeed grant handsome rewards to both Lindsay and Dalziel.[6]

Sir William Dalziel was a Lanarkshire knight. He saw action at the battle of Otterburn in 1388 and reputedly served as standard bearer to the King of Scots.[7] In January 1390, he obtained a safe conduct to come to England to make arrangements on behalf of John Dunbar, Earl of Moray, who had challenged Thomas Mowbray, the Earl of Nottingham.[8] Dalziel's prominent role in the feats of arms in May is documented in both the English and Scottish sources. Though only a child in the 1390s, Bower may well have heard many stories about him. He presents him as a larger-than-life figure, notable for both his prowess and wit. After reporting his words at the meal, Bower cannot resist relating another incident concerning Dalziel "in London at another time," presumably when he came on the preparatory mission earlier in the year.[9] The episode itself is positively Pythonesque. Dalziel first spotted Sir Piers Courtenay, brother of the Archbishop of Canterbury and one of England's leading jousters, in the streets of London. He was sporting a new surcoat with a falcon embroidered on the sleeve with the words: "I beer a falcon fairest of flicht: qwha so pinchez hir his deth is dicht." Dalziel rose to the challenge and had a surcoat made for himself displaying a magpie pecking at a pea, with the words: "I beer a py pikkand at a pese; qwha so pikkis at hir I pik at his nose in faith." The provocation led to a meeting in the lists in front of a large audience, including Richard II. In one encounter, Dalziel knocked out Courtenay's teeth, prompting him to appeal to the king that the fight was no longer fair. Dalziel protested his readiness to continue the fight in exactly the same physical condition, provided that Courtenay was prepared to reciprocate the arrangement and wager £200 on the outcome. After the English knight accepted the challenge, Dalziel revealed that he had only one eye, having lost the other at the battle of Otterburn. Needless to say, Courtenay again called foul. After a heated argument, the king awarded the prize to the Scots knight as having won "in both deeds and words."[10]

Humor does not always cross cultural boundaries. Robert Darnton has written about the challenges and opportunities in understanding what the past found humorous. "When you realize," he observes in relation to the "great cat massacre" in eighteenth-century Paris, "that you are not getting something—a joke, a proverb, a ceremony that is particularly meaningful to the natives,—you can see where to grasp a foreign system of meaning in order to unravel it." His approach is to conduct a close ethnographic reading of his text, and his argument is that in killing the cats, the apprentices were cleverly deploying the symbolic resources of their culture to avenge themselves on their master. He goes on to declare that by "getting the joke" of the game in which Parisian apprentices slaughtered the cats of their masters, "it may be possible to 'get' a basic ingredient of artisanal culture under the Old Regime."[11] Needless to say, not everyone has been persuaded by his methodology or his specific interpretation of the episode.[12] Darnton may not have escaped the danger of reading too much into adolescent high jinks. As the mother in the *Life of Brian* might have told him, they were just very naughty boys. Still, Darnton's approach seems the only way of proceeding when confronted with episodes from the past that seem alien and opaque. There are several episodes of this sort in *Scotichronicon,* including one in which a canon of Scone organized a mock procession to prompt Robert III to compensate the villagers for the destruction of their crops by the crowd attending his coronation, that has formed the focus for an illuminating study of popular culture and Robert's kingship.[13] Bower's account of Dalziel's encounter with Courtenay might likewise support closer analysis of the symbolism of the falcon's pinch and the magpie's peck and the smashed teeth and gouged eye. In terms of the reported exchange after Lindsay's triumph in the lists, however, the comic elements are all too apparent. The English knight's backhanded compliment to Lindsay's prowess needs little explication. The humor of Dalziel's repartee is all too clear. For the historian, the problem is not in "getting" Dalziel's joke. The problem is more in understanding how he got away with it. In theory, a royal and noble audience should not have found it humorous. The patrilineage and the honor of its women, it might be assumed, were deadly serious matters in medieval Europe. Increasing stress on the bloodline, from the twelfth century onward, made the royal family and the aristocracy vulnerable, in honor and self-regard if not in law, to allegations of bastardy.

Fantasies about the wives of kings and lords taking lovers were by no means confined to the locker room. Adultery by royal women looms large in the courtly literature of the Middle Ages. King Arthur's wife, Guinevere, had her Sir Lancelot, and Mark's wife, Iseult, had her Tristan. A number of scholars, historical and literary, have sought to explore the seemingly paradoxical relationship between the conventions of courtly love and the increasing emphasis in feudal society on the male bloodline, and shown how stories about royal and aristocratic women taking knightly lovers may have functioned in the French-speaking world in the twelfth and thirteenth centuries.[14] Focusing on French romances of the late twelfth and thirteenth centuries, Peggy McCracken has further explored "how romances about adulterous queens" fit into "the cultural construction of queenship in medieval France."[15] She stresses the fictionality of the representations, as exemplified in the barrenness of the adulterous queens, and how they reveal anxieties about women and power. In seeking to explain "the disappearance of the courtly adulterous queen as the subject of romance," she suggests an association with the major scandal at the French court in 1314.[16] The ageing Philip IV became aware of a scandal involving his three daughters-in-law, the wives of the future Louis X, Philip V, and Charles IV. It was established that two of them, the wives of Louis and Charles, had conducted adulterous affairs with two Burgundian knights. The knights were tortured, castrated and hung, drawn and quartered, and the ladies were humiliated and imprisoned for life. The scandal challenged the fictional status of the adulterous queen. Thenceforward, McCracken argues, the representation of a queen "whose transgressive sexuality contributes to the political stability of her husband's court is no longer a viable way to imagine a relationship between women and power."[17]

The French royal scandal had far-reaching consequences on both sides of the English Channel. Louis X was able to marry a second time after the suspiciously convenient death of his disgraced wife. He died in 1316, leaving his second wife pregnant. The child turned out to be male, but King John the Posthumous only lived five days. Doubts regarding the legitimacy of Jeanne, Louis's daughter by his first marriage, informed the political context of the edict in 1317 that declared that the succession to the French crown should pass through and to males.[18] The reigns of Philip V and Charles IV proved as short and unproductive in terms of a surviving male heir as that of their elder brother. In its disruption of the marriages of the three princes, adultery, real or alleged, can be seen as playing a significant role in the succession crisis of 1328 and setting the scene for the Plantagenet claim to the French crown and the Hundred Years' War.

As the grandson of Philip IV, Edward III of England was closer in blood to the last Capetians than Philip of Valois, who succeeded as Philip VI in 1328. Edward's mother, Isabella of France, was in Paris when the scandal that engulfed her sisters-in-law broke. There was some suspicion that she was instrumental in revealing the scandal.[19] Insofar as she sought to uphold the honor of the French royal house, her own role in precipitating a crisis in England is deeply ironic. Her marriage to Edward II had begun auspiciously enough, but her husband's indulgence of favorites and misrule led to her alienation and, ultimately, to her making common cause with his enemies. Her defection in France in 1325 and her alliance with Roger Mortimer were body blows to Edward's regime and reputation. In 1326, Edward responded in kind, coming close to accusing her of adultery.[20] Isabella and Mortimer invaded England and launched a rebellion that led to her husband's defeat, deposition, and death. The 14-year-old Edward III became king in 1327, with Mortimer the power behind the throne. The young king and a group of noblemen brought this shabby episode to an end in Nottingham Castle in 1330 when they dragged Mortimer from his mother's chamber. He was condemned as a traitor and hanged. Isabella was banished to one of her country seats.

The coincidence of the two royal scandals has attracted some attention from historians. After all, Queen Isabella played some part in both episodes. It was Charles Wood, though, who highlighted, and sought to explain the strikingly different outcomes to the two episodes in France and England.[21] There seems to have been a general backlash against women at the French royal court. More specifically, the scandal has been associated with an edict barring women from the royal succession. The edict certainly sidestepped the issue of the paternity of Joan, putative daughter of Louis X. In England, Isabella's adultery was not the major issue in the crisis of 1326–27. It was Edward II who was deposed, not his adulterous queen. Far from feeding speculation about the paternity of Edward of Windsor, the crisis was resolved satisfactorily by Edward II's abdication in favor of his son. In seeking to explain this divergence, Wood points to differences between the two kingdoms in relation to public law. The legitimacy of both monarchies depended on both heredity and recognition, but the balance in France was tilted far more to the bloodline than in England. Though kings and kingdoms are not private persons and property, it is worth noting how allegations of bastardy were dealt with in the law courts. As Wood explains, paternal recognition was all-important in English common law. If a father acknowledged a son conceived during his absence, for example, the son could not be denied his inheritance. Edward II always recognized Edward of Windsor as his son, the key point at common law. Still, it is not clear that attempts to disinherit children by disputing their paternity were dealt with any differently in French courts. It was presumably Louis X's acknowledgment of Joan as his daughter that made the edict of 1317 the more necessary. While the two episodes do illustrate differences in public law, it may be that the ways in which they unfolded owed most to the specifics of the situation. Early accounts of the French adultery scandal of 1314 place some emphasis on the impetuous and suspicious nature of the ageing Philip IV. At the same time, the edict of 1317 that barred women from succession to the French throne cannot be presented merely as a response to the scandal. A move of this sort had been foreshadowed in Philip IV's time, evidently prompted by the fact that his eldest son had died, leaving brothers but no sons.[22] The major problem in England in 1326–27 was not the queen's adultery, but Edward II himself.

According to McCracken, the scandal in France in 1314 brought to an end a cultural tradition in which adulterous queens could be innocently imagined. In this case, the adultery of Isabella of France should have been the final nail in the coffin. Still, it does not appear that attitudes and tastes changed quite so precipitately. There were broader social and cultural trends in the late thirteenth and early fourteenth centuries that would already have made the stories of Guinevere and Iseult appear old-fashioned in tone and style. The romance narrative was giving ground among courtly writers and audiences to more lyrical forms of expression. Conversely, the old-style romances continued to be read for pleasure, even in royal and aristocratic circles, well into the fourteenth century. It is striking that the scandal seems not to have greatly altered either the behavior or the tastes of Isabella of France. In the early years in England, she shared an interest in French romance with her husband, and in 1326 she found her life imitating art, as she played Guinevere to Mortimer's Sir Lancelot. After her disgrace and rustication in 1330, Isabella continued to enjoy reading French romances, many of which passed on her death in 1358 to her son Edward III and her daughter Joan, Queen of Scotland. Earlier in the year she lent her copies of the *Holy Grail* and *Sir Lancelot* to King Jean of France, who was in England as a prisoner of war. Given Isabella's past, her ownership of *Sir Lancelot*—and her lending it to the French king—is particularly notable.[23] More generally, the storylines of the Arthurian romances, like the storylines of the Bible, classical literature, and history, continued to be widely known in fourteenth-century England. They provided a rich store of allusion and nourished the imagination. Among noblemen and knights, and perhaps among ladies, the old fantasies of adulterous love remained potent.

Edward III did not let the scandals of his parents cramp his own style. In staging his coup in 1330, he acknowledged the dishonor that his mother had brought the realm. The focus on Mortimer's special culpability likewise enabled him to set the scene for some rehabilitation of the reputation of his father.[24] Needless to say, Edward took some care that his own queen did not stray. Philippa of Hainault bore him 12 children, 11 of them between 1330 and 1348. She often accompanied him on campaign: indeed two of her sons, Lionel of Antwerp and John of Gaunt [Ghent], were born in the Low Countries. Still, Philippa and her ladies were active participants in the courtly festivities of the 1340s and 1350s that combined chivalry and love play. The tournaments presided over by the king and queen at Windsor and elsewhere brought young lords and ladies together in a range of courtly entertainments. The monastic chroniclers were horrified by the debauchery associated with tournaments held in a number of cities and towns in 1348.[25] According to the Monk of Meaux, the princes and magnates summoned to them ladies who were then paired with and lustfully used by men other than their husbands.[26] Henry Knighton, canon of Leicester, wrote about the appearance at the lists of troops of damsels, 40 or 50 strong, "all very eye-catching and beautiful," dressed in men's clothes and showing their figures, letting slip the ties of marital chastity.[27] The king himself was not without personal reproach. There is a circumstantial and disturbing story of how, around 1342, his desire for the beautiful wife of a nobleman led ultimately to his raping her.[28] Jean le Bel, the French chronicler who provides the most detailed account, is obviously mistaken in identifying the lady as the Countess of Salisbury and in other points of detail. Given the story's circulation of France, it is hard to escape the conclusion that it had its origin in French propaganda against Edward III.[29] Jean Froissart, who used le Bel as a major source, disputed its veracity on the grounds of what he knew about the king and what he had learned in England. It is nonetheless quite striking if, as he himself says, he "asked people about it who must have known if it ever happened."[30] Even if the story, in its specificity, is preposterous, its rehearsal by le Bel, who was generally well inclined to England, is evidence that he had made himself vulnerable to allegations of lasciviousness.[31] It has been well argued by Francis Ingledew that the adoption of the garter as a badge and the motto *Honi soit qui mal y pense* (Shame upon him who thinks evil upon it) was "a statement of royal defiance" with respect to canards of this sort.[32]

Edward had some success in channeling the energies and urges of the English aristocracy. His splendid court provided a framework for chivalric competition and courtly emulation. The Order of the Garter became the apex of the community of honor. Still, there was always a frisson of danger. Marital prowess and sexual desire could prove highly destructive and disruptive. The fine line that the king sought to maintain is no more evident than in the life and loves of Joan of Kent, his young cousin.[33] The ward of the Earl of Salisbury, the king's close friend, Joan married Sir William Montagu, the future second earl, around 1341. In 1347, however, Sir Thomas Holland came forward to claim that Joan was his wife and announce his intention to petition the pope for the annulment of her second marriage. Holland's story was that after a clandestine marriage around 1340, he had gone overseas. On his return, he learned that her guardian had forced her into the marriage with his son, and though he protested he could not get a hearing. Rather surprisingly, he took service as steward of Salisbury's household. The celebrity and a modest fortune he won through his prowess at Crécy enabled him to contemplate a costly and possibly destructive suit. After the papal curia at Avignon accepted his claim in 1349, he was able to take Joan as his wife.[34] As Ian Mortimer has observed, it is remarkable that while the case was under adjudication, Holland and Montagu came together at Windsor in April 1349 in the inaugural tournament of the Order of the Garter.[35] All in all, there has to be some suspicion that Holland's story was a legal fiction. The likelihood is that Joan's marriage to Salisbury had failed, and, whether as a cause or consequence of this failure, she formed a liaison with her husband's steward.[36] The story of the premarriage might well have been designed to save the honor of the principal parties, masking either Salisbury's inadequacy or Joan's forwardness. *Honi soit qui mal y pense.*

Sexual misconduct and marital irregularities in royal and aristocratic circles continued to have political consequences in the 1360s and 1370s. After Queen

Philippa's death in 1365, Edward III increasingly found solace with Alice Perrers, who came as close as any woman in medieval English royal history to the formal status of king's mistress. Her influence over the king and the flow of royal patronage was a matter of considerable political concern in the last decade of the reign. The revelation in 1376 that she had secretly married Sir William Windsor massively compounded the problem. It made the king's relationship explicitly adulterous and had the potential to produce suppositious royal bastards. Even the issue of the royal succession was somewhat confused by marital uncertainties. It seems likely that Edward, Prince of Wales, had been enamored of his alluring cousin, Joan of Kent, for some time. He secretly married her in spring 1361, indecently soon after Sir Thomas Holland's death in Rouen in the last days of 1360. According to a chronicle seemingly written in Rouen, Joan boldly flirted with the prince when he pressed the suit of one of his knights.[37] When the marriage came to light, the king was furious. The Archbishop of Canterbury declared it invalid on the grounds of affinity. The prince and Joan were not only cousins but also the prince was godfather of her oldest son. By summer, the king gave in to his son's resolve to have Joan as his wife and petitioned the pope for a dispensation. After reprimanding the couple and imposing heavy penance, the pope released them from excommunication and issued a dispensation that made possible a wedding in October.[38] In 1362, the prince and princess set out for Aquitaine, where sons were born in 1365 and 1367. In spite of the papal judgments and dispensations, the marital adventures of Joan of Kent continued to give hostages to fortune. In 1370, the pope reputedly used the threat of declaring the children of the marriage illegitimate to put pressure on the Black Prince not to execute the bishop of Limoges.[39] In the meantime, Lionel of Antwerp, the king's second son, had died in 1368, leaving only a daughter, Philippa, by his first marriage. Though it is not documented until the 1460s, when it was used to impugn the Yorkist title to the crown, the claim that Lionel's wife had an affair with Sir James Audley, the steward of her household, and that Philippa was not Lionel's daughter, may have its origins in earlier times. According to the story, Edward ordered the summary execution of the knight and subsequently required Philippa to renounce her place in the royal succession.[40] Though the canard may have been a later invention, there are elements that may reflect machinations and indeed events of the 1370s. After all, Philippa's husband was Edmund Mortimer, Earl of March and grandson of the "great traitor." His leadership of the attack on the court in the Good Parliament in 1376 indicates that his relations with senior members of the royal family were under some strain.[41]

The succession to Edward III proved less clear-cut, legally as well as practically, than could have been imagined at the height of his reign. The Black Prince had taken care to take Joan with him when he went out to Aquitaine in 1362. Two sons were born there: Edward of Angoulême in 1365, who died in 1372, and Richard of Bordeaux in 1367. After the Black Prince's return to England, broken in health, there were grounds for concern as to what would happen if, as seemed likely, he died before Richard reached adulthood and indeed if Richard himself did not survive childhood. From the death of Lionel, Duke of Clarence, in 1368, John of Gaunt, Edward III's third son, must have been seen as a serious prospect for the succession. Rumors regarding Gaunt's designs on the crown began surprisingly early. Some time between 1372 and 1376, the King of Navarre informed the Count of Flanders that Gaunt was planning to have the prince's children declared illegitimate and succeed his father on the throne.[42] Though the report presumably originated in misinformation designed to discredit Gaunt, it was taken seriously in some quarters. According to Thomas Walsingham, Gaunt made moves in parliament in 1376 to bar women from the royal succession.[43] Though there is no record of a challenge to the legitimacy of Philippa, there would have been interest in Lancastrian circles in rumors about her mother. The main focus of concern, of course, was that Gaunt was positioning himself to set aside Richard and claim the throne. Until recently, Walsingham's statements about plans to alter the succession were dismissed as evidence of the depth of his prejudice against Gaunt.[44] The revelation that Edward put his seal to a draft of an entail of the crown, probably in October, shows that such a scheme was actually in train.[45] It included a family compact involving the king, his sons, and Joan of Kent, on behalf of her son. Philippa may well have been called on to accept the terms of the entail and, in effect, to renounce her title.

The crisis and agitation served at least to confirm Richard's status as heir to the throne. The proceedings, however, do reveal some slight defensiveness. It was the parliament, exasperated by corruption at court and deeply suspicious of Gaunt, that petitioned the ailing Edward to acknowledge his grandson as his heir. Archbishop Sudbury of Canterbury presented Richard to parliament and, on the king's behalf, declared that though the Prince of Wales has been called to God, nonetheless he remained, as it were, with them "because he had left behind him such a noble and fine son, who is his exact image and true likeness."[46] Even the entail of the crown, drawn up in autumn 1376 but subsequently set aside, was as much designed to support Richard's position as heir as to consolidate Gaunt's reversionary interest. After all, it bound Richard's uncles to support his accession. Throughout the turmoil of 1376–77 the concern was that Richard was vulnerable, and not simply on account of his tender age. The impression that his legitimacy was in question can be supported, ironically perhaps, by the manner in which the loyalists attacked Gaunt. They did not stick to attributing to him treasonous intentions but alleged that he himself was not his father's son. Interestingly, there were no allegations of adultery on Queen Philippa's part. Rather it was claimed that she had accidentally overlain her child and, fearful of the consequences, had found a substitute. The canard probably began in Flanders, but it was claimed that the Queen had confessed the substitution to Bishop Wykeham to be revealed if Gaunt ever came close to the succession. In 1377, there was a violent demonstration against Gaunt in London in which his coat-of-arms was displayed reversed as a traitor and bills were distributed denying his paternity. The claim that he was the son of a butcher of Ghent was "great noise and clamor" throughout the realm.[47]

There was a strong popular element in securing Richard's accession. In the early years of his reign, his relative youth and innocence proved as much an asset as a liability. The coronation consecrated his status as the true heir to the throne. It is possible, however, that doubts about his legitimacy lingered. The reputation of Joan of Kent proved a problem.[48] Froissart described her as "in her time the most beautiful in all the kingdom of England—and the most amorous."[49] The behavior of the rebels toward her in 1381, though it is hard to interpret, suggests that this was a popular assessment as well. Though they tell slightly different stories, Froissart and Walsingham report that some rebels behaved overly familiarly with her, including sitting on her bed and demanding a kiss.[50] While Joan played an important role as peacemaker in the factionalized politics of the early 1380s, she was less politically involved after Richard's marriage. In the months before her death in August 1385, she faced two scandals involving Sir John Holland, Richard's half-brother, that refocused attention on her checkered past. First of all, Holland seduced Elizabeth, the wife of the Earl of Pembroke and the daughter of John of Gaunt. Since Elizabeth's marriage had not been consummated, an annulment was sought, allowing Holland to marry his lover.[51] A second and more serious incident in May 1385 reputedly brought Joan to an early grave. In a senseless affray at York, where Richard was assembling an army to invade Scotland, Holland slew the eldest son of the Earl of Stafford and fled to sanctuary. The king was furious at his half-brother, who was indicted for the homicide. Joan died believing that her pleas for mercy had been in vain. In any event, Holland secured a pardon at the urging of his father-in-law. In the summer of 1386, when Holland set out with Gaunt on a military expedition to Castile, he wisely took Elizabeth with him.

Richard grew to manhood without a close sense of family. Born in Bordeaux in 1367, he came to England for the first time in 1372. By this stage his father was broken in health, and he had lost his elder brother, Edward of Angoulême. Richard can have had few happy memories of his father. In 1376, the nine-year-old prince witnessed his father's final illness and heard his will and the curses laid on him if he failed to perform its terms.[52] Richard paid for his father's tomb at Canterbury, but made no special effort to honor his memory. In contrast, he was attached to the memory of his great-grandfather Edward II, whose canonization he actively promoted from the mid-1380s to the mid-1390s, and was devoted to the cult of St. Edward the Confessor, whose personal and family circumstances were so close to his own and whom he clearly revered as his spiritual father.[53] His relationship with his mother seems not to have been close. Shortly before her death in 1385, she resolved to be buried not with Richard's father at Canterbury but with Sir Thomas Holland at Stamford. Richard attended her funeral but seemingly not her interment. By comparison with his grief at the loss of Queen Anne and some of his friends, and the honoring in death of many members of his circle, his neglect of his mother is striking.[54] In a remarkable gesture, Richard had the remains of his elder brother brought back from Bordeaux for reburial at Langley. Shortly after his visit to Stamford in June 1392, he authorized expenditure to secure the ironwork around Edward's tomb.[55]

At the end of 1386, Richard was threatened with deposition by Thomas of Woodstock, his youngest uncle, and a powerful coalition of magnates.[56] Insofar as they seriously considered such a move, it is probable that they would have proceeded, for want of better grounds, by denying his legitimacy. Even after Richard took the reins of power in May 1389, he seems not to have been able to still the murmurs. In July, he ordered the arrest of certain people in the Forest of Dean who had "blasphemed" the king's person.[57] Around this time, too, a Londoner allegedly declared that Richard "was unfit to govern and should stay in his latrine."[58] In all likelihood such seditious utterances involved allegations of bastardy. Since he had been publicly acknowledged as his father's son, his legitimacy was most easily impugned by reference to the possible irregularity of his parents' marriage. In 1394, Richard took steps to secure the papal bulls and other legal instruments relating to it. On November 25, the abbot and convent of Westminster issued the king a receipt for a coffer containing this sensitive material. The transaction was witnessed by three of Richard's most trusted counselors. The fact that it was Thomas Arundel, Archbishop of York and Chancellor, who delivered the coffer to the monks might indicate that the documents had previously been in Chancery and indeed in the hands of Richard's opponents in 1386–88.[59] Richard would have felt safer with them in Westminster Abbey. In the meantime he sought to rebuild the edifice of monarchy, honoring and binding to him princes and nobles of royal descent, and associating his kingship with his saintly forebear, St. Edward the Confessor.[60]

The overthrow of Richard II in 1399 was associated with aspersions regarding his paternity. Froissart reports that around 1398, Londoners were becoming disaffected with his rule and expressing doubts that he was really the son of the Prince of Wales.[61] The author of *Traison et Mort* (Treason and death) states that when he was brought to London a prisoner in August 1399, a boy in the crowd called out, to general approval, "down with the bastard!" Adam of Usk, another close observer of events, likewise reports the clamor against the king and that "unsavory things" were said about his birth, "namely that he was not born of a father of the royal line, but of a mother given to slippery ways—to say nothing of many other things I have heard."[62] According to Froissart, Henry of Bolingbroke attempted to browbeat Richard in the Tower of London by reference to such stories. In addition to condemning Richard's failings as king, he allegedly referred to their grandfather's opposition to the marriage of the Prince of Wales to Joan of Kent and to the widespread rumor that Richard, like his older brother, was the son not of the prince but of a clerk or canon.[63] Though circulating at the time of Richard's deposition, the canards were not new in 1399 and cannot be assumed to be Lancastrian propaganda. It is telling that Froissart, who knew and was broadly sympathetic to Richard, did not present them as novel or opportunistically confected. The only chronicler in England who attests the circulation of such stories in 1399 is Adam of Usk, who was no friend of the house of Lancaster.

To return to Sir William Dalziel's joke and to its reception. It was a rhetorical tour de force. It would have been hard not to acknowledge Dalziel's spirit, delivery, and wit. In the representation of women—whether as the spoils of war in Scotland, or as libidinous wives in England—here was certainly a crass locker-room humor. The joke, though, needs to be set in the context of a wider discourse on adultery that is evident in the romances that were enjoyed, it would appear, by both sexes. The scholarly theorizing about the relationship of courtly love to feudal society may still be broadly applicable in the later Middle Ages. For knights and courtiers seeking to make their way in the world, noble ladies were both patrons and prizes. Such relationships were not wholly fanciful. Royal and aristocratic women in England enjoyed a surprising measure of personal freedom. Bold knights succeeded sufficiently often with heiresses and widows, and sometimes with married women, to make their love service seem worth the pain. The heroes in this world were men like Sir Thomas Holland who won the hand of the "Fair Maid of Kent," and Sir John Holland who seduced John of Gaunt's daughter. Still, it is hard to see how kings and noblemen could have countenanced the romance of adultery with any degree of equanimity. The discourse of wifely infidelity perhaps helped in some ways to support the existing social and moral order. It was part of the ideological armory of patriarchy. It justified moves to control women, daughters, wives, and even mothers. The law turned on its head the adage that it is a wise child who knows its father. Legitimacy was a matter of paternal recognition. The notion that wives might be untrue served at both an individual and general level to paper over the cracks of patrilineage. A father might disinherit an unworthy son. Society might explain to itself its own degeneracy. The point was often made by preachers and moralists. John Audley, a chaplain and author of a great deal of rather bleak religious verse, saw adultery as central to the decay of the times: "Now a lady will take a page / For no love but for fleshly lust / And all her blood disparage" and "Lords and lordships they waste away / That make false heirs."[64] In claiming that the poor showing of English knights in the late fourteenth century was attributable to the corruption of the bloodline, Dalziel was saying no more than many contemporary English moralists.

Sir William Dalziel was bold indeed to say what he did in England and in the company of Richard II. The king must surely have been sensitive to jokes about sons whose failure to match the martial prowess of their fathers raised questions about their real paternity and their mothers' chastity. In 1390, he was seeking to renew his kingship and enhance the prestige of the monarchy by stressing the sacredness of his office and presenting himself, perhaps more symbolically than genealogically, in the long line of English kings. It is worth noting two of his concerns in the months before and after the tournaments. In March, Richard sent to Westminster Abbey a pair of red velvet shoes, set with pearls, to replace the shoes that he had worn at his coronation as part of the regalia, one of which had slipped from his foot and been lost as he was carried out of the church after the ceremony. This restoration was no whim. He arranged for their manufacture shortly after declaring his majority in May 1389. They had then been sent to Rome where they had been blessed by Urban VI prior to his death in October.[65] In June, Richard went to Gloucester, the burial place of Edward II, to discuss the evidence of miracles at his tomb, the compilation of a book of miracles to send to Rome to support the case for his canonization, and the possible translation of his remains, presumably to Westminster Abbey.[66]

Richard was not discouraged by the successes of the Scottish knights. He set about calling a grand tournament to be held at Smithfield in October.[67] It was scheduled for the three days before the feast of St. Edward the Confessor, when Richard and his chapel joined the monks in the liturgy and processions.

Richard himself may have entered the lists at Smithfield.[68] Presumably less was left to chance in October than six months earlier. It is well known that Geoffrey Chaucer was involved in organizing the Smithfield tournament.[69] In his capacity as clerk of the king's works from 1389, he presumably had some involvement in and gained some experience from the passages of arms in May, including perhaps the erection of the "summer palace" from which the royal couple watched the duel on London Bridge. Though some Scots returned to London in October, they were not able to repeat their earlier triumphs. Nonetheless they brought home to Scotland in 1390 reports that established Richard's reputation there as a chivalric and magnanimous king.[70] If Richard had been offended by Dalziel's speech, he had had the good sense and restraint not to show it. The occasion demanded that he lead the company in laughter, and that is what he seemingly did. As Terry Jones has shown, Richard could do "stern" like the best of kings.[71] Richard was certainly sharp with the pompous English knight, who through his lack of courtesy had created a situation that could well have got out of his hand. Nonetheless he had nothing but praise for Dalziel and rewarded him very generously. Interestingly, in discussions of Richard's personality, it has been little considered whether he had a sense of humor. Bower's story suggests that he did.

Notes

1. The passages of arms are reported in a number of English and Scottish chronicles, notably *The Westminster Chronicle 1381–1394*, ed. L. C. Hector and Barbara F. Harvey (Oxford: Clarendon Press, 1982), 432–37; F. J. Amours, ed., *The Original Chronicle of Andrew of Wyntoun*. 6 vols. (Edinburgh: The Scottish Text Society, 1903–14), 6: 359–62, lines 1125–1226; D. E. R. Watt, ed., *Scotichronicon by Walter Bower in Latin and English*. 9 vols. (Aberdeen, Scotland: Aberdeen University Press, 1987–1998), 8:14–19. There is documentary corroboration of Richard II's grants of safe conducts and rewards to the Scottish knights: D. Macpherson, ed., *Rotuli Scotiæ in turri Londinensi et in domo capitulari Westmonasteriensi asservati*. 2 vols. (London: Record Commission, 1814–19), 2:103–4; Frederick Devon, ed., *Issues of the Exchequer, Henry III-Henry VI* (London: Record Commission, 1847), 239. London, The National Archives (hereafter TNA), E 403/151, m. 6.
2. Michael J. Bennett, *Richard II and the Revolution of 1399* (Stroud, Glos: Sutton, 1999), 42; Christopher D. Fletcher, *Richard II: Manhood, Youth, and Politics, 1377–99* (Oxford: Oxford University Press, 2008), 200. In general see James L. Gillespie, "Richard II: Chivalry and Kingship," in *The Age of Richard II*, ed. James L. Gillespie (Stroud, Glos: Sutton, 1997), 115–38.
3. Amours, *Chronicle of Andrew of Wyntoun*, 360–62, lines 1155–1211.
4. Watt, *Scotichronicon by Walter Bower*, 8:14–19.
5. Terry Jones, *Chaucer's Knight: The Portrait of a Medieval Mercenary* (London: Methuen, 1985); Terry Jones, et al., *Who Murdered Chaucer? A Medieval Mystery* (London: Methuen, 2003); Terry Jones, "Was Richard II a Tyrant? Richard's Use of the Books of Rules for Princes," in *Fourteenth Century England*, V, ed. Nigel Saul (Woodbridge, Suff.: The Boydell Press, 2008), 130–60.
6. Richard's grant of £100 and a silver and gilt ewer to Lindsay and £40 to Dalizel, along with gifts to other Scottish knights and squires, were recorded on the exchequer issue roll on May 25, 1390: TNA, E 403/151, m. 6.

7. John Almon, *The Peerage of Scotland: A Genealogical and Historical Account of All the Peers of That Ancient Kingdom* (London, 1767), 293.
8. Macpherson, *Rotuli Scotiæ*, 2:103.
9. Watt, *Scotichronicon by Walter Bower*, 8:156. An English source records a duel between Sir Piers Courtenay and an unnamed Scottish knight, "who was not wanting in vigour or mettle," on May 28: *Westminster Chronicle*, 436–37. Since Courtenay won the laurels in this duel, it seems not to be the encounter described in *Scotichronicon*. The story likewise only makes sense on the assumption that Courtenay did not know that Dalziel lacked an eye, making it more likely that the incident took place during Dalziel's first visit.
10. Watt, *Scotichronicon by Walter Bower*, 8:156.
11. Robert Darnton, *The Great Cat Massacre and Other Episodes in French Cultural History* (New York: Basic Books, 1984), 75–104, 78.
12. Harold Mah, "Suppressing the Text: The Metaphysics of Ethnographic History in Darnton's Great Cat Massacre," *History Workshop Journal* 31 (1991): 1–20.
13. John J. McGavin, "Robert III's 'Rough Music': Charivari and Diplomacy in a Medieval Scottish Court," *The Scottish Historical Review* 75 (1995): 144–58.
14. Herbert Moller, "The Social Causation of the Courtly Love Complex," *Comparative Studies in Society and History*, 1 (1958–9): 137–63; Georges Duby, "Dans la France du Nord-Ouest, au XIIe siècle: Les jeunes dans la société aristocratique," *Annales. Economies—Sociétés—Civilisations*, 19 (1964): 835–46; R. Howard Bloch, *Medieval French Literature and Law* (Berkeley: University of California Press, 1977); R. Howard Bloch, *Etymologies and Genealogies: A Literary Anthropology of the French Middle Ages* (Chicago: University of Chicago Press, 1983).
15. Peggy McCracken, *The Romance of Adultery: Queenship and Sexual Transgression in Old French Literature* (Philadelphia: University of Pennsylvania Press, 1998), 20.
16. McCracken, *The Romance of Adultery,* 173.
17. McCracken, *The Romance of Adultery,* 173.
18. Andrew W. Lewis, *Royal Succession in Capetian France: Studies on Familial Order and the State* (Cambridge, MA: Harvard University Press, 1981), 149–51.
19. The claim that she engineered their disgrace has been challenged by Elizabeth A. Brown in "Diplomacy, Adultery and Domestic Politics at the Court of Philip the Fair: Queen Isabelle's Mission to France in 1314," in *Documenting the Past. Essays in Medieval History presented to George Peddy Cuttino*, ed. Jeffrey S. Hamilton and P. J. Bradley (Woodbridge, Suff.: Boydell & Brewer, 1989), 53–83.
20. Ian Mortimer suggests that the romance between Isabella and Mortimer began as early as 1323: Ian Mortimer, *The Greatest Traitor: The Life of Sir Roger Mortimer, 1st Earl of March, Ruler of England, 1327–1330* (London: Jonathan Cape, 2003), 129, 145–57. For a cooler assessment of their relationship as late as 1326, see Seymour Philips, *Edward II* (New Haven, CT: Yale University Press, 2010), 488–91.
21. Charles T. Wood, *Joan of Arc and Richard III: Sex, Saints, and Government in the Middle Ages* (Oxford: Oxford University Press, 1988), 12–14.
22. Lewis, *Royal Succession in Capetian France*, 152.
23. London, British Library, Cotton MS. Galba E. XIV, f. 50 r; Michael Bennett, "Isabelle of France, Anglo-French Diplomacy and Cultural Exchange in the late 1350s," in *The Age of Edward III*, ed. James S. Bothwell (Woodbridge, Suff.: Boydell & Brewer for York Medieval Press, 2001), 219 (215–25).
24. W. Mark Ormrod, "The Sexualities of Edward II" in *The Reign of Edward II: New Perspectives*, ed. Gwilym Dodd and Anthony Musson (Woodbridge, Suff.: Boydell & Brewer for York Medieval Press, 2008), 40–46 (22–47).

25. Ian Mortimer, *The Perfect King: The Life of Edward III, Father of the English Nation* (London: Jonathan Cape, 2006), 267.
26. Bond, Edward A., ed., *Chronica Monasterii de Melsa*. 3 vols. (London: Rolls Series, 1868), 3:72.
27. Knighton, Henry, *Knighton's Chronicle 1337–1396,* ed. G. H. Martin (Oxford: Clarendon Press, 1995), 92–95.
28. Antonia Gransden, "The Alleged Rape by Edward III of the Countess of Salisbury," *The English Historical Review* 87 (1972): 333–44.
29. Gransden,"Alleged Rape by Edward III," 340–41.
30. Gransden,"Alleged Rape by Edward III," 334.
31. Mortimer, *The Perfect King*, 191–98.
32. Francis Ingledew, *Sir Gawain and the Green Knight and the Order of the Garter* (Notre Dame, IN: University of Notre Dame Press, 2006), esp. 112–19.
33. Margaret Galway, "Joan of Kent and the Order of the Garter," *University of Birmingham Historical Journal*, 1 (1947–48): 13–50.
34. K. P. Wentersdorf, "The Clandestine Marriages of the Fair Maid of Kent," *Journal of Medieval History* 5 (1979): 203–31.
35. Mortimer, *The Perfect King*, 267–68.
36. Chris Given-Wilson and Alice Curteis, *The Royal Bastards of Medieval England* (London: Routledge, 1984), 15–16. The standard biographical account accepts the story of the earlier marriage between Joan and Holland: Richard Barber, "Joan, suo jure Countess of Kent, and Princess of Wales and of Aquitaine [*called* the Fair Maid of Kent] (*c*.1328–1385)," *Oxford Dictionary of National Biography* (Oxford: Oxford University Press, 2004).
37. Siméon Luce, ed., *Chronique des Quatres Premiers Valois (1327–1393)* (Paris: Renouard, 1862), 123–34.
38. Wentersdorf, "Clandestine Marriages of the Fair Maid of Kent," 217–19.
39. Jean de Cros, Bishop of Limoges, had encouraged the revolt by claiming that the Prince of Wales was dead and that he had attended his funeral at Angoulême. Since he was godfather to the prince's eldest son, Edward of Angoulême, his rebellion was seen as an especially egregious act of betrayal. Jean Froissart, *Chroniques*, ed. Kervyn de Lettenhove, 26 vols. (Osnabrück: Biblio Verlag, 1967), 8: 424.
40. Sir John Fortescue, *The Governance of England*, ed. Christopher Plummer (Oxford: Clarendon, 1885), 354.
41. Michael Bennett, "Edward III's Entail and the Succession to the Crown, 1376–1471," *The English Historical Review* 113 (1998): 586–94.
42. The letter refers to the children of the Prince of Wales, although Richard was the sole surviving child of the marriage. Froissart, *Oeuvres*, ed. Kervyn de Lettenhove, 8: 460–62.
43. E. M. Thompson, ed., *Chronicon Angliae* (London: Rolls Series, 1874), 92–93. *The St. Albans Chronicle: The Chronica Maiora of Thomas Walsingham, Volume 1: 1376–1394,* ed. John Taylor, Wendy Childs and L. Watkiss (Oxford: Clarendon Press, 2003), 38–41.
44. V. H. Galbraith, ed., *The Anonimalle Chronicle, 1333–1381* (Manchester: Manchester University Press, 1927), xli.
45. Bennett, "Edward III's Entail and the Succession to the Crown," 590–94.
46. Myers, A.R., ed., *English Historical Documents, Vol. IV. 1327–1485* (London: Eyre and Spottiswoode, 1969), 122.
47. Galbraith, *Chronicon Angliae*, 121–26; *The St. Albans Chronicle*, I, 60–61; Anthony Goodman, *John of Gaunt. The Exercise of Princely Power in Fourteenth-Century Europe* (London: Longman, 1992), 61.

48. Joanna Chamberlayne, "Joan of Kent's Tale: Adultery and Rape in the Age of Chivalry," *Medieval Life* 5 (1996): 7–9.
49. Froissart, *Oeuvres*, ed. Kervyn de Lettenhove, 2:243.
50. W. Mark Ormrod, "In Bed with Joan of Kent: The King's Mother and the Peasants' Revolt," in *Medieval Women: Texts and Contexts in Late Medieval Britain. Essays for Felicity Riddy*, ed. Jocelyn Wogan-Browne, Rosalynn Voaden, Arlyn Diamond, Ann Hutchinson, Carol M. Meale, and Lesley Johnson (Turnhout: Brepols, 2000), 277–92.
51. Knighton, *Knighton's Chronicle*, 342–43. The Latin does not make it clear whether the divorce was made on account of Holland's desire for her, or her desire for Holland. In his translation, G. H. Martin renders it as Holland's "desire for her."
52. *A Collection of All the Wills, now known to be Extant, of the Kings and Queens of England, Princes and Princes of Wales, and Every Branch of the Blood Royal*, ed. J. Nichols (London, 1780), 75. *The St. Albans Chronicle*, I, 32–35.
53. Mark Ormrod, "Richard II's Sense of English History," in *The Reign of Richard II*, ed. Gwilym Dodd (Stroud, Gloss.: Sutton, 2000), 97–110; Nigel Saul, *Richard II* (New Haven, CT: Yale University Press, 1997), 311–14.
54. He does not seem to have spent a great deal on her funeral or commemoration. The tenth anniversary of her death, in August 1395, though, prompted him to equip 24 paupers as mourners with black cloth and wax torches at a cost of over £20: TNA, E 403/551, m. 16.
55. The payment was made some time before July 17, 1392: TNA, E 403/539, m. 13.
56. For a discussion of this episode, see Saul, *Richard II*, 189–90.
57. Frederick Devon, ed. *Issues of the Exchequer, Henry III-Henry VI*, (London: Record Commission, 1847), 239.
58. Caroline M. Barron, "The Quarrel of Richard II with London," in *The Reign of Richard II. Essays in Honor of May McKisack*, ed. Caroline M. Barron and F. R. H. Du Boulay (London: Athlone, 1971), 179–80.
59. London, Westminster Abbey, Muniments, no. 9584 .
60. Bennett, *Richard II and the Revolution of 1399*, ch. 3.
61. Froissart, *Oeuvres*, ed. Kervyn de Lettenhove, 16:159–60.
62. *The Chronicle of Adam Usk 1377–1421*, ed. Chris Given-Wilson (Oxford: Clarendon Press, 1997), 62–63.
63. Froissart, *Oeuvres*, ed. Kervyn de Lettenhove, 16:199–201.
64. *The Poems of John Audelay*, ed. Ella Keats Whiting (EETS, o.s 184, 1931 for 1930), 4.
65. *Westminster Chronicle*, 414–17.
66. *Westminster Chronicle*, 436–39.
67. Bennett, *Richard II and the Revolution of 1399*, 42; Juliet R. V. Barker, *The Tournament in England 1100–1400* (Woodbridge, Suff.: Boydell & Brewer, 1986), esp. 100, 108–09; Sheila Lindenbaum, "The Smithfield Tournament of 1390," *Journal of Medieval and Renaissance Studies*, 20 (1990): 1–20.
68. According to one chronicle, Richard won the honors on the first day: *Westminster Chronicle*, 436–39. Froissart does not mention his active participation, which was probably merely ceremonial: Saul, *Richard II*, 453.
69. Derek Pearsall, *The Life of Geoffrey Chaucer. A Critical Biography* (Oxford: Blackwell, 1992), 210–12.
70. During May 1390 Richard II spent over £300 in gifts to Scottish knights and squires participating in the passages of arms: TNA, E 403/151, m. 6. Andrew of Wyntoun refers to Richard as then reigning "in his flowris": *Original Chronicle*

of Andrew of Wyntoun, 6:362, line 1216. Anthony Goodman, "Anglo-Scottish Relations in the Later Fourteenth Century: Alienation or Acculturation" in *England and Scotland in the Fourteenth Century: New Perspectives*, ed. Andy King and Michael A. Penman (Woodbridge, Suff.: Boydell & Brewer, 2007), 236–53.

71. Jones, "Was Richard II a Tyrant?," 147–51.

CHAPTER 11

NEEDY KNIGHTS AND WEALTHY WIDOWS: THE ENCOUNTERS OF JOHN CORNEWALL AND LETTICE KIRRIEL, 1378–1382[1]

W. Mark Ormrod

The publication of Terry Jones's study of *Chaucer's Knight: The Portrait of a Medieval Mercenary* marked an important moment in the study of later medieval knighthood. Jones's representation of the Knight as a "medieval mercenary" sent something of a shockwave through the academy and produced significant reassessments of the motives, values, and social mores of the knightly class in the era of the Hundred Years' War. Not everyone concurred with Jones's interpretation of the *Canterbury Tales*, and some scholars firmly dissociate themselves from any notion that knights were motivated solely by material gain.[2] Yet Jones's study may be seen to have bred a new understanding that the profession of arms was, for some men in the fourteenth century, not merely a matter of vocation but also emphatically a career. Much more attention has recently been given to the landless younger sons of English gentry families who did long-term service to the English crown—and, after 1360, to the Great Companies—in the long series of campaigns and military occupations in France, Iberia, and Italy. The ability of such men to establish themselves as members of the landholding and office-holding aristocracy back home in England depended to a large degree on their ability to seek out the patronage of the Crown and nobility, to invest their fortunes of war into land, and not infrequently to indulge in the kinds of violent, direct action that earned them an abiding reputation as ruthless lawbreakers.[3]

One of the more controversial elements of these strategies of self-advancement was the habit of abducting and marrying heiresses and widows whose wealth might be appropriated to support needy knights. The fourteenth century is full of real and fictional accounts of the crime of *raptus* (abduction or ravishment), in which defenseless women were taken from their homes and forced into the exchange of marriage vows by unscrupulous men-on-the-make.[4] Under certain circumstances, *raptus* could be as emotive an issue as the associated, but formally distinct, crime of rape: Christopher Cannon has argued that the famous charge of *raptus* brought against Geoffrey Chaucer for the abduction of Cecily Chaumpaigne of London may have included specific allegations of sexual violence.[5] Given the absence of a recognized judicial action against attempted *raptus*, however, the only formal recourse against those who tried but failed to abduct women of property lay in the range of actions covering forced entry and damage to property. Not surprisingly, therefore, modern commentators have often been struck by the way that the law of *raptus* seemed more concerned to protect the landed interests of the victim's male relatives than to uphold her own rights to control her body and to make free choice in marriage. The position was especially tense in the case of young, unmarried women: the Statute of Rapes of 1382 was devised specifically in order to reinforce patriarchal authority and prevent young heiresses from eloping with unsuitable secret lovers.[6] But in the case of widows, too, the situation was hardly less fraught: because male relatives could not take legal actions on behalf of independent widowed women, the latter were forced to enter the very male, public world of the law courts in pursuit of their claims against threatening suitors.

One case from many offers a powerful representation of the way in which landless career soldiers preyed on women of property. Here is the petition of Alice Kirriel alleging a series of violent encounters with the old soldier Sir John Cornewall early in the reign of Richard II:

> To the noble lords of Parliament, Lettice who was the wife of John Kirriel, knight, requests that, whereas she was at her castle of Westenhanger in the county of Kent on the Sunday after the feast of the Purification of Our Lady in the first year of the reign of the king who now is [February 8, 1378], there came John Cornewall, knight, in a friar's habit; and he deprived Lettice's servants of their clothes and dressed his own servants in them; and he came to the castle with forty armed men; and he broke the doors of the hall and the chambers of the castle, and he held Lettice in torment for four hours until the country was raised, for fear of which he went away. And he has several times made assault against Lettice, and comes and goes from time to time such that she dare not leave the castle without a multitude of people and holds vigil inside the castle as in times of war. And now at the feast of Sts Simon and Jude last [October 28, 1381], John Cornewall came to the castle by night, with sixty armed men with ladders of war; and they scaled the castle, broke the doors and windows, and chased Lettice into some water where she stayed, out of fear, for four hours until she was close to death. And the said John Cornewall, understanding that Lettice was dead, took her horses and other goods and chattels, to the value of a thousand marks, and went away; of which offenses John is indicted. May it please you, as a work of charity, to ask our lord the king that writs be sent to all the sheriffs of England to arrest [John] and put him in prison and, for those counties from which passage abroad may be made, to forbid him from leaving the country to Lettice's detriment; and that no protection or charter of pardon be granted to John in relation to the suits that Lettice has begun, or will begin against him, for the horrible misdeeds above named.[7]

Many aspects of this highly dramatized text cry out for attention. Sir John's ruse of dressing up as a friar is a direct playing out of the convention, satirized by Chaucer, in which members of the mendicant orders abused their role as confessors and spiritual advisors to indulge in illicit intimacies with ladies of fashion.[8] Equally, the knight's deployment of the arts and equipment of the siege is an ironic reminder that Westenhanger Castle stood very much in a war zone, the southeast corner of Kent, which was regularly subject to French raids during the later 1370s; Lettice's ability to withstand Cornewall's repeated attacks reflects her capacity to mobilize local retainers and tenants for the defense of a strategically important position on the very frontier of England.[9] We might also reflect that Sir John's final attack on Westenhanger occurred just a few months after a great eruption of popular violence across many parts of Kent in the summer of 1381, and note that his violent actions against the widow Kirriel thus represented a particularly gross betrayal of their social order's desire for stability in the aftermath of the Peasants' Revolt.[10]

On the other hand, we must not be too easily beguiled by Lettice's construction of womanly victimhood. Petitions, like all legal documents, were subject to the constraints and conventions of form, and the rhetorical devices employed were part of an established technique to draw the sympathy of those—in this case, the lords of Parliament—to whom they were directed.[11] As a widowed woman with independent rights at law, Lettice Kirriel had plenty of opportunities to sue Sir John Cornewall: indeed, she made clear in her petition that legal proceedings were already under way. Her nervousness was not brought on by any ignorance of the formalities of the law, then, but rather by the understanding that the male establishment sometimes conspired with the abductor to present the independent woman as a willing party to her own ravishment. Two particularly high-profile cases from earlier in the fourteenth century—those of Elizabeth de Burgh and Alice de Lacy—had revealed that the Crown was quite prepared to pardon acts of abduction committed by knights of the royal household against even some of the highest-born ladies of the land.[12] As we investigate further the careers of John Cornewall and Lettice Kirriel, we find that the balance of power between them had rather less to do with gender and much more with the connections and influence that the parties were able to bring to bear from above. Indeed, what starts as a story of the violent affray between the knight and the lady ends up as something of a parable on the transformative impact of royal patronage upon late medieval gentry society.

First, then, to the defendant: who precisely was Sir John Cornewall? He may be plausibly identified as one of the numerous descendants of the illegitimate offspring of Richard Plantagenet, brother of King Henry III, and specifically as the third son of Sir Geoffrey Cornewall (d. 1335), baron of Burford.[13] This Sir John Cornewall was born in the early 1320s. Together with his middle brother, Geoffrey, John was taken into service in the household of Edward III and rose to the rank of esquire of the chamber, accompanying the king on his first expedition against the French in 1338–40.[14] By 1357, John had been knighted and retained by the Black Prince and was serving with the latter in Gascony following the great victory at Poitiers.[15] Later family tradition had it that Sir John married an unnamed niece of John de Montfort, the pro-English Duke of Brittany; their son, also John (on whom much more anon), was probably born in the 1360s. The connection is significant, for Sir John may have been one of those English military professionals who, in the aftermath of the Anglo-French peace of 1360, sought to continue their careers in the ongoing civil war in Brittany.[16] After the reopening of Edward III's hostilities with France in 1369, Cornewall emerged as captain of the Anglo-Breton garrison at Auray and served under John de Montfort in the Earl of Buckingham's naval expedition to Brest over the winter of 1377–78.[17] In spite of his exalted connections, however, John remained very much an impoverished younger son clinging to gentility: significantly, there is no evidence that he invested any of the profits of his military career into building up a landed estate of his own in England.[18] A ready backstory therefore emerges to John's first attack on Lettice Kirriel in February 1378. With his Breton wife dead and their young son growing to maturity, the ageing John's thoughts turned increasingly to economic imperatives. Upon his return from the Breton campaign in January 1378, Cornewall gathered together an impromptu force of recently demobilized soldiers and local thugs, and began to focus his social and financial aspirations on the abduction of a suitably distinguished and well-endowed English gentle widow.[19]

Lettice Kirriel fitted the specification perfectly. While we know nothing of her natal family, a great deal can be reconstructed about Lettice's notably eventful career as wife and matriarch. By 1378, Lettice was a widow twice over. Her first husband was John Bricklesworth (or Brixworth), son of a London merchant and alderman, who on several occasions had represented the city in parliament.[20] John rose through service in the civic courts to become the common sergeant (public prosecutor) of the city by 1365 and sheriff of London in 1365–66.[21] The Bricklesworths had at least four children; since the eldest, also Lettice, was already professed as a nun Stratford atte Bowe by 1368, our Lettice may be assumed to have been born in the 1330s and to have married her first husband around 1350. John Bricklesworth died in 1368, leaving as his heir the eldest of three sons, Richard, then aged ten, who was put into wardship by the city authorities. John made ample provision for his widow's dower.[22] Like many London women, Lettice was well versed in business and law, and was to use the experience gained in her first marriage to good effect in her later engagements in the courts. But although London custom gave widows strong rights, Lettice seems to have found it difficult to recover a number of the properties that her deceased husband had earlier leased to Henry Picard (d. 1361), the prominent vintner and one-time mayor of London. It was probably the arduous litigation with Picard's heirs, then, that prompted Lettice, like other city widows of her generation, quickly to seek the support of a new husband. By July 1371 at the latest, Lettice had remarried, taking as her new husband Sir John Kirriel.[23]

Kirriel was a man of very different background from Bricklesworth. He was the descendant of a distinguished gentry family originating in Leicestershire but settled since the thirteenth century in Kent, with their main residence first at Walmer and later at Westenhanger. The Kirriels had become prominent figures in the Cinque Ports, and John's father, Sir Nicholas (d. 1327), served briefly as admiral of the western fleet to Edward II.[24] John, born in 1307, rapidly emerged as a great stalwart of Edward III's wars. In 1335, he sold his Leicestershire manor of Croxton Kerrial for the considerable sum of 1,000 marks to John, Lord Seagrave, the new husband of the king's cousin, Margaret of Brotherton.[25] But John's good connections with the court were principally determined by his service to one of Edward III's closest friends, William Clinton, Earl of Huntingdon, and the latter's wife, the great Kentish heiress Juliana de Leybourne. It was fitting testimony to the heightened social aspirations of the family that in 1343–45 John Kirriel secured license to crennelate his residence at Westenhanger and founded a chantry in the local parish church for the good estate of the king and the Earl of Huntingdon. John served on two of the great military set pieces of the period, the Crécy-Calais campaign of 1346–47 and the Reims campaign of 1359–60.[26] And although he was over 60 when the French war resumed in 1369, he showed little sign at first of letting up. An extant dossier of his expenses tells in vivid detail Kirriel's various efforts to recruit men-at-arms and archers for successive planned (and aborted) expeditions over the period 1369–71 and his many comings and goings between Westenhanger, Sandwich, and Dover upon the urgent business of defending the coasts.[27] It was only after he broke his leg in August 1371 that Sir John finally withdrew from active service abroad, and even then he remained actively engaged in the administration of the home front.[28]

It was in the midst of these travails that John had taken the widow Bricklesworth to wife. John had also been married before, and had two adult sons, John and Nicholas. It was not unusual in this period for members of the landed gentry and even the baronage to marry into the mercantile elites of London, and John was clearly mindful of the advantages he might gain from assisting Lettice in the management of her property in the capital.[29] As things turned out, though, it was Lettice who ended up as the main beneficiary of this new match. A series of misfortunes befell the Kirriels in the course of the late 1370s with the deaths, in quick succession, of three key family members: Sir John's eldest son (before 1377), Sir John himself (in January 1377), and his second son and successor in the family estate, Sir Nicholas (in December 1379).[30] The latter's heir, William, was only a few months old at Nicholas's demise and was taken into royal custody. The Kirriels' fortunes now rested largely on the resourcefulness of two dowagers: Lettice, widow of the older John, and Elizabeth (d. 1419), relict of Nicholas and mother of the infant William. Both had done well in their dower arrangements, with Lettice securing a life interest in Westenhanger, and Elizabeth enjoying possession of one of the Kirriels' other principal manors at Stockbury.[31] The dates serve further to emphasize the ruthless opportunism shown by John Cornewall in his attacks on Westenhanger from 1378 to 1381. The fact that the knight made his first advances almost exactly a year after the death of Sir John Kirriel compounds the point: Cornewall struck at the very moment when the widow emerged from her year of mourning and was thus, by social convention, available once more as a prospective bride. And although John's immediate expectation of a forced marriage could only extend as far as a life interest in Lettice's dower, who was to say what the apparent imminent extinction of the Kirriel dynasty might also do for the longer-term fortunes of the Cornewalls?[32]

All of this was to reckon without the resourcefulness of Lady Kirriel. Since the death of her second husband, Lettice had once more been active in her own right in the courts, vigorously defending her dower rights in London.[33] The lady of Westenhanger may have been left "close to death" by the trauma of Cornewall's attack, but her experience of hiding for four hours in the castle moat made her all the more determined for action at law. Over the winter of 1381–82, Lettice secured an indictment of Sir John and ten named followers for his most recent attack on Westenhanger, claiming £40 for the loss of 12 horses and other unspecified damages. Using the legal know-how of her attorneys, Lettice tried to jump the queue for justice by having the indictment referred for trial not before the justices of the peace or the court of king's bench but by a special commission of oyer and terminer purchased from the royal Chancery for the sum of £1 in February 1382. This tribunal was to be headed by no less a person than the Chief Justice of Common Pleas, Sir Robert Belknap, himself a prominent and well-connected figure in Kent.[34] Nor was Lettice as yet content. Taking advantage of the summoning of a new parliament to meet at Westminster on May 7, 1382, she submitted the petition quoted at the beginning of this study with the express intent of preventing John Cornewall from wriggling free and escaping abroad. Lettice was especially concerned that John might obtain license for further nefarious deeds by suing a retrospective pardon from the crown in recognition of his military record. Such trading of justice was a regular element of gentry life in the period: John Cornewall's eldest brother, Richard, had himself secured a pardon of homicide in 1340 on the grounds of service in Scotland and France.[35] Insecurities over John's ability to manipulate his connections may also explain why Lettice also notably upped the stakes in her petition, now claiming damages of 1,000 marks (£667) for John's recent attack on Westenhanger—a figure that represented the annual income of a well-endowed baron and would clearly have driven the already impoverished Cornewall into rapid ruin.

It is typical of the kind of process that Lettice Kirriel attempted in the spring of 1382 that we do not have a precise record of what happened next. But the imperfect trail strongly suggests that it took some time to bring the case to conclusion. Contrary to common practice, Lettice Kirriel's petition to the lords in parliament was not annotated for further actions to be taken in the chancery or the law courts. It is possible that it was rejected, for the kinds of intervention that Lettice sought could easily be read as presuming John's guilt and thus seeking unduly to influence the processes of the common law. Chief Justice Belknap was also a very busy man, not least in dealing with the judicial aftermath of the Peasants' Revolt, and there is no reason to think that he necessarily put the Kirriel case at the top of his agenda. The most likely hypothesis, however, is that John Cornewall did exactly as Lettice had feared and successfully evaded arrest. His protector was Sir Thomas Trevet, a well-connected career soldier who had served alongside Cornewall in the Brittany campaign of 1377–78 and led an important military expedition to Gascony in 1378–79. In April 1383, when the final arrangements were being put in place for the Bishop of Norwich's infamous crusade against Flanders, Trevet seems to have secured for Cornewall the expectation of a full retrospective pardon. The deal took some time to work its way out, not least because Trevet was charged with an act of treason during the Flemish campaign and was temporarily disgraced.[36] By January 1385, however, Thomas was restored to royal favor and was at last in a position to secure the delayed pardon for Sir John Cornewall. Tellingly, the resulting royal letters patent declared John released of liability for "all manner of felonies, *abductions of women*, and trespasses" committed before 1383.[37] Seven years after his first attack on Westenhanger Castle, and four years since his last attempted abduction of Lady Kirriel, John Cornewall had finally extricated himself from his liability to Lettice.

The various stages through which the Cornewall-Kirriel dispute passed help us to understand the fine balance of power between the two principal parties. The explicit reference to *raptus* in John's pardon provides strong grounds for interpreting his violent attacks on Westenhanger as attempted acts of abduction, and thus gives special force to the rhetorical conventions that the defenseless widow deployed in the petition with which we began. Yet Lettice's expectations of justice, and her knowledge of and confidence in the rights that the legal system bestowed on single women, make it inappropriate to read the controversy solely in terms of gender. Status was also at least as important. In spite of his distinguished lineage, John Cornewall knew full well that his lack of landed property rendered him in certain respects less powerful than the wealthy widow of Westenhanger. And in spite of the official condoning of the knight's harassment, Lettice clearly remained firmly in possession of her estate, which on her death some time later was duly divided and passed on, without interruption, to her son Richard Bricklesworth and her step-grandson William Kirriel.[38] Indeed, a functionalist reading of the case might suggest that Sir John was only allowed his pardon of 1385 on the strict understanding that he would sin no more against ladies of his kind.

Most strikingly, the outcome of the case depended to a significant degree on issues of lordship and grace. John Cornewall had put his trust in the fact that, since the deaths of the Earl and Countess of Huntingdon in 1354 and 1367, the Kirriels had been without noble patrons. Cornewall was also at first quite vulnerable in this respect, particularly since his chief patron, the Duke of Brittany, was increasingly inclined to distance himself from the Plantagenet court after the death of Edward III.[39] Both parties therefore put their principal trust in the English Crown, Lettice by mobilizing the king's public commitment to the protection of the defenseless and John by exploiting his connections in the military elite. It is this double dependence on the royal pleasure that may also explain why it took so long to resolve the dispute. The deaths of the Black Prince and Edward III and the succession of the boy-king Richard II meant that, for much of the late 1370s, the personal will of the monarch was in abeyance. It is significant that when Lettice sought a decisive intervention in 1382, she used a new mechanism developed over the previous half-decade to address the absence of royal will and directed her petition not directly to the king but to the lords in Parliament.[40] It was only with the emergence of Richard II into the full exercise of his kingship during the early 1380s that Cornewall was finally able to call in the royal favor that left him free of any further culpability to the attempted abduction of Lady Kirriel.

It was royal grace that also very much determined the long-term fortunes of the Kirriel and Cornewall clans. William Kirriel and his descendants remained firmly in control of their Kentish estates for the next hundred years and more. But they never again achieved the kind of distinction that had attached to their ancestors Sir Nicholas and Sir John. William's son, Sir Thomas, married a Devon heiress, Cecily (d. 1472), widow of John Hill, but the family became embroiled in disputes over her property.[41] In 1483, by way of fulfillment of the very arrangement that John Cornewall had so keenly sought a century earlier, Elizabeth Kirriel, widow of Sir Thomas's son, John, married Sir Ralph Ashton, a prominent Yorkist who served the regime of Richard III as Knight of the King's Body and Vice-Constable of England. Like Lettice before her, this Elizabeth had been given a life interest in her first husband's castle and manor of Westenhanger. Ashton, with a determination that would have been the envy of Sir John Cornewall, entered into litigation with Elizabeth's son John Kirriel to ensure effective possession of the property, which he subsequently turned into his principal place of residence. After Ashton's death, Elizabeth moved still further up the social hierarchy by taking as her third husband John Bourchier, a younger son of the Earl of Essex.[42] All of this, however, was at the direct expense of the Kirriel family itself. It is strongly indicative of their declining fortunes that Sir Thomas's grandson John was content with the modest rank of gentleman.[43] Significantly, then, the decline of the Kirriels owed itself in no small part to the very situation that had first attracted the attention of John Cornwall in the late 1370s: the phenomenon whereby generous provision for widows tended to strip the main estate of significant assets and render it at risk of permanent depletion through the ruses of wily suitors.[44]

How much happier the fate of those gentry families that caught and kept the attention of the crown! Though the precise date remains unknown, Sir John Cornewall must have died shortly after his pardon of 1385. By that stage his son John, now in his early twenties, was already embarked on an active military career, serving on the Scottish campaign of 1385 and subsequent expeditions to France.[45] In the 1390s, John the younger emerged as a strong supporter of Richard II with a generous annuity of 190 marks. It was this favored status that also allowed John to succeed where his father had only aspired: to woo and marry a wealthy widow, Philippa Cergeaux, and take over custody of her late husband's estates in Cornwall. John was a skilled political trimmer, and his close links with John of Gaunt helped him to ingratiate himself with the new regime of Henry IV after 1399. The convenient death of his first wife allowed him to play for even higher stakes on the marriage market, and in or shortly after 1400 he married the new king's sister, Elizabeth of Lancaster, dowager Countess of Huntingdon. Once more, the rights that had eluded the father fell, in truly spectacular fashion, to the son, for John was given a life interest in Elizabeth's royal annuity of 1,000 marks, and the couple won rights of dower in the forfeited estates of the disgraced Earl of Huntingdon. On Elizabeth's death in 1425, John rapidly invested the money he had made from their business deal and the profits of French ransoms by purchasing Ampthill in Bedfordshire, where he built a great castle. The apogee of his career came in 1432, when he was raised to the peerage in his own right as Lord Fanhope. John's only son, yet another John, was killed at the siege of Meaux in 1421 while still a teenager, and the rising dynasty fell extinct. A story attributed to Jean Juvenal des Ursins has it that John senior was so horrified at the extinction of his line that he immediately declared the war unjust and vowed never to fight again except on crusade.[46] Had the son lived, we can only guess at the later fortunes—and no doubt the perils—of a family that shared its blood with the house of Lancaster.

Public attitudes to violence in late medieval England were very different from those that prevail in modern liberal-democratic societies. Physical force was condoned and even celebrated when it was used as a form of social control. It was also frequently justified as a form of rough justice. Its extent could often be exaggerated as a means to an end, for the law of trespass did not admit disputes unless the plaintiff could prove that an unwarranted entry had been committed *vi et armis* (with force and arms).[47] Perhaps most strikingly, knightly society readily imagined amorous adventures as acts of war: the medieval allegory of the *Assault on the Castle of Love* was replete with images of lustful knights breaching the defenses of demure ladies.[48] None of this is to deny the very real fear that Sir John Cornewall's successive hostile attacks excited in the heart of the resourceful Lettice Kirriel. In the hands of a skilled communicator such as Terry Jones, the siege of Westenhanger Castle would lend itself readily to reflections on the grim brutality of medieval life. And in pursuing the more complex motives and deeper meanings behind such knights' tales, we can all learn a good deal more about the social practices and cultural values of gentry society in Chaucer's England.

Notes

1. I am grateful to my colleagues Jeremy Goldberg and Craig Taylor for advice, references, and critical readings, and to former colleagues Shelagh Sneddon and Jocelyn Wogan-Browne for expert assistance with editing and translating.
2. Terry Jones, *Chaucer's Knight: The Portrait of a Medieval Mercenary*, further rev. ed. (London: Methuen, 1994), vii-xxii, summarizes responses to the first (1980) edition.
3. See, *inter alia*, Philip Morgan, *War and Society in Medieval Cheshire, 1277–1403*, Chetham Society, 3rd series, (Manchester: Chetham Society, 1987), 34; Kenneth Fowler, *Medieval Mercenaries, I: The Great Companies* (Oxford: Blackwell, 2001); Adrian R. Bell, "The Fourteenth-Century Soldier: More Chaucer's Knight or Medieval Career," in *Mercenaries and Paid Men: The Mercenary Identity in the Middle Ages*, ed. John France (Leiden: Brill, 2008), 301–16.
4. The large literature on *raptus* is recently summarized conveniently by Jeremy Goldberg, *Communal Discord, Child Abduction, and Rape in the Later Middle Ages* (Basingstoke: Palgrave, 2008), 159–75.
5. Christopher Cannon, "Raptus in the Chaumpaigne Release and a Newly Discovered Document Concerning the Life of Geoffrey Chaucer," *Speculum* 68 (1993): 74–94. For other treatments of the case, see Henry Ansgar Kelly, "Statutes

of Rapes and Alleged Ravishers of Wives: A Context for the Charges against Thomas Malory, Knight," *Viator* 28 (1997): 361–419; Carolyn Dinshaw, "Rivalry, Rape, and Manhood: Gower and Chaucer," in *Violence Against Women in Medieval Texts*, ed. Anna Roberts (Gainesville: University Press of Florida, 1998), 137–60; Suzanne Edwards, "The Rhetoric of Rape and the Politics of Gender in the *Wife of Bath's Tale* and the 1382 Statute of Rapes," *Exemplaria* 23 (2011): 3–26.

6. John B. Post, "Sir Thomas West and the Statute of Rapes, 1382," *Bulletin of the Institute of Historical Research* 53 (1980): 24–30.
7. Kew, The National Archives (hereafter TNA), SC 8/55/2713: *A nobles seignurs de parlement supplie Letice, qi fuit la femme Johan de Keryell chivaler, qe come ele estoit en soun chastel de Ostrynghangre, en le counté de Kent, le dismaynge prochein apres la fest del Purificacioun de Nostre Dame, l'ane du regne nostre seignur le roy q'ore est primere, la vient Johan de Cornwaille chivaler en abit de freres et entra le dit chastel; et despoila les servauntz la dite Letice de lour draps et en*[t] *vesti sez servauntz de mesme; et amena en le dit chastel xl hommes armés; et debrusa les eous de la sale et de les chambres du dit chastel; et tient la dit Letice en torment par quatre houres, tanke le pais se leva, et pur doute de eux, il s'en ala. Et plusours foitz il ad fait assaut a dite Letice; et iese en agait de temps en temps, issint q'ele n'osa quatre anz passez isser de son dit chastel saunz multitude de gentz, mes deynz le dit chastel tenu veille come en terre de gurre. Et ore a le fest de seintz Simond et Joud darryn passé, le dit Johan Cornwaille vient a dit chastel nuttandre, ou sessante homes armés ou diz escales de gurre; et escala le dit chastel, debrossa les eous et les fenestres de dit chastel, et chasa la dite Letice en un ewe; et illoeques, pur pouer, ele demeura pur quatre heurs, tanke ele feust bien près morte. Et le dit Johan Cornwaille, entendant la dite Letice esté morte, prist ovesque luy les chivals del dite Letice et autres biens et chateux, a la value de mille livres, et s'en ala: des quex choses le dit Johan est endité. Qe vous plese, en oevre de charité, de prier nostre tres redouté seignur le roy d'envoier brefs a touz viscountes D'Engleterre de luy prendre et metre en prison, et luy defender passage, par les ditz bres, en touz les counteez ou passage sount, al costages le dite Letice; et qe nule protectioun ne charter de pardon soit granté a dit Johan Cornwaille en les suytz qe la dite Letice ad commence, ou est a commencer, devers luy pur les oribles malfauz souditz.*
8. Arnold Williams, "Chaucer and the Friars," *Speculum* 28 (1953): 499–513.
9. Eleanor Searle and Robert Burghart, "The Defense of England and the Peasants' Revolt," *Viator* 3 (1972): 365–88.
10. Anthony Tuck, "Nobles, Commons and the Great Revolt of 1381," in *The English Rising of 1381*, ed. R. H. Hilton and T. H. Aston (Cambridge, UK: Past and Present Society, 1984), 194–212. For attacks on women in the Peasants' Revolt, see Sylvia Federico, "The Imaginary Society: Women in 1381," *Journal of British Studies* 40 (2001): 159–83.
11. Gwilym Dodd, *Justice and Grace: Private Petitioning and the English Parliament in the Late Middle Ages* (Oxford: Oxford University Press, 2007), 302–16.
12. J. Enoch Powell and Keith Wallis, *The House of Lords in the Middle Ages* (London: Weidenfeld & Nicolson, 1968), 319–21; Frances A. Underhill, *For Her Good Estate: The Life of Elizabeth de Burgh* (New York: St. Martin's Press, 1999), 15-17; Linda E. Mitchell, *Portraits of Medieval Women: Family, Marriage, and Politics in England, 1225–1350* (Basingstoke: Palgrave, 2003), 117–21. That Alice de Lacy actively resisted her abduction by Hugh Frene is demonstrated by her own petition of protest (not examined by Mitchell): TNA, SC 8/64/3163.
13. G. W. Marshall, "The Barons of Burford, I," *Genealogist* 3 (1879): 225–30; Cecil G. S. Foljambe, Earl of Liverpool, and Compton Reade, *The House of Cornewall* (Hereford: privately printed, 1908), 166–88. The other main branch of this

family, the Cornewalls of Kinlet and Thonock, produced no known Sir John in the appropriate generation: Foljambe and Reade, *House of Cornewall*, 53–72; and see below, n. 45.

14. *The Wardrobe Book of William de Norwell*, ed. Mary Lyon, Bryce Lyon, Henry S. Lucas and Jean de Sturler (Brussels: Académie Royale de Belgique, 1983), 35.
15. *Register of Edward the Black Prince*, 4 vols. (London: His Majesty's Stationery Office, 1930–3), 4:208. In ca. 1360 the Hainaulter Mary de Maubuge petitioned for the release of her husband from arrest as a spy in England on the grounds that he had served the Black Prince in the company of John Cornewall: TNA, SC 8/60/2994.
16. Fowler, *Medieval Mercenaries*, 327.
17. *Foedera, conventions, litterae, et cujuscunque generic acta publica*, ed. Thomas Rymer, 3 vols. (London: Record Commission, 1816–30), 3: 1062; Michael Jones, *Ducal Brittany, 1364-1399* (Oxford: Oxford University Press, 1970), 186; TNA, E 101/42/13, m. 1, cited in "The Soldier in Later Medieval England," http://www.icmacentre.ac.uk/soldier/database; Jonathan Sumption, *The Hundred Years War III: Divided Houses* (London: Faber & Faber, 2009), 308–10.
18. Caroline Shenton, "The English Court and the Restoration of Royal Prestige, 1327–1345," (unpublished thesis, University of Oxford, D.Phil. 1995), 55–56, assumes that John had interests in Oxfordshire, but her reference does not justify this: *Calendar of the Patent Rolls Preserved in the Public Record Office, Edward II-Richard II*, 27 vols. (London: Her/His Majesty's Stationery Office, 1894-1916) (hereafter *CPR*), 1340–43: 214.
19. For Cornewall's followers see *CPR*, 1381–85: 133.
20. TNA, E 40/1844; Alfred P. Beaven, *The Aldermen of the City of London*, 2 vols. (London: Eden Fisher, 1908-13), 1: 261–97.
21. Caroline M. Barron, *London in the Later Middle Ages: Government and People, 1200–1500* (Oxford: Oxford University Press, 2004), 332, 359.
22. *Calendar of Wills Proved and Enrolled in the Court of Husting, London*, ed. Reginald R. Sharpe, 2 vols. (London: Corporation of the City of London, 1889–90), 2: 119–20; *Calendar of Letter Books of the City of London*, ed. Reginald R. Sharpe, 11 vols. (London: Corporation of the City of London, 1899–1912), *Letter Book G*: 286; *The Church in London, 1375–1392*, ed. Alison K. McHardy (London: London Record Society, 1977), no. 366.
23. *Calendar of Inquisitions Post Mortem, Edward I-Henry VI*, 26 vols. (London, Her/His Majesty's Stationery Office/TNA, 1904–2009) (hereafter *CIPM*), 15: nos. 279–80; Barbara A. Hanawalt, "The Widow's Mite: Provisions for Medieval London Widows," in *Upon My Husband's Death: Widows in the Literature and Histories of Medieval Europe*, ed. Louise Mirrer (Ann Arbor: University of Michigan Press, 1992), 21–45.
24. George Edward Cokayne, *The Complete Peerage of England, Scotland, Ireland, Great Britain and the United Kingdom*, 13 vols. (London: St. Catherine Press, 1910–59), 3: 542; Bruce Webster, "The County Community of Kent in the Reign of Richard II," *Archaeologia Cantiana* 100 (1984): 219–20 [217–29]; Charles R. S. Elvin, *Records of Walmer* (London: H. Gray, 1890), 61, 68–69; *Calendar of the Fine Rolls Preserved in the Public Record Office, Edward II-Richard II*, 10 vols. (London: His Majesty's Stationery Office, 1912–29) (hereafter *CFR*), 1327–37: 1.
25. Berkeley (Eng.), Berkeley Castle Muniments, D/5/20/17, 18.
26. *CIPM*, 7: no. 249; George Wrottesley, "Crécy and Calais, AD 1346–1347, from the Rolls in the Public Record Office," *Collections for a History of Staffordshire* new

ser. 18 (1896): 38, 99, 102, 155, 182 [1–284]; *CFR*, 1337–47: 161; *CPR*, 1343–45: 19, 23, 106, 184, 306, 483; *CPR*, 1358–61: 381, 565; *CPR*, 1364–67: 365, 430; *Calendar of the Close Rolls Preserved in the Public Record Office, Edward II-Richard II*, 24 vols. (London: Her/His Majesty's Stationery Office, 1892–1927) (hereafter *CCR*), 1360–64: 398.

27. TNA, E 101/29/40.
28. *CPR*, 1370-4: 107–8; *Foedera*, ed. Rymer, 3: 952.
29. Simon J. Payling, "Social Mobility, Demographic Change, and Landed Society in Late Medieval England," *Economic History Review* 2nd ser. 45 (1992): 66 n61 [51–73]. In 1374, John Kirriel was recorded as holding Bricklesworth's London property: TNA, CP 40/749, rot. 474, cited in "Londoners and the Law: Pleadings in the Court of Common Pleas, 1399–1509," http://www.british-history.ac.uk
30. John the younger left a daughter, Joan, born ca. 1373, who married John Wykes: *CIPM*, 21: nos. 219–20.
31. *CIPM*, 14: no. 313; 15: no. 245; 21: nos. 219–20; *CPR*, 1377–81: 109; *CCR*, 1377–81: 491.
32. Compare the case of Lettice's contemporary Alice Perrers, whose estate ought to have passed to her illegitimate daughters by Edward III but whose wishes were confounded by the male relatives of her husband, William Windsor: see T. R. Gambier-Parry, "Alice Perrers and her Husband's Relatives," *English Historical Review* 47 (1932): 272-76; W. Mark Ormrod, "The Trials of Alice Perrers," *Speculum* 83 (2008): 386–92 [366–96].
33. *CCR, 1377–81*: 111, 388: *Calendar of Plea and Memoranda Rolls Preserved among the Archives of the City of London, 1364–1381*, ed. Arthur H. Thomas (Cambridge: Corporation of the City of London, 1929), 261.
34. *CPR, 1381–85*: 133; John L. Leland, "Bealknap, Sir John (d. 1401)," *The Oxford Dictionary of National Biography*, ed. H. Colin G. Matthew and Brian H. Harrison, 60 vols. (Oxford: Oxford University Press, 2004) (hereafter *ODNB*), 4: 528–29.
35. TNA, SC 8/244/12186; *CPR, 1338–40*: 343; Helen Lacey, *The Royal Pardon: Access to Mercy in Fourteenth-Century England* (York: York Medieval Press, 2009), 100–06.
36. Jonathan Sumption, "Trevet, Sir Thomas," *ODNB*, 55: 352–53.
37. ...*omnimodis feloniis, raptibus mulieribus, et transgressionibus*...: TNA, C 66/319, m. 39. *CPR, 1381–5*: 517 renders *raptibus mulieribus* as "rapes." The privy seal warrant authorizing the letters patent is TNA, C 81/488/3530.
38. For William see *CIPM*, 20: no. 28.
39. Jones, *Ducal Brittany*, 60–92.
40. Dodd, *Justice and Grace*, 97–98.
41. TNA, C 1/48/306; C 1/79/2; *CIPM*, 26: no. 466.
42. TNA, C 1/76/3; C 1/79/2; Rosemary Horrox, "Ashton, Sir Ralph," *ODNB*, 2: 682–83.
43. TNA, C 1/48/306.
44. For the wider context of this practice see Rowena E. Archer, "Rich Old Ladies: The Problem of Late Medieval Dowagers," in *Property and Politics: Essays in Later Medieval English History*, ed. Anthony J. Pollard (Stroud, Glos.: Alan Sutton, 1984), 15–35.
45. Foljambe and Reade, *House of Cornewall*, 166–67; Adrian R. Bell, *War and the Soldier in the Fourteenth Century* (Woodbridge, Suff.: Boydell Press, 2004), 161–62. There is little clarity in the literature as to the distinction between the two Johns: Cokayne, *Complete Peerage*, 5: 253–54; A. Compton Reeves, *Lancastrian Englishmen* (Washington, DC: University Press of America, 1981), 139–202.

Simon J. Payling, "Cornewall, John, Baron Fanhope," *ODNB*, 13: 446–47, on which I generally rely, suggests that the father lived into the early 1390s and that the son was born in the 1370s. The position is complicated by the entry into public life during the 1380s of Sir John Cornewall of Kinlet and Thonock (ca. 1366–1414), another descendant of Richard of Cornewall: John S. Roskell, Linda Clark, and Carole Rawcliffe, *The House of Commons, 1386–1421*, 4 vols. (Stroud, Glos.: Alan Sutton, 1993), 2: 661–62.

46. Jean Juvenal des Ursins, "Histoire de Charles VI," in *Nouvelle collection de memoires relatives à l'histoire de France*, ed. Joseph François Michaud and Jean Joseph François Poujoula, 1st ser. 2 (Paris: Adolphe Everat, 1857), 562 [335–569].
47. Philippa C. Maddern, *Violence and Social Order: East Anglia, 1422–1442* (Oxford: Clarendon Press, 1992).
48. Roger Sherman Loomis, "The Allegorical Siege in the Art of the Middle Ages," *American Journal of Archaeology* 23 (1919): 255–69.

CHAPTER 12

MAKING MEDIEVALISM: TEACHING THE MIDDLE AGES THROUGH FILM

Martha Driver

Terry Jones is a funny man. He is also instructive, whether talking about Richard II or the Crusades or about the Ellesmere manuscript of Geoffrey Chaucer's *Canterbury Tales*. In 2008, Pace University in New York City awarded Jones an honorary doctoral degree, describing him as "Historian, Actor, Co-Founder of Monty Python."[1] The primary emphasis on "Historian" aptly alludes to the knowledge that underpins many of his film projects. Through film Jones has shaped the modern vision of the Middle Ages, has influenced the ways in which the medieval period is taught and received by scholars and students, and has informed hundreds of thousands of people about the past. His approach is reminiscent of medieval notions of carnival, or "the world turned upside down," an upending of the expected order. If medievalism is "the idealization of medieval life and culture, with an emphasis upon a rich, mysterious and imaginary world of nobility," as Morton W. Bloomfield says,[2] Jones's work might be said to promote the underbelly of the idealized past, forcing viewers to question medieval stereotypes that they have not fully examined previously. And if "Medievalism is the seed-bed of medieval scholarship,"[3] as Bloomfield further writes, Jones's films send scholars and students back to their books with many questions: Which modern assumptions about the medieval past are in fact incorrect? What is the true story? What do primary sources suggest? And what (perhaps most importantly) is so funny about the Middle Ages?

Jones has shown that film is one of the most useful tools for talking about the Middle Ages to a general audience or a college class and for conveying with graphic immediacy subjects not fully conjured by the written word. As the historian and film expert Robert A. Rosenstone suggests, the past created by movies "is not the same as the past provided by traditional history, but it certainly should be called history—if by that word, we mean a serious encounter with the lingering meaning of past events."[4] This paper examines Terry Jones's rereading of medieval history, which is most fully realized in *Medieval Lives, Monty Python and the Holy Grail,* and *Erik the Viking,* films in which Jones brings his creative forces to bear on medieval subjects, energizing the field and its students in the process.

Isn't Chivalry Just Full of Little Surprises?[5]

Part of Jones's approach to history is also the technique employed more generally by Monty Python, the British comedy troupe that Jones cofounded and that grew out of *Monty Python's Flying Circus,* which premiered on BBC TV (British Broadcasting Corporation TV) in October 1969 (and made its American debut on the PBS (Public Broadcasting Service) channel in 1974 in Dallas). The show, like Jones's subsequent films, was episodic, mocking, parodic, irreverent, self-reflexive, full of surprises, and seen as postmodern in style by its critics.[6] This self-reflexivity, along with persistent upending of expectation (or perhaps puncturing of easy surmise), occurs as well in *Medieval Lives,* an eight-part series that appeared on BBC TV in 2004.

In each episode of *Medieval Lives,* Jones dresses like a medieval character (as Robin Hood for "Outlaws" and in drag for "Damsels," for example) and tells historical anecdotes while visiting castles, towns, and other locations associated with the subjects under discussion. There are also animated manuscript illuminations that are both graphic and demonstrative; Jones actually jumps into the medieval scenes at points and engages with cutout characters in the illustrations, a literal leaping back into time and into the picture (in "Peasant," there is a comic animation of one of the calendar pages from the Limbourg brothers' *Belles Heures,* for example, and "Knight" contains graphic close-ups of manuscript scenes of terrible mayhem). Medieval manuscripts and documents are further featured in many of the episodes; the primary source texts that comprise the historical record are shown and read aloud (or paraphrased). The series is visually sumptuous, comic, and educational. Because film is by definition visual, the main narration is primarily emphatic and simplified, supplemented by interviews with a range of experts who, like Jones, explain concepts clearly for a general audience.

If used in teaching (and it should be), the series is best supplemented with chapters from the accompanying book, *Terry Jones' Medieval Lives,* which presents a more nuanced and detailed account of the history, has a helpful bibliography and some reproductions of medieval scenes, and is also simply hilarious.[7] In the TV series, for example, the story of the English mystic Christina of Markyate (ca. 1096–ca. 1155) is dramatized by puppets as a sort of Punch-and-Judy show ("Damsels"), whereas in the book, the story, while wittily told, is elaborated and includes references to primary sources; one medium in each case affirms the other.

Among other commonplaces (the notion that all peasants were poor or, for that matter, that monks were), the notion of medieval knighthood and the ideals of chivalry are carefully dissected and examined, and we learn that far from rescuing damsels in distress and slaying dragons, the goals of medieval knights were really "fame, money and God's approval," found most directly in prowess in battle.[8] The episode on the knight includes examples of renowned warriors like William the Marshal, the fourth son of an English baron of middle rank who made his reputation and much of his money in the tournament. Marshal was originally a landless knight whose skill at tourneying and warfare won him the hand in marriage of Isabel de Clare, heiress to the earldom of Pembroke (and the series takes viewers to the ruins of her castle). In Jones's book, the famous story of William's helmet is recounted: after one tournament, his helmet was so battered that "he was discovered with his head on the blacksmith's anvil having the dents hammered out."[9] This anecdote is told originally in *L'histoire de Guillaume de Maréchal,* the biography of William the Marshal commissioned by his son, and figures in the plot line of another film, *A Knight's Tale,* directed by Brian Helgeland and released in 2001, about a thatcher's son who makes his way up the social and economic ladder through his skill at jousting.[10]

The fictive William Thatcher in Helgeland's film seems, in fact, not to be entirely a fiction. The series episode "Knight" is framed by Jones's discussion of the mercenary knight Sir John Hawkwood, the son of a tanner from Essex, who exemplifies the opportunistic warrior of the fourteenth century. Mercenaries are discussed as well in *Terry Jones' Medieval Lives,* the information in part being taken from Jones's earlier book, *Chaucer's Knight: Portrait of a Medieval Mercenary,* which was published in 1980 and, unlike many scholarly books, is still in print.[11] In the latter volume, Jones argues that Chaucer's Knight, clad in rusty armor and dingy tunic and lacking in armorial bearings, is intended as a comic portrait of a mercenary. To support this rather persuasive theory that makes sense of many odd details (like the presumably hyperbolic catalogue in the "General Prologue" of the Knight's battles fought over a 40-year period from 1344 to 1386), there is recourse time and again to primary sources, for example, the legislation passed by Parliament in 1376 to control "down-at-heel ex-soldiers":

> And as for the others who claim to be "gentils," and men-at-arms or archers who have fallen on hard times because of the wars or for some other reasons, if they cannot prove their claim, and it can be proved they are craftsmen and not in any service, they shall be made to serve or to return to their crafts which they practised thereto.[12]

The notion of medieval craftsmen taking up arms is not as far-fetched as one might initially think. The mercenary soldier sans noble antecedents was a fact by the fourteenth century, discussed by Jones on film and in print. In both cases, the message is the same: battle meant money and could further a rise in rank and power. This puncturing of illusions about "knights in shining armor" is historically valid and carries over into fiction, too. As John Ganim remarks, "Jones's fiercely antiaristocratic demolition in his book, *Chaucer's Knight: Portrait of a Mercenary,* in fact, underlines the comedy of *Monty Python and the Holy Grail,*" which Ganim aptly describes as an "anarchic attack on social illusions."[13]

Perhaps He Was Dictating[14]

Monty Python and the Holy Grail (1975) is comprised of classic scenes that can be readily appreciated by the pedagogue, along with everyone else. Shot in under six weeks on a minuscule budget (hence coconuts for horses), the film was a group effort, directed alternately by Jones and the animator-cartoonist-director Terry Gilliam (neither had directed before). Jones oversaw the narrative while Gilliam focused on visual detail; Jones dealt with the actors while Gilliam handled the camera. Both Terrys were keen on the films of Italian director Pier Paolo Pasolini and tried, according to Gilliam, to recreate "the time and place and the filth."[15]

Drawing on a sketch by Michael Palin and Jones about Arthur and Camelot, the entire troupe wrote and revised the script. The film was backed by rock bands, including Pink Floyd and Led Zeppelin (and much admired by Elvis when completed!). The sound track was supplied partly by tunes composed by Neil Innes ("Brave Sir Robin") but mainly by music found by Jones in a music library, which, in this context, adds to the spoofy mockery; here canned themes that more usually accompany straight scenes of warfare, for example, underscore the comic inversions of expectation. Though the Pythons had earlier scouted several castle locations in Scotland and thought they had secured them for the shoot, Jones, just prior to filming, received a letter from the Department of the Environment for Scotland that said their jokes were thought to be "inconsistent with the dignity of the fabric of the buildings."[16] So the castle scenes were shot at the privately owned Doune Castle, the stand-in for all the medieval castles in the film (some are sets).

Monty Python and the Holy Grail remains the best of all movies with medieval themes for a variety of reasons, including its subversion of ready assumptions about the Middle Ages, the engagement of viewers, and the multivalenced commentary: on the Middle Ages; on medieval culture, values, and politics; and on modern reception and interpretation of the past. The interruptions in the Pythons' narrative and the intermingling of stories are typical of medieval stories, as any student of *Perceval, Tristan and Isolt,* or Chaucer will have noticed. Alan Lupack comments on this playful adaptation in the film based on themes from medieval literature:

> The fabulous beasts, the dangerous trials, the perilous bridge crossing, the combat that continues when one knight is severely wounded, the rescue of a maiden imprisoned in a tower, the fabulous ship that takes the knights to the Grail castle—all these stock motifs from medieval romance are parodied in the film. Also parodied is the kind of anachronism found both in medieval literature and in modern renderings of the medieval.[17]

There are also historical references running throughout. The Pythons' Arthurian narrative is set in AD 932, but the historical period in which the film is set is in fact fluid: Arthur seems to live "in the sixth, twelfth, and fourteenth centuries—an embodiment of the contradictions inherent in the popular understanding of a thousand years as a single historical period."[18]

The opening credits with subtitles in pseudo-Swedish pay homage to *The Seventh Seal,* Ingmar Bergman's famous film, but also slyly refer to *Beowulf* and other early English epic literature that features battles between Norsemen

(Danes and Swedes) rather than Englishmen. The early Britons were conquered and ruled by the Anglo-Saxons, tribes from Germany and Scandinavia. Carol O'Sullivan notes that the mock-Swedish subtitles not only comment "on the general untrustworthiness of subtitles and subtitlers but also recall the 'translated' medieval aesthetic enshrined in art cinema by European auteurs such as Eric Rohmer (*Perceval ou le Conte du Graal,* 1965), Robert Bresson (*Lancelot du Lac,* 1974) and, preeminently, Bergman (*The Seventh Seal,* 1957; *The Virgin Spring,* 1960)."[19] The send-up in the opening subtitles works on several levels, alluding both to medieval history and literature and to films with medieval themes.

As medievalists know, the cry "Bring out your dead" was heard during the outbreaks of plague, also known as the Black Death, that swept across Europe periodically. The Python's Plague Cart episode is a humorous way to begin discussion in the classroom of the major plagues that wiped out a large proportion of the European population in the fourteenth century. The scene can further introduce the graphic description of the effects of the plague in Florence recounted in the prologue to *The Decameron* by Giovanni Boccaccio. Boccaccio's prologue vividly presents the reader with details of mass burials, the carting of bodies, and the destruction of human life as well as of religious and moral values. In the Python sketch, the man pushing the death cart seems to be receiving a fee from the family member who is trying to get him to take away the old man (called Body in the screenplay), who is not quite dead yet, as he keeps pointing out in statements like, "I feel happy," and "I think I'll go for a walk."[20]

A similar grim humor informs a related scene in *Monty Python and the Holy Grail* that shows the chant of the flagellants, hooded men in monks' robes hitting themselves over the head with wooden boards. The screenplay points out that this "is a line of monks à la *Seventh Seal* flagellation scene," a serious scene of crowd hysteria in the latter film.[21] From the twelfth century on, many groups of flagellants roamed the English and French countrysides, particularly during times of famine or plague, though they are more usually described in contemporary accounts as whipping or scourging themselves.[22] The Children's Crusade was one specific example of a group engaged in a form of hysteria. This crusade was undertaken by children in 1212, who, inflamed by stories of Christians battling the infidel (or Muslims) in the Holy Land, walked barefoot through the mountains spreading the word that Christ's Cross and belief would help them to conquer the Holy Land. Thousands died before they arrived in Jerusalem.[23]

The nature of hysteria and the irrational action of crowds, which could become carried away by violence, is further represented in another scene in which the villagers bring a woman before their lord with the charge that she is a witch.[24] This sort of unthinking hysteria was horribly observed in Nazi Germany in the modern period, but also occurred in the witch trials that persisted in Europe from the later Middle Ages (notably with the trial of Joan of Arc) through the eighteenth century in America. When the lord (who turns out to be Sir Bedivere [Jones]) inquires, "Why do you think she is a witch?" one peasant (John Cleese) replies, "She turned *me* into a newt!" As Bedivere inquires, "A newt?" the peasant, who does not seem the worse for wear, weakly explains, "I got better." After a long conversation about how to determine whether or not the woman is a witch, Bedivere and the villagers then deduce the following: "'If she weighs the same as a duck... she's made of wood.' 'And therefore?' 'A witch!'"[25] This sketch pokes fun at medieval notions of science and fallacious reasoning but also more generally at the human tendency to judge and condemn others, which has not changed perceptibly since the sixth, twelfth, fourteenth, or twentieth centuries.

The hilarious episode in which King Arthur meets Dennis the peasant (and member of an "anarcho-syndicalist commune") points up the problematic relationship between peasants and nobles in the Middle Ages, while Arthur's scene with the Black Knight (played by Jones) shows the completely irrational bravery of the latter warrior, who is courageous to the point of stupidity. The Black Knight is iconic in more ways than one. An exhibition at the Musée de Cluny, Musée National du Moyen Age, featured an illuminated fifteenth-century manuscript of the *Histoire du chevalier Zifar*. In this medieval Spanish tale, a knight cuts off the head and feet of the enemy, but the enemy does not die: "Cette scène utilise le même ressort comique que le combat opposant Arthur et le chevalier noir dans *Monty Python, Sacré Graal* (This scene uses the same comic energy as the combat between Arthur and the Black Knight in *Monty Python and the Holy Grail*)" Beside the exhibition case with the manuscript, there was a screen showing the Black Knight clip to demonstrate the similarities between stories. Various critics further point to this vignette as spoofing Robert Bresson's *Lancelot du Lac,* which appeared a year earlier.[26] The scene is anti-idealization, an upending of the supposed nobility of medieval battle, chivalry, and warfare, a persistent theme in Jones's scholarship and in his pedagogy.

Another scene shows Lancelot relentlessly killing guards and eight wedding guests at Swamp Castle in order to rescue someone he thinks is a fair maiden in distress (who turns out to be Herbert, a stage-struck young man).[27] In the Arthur legends, Lancelot has the reputation of a knight who slaughters violently without always knowing who his victims are (this is specifically recounted in Sir Thomas Malory's *Morte Darthur,* in which Lancelot kills Gawain's brothers by mistake as he is rescuing Guinevere from being burnt at the stake).[28] Lancelot is a well-trained athlete and a courageous knight who shows great prowess in swinging a variety of large steel weapons, but he is not the best guest, even uninvited, at a wedding.

The scene in which Arthur and his knights encounter the French knights in the castle in England can be analyzed from a number of perspectives. In the fourteenth century, there was an exchange of nobility in the French and English courts, and French nobles mixed readily with English ones without a clear definition of nationality. During the Hundred Years' War in the fifteenth century, the English invaded France and held certain towns for a number of years (for example, Calais), and these towns became outposts of English culture. This led to a long-standing enmity and competition between the French and the English (and to the rise of French nationalism). French, however, remained the language of English law books from manuscript to print, was used in English law courts, and was spoken in English royal courts until the time of Elizabeth I.

In the scene presented by the Pythons, the French knight taunts Arthur from the castle walls. Taunting, or the exchange of formal insults, was part of formal warfare in the Middle Ages, though it is very doubtful that the insults exchanged were quite like those imagined by Monty Python. The French knight calls Arthur an "English pig-dog," saying further, "I blow my nose on you, so-called Arthur King." His other insults include: "I fart in your general direction" and "Your mother was a hamster, and your father smelled of elderberries." The French knight also makes fun of Middle English pronunciation of the word "knights," which would originally have been pronounced with the "k" sound: "silly English k... niggets."[29]

These are just a few episodes that are worth a second and third look by students of the Middle Ages and their teachers. Aspects of medieval narrative and the playful use of language more generally, both in medieval stories and in this film, may be more fully explored in the scene of the "Knights Who Say Ni," for example, in which words are imbued with irrational power. The resourceful teacher might further use the knights' adventure in the cave of Caerbannog to discuss the writing of medieval manuscripts. Brother Maynard, the monk deciphering the inscriptions made by Joseph of Arimathea on the wall of the cave, says the Holy Grail is located in "the aaaaaarrrrrgggghhh"; when Arthur and Bedivere point that this does not make much sense, Galahad then suggests that "Perhaps he was dictating," one of the suppositions sometimes made about medieval writers and their scribes.[30] In *Monty Python and the Holy Grail,* the rich narrative entertainments of the medieval past have been recast and reimagined to create the entertainment of the present, attractive perhaps because they remind us of the medieval stories we love so much, sending scholars and students alike back to their books.

I Think You'll Find It's All a Question of What You Want to Believe In[31]

As Jones has repeatedly shown, illusion is seductive, and misinformation can be dangerous. In *Erik the Viking* (1989), just at the moment his Atlantis-like island is about to sink into the sea, King Arnulf (Jones) exclaims that none of this is happening. This film, written and directed by Jones, debunks Viking stereotypes, the received notion of Viking raiders gleaned from film and general histories, and presents instead a peaceable hero who prefers conversation to pillaging and who would rather have a romantic relationship with a woman than rape her. The film includes accurate renderings of several characters from Norse mythology and, like its hero, is kinder and gentler than previous Python films in the comedy it employs.

The screenplay of *Erik* was drawn in part from Jones's *The Saga of Erik the Viking,* written by Jones for his young son, Bill. The original source may have influenced the sweeter tone of the humor as well.[32] In the children's book, Erik is married and makes a vow not to sleep in his own bed until he finds "the land where the sun goes at night."[33] In the film, the unmarried hero mistakenly kills a pretty Viking woman during a raid and quests to wake the gods to end the age of Ragnarok, seeking his lost ladylove in the process. Though there is physical humor, the prose of the novel is lofty and formal, rather like the style of J. R. R. Tolkien's *Lord of the Rings* trilogy. The children's book also includes an homage to Bergman's *Seventh Seal:* the climax of the novel is Erik's chess game with Death, a story element not seen in the film. The film is more lighthearted; the magical and mythic become humorous slapstick, with physical comedy as the main focus.

Episodes retained from the novel include "Erik and the Sea Dragon" and "At the Edge of the World"; in the film, both scenes employ spectacular special effects that hold up against more modern techniques, including computer-generated imagery (CGI). In the novel, the Vikings aboard Erik's ship, the *Golden Dragon,* notice a strange mist, and the sea dragon's roar is at first mistaken for thunder; there is a most peculiar sun that turns out to be the eye of the dragon.[34] One of Erik's men, Ragnar Forkbeard, straps two bolsters on his back, climbs onto the dragon's nose, plunges the bolsters into the dragon's nostrils and slices the bolsters open; the dragon inhales the feathers and sneezes mightily, sending the ship flying out of harm's way: "the ship shot out of the Dragon's jaws and across the waters...and over the sea it flew through the air as if it were a bird, not a ship, and at last landed with a great splash."[35]

In the film, just before Erik's ship (also called the *Golden Dragon*) leaves port, his mother ceremonially offers Erik his father's pillow and explains: "It was the pillow HE took with him. He said it once saved his life."[36] This sentimental scene is greeted with tittering from the other Vikings, although, as the screenplay explains, "They've ALL been embarrassed by their mums at one time or another."[37] As in the novel, the dragon's eye is mistaken for the sun, and just as the monstrous creature is about to devour the Viking ship, Erik climbs up on its nose and inserts his father's pillow with the same effect: the Viking ship is blown clear by the dragon's sneeze. The joke added here is made by Snorri, one of Erik's men, who remarks, "Urgh! What's it been eating?"[38]

In the film, there is compression of narrative detail; while other Vikings are shown as heroic in the novel, Erik is the main actor in the film. The less-than-heroic Vikings accompanying the film's Erik are recognizable as imperfect humans who say what we might think in private. Ashamed of their emotional mums and cracking jokes about halitosis, these Vikings behave like silly adolescents in counterpoint to the idealistic Erik, catching viewers off guard and making them laugh.

In both print and film, the scenes at the Edge of the World are terrifying and exhilarating; in both cases the episode is used to move the plot along. Near the end of the novel, the *Golden Dragon* is caught in the flood and is whirled toward a waterfall. Ragnar Forkbeard tethers the ship to a rock that sticks out of the sea. Erik and Sven the Strong tie themselves to the main boat and attach a line to their rowboat, with which they go over and through the falls and find themselves in a cave. They then return to the surface, and the *Golden Dragon* and its men sail over the falls and into the caverns beneath the Edge of the World.[39] In the film, when Princess Aud blows the Horn Resounding, the *Golden Dragon* flies off the Edge of the World and lands near the bridge that will take the men to Asgaard, the home of the gods.

In the novel, Erik's chief antagonist is the Old Man of the Sea, a deceptive trickster and shapeshifter who wants to entrap Erik and his men beneath the waves. Near the end of the novel, Erik's lost father, thought dead, is freed by Erik from the Old Man's dungeon. In the film, Erik's opponent is the cruel Halfdan the Black (John Cleese), who is portrayed as a relentlessly polite, finicky sadist, a refined yet amoral businessman. Aronstein points out: "the contrast between Cleese's calm businessmen [*sic*] and the violence he perpetuates is pure Python in its implication that, in spite of all of our progressive myths about the disjunction between an [*sic*] civilized present and a barbaric past, the past is very much with us."[40]

While the film character is a riff on present-day corporate corruption, the historical Halfdan the Black (Halfdan Svarte), a ninth-century Norwegian king, was viewed as a good ruler under whom the Norwegians prospered and who developed a collection of laws for his people. After his premature death when his sledge fell through the ice, his body was divided into four pieces and buried in four places in the lands he held in order to insure the fields would be fruitful. In a related saga of Halfdan the Black in the *Helmskringla* (Chronicle of the kings of Norway), Halfdan's father is said to have descended from the goddess Freya.[41]

Freya the goddess also appears in the film in the person of Eartha Kitt and is shown as a seer and storyteller. It is she who first inspires Erik to go on his quest and accurately describes for him the age of Ragnarok:

> when Fenrir the Wolf would swallow the sun, and a Great Winter would settle upon the world. It was to be an axe age, a sword age, a storm age, when brother would turn against brother, and men would fight each other until the world would finally be destroyed.[42]

John Aberth comments that the film "gives the fullest treatment to Viking religion and beliefs of any English-language film."[43] In Norse mythology, Fenrir the hell-wolf will fight and eventually kill Odin, the chief of the gods, during the Ragnarok.[44] In *Erik the Viking,* Erik ultimately chases Fenrir the Wolf from the sky to signal the ending of Ragnarok. The father of Fenrir, the Norse trickster god Loki, is shown in the film as a treacherous blacksmith's assistant, eager to produce weapons and to promote the Age of Ragnarok because it is good for trade. Once the *Golden Dragon* has flown over the Edge of the World, the Vikings must cross Bifröst, the rainbow bridge that connects Midgaard (middle earth) to Asgaard, a reference familiar from the poetic and prose Eddas, the latter composed by Snorri Sturluson in the thirteenth century.[45] The Norse gods of Asgaard are represented in the film as wayward children, emphasizing "their capricious quality, particularly of Odin. We also get the message that their power is limited, which is demonstrated in Viking mythology by the fact that during the time of Ragnarok, the gods who do battle with the giants will be defeated."[46]

The film *Erik the Viking* is a fractured fairy tale, a broadly comic rendering of well-researched Viking beliefs and practices, and like the novel, it has a happy ending. In the novel, Eric learns that "our true goal lies within ourselves and in what we do, and not in the things we think we are looking for."[47] The film ends rather less philosophically but stays true to the consistent physicality of the humor: the *Golden Dragon* flying back through the air from Asgaard lands on the wicked Halfdan the Black, satisfactorily squashing him, and the sun is restored to Erik and his people.

Through his films, Terry Jones has made us laugh, and, by persistently raising valuable questions and exploding generally accepted stereotypes, he has also taught us to look more closely at aspects of the Middle Ages we overlook or take for granted. The satiric recreation of the period in Jones's films invites lively discussion about the ways in which historical narrative is perceived, edited, written, and retold. Film also profoundly influences historical memory. Jones's work challenges the idealization of the medieval past and unthinking acceptance of superficial commonplaces, making us think of medieval people as being like people we might know, with all their faults included. Like other films with medieval themes, Jones's movies are perhaps best read in context, alongside and in conjunction with literary and historical sources, and provide a rich resource for the students and teachers of the Middle Ages. As Bloomfield writes, "The history of the Middle Ages will continue to stimulate lovers of Medievalism just as Medievalism stimulates study of the Middle Ages. They both need each other."[48] In his films, Jones has alluded to the work of other filmmakers and the writing of literary scholars and historians, as well as to contemporary politics and the sillier and profounder aspects of human nature, among other subjects. In homage to him, I thought I would write this essay entirely in the nude, but I found I lacked Terry's inherent facility for funniness (and it was also rather drafty).[49] Hats (if not clothes) off to Terry Jones for all he has taught us!

Notes

1. As artist-in-residence, Terry Jones has lectured at Pace University on three occasions, speaking to Chaucer classes and presenting public lectures drawn from Terry Jones et al., *Who Murdered Chaucer? A Medieval Mystery* (New York: St. Martin's Press, 2004), from Terry Jones and Alan Ereira, *Terry Jones' Barbarians* (London: BBC Books, 2007), as well as lectures on films and filmmaking. The honorary degree was awarded in 2008; the quotation is taken from "Recent Recipients of Honorary Degrees," Commencement Ceremonies Class of 2011, New York, Pace University, 2011, 52.
2. Morton W. Bloomfield, "Reflections of a Medievalist: America, Medievalism, and the Middle Ages," in *Medievalism in American Culture, Medieval & Renaissance Texts and Studies*, ed. Bernard Rosenthal and Paul E. Szarmach, 55 (Binghamton, NY: Center for Medieval and Early Renaissance Studies, 1989), 14 [13–29].
3. Bloomfield, "Reflections," 26.
4. Robert A. Rosenstone, ed., *Revisioning History: Film and the Construction of a New Past* (Princeton, NJ: Princeton University Press, 1995), 5.
5. Terry Jones, "The Knight," *Medieval Lives*, BBC2, 2004 TV, YouTube video, 29:10, posted by BBCWorldwide on April 9, 2009.
6. See, e.g., Susan Aronstein, *Hollywood Knights: Arthurian Cinema and the Politics of Nostalgia* (New York: Palgrave Macmillan, 2005), 110, who comments: "Their Flying Circus uses postmodern techniques—pastiche, self-reflexiveness, an abandonment of continuity and closure, and parody—to tear apart social and narrative conventions, calling their audience's attention to the fact that all narratives, from genres to political and social discourses, are assembled out of

disparate parts and bound together only by conventions of closure and continuity designed to make them seem natural and transparent."

7. Terry Jones and Alan Ereira, *Terry Jones' Medieval Lives* (London: BBC Books, 2005). Also worth reading is Terry Jones and Alan Ereira, *Crusades* (London: Penguin BBC Books, 1994), the book accompanying the documentary series (1995; DVD, A&E Home Video, 2002). It, too, contains bibliography, notes and a comprehensive index.
8. Jones and Ereira, *Terry Jones'*, 145.
9. Jones and Ereira, *Terry Jones'*, 143–44.
10. Georges Duby, *L'histoire de Guillaume de Maréchal ou le meilleur chevalier du monde*: *William Marshal the Flower of Chivalry*, trans. Richard Howard (New York: Pantheon, 1985). Brian Helgeland, *A Knight's Tale: The Shooting Script* (New York: Newmarket Press, 2001), viii, explains his inspiration for the lead character in the film, the craftsman William Thatcher, born in Cheapside, who becomes a knight. Looking through some old notes on medieval jousting, he found underlined, "You had to be of noble birth to compete" and invented, apparently on the spot, the peasant William "who wanted to be a knight only he had to fight the prejudices, laws, and roadblocks set up by the powers that be." He then read medieval histories and "biographies on Chaucer, Edward the Black Prince, and William Marshall—the jousting Mickey Mantle of his day. I reread *The Canterbury Tales*.... All of it to steep me in medievalism, all of it to add a realism, a sense of the smell of the place."
11. Terry Jones, *Chaucer's Knight: The Portrait of a Medieval Mercenary* (1980; New York: Methuen, 1985). Derek Brewer, the esteemed Chaucer scholar, aptly described the style of this volume: "Jones... writes with considerable verve and the insight of a successful creative writer. He also writes as an entirely serious and responsible historian of the period" (*Times Educational Supplement*, 1980, quoted on the back of Jones's volume). For other responses to Jones's book, see David Aers's review, "Chaucer's Knight: A Portrait of a Medieval Mercenary," *Studies in the Age of Chaucer* 4 (1982): 169–75, which admires the questions raised by Jones ("the first part of the book... sets orthodox medievalists problems which they must take seriously," 172). For more on mercenaries, see also John H. Pratt, "Was Chaucer's Knight Really a Mercenary?" *Chaucer Review* 22.1 (1987): 8–27; Terry Jones, "The Monk's Tale," *Studies in the Age of Chaucer*, ed. Larry Scanlon, 22 (2000): 389–91, 395–97 [387–97]. For Chaucer's pacifism, see R. F. Yeager, "Pax Poetica: On the Pacifism of Chaucer and Gower," *Studies in the Age of Chaucer* 9 (1987): 97–121.
12. Jones, *Chaucer's Knight*, 26–27.
13. John M. Ganim, "The Hero in the Classroom," in *The Medieval Hero Onscreen: Representations from Beowulf to Buffy*, ed. Martha W. Driver and Sid Ray (Jefferson, NC: McFarland, 2004), 244–45 [237–49]. David D. Day, "Monty Python and the Holy Grail: Madness with a Definite Method," in *Cinema Arthuriana*, rev. ed., ed. Kevin J. Harty (Jefferson, NC: McFarland, 2002), 127–35, remarks upon the prescience with which the Pythons critique medieval historiography in the film: "When the troupe satirizes the ways we know the past and our motives in doing so, they seem to be treading the same intellectual path or one very similar to that which serious academics whom they satirize have trodden"(134).
14. *Monty Python and the Holy Grail* (MPHG), dir. Terry Gilliam and Terry Jones, with Terry Jones, Terry Gilliam, Graham Chapman, John Cleese, Eric Idle, Michael Palin (London: Python [Monty] Pictures Limited, 1975). Elisabetta Girelli,

writing about Jones in biographies provided by the British Film Institute, comments: "Jones's directing career has been overshadowed by Python's collective formula, yet he was largely responsible for the stylistic presentation of the group's work" (Elisabetta Girelli, "Jones, Terry (1942 –), in *Reference Guide to British and Irish Film Directors*, available at BFI Screenonline, http://www.screenonline.org.uk/people/id/499825/index.html). MPHG was produced by John Goldstone, described by Jones as the perfect producer who "always trusted the creativity of the director with whom he was working"; discussion in Lloyd Kaufman with Ashley Wren Collins, *Produce Your Own Damn Movie!* (New York: Focal Press, 2009), 78 [77–79]. Some of this discussion appears in Martha W. Driver, "'Stond and Delyver': Teaching the Medieval Movie," in *Medieval Hero*, 212–15.

15. Derived from interviews on the DVD of *Monty Python, Almost the Truth: The Lawyer's Cut* (DVD, disc 2, episode 4, "The Ultimate Holy Grail Episode," Eagle Rock, dir. Bill Jones, Alan G. Parker, and Benjamin Timlett, 2009). The coconuts are also a BBC joke. BBC Radio's sound effects studio was known for using everyday objects to make sounds for radio plays (thanks for this information to Gill Kent).
16. This story is told in "The Ultimate Holy Grail Episode" and also in Michael Palin and Terry Jones, "The Quest for the Holy Grail Locations," in *Monty Python and the Holy Grail: The Ultimate Definitive Final Special Edition* DVD (disc 2), 2001. Brian Levy and Lesley Coote, "The Subversion of Medievalism in Lancelot du Lac and Monty Python and the Holy Grail," *Studies in Medievalism* 13 (2004): 99–126, analyze the role of the castle in MPHG (113–14), but note that all the castles shown in the film are "the same castle shot from different angles" (125, n. 60).
17. Alan Lupack, *The Oxford Guide to Arthurian Literature and Legend* (Oxford University Press, 2005), 279. See also Sarah Salih, "Cinematic Authenticity-Effects and Medieval Art: A Paradox," in *Medieval Film*, ed. Anke Bernau and Bettina Bildhauer (Manchester, UK: Manchester University Press, 2009), 23 [20–39]: "The antimimetic Monty Python and the Holy Grail (1975), in which various modes of the illusory medieval—chivalric glamour, earthy squalor, quotations of medieval forms—jostle with the rude interruptions of modernity, may be the paradigmatic medieval film, and is certainly a favourite of many medievalists." Mark Burde, "Monty Python's Medieval Masterpiece," *The Arthurian Yearbook* 3 (1993): 3–20, says the film is "the product of too much research and knowledge to dismiss lightly" (4). Burde cites the Pythons' appropriation of medieval interlace technique in the narrative (6) and summarizes the targets of the film's lampoons (7–9). For more medieval references, see Christine M. Neufeld, "Coconuts in Camelot: Monty Python and the Holy Grail in the Arthurian Literature Course," *Florilegium* 19 (2002): 127–48; and Raymond H. Thompson, "The Ironic Tradition in Arthurian Films Since 1960," in *Cinema Arthuriana*, rev. ed., ed. Kevin J. Harty (Jefferson, NC: McFarland, 2002), 114–17 [110–17].
18. Nickolas Haydock, *Movie Medievalism: The Imaginary Middle Ages* (Jefferson, NC: McFarland, 2008), 10.
19. Carol O'Sullivan, "A Time of Translation: Linguistic Difference and Cinematic Medievalism," in *Medieval Film*, ed. Anke Bernau and Bettina Bildhauer (Manchester, UK: Manchester University Press, 2009), 68 [60–85]. O'Sullivan further notes the subtitles added to *The Ultimate Definitive Final Special Edition* DVD (disc 1, "Subtitles for People Who Don't Like the Film"). In this case, subtitles supplied randomly from William Shakespeare's *Henry IV*, Part II, consistently contradicting everything King Arthur says, reflect a persistent human tendency

to impose modernity on the past while also "overwriting a purportedly tenth-century tale with fragments of a sixteenth-century retelling of fourteenth-century events" (69). There is also use of comic subtitling in Jones's *Erik the Viking*, dir. Terry Jones, with John Cleese, Terry Jones, Eartha Kitt, Tim McInnerny, Tim Robbins, Antony Sher, Mickey Rooney, Imogen Stubbs (London: Prominent Features, 1989).

20. Graham Chapman, John Cleese, Terry Gilliam, Eric Idle, Terry Jones and Michael Palin, *Monty Python and the Holy Grail: The Screenplay* (London: Methuen, 2003), 5. Richard Burt, *Medieval and Early Modern Film and Media* (New York: Palgrave Macmillan, 2008), 53, points out that "the film calls into question both the authority and meaning of the written record of history," and "The shot of the police car entering the frame near the end of the film is followed by handheld cinéma verité shots of the police that continue to the end, making it seem as if we are witnessing a documentary about reenactors of a medieval battle" (55).
21. Chapman et al., *Monty Python*, 15.
22. For more on the effects of mass hysteria in the Middle Ages, see Norman Cohn, *The Pursuit of the Millennium: Revolutionary Millenarians and Mystical Anarchists of the Middle Ages*, rev. ed. (London: Maurice Temple Smith, 1970); Mark Pegg, *The Corruption of Angels: the Great Inquisition of 1245–1246* (Princeton, NJ: Princeton University Press, 2001).
23. See also Norman Housley, *Fighting for the Cross: Crusading to the Holy Land* (New Haven, CT: Yale, 2008), 15, 30, 36, 200.
24. The title of Timothy R. Tangherlini's "'How Do You Know She's a Witch?': Witches, Cunning Folk, and Competition in Denmark," *Western Folklore*, 59.3/4 (Summer–Autumn 2000): 279–303, an article that does not actually discuss the Python film, demonstrates how lines from MPHG are instantly recognizable wherever they appear.
25. Chapman et al., Monty Python, 17–18.
26. Exhibition caption, "L'epée: Usages, mythes et symboles," Musée de Cluny, Musée National du Moyen Age, Paris, April 28 to September 26, 2011. The comparison of the manuscript of the *Histoire du chevalier Zifar* (BNF MS. Esp. 36) with the clip from the film aptly illustrates the educative reach of Monty Python and the Holy Grail. Haydock, *Movie Medievalism*, 12, comments that the Pythons are making fun of Bresson's *Lancelot du Lac* (1974), which "often frames shots of bodies from the torso down, and includes a great deal of un-synced [sic], extradiegetic sound," as well as "avant-garde cinema as a whole." See also John Aberth, *A Knight at the Movies: Medieval History on Film* (New York: Routledge, 2003), 25, who suggests that the scene of Arthur's fight with the Black Knight specifically comments on Bresson. Levy and Coote, "Subversion of Medievalism," describe both films, but do not compare them directly.
27. Aronstein, *Hollywood Knights* (see above, n6), misidentifies Herbert as "Irvin, the Singing Groom" (115). Herbert (Jones again) has show-business aspirations and is described in the screenplay as "[a] young, quite embarrassingly unattractive prince" (47). Both father and son are confused about gender, Herbert calling his father "Mother" and his father (Palin) calling Herbert "Alice" (48–49), also noted briefly in Levy and Coote, "Subversion of Medievalism," 114–15.
28. Malory is clearly one source for MPHG, and as Levy and Coote, "Subversion of Medievalism," point out, for Malory "and his contemporaries, the Arthurian legend provided a means for considering and criticizing their own political situation.... In *Monty Python and the Holy Grail*, the legend is being used in the same

way…as a means of criticizing contemporary society and politics" (118). In the confusingly titled novel by Terry Jones, *Douglas Adams' Starship Titanic: A Novel by Terry Jones* (New York: Ballantine, 1997), 151–52, there is another seeming allusion to Malory. Knightly catalogues in the *Morte Darthur* are used dramatically, as in the attack in "Slander and Strife" by Gawain's kin upon Lancelot in the queen's chamber: "Then sir Agravain and sir Mordred got to them twelve knights and hid themself in a chamber.…And these were their names, sir Collgrevaunce, sir Mador de la Porte, sir Gingaline, sir Meliot de Logres, sir Petipace of Winchelsea, sir Galleron of Galloway, sir Melion de la Mountain, sir Ascomore, sir Gromoresom Erioure, sir Cursesalain, sir Florence and sir Lovel"; Derek Brewer, *The Morte Darthur: Parts Seven and Eight* (Evanston, IL: Northwestern University Press, 1996), 102. In Jones's science-fiction comedy, there is a funny list of the corporals of the planet Yassaccanda that resembles medieval catalogues of knights: "Corporals Yarktak, Edembop, Raguliten, Desembo, Luntparger, Forzab, Kakit, Zimwiddy, Duterprat, Kazitinker-Rigipitil, Purzenhakken, Roofcleetop, Spanglowiddin, Buke-Hammadorf, Bunzywotter, Brudelhampton, Harzimwodl.…" As in the medieval example, the names sound at once lofty and impossible. The novel includes a plot as intricately designed as Chaucer's "Miller's Tale," in which small details introduced early on become significant later.

29. Chapman et al., *Monty Python*, 26.
30. Chapman et al., *Monty Python*, 77.
31. Immortal words spoken by King Arnulf just before his island sinks into the sea in *Erik the Viking*, screenplay by Terry Jones, available online at http://www.dailyscript.com/scripts/Erik+The+Viking.txt. *Erik the Viking*, dir. Terry Jones, with John Cleese, Terry Jones, Eartha Kitt, Tim McInnerny, Tim Robbins, Antony Sher, Mickey Rooney, Imogen Stubbs (London: Prominent Features, 1989).
32. Bill Jones later recut the film, which is the current version available on DVD (December 4, 2007). The book won the 1984 Children's Book Award. Terry Jones is also the author of several other books for children, including *Nicobobinus* (1986; London: Puffin, 1987); *Fairy Tales* (London: Puffin, 1987); *Fantastic Stories*, which won the 1992 Smarties Prize (London: Viking, 1993); and the series *The Knight and the Squire* (London: Anova Books, 1997) and *The Lady and The Squire* (London: Anova Books, 2000), which were shortlisted for the 2002 Whitbread Prize. Children know Terry for his portrayal of Toad in *Mr. Toad's Wild Ride*, drawn from Kenneth Grahame's *Wind in the Willows* (Terry also contributed songs, directed, and wrote the screenplay, *Mr. Toad's Wild Ride*, dir. Terry Jones, with Steve Coogan, Eric Idle, Terry Jones, Antony Sher, Nicol Williamson, Stephen Fry and Michael Palin, 1996, DVD, Los Angeles/London: Walt Disney Video, March 2, 2004), and teenagers might be aware that Jones wrote the script for *Labyrinth*, dir. Jim Henson, with David Bowie, Jennifer Connolly, Frank Oz, Los Angeles/London: Henson Associates, Lucasfilm, 1986.
33. Terry Jones, *The Saga of Erik the Viking* (London: Penguin, 1988), 9.
34. Jones, *Saga of Erik the Viking*, 17–18.
35. Jones, *Saga of Erik the Viking*, 20.
36. Jones, *Erik the Viking*, screenplay.
37. Jones, *Erik the Viking*, screenplay.
38. Jones, *Erik the Viking*, screenplay.
39. Jones, *Saga of Erik the Viking*, 110–123.
40. Susan Aronstein, "When Civilization Was Less Civilized: Erik the Viking (1989)," in Kevin J. Harty, ed., *The Vikings on Film: Essays on Depictions of the Nordic Middle*

Ages (Jefferson, NC: McFarland, 2011), 79 [72–82]. Aronstein also notes with disappointment that there is just one glimpse of a horned helmet in the film, and "we all know Vikings wore horned helmets" (77), but this is another erroneous commonplace, as shown in Roberta Frank, "The Invention of the Viking Horned Helmet," in *International Scandinavian and Medieval Studies in Memory of Gerd Wolfgang Weber*, ed. Michael Dallapiazza et al., *Hesperides: Letterature e Culture Occidentali* 11 (Trieste, Italy: Edizione Parnaso, 2001), 199–208. The simple leather helmets worn by Erik and his men in the film are closer to the original headgear worn by Viking warriors.

41. See Thomas B. Willson, *History of the Church and State in Norway from the Tenth to Sixteenth Centuries* (Westminster, UK: Archibald Constable, 1903), 10–11. For the saga, see "Heimskringla or The Chronicle of the Kings of Norway: Halfdan the Black Saga," Online Medieval and Classical Library Release #15b, The Online Medieval and Classical Library, http://omacl.org/Heimskringla/halfdan.html. The historical Halfdan the Black is also briefly mentioned in John Aberth, *A Knight at the Movies: Medieval History on Film* (New York: Routledge, 2003), 58–59.
42. Jones, *Erik the Viking*, screenplay.
43. Aberth, *Knight at the Movies*, 58–59.
44. Bernard Scudder, trans., "Egil's Saga," in *The Sagas of the Icelanders: A Selection*, preface by Jane Smiley, intro. by Robert Kellogg (New York: Penguin, 2000), 157–158 [3–184].
45. Bifröst or Bilröst is the rainbow bridge that connects Midgaard (Middle Earth) with Asgaard, the realm of the gods. The bridge also appears at the end of Richard Wagner's *Das Rheingold*; on the opening night of Robert Lepage's version at the Metropolitan Opera House (September 27, 2010), New York, the special effects were not working properly. Eric Owens, who sang the role of Alberich, played the part of Grendel in Julie Taymor's *Grendel* at the Lincoln Center Festival, July 11, 2006.
46. Aberth, *Knight at the Movies*, 57.
47. Jones, *Saga of Erik the Viking*, 176.
48. Bloomfield, "Reflections of a Medievalist" (see above, n2), 27.
49. "From 'Naked Man Playing Organ' and 'Man in Bed with Carol Cleveland' from the Monty Python TV show, to 'Naked Hermit in Pit' in Monty Python's *Life of Brian* (a movie that he directed naked, while the rest of the cast remained largely clothed), the creative life has been one long nudist romp for Mr. Jones"; Douglas Adams, "Introduction," in Terry Jones, *Douglas Adams' Starship Titanic: A Novel by Terry Jones* (New York: Ballantine, 1997), x.

CHAPTER 13

THE "SILLY" PACIFISM OF GEOFFREY CHAUCER AND TERRY JONES

William A. Quinn

et dissipabitur arcus belli et loquetur pacem gentibus
(And the bow for war shall be broken. And he shall speak peace to the Gentiles.)

Zaccharias 9:10

As a member of *Monty Python's Flying Circus,* Terry Jones was, is, and shall ever seem brilliantly silly. As a medievalist, however, Jones has taken Geoffrey Chaucer, the father of English comedy, most seriously. In *Chaucer's Knight,*[1] first published only seven years after Richard M. Nixon declared "peace with honor" in Vietnam, Jones challenged a longstanding critical consensus that Chaucer intended his portrayal of a worthy, perfect, and gentle Knight in the "General Prologue" to *The Canterbury Tales (CT* I, 43-78)[2] to be taken sincerely. Instead, Jones argued that the historical details of Chaucer's description (rather than its doting adjectives) represent the career of a brutal mercenary. Many Chaucerians did not immediately welcome Terry's revisionist reading. So, with typical (and very Chaucer-like) self-effacement, he conceded in the introduction to his study's second edition that, "We may not know for certain what Chaucer thought about war or crusading."[3] In light of subsequent scholarly developments, there seems little reason for him to have been so conciliatory.

Now, more than thirty years since the original publication of *Chaucer's Knight* and more than eight years since George W. Bush declared "Mission Accomplished" in Iraq (May 1, 2003), the Knight retains for many readers his admirable status as a paragon of chivalry—whatever that, in fact, might mean. Many Chaucerians still resist Terry's effort to draft Chaucer as an antiwar protester—primarily because the majority prefer to keep Chaucer funny. Unlike William Langland or John Gower, Chaucer made no explicit objection specifically to crusading or to the Hundred Years' War. For this reason alone, this lack of an explicit, direct, and negative declaration against these particular wars by Chaucer *in propria persona,* Chaucerians hesitate to think of Chaucer as a conscientious objector. After all, Chaucer was once fined for assaulting a Franciscan, whose order (like the Lollards) did profess pacifism. Not unpricked by Terry's critique of Chaucer's Knight, however, several subsequent scholars, including R. F. Yeager, Helen Barr, Nigel Saul, and Kate L. Forhan, have argued with increasing persuasiveness that Chaucer was himself indeed a pacifist of sorts.[4] The term "pacifist" may seem anachronistic when applied to Chaucer, but not necessarily the concept.[5] And it makes extraordinary sense that Terry should be among the first to comprehend that Chaucer-the-humorist was Chaucer-the-pacifist as well, because it takes one to know one.

More recently and at least as provocatively, Terry and others have proposed that King Henry IV and Archbishop Thomas Arundel may have had Chaucer *disappeared* because he "fell short of the sycophancy required of the new regime."[6] Dismissing slanders originally perpetuated by Lancastrian propaganda, Terry questions a common perception of the last Plantagenet as a tyrant. He argues, instead, that King Richard II was far more tolerant of dissent for most of his reign. And Terry especially laments the usurpation of this true king because he was apparently so reluctant to fight: "In fact, the pursuit of peace is one of the most remarkable and yet least celebrated characteristics of Richard's rule."[7] Among historians, King Richard's motivation, indeed his mental health, remains debatable. The pertinent point here, however, is that Terry never misses an opportunity to celebrate such a political leader who tried, at least, for whatever reasons, to keep the peace.[8]

Terry has most recently provoked an entirely different type of contentiousness by making explicit, direct, and negative declarations against a particular war *in propria persona.* In a series of articles first appearing between 2001 and 2004, he renounced the then-extremely popular "shock and awe" show—more specifically, the United Kingdom's participation in the war against Saddam Hussein. He found the official justification for a preemptive strike against Iraq (i.e., on the basis of an illusory threat posed by weapons of mass destruction) more ludicrous than laughable. For Terry, the real threat to the One True and Holy West was its own bellicose fuzzy-headedness: How can one fight an abstract noun like "terrorism" per se? by bombing "it" into oblivion? or by catching "it" once and for all in a spider hole?[9] How is the bombing of terrorists throughout Iraq substantially different from bombing the Provisional Irish Republican Army (IRA) in Dublin... or a few "training bogs in Tipperary"... or even the target-rich Irish enclaves of several U.S. cities?[10] How was Saddam's deplorable use of nerve gas not analogous to the spraying of Agent Orange in Vietnam? As an acerbic critic of contemporary events, Jones usually sounds far more Swiftian than Chaucerian.[11]

Chaucer was never so explicitly barbed. He was not so outraged as Langland nor so didactic as Gower. Happily, however, Chaucer's humor remains funny and influential largely because he deliberately avoided occasionality. His advocacy of peace was not restricted to his immediate historical milieu. So too, his pacifism was not voiced as strident indignation. Chaucer's intermittent silliness in the

Canterbury Tales does not undermine the framing integrity of his serious themes, however. Rather, his silliness often seems a conscientious "strategery" intended to subvert the sort of dangerous earnestness that often justifies violence. For Chaucer (as for Terry-the-Pythoner), humor is a weapon, sometimes the only effective weapon against the deadly serious sins of *superbia* and *ira* that welcome war.

Though he has been one of the most successful promoters of medieval studies for the last several decades, Terry has also frequently exploited the alterity of the Middle Ages for comic effect. His sometimes silly fabrications of a "medieval" past provide a mere ruse, however, for gaining some objective distance with which to view contemporary absurdities.[12] Conversely, Terry-the-political-satirist often sees medieval history as immediately relevant to our times because he has both the historical memory and the political foresight to do so. In his antiwar essays, Terry occasionally proposes what must seem (to nonmedievalists) strange parallels between the horrors of warfare in the late fourteenth century and today's more remote-controlled atrocities. For example, when considering state-sponsored terrorism, he remarks, "One thinks, for example, of Edward III's *chevauchée* across Normandy in 1359 (or possibly one doesn't)."[13] Similarly, in order to debunk the political pose of "deniability" (such as claimed by Adolf Hitler regarding his death camps), Jones recalls: "Same with Henry II and the murder of Thomas Becket, I suppose."[14] With a seemingly silly but compelling elenchus, Jones even comes to the logical conclusion that "George W. Bush is an Al Qaeda agent working for the destruction of the Western World as we know it"—QED.[15] Perhaps, simply because Terry often argues (in good scholastic fashion) by analogy, his antiwar reasoning might be dismissed as quaintly "medieval." He himself, of course, has repeatedly objected to such common use of the adjective "medieval" as a synonym for "silly" or "stupid" or even "cruel" (as in the expression "medieval torture," though the modern era far excels the Middle Ages in this art too). Having corrected our historical lenses, Terry would target instead these dark ages now.

Terry has, therefore, alienated a number of his worthy, perfect, gentle, and former fans. Chaucer too has disappointed many Chaucerians when he becomes surprisingly sincere as in "The Former Age," "Lak of Stedfastnesse," the "Tale of Melibee," and the "Parson's Tale."[16] Few readers enjoy the "Tale of Melibee," but Terry insists that we admire Chaucer's choice:

> as his own Tale, he chose to translate an uncompromising pacifist tract. Critics have, in the past, tended to minimize Chaucer's anti-war statements yet... Chaucer was bold enough to present as his own personal statement as pacifist tract—and a French one at that—opposing all wars.[17]

The three "olde foes" (*CT* VII, 970) who assault Melibee's wife and daughter are not initially specified in Chaucer's tale; they are clearly not France nor Iraq. Prudence later identifies them as the World, the Flesh, and the Devil, "thou hast suffred hem to entre in to thyn herte willfully... and hast nat defended thyself suffisantly agayns hire assaultes"(*CT* VII, 1421-3). Peggy A. Knapp has questioned how Prudence could logically "urge peacemaking" with three such enemies.[18] If Melibee's foes are interpreted as his own motives for vengeance—the constant demands of pride, cupidity, and anger—rather than external enemies, the interpretive problem may be somewhat resolved: Melibee must struggle to achieve reconciliation with his own temptations, by silencing them. These internal adversaries cannot be exiled; they must be overruled "and in this nede ye caste yow to overcome youre herte" (*CT* VII, 1847-58). This is the only legitimate jihad. Such a radical commitment to nonviolence as that voiced by Lady Prudence cannot be overstated or repeated too often.

Irate Melibee, at first, wants to be imprudent; he fears his inaction will be construed as impotent appeasement: "But whoso wolde considere in alle vengeances the perils and yveles that myghte sewe of vengeance-takynge, / a man would nevere take vengeance, and that were harm" (*CT* VII, 1429-30). Prudence affirms that peace is the true antidote to violent assault, not war. Mercy is the true contrary to vengeance; eager enforcement of the *lex talionis* (law of retaliation) is merely a reiteration of vengeance (*CT* VII, 1275-90). Probably the hardest lesson for a clearly wronged party to hear is Prudence's suggestion that Melibee himself is "peraventure" not entirely innocent.[19]

Wise men—including doctors (*CT* VII, 1011, 1267) and lawyers (*CT* VII, 1021) and elders (*CT* VII, 1037) and some humorists—all oppose war. It is only false friends (*CT* VII, 1017) and foolish young people (*CT* VII, 1035) who are always eager for a good fight; this bellicose majority, though "the greteste partie" (*CT* VII, 1049), is entirely dismissed by Prudence as "a gretter nombre of fooles" (*CT* VII, 1258) because the outcome of combat is ever at the whim of Fortune (*CT* VII, 1448).

Prudence does concede, only most reluctantly, that legal retribution and self-defense may rarely justify fighting. But there can be no enthusiasm for violent action:

> And therfore ye shul venge yow after the ordre of right; that is to seyn, by the lawe and noght by excesse ne by outrage. . . . And if ye seye that right axeth a man to defenden violence by violence and fightyng by fightyng, / certes ye seye sooth whan the defense is doon anon withouten intervalle or withouten tariyng or delay, / for to defenden hym and nat for to vengen hym. / And it behoveth that a man putte such attemerance in his defense / that men have no cause ne matiere to repreven hym that defendeth hym of excesse and outrage, for ellis it were agayn resoun. (*CT* VII, 1528-35)

Prudence likewise warns that war brings economic disaster; she recalls the Biblical rebukes of perilous adventurism. Vengeance is ultimately the Lord's, and so is ultimate victory (*CT* 1655–56). Prudence thus makes the "just war" theory all but unjustifiable in practice. Like many an obtuse husband, Melibee eventually sees: "I see wel, dame Prudence, that by youre faire wordes and by your resouns that ye han shewed me, that werre liketh yow no thyng" (*CT* VII, 1672). Unity and peace trump even knightly honor (*CT* VII, 1675-1681)—"mieulx vault perdre a honneur que gaignier a honte."[20] Pride must yield to peace. Most of Prudence's rhetoric is caressing, but she does eventually adopt a "semblant of wrathe" (*CT* VII, 1696); such a pacifist voice should sound neither effeminate nor naive (*CT* VII, 1082–88) nor individual. Whether as translator or author or tale-teller or narrative persona or rehearser, Chaucer thus assumes the semblance of both sincere and absolute truth, just another mouthpiece of peace.

Chaucer's Parson only extends Prudence's antiwar sentiments to address all forms of violent action as anger. Indeed, the Parson condemns both war and capital punishment as mere manifestations of *ira*. "Hasty" or sudden and unconsidered retaliation—that is, revenge as a reflex—is bad. But well-planned, reflective vengeance is far worse:

> Another Ire is ful wikked, that comth of felonie of herte avysed and cast biforn, with wikked wil to do vengeance, and therto his resoun consenteth; and soothly this is deedly synne. This Ire is so displeasaunt to God that it troubleth his hous and chaceth the Hooly Goost out of mannes soule, and wasteth and destroyeth the liknesse of God–that is to seyn, the vertu that is in mannes soule— / and put in hym the liknesse of the devel, and byneymeth the man from God, that is his rightful lord. /" (*CT* X, 542–45)

Even, most rarely, when the law or self-defense mandate manslaughter (a term that the Parson uses interchangeably with "homicide"),[21] there can be no eagerness for conflict and no romanticizing of bloodshed:

> But lat the justice be war that he do it rightfully, and that he do it nat for delit to spille blood but for kepynge of rightwisnesse. Another homycide is that doon for necessitee, as whan a man sleeth another in his defendaunt and that he nay noon otherwise escape from his owene deeth. / But certeinly if he may escape withouten slaughter of his adversarie, and sleeth hym, he dooth synne and he shal bere penance as for deedly synne. (*CT* X, 571–72)

None of this argumentation seems silly or medieval or irrelevant to Terry. Indeed, perilously Parson-like himself, Terry once imagined calling Tony Blair to confession: "Imagine the effect on voters, if the prime minister were to make public the guilt he must now be feeling.... And just suppose he starts blabbering about his remorse, as a Christian."[22] Whereas the Parson prays for "wit.../ To shewe you the wye" (*CT* X, 48–49), Terry's wittiness actually conveys less optimism.

For purely aesthetic reasons—primarily a preference among modern readers for clever irony—Chaucerians hesitate to hear Chaucer per se confirming the relentlessly straightforward statements of Prudence and the Parson. John Barnie, for example, does attribute Chaucer's muted quietism to his disillusionment with war, but finds all his personal convictions masked by fictional personae or commonplace expressions.[23] This is true to the extent that modern readers perceive the allegory of the "Melibee" and the homily of the Parson (itself another rather straightforward translation by Chaucer) as *tales*—that is, as the fictional expressions of individualized pilgrim-narrators. But neither the "Tale of Melibee" nor the "Parson's Tale" present one individual's point of view. For Chaucer, neither "his own" allegory nor the penitential he hands over to his

Parson echoes a singular voice. Both merely re-present the statements of irrefutable, so universal, so individually applicable truth, like the reiteration of "dona nobis pacem" with every "Agnus Dei." It is silly for Chaucerians to insist, since Chaucer never explicitly said "Thou shalt not kill Frenchmen," that he had not heard "Thou shalt not kill. Period!" In sum, Terry's critique of the military adventurism exemplified by Chaucer's portrait of the Knight seems utterly supported by the testimony of Chaucer's sincerest *Tales*. We do know what Chaucer thought about the Crusades and the Hundred Years' War and "Operation Iraqi Freedom"—in an absolutist sense.

Often—it seems as often as possible—Chaucer dismisses any positive descriptions of combat in his narratives. For martial excitement, "Rede Dares" (*T&C* V, 1771), not *Chaucer*. Chaucer frustrates Troilus's desire not only to regain Criseyde but also to have personal revenge against Diomede. When not reticent or dismissive, Chaucer's representation of combat (excepting the Knight's career) never even seems truly celebratory. On the contrary, Chaucer's description of the temple of red Mars "armypotente" (*CT* I, 1967–2040) is quite horrific. Chaucer's "derke imaginying" portrays a sacristy dedicated to murder and mayhem, not battle and tournament. Arcite—whose pseudonym "Philostrate" might as readily be translated "war-monger" as "laid low by love"—prays for victory to this "fierse Mars" (*CT* I, 2369), and gets it, and dies frustrated by a Saturnine twist. Saturn's own self-portrait hardly makes "vengeance and pleyn correccioun" (*CT* I, 2461) attractive. Terry seriously questioned the heroism of a ferocity that some readers see applauded throughout the "Knight's Tale" (e.g., *CT* I, 1640, 1656–57). The Knight does describe the contestants in Theseus's melee to be as "fierce as tigers cruel as hunters or dangerous as lions mad with hunger (*KT*, 2599–2635) but he makes no mention of their courage, skill or generosity to opponents."[24]

The adjective "fierce" did have both positive and negative applications in late fourteenth-century usage. It could describe a "proud, lofty, noble" person as well as someone "violent, cruel; wild, untamed."[25] Its primary denotation is negative, however: "Of formidably violent and intractable temper, like a wild beast; vehement and merciless in anger or hostility."[26] The English adjective "fierce" (< French *fier*) is, in fact, curiously derived from the far more bestial Latin adjective *ferus* rather than *ferox*.[27] "Fierce" could also be used in certain now-obsolete senses to mean "high-spirited, brave, valiant" or "proud, haughty."[28] (Regrettably, "wild, merciless haughtiness" itself has not yet become obsolete.) And Chaucer never uses "fierce" unequivocally as a compliment.[29] In the "Knight's Tale," perilous Arcite is described as madly fierce (I, 1598, 2676), but not Palamon. Mars is readily fierce (cf. "Anelida and Arcite," and *T&C* III, 22), as is "Outrage" (*CT* I, 2012). The "corage" of Turnus (*CT* I, 1945) is fierce, and so—absurdly—is that of Sir Thopas (*CT* VII, 1970).

So it seems, in truth, there was no need (besides courtesy) for Terry to have conceded that Chaucer's own convictions about war are now irretrievable because Chaucer's pacifism was in no way peculiarly his own. For once, Chaucer's theme is simple and straightforward and entirely translatable and not very entertaining as such. Most modern readers prefer the seemingly pointless fun of "Sir Thopas" instead of the lugubrious lecturing of Prudence. Some have even tried to read the "Melibee" as a joke, another act of self-parody on Chaucer's part because it seems such a conspicuous failure to tell "a lytel thyng in prose" (*CT* VII, 937). This supposedly comic premise alone does not sustain the proposed humor, however; the "moral tale vertuous" (*CT* VII, 940) seems in its entirety entirely tiring: "too slow moving to be funny."[30] Both Geoffrey Chaucer and Terry Jones have disappointed some fans by sounding rather too serious. We prefer Chaucer of the "Miller's Tale" and Jones of *The Holy Grail*.

Nevertheless, the same perspicacity reconciles a libertine indulgence of sheer silliness to a completely sincere renunciation of war—for both Jones and Chaucer. Indeed, Terry's direction of *Monty Python* episodes has several points of comparison with Chaucer's compilation of the *Tales*, including the dynamic flow of the whole show, the interplay of discrete scenes, the deliberate abandonment of segments, and a relentless irreverence. Jones's subsequent objections to the war in Iraq should be recognized as very Chaucerian too. Conversely, a profound dedication to pacifism motivates even Chaucer's most ludicrous, most Pythonesque tale, his "Rime of Sir Thopas."

Chaucer's likewise self-assigned tale of "Sir Thopas" is normally read as a brilliant but primarily formal parody.[31] Long ago, John M. Manly thought that Chaucer meant to mock the Flemish bourgeoisie.[32] And Donald R. Howard has suggested that Chaucer wished to debunk "gentilesse," or class pretentiousness—a jibe at the Squire, perhaps. Nevertheless, most readings of "Sir Thopas" foster an interpretation of Chaucer's tale as a burlesque of minstrelsy in general and of the genre of tail-rhyme romance in particular.[33] The absurd content of Chaucer's *Chanson de Thopas*—insofar as this tale has any plot at all—is now obvious, though it has not always been read as a deliberate travesty.[34] Indeed, Chaucer has his Host miss its humor. However, "most scholars have maintained, following the lead of Richard Hurd, who in 1911 claimed *Thopas* was 'Don Quixote in little,'"[35] that Chaucer's burlesque is both deliberate and hilarious. Flanders is hardly a far country (*CT* VII, 718). The birthright of "Sir" Thopas is hardly that of a "lord" (*CT* VII, 722). Though Thopas may be a poacher of privilege (like Alison of Bath), he prefers archery and wrestling to the more noble (and predatory) pastimes of hunting and hawking. He braves a forest that is "fair" (*CT* VII, 754) not "wod"; if he rides too far north and east, he may end up in the sea. His overly pricked horse bleeds like a wash rag (*CT* VII, 776). The fierce beasts that threaten gentle Thopas are not lions and tigers and boars, but deer and conies. Though the country of Fairye is so wild that neither woman nor child dare ride as his companion (*CT* VII, 806), Thopas himself is girly.[36] But his queer beauty only mirrors—in a fun-house fashion—the attractiveness of the Knight's son; like the Squire, Thopas seems a more Venereal rather than Martial cavalier, more like a Palamon than an Arcite.[37] The conspicuous silliness of Thopas's devotion to an unseen Elf-Queen[38] shatters the illusion of an Emily and garbles Amor's lexicon (*CT* VII, 772, 850, 895, 900). When an extremely unchivalric giant threatens to kill our hero's sissy horse (*CT* VII, 813), Thopas runs away like brave Sir Robin. When Thopas puts on his very pretty armor (*CT* VII, 845–87), it is a traditional scene made tired by time and silly by details.[39] Indeed, the humor of "Sir Thopas" now seems so obvious, the true wonder is that its absurdity could have ever been missed. Analogously, if Terry's reading of the Knight's portrait prevails, future readers may wonder how Chaucer's excessive praise in the "General Prologue" could have ever seemed other than parodic.

Chaucer's two self-assigned tales hardly comprise a well-balanced diptych. Each tale alone seems an oversimplified projection of only half of the poet's identity, his earnestness or game, his sweetness or usefulness. But it is the conjunction of these two simpleton tales that reflects Chaucer's sophisticated self-consciousness as a comic teacher.[40] Regarding Chaucer's attitude toward chivalry, V. J. Scattergood has suggested that there is little difference between the themes of Chaucer's self-assigned tales.[41] R. F. Yeager too affirms that reading "Sir Thopas" as intended "in some measure a criticism of the knightly class... offers a logical answer to the question of connection" to the "Melibee."[42] Whereas the "Miller's Tale" attacks that of the Knight's romance from the rear, Chaucer deploys the absurdity of "Sir Thopas" as a preemptive strike; it provides the shock and guffaw preceding the high seriousness (pace Matthew Arnold) of Prudence's pacifism.[43] As Christopher Crane has observed, "During the Middle Ages, laughing and learning—indeed, flatulence and faith—were not necessarily opposed."[44]

In short, Chaucer has much the same target in both "Thopas" and the "Melibee"—the foolishly irate arrogance of "gentle" *bellatores* (warriors). As a prelude to proposing the Christian ideal of pacifism, Chaucer's "Tale of Sir Thopas" inflates the inherent silliness of romantic chivalry until it becomes "far too silly," requiring the Host (rather than a Colonel of the "Anti-Silliness Patrol") to interrupt. The only plot alternative for the Host's intercession would have been for Chaucer's tale to explode after one more (wafer-thin) fit of rhyme. The silliness of "Sir Thopas" is, thus, disarming.

Although classical rhetoricians considered humor simply an attention-getting device, and although medieval rhetoricians neglected to theorize further about humor, Christopher Crane has proposed that for medieval audiences:

> laughter arises as they identify themselves with the clearly superior of the two incongruous elements [God and man].... Finally, medieval English comedy celebrates the superiority of God over man and the Christian hope for man's ultimate reunion with God.[45]

Mutatis mutandis, the comedy of both Terry Jones and Geoffrey Chaucer invites their mutual fans to identify with peace rather than war.

Such trenchant silliness achieves the comic equivalent of "objective distance"—the ability to step away from current predispositions—in other words, the playful equivalent of a sincere historian's wider perspective. This generic silliness allows for a more critically insightful perception of the *alterity* of contemporary absurdities. Knapp explains how: "The usual censors operating in everyday life are circumvented by comedy's bribe of pleasure, producing imaginative freedom."[46] Both classical and medieval rhetoricians recognized the persuasiveness of strategic silliness, especially when addressing a hostile audience. Chaucer's silliest tale thus cries peace too.

But Herry Bailey does not get Chaucer's joke. The Host, being sanguineous, sounds extremely rude, possibly irate because the end-rhymes of "Sir Thopas" have made his ears ache. But, after hearing the "Melibee," the Host confesses his own "perilous" nature; he admits (or brags) that he is especially virulent when prodded to take murderous vengeance "lik a wilde leoun, foolhardy" by his imprudent wife. This whole vignette of Herry and Goodelief (*CT* VII, 1189-1923) plays as a parody of some lady provoking her champion to combat. It is also one small step toward Canterbury and reluctant pacifism.

All in all, silly Chaucer should not be thought suddenly sympathetic toward pacifism in 1399—nor should we think that of Terry in 2001. Though the madly amusing 41 episodes of *Monty Python's Flying Circus* (first broadcast on the BBC [British Broadcasting Corporation] from 1969 to 1974) made little or no explicit reference to the double-decade war in Vietnam (1955–75)—other than that the country itself is, indeed, lots of miles away from Finland—Jones and company clearly opposed the always-earnest mentality that advocates every war. Like Chaucer's comedy, the humor of *Monty Python* has escaped ephemeral occasionality and so does not require so many footnotes as Aristophanes's *Lysistrata*. Unfortunately, such Chaucerian silliness also remains vitally amusing because its target, pernicious pomposity, regrettably remains always au courant.

It is possible to argue that Terry reading of Chaucer's Knight may, perhaps, be a bit too unforgiving. I myself hold some hope that this one Knight is presently *as a pilgrim* on the road to recovery. Chaucer does allow some glimpse of the penitent warrior; his "bismotered habergeon" (*CT* I, 76) may or may not be seen as a sign of humility.[47] Chaucer's parody of the investiture topos in "Sir Thopas" highlights the idea that a knight's romantic identity *as a knight* is largely a put-on. In sharp contrast, Chaucer's pilgrim-Knight has removed his armor. Subsequently, the Knight as narrator also seems to express a certain nervousness while reporting Arcite's funeral. Terry thinks this peculiarly prolonged *occupatio* (*CT* I, 2913-66) has "a ludicrous ring"[48] with the intent of mocking lavish, contemporary funerals. The splendid extravagance of the funeral fire is patently silly because "Arcite is coold" (*CT* I, 2815). Perhaps, however, the ultimate futility of Arcite's martial victory, the final wages of the character with whom the Knight should most closely identify, has now become all too apparent—even to the narrating Knight. The Knight later prevents a fight between the Pardoner and the Host, and this gesture itself functions as a redemptive moment: the mercenary becomes a peacekeeper with the invitation: "lat us laughe and pleye" (*CT* VI, 967).

Terry, however, sees the Knight as a static fraud whose interruption of the Monk is simply quite rude because the Monk's tale "'quits' the Knight's authoritarian and materialistic vision of the world... by asserting the right of the people to bring down tyrants" and so affirming a Boethian contempt for the folly of desiring "worldly power and glory."[49] Realistically speaking, therefore, embracing pacifism requires an otherworldly perspective (*contemptus mundi*) that sounds rather silly to most world leaders. Like everything else in our postlapsarian world, the word "silly" itself has unhappily fallen to mean little more than "associated with foolishness." Once upon a time, however, the Old English adjective *saelig* glossed *beatus* as well as *felix*, and so was used to translate "beati pacifici quoniam filii Dei vocabuntur" (*Matt.* 5: 9). In Middle English, *seli* retained a strong sense of "spiritually favored, blessed; holy, virtuous."[50] Chaucer used the adjective some 24 times in *The Canterbury Tales*. At one semantic extreme are his references to the dupability of John the Carpenter and Absolon. At the other extreme are his references to the patient sanctity of Custance and Griselda. It may sound profoundly silly to call either Moral Chaucer or Philosophical Jones "saintly" in this redeemed sense. Both, however, surely invite us to take a silly walk on the path to peace.

Notes

1. Terry Jones, *Chaucer's Knight: The Portrait of a Medieval Mercenary*, rev. ed. (London: Methuen, 1994 [1st Ed., 1980]).
2. Chaucer, *The Riverside Chaucer*, 3rd ed., gen. ed. Larry D. Benson (Boston: Houghton Mifflin, 1987).
3. Jones, *Chaucer's Knight*, xxi.
4. See R. F. Yeager, "'*Pax Poetica*': On the Pacifism of Chaucer and Gower," *Studies in the Age of Chaucer* 9 (1987): 97–121; Helen Barr, "Chaucer's Knight: A Christian Killer?" *English Review* 12.2 (2001): 2–3; Nigel Saul, "A Farewell to Arms? Criticism of Warfare in Late Fourteenth-Century England," *Fourteenth Century England* 2 (2002): 131–45; Kate L. Forhan, "Poets and Politics: Just War in Geoffrey Chaucer and Christine de Pizan," in *Ethics, Nationalism, and Just War: Medieval and Contemporary Perspectives,* ed. Henrik Syse and Gregory M. Reichberg (Washington, DC: Catholic University Press, 2007), 99–116.
5. See Yeager, "*Pax Poetica*," 98 n.7. See too John H. Pratt, *Chaucer and War* (Lanham, MD: University Press of America, 2000). Medieval elaborations of the Augustinian conception of "just war" are very nuanced in theory; in practice, however, every war has been thought "just" by all sides.
6. Terry Jones, et al., *Who Murdered Chaucer? A Medieval Mystery* (New York: Thomas Dunne Books/St. Martin's Press, 2003), 182.
7. *Who Murdered Chaucer?* [9]. Jones *et al.* add "For although Richard is often accused of vindictiveness, he actually seems to have shown unaccountably little interest in that favourite hobby of medieval rulers: 'cruel and unusual punishments'" (*Who Murdered Chaucer?* 142).
8. Jones *et al.* concede "Richard (or whoever was directing court policy at this time [the 1380s]) was determined to have peace, but his (or their) reasons were not necessarily idealistic or pacifist. Peace made economic sense" (*Who Murdered Chaucer?* 15). See Nigel Saul, *Richard II* (New Haven, CT: Yale University Press, 1997).
9. Terry Jones, *Terry Jones's War on the War on Terror* (New York: Nation Books, 2005), a collection of "little outbursts of indignation" (xix) originally published from December 28, 2001, to July 7, 2004, in *The Guardian*, *The Observer*, and *The Independent*, and in Anna Kiernan, ed., *Voices for Peace* (London: Scribner, 2001).
10. Jones, *Terry Jones's War*, 28.
11. The sang-froid of "How to Bomb and Save Money" (*Terry Jones's War*, 59–62) comes closest to Jonathan Swift's "Modest Proposal." Like Chaucer, however, Jones seems uncomfortable in the role of a sincere *vox clamantis* (voice of one crying) he never claims to be our new Isaiah or John the Baptist or John Gower. In "A Scared Prophet" (*Terry Jones's War*, 93–5), Jones rehearses his conversation (or internal dialogue) with a "Prognosticator of Political Poppycock," a "Brain of a Christmas Turkey without

the Stuffing," who is utterly scared by reading the future and thought, therefore, mad.

12. In his episode on "The Knight" for a 2004 BBC series, Jones describes the deromanticized reality of chivalry as little more than "learning how to kill people, making money and becoming famous" <http://www.youtube.com/watch?v=NhWFQtzM4r0&list=SL>. See Terry Jones and Alan Ereira, *Medieval Lives* (London: BBC, 2004).
13. Jones, *Terry Jones's War*, 3.
14. Jones, *Terry Jones's War*, 110.
15. Jones, *Terry Jones's War*, 49.
16. Yeager also looks to the "Retraction" for echoes of Chaucer's own addenda to his source for the *Melibee*, phrases that show Chaucer personally affirming Prudence's pacifism ("*Pax Poetica*," 120).
17. Jones, *Chaucer's Knight,* 145. Here, Jones is specifically taking a stand against Muriel Bowden who—initially in a post-World War II milieu—denied that Chaucer was so explicitly a pacifist as Gower on the assumption that Chaucer enjoyed the "excitement" of combat (Jones, *Chaucer's Knight,* 280, n. 20, citing Muriel Bowden, *A Commentary on the "General Prologue" to The Canterbury Tales*, 2nd ed. [London: Macmillan, 1969]; 1st ed., 1948).
18. Peggy A. Knapp, *Chaucerian Aesthetics* (New York: Palgrave Macmillan, 2008), 146.
19. For the philosophical and legal implications of assigning culpability, see Yeager, "*Pax Poetica*," 101–03.
20. Chaucer's translation somewhat softens this saying (*CT* VII 1842–45); see William R. Askins, "The Tale of Melibee" in Robert M. Correale and Mary Hamel, ed., *Sources and Analogues of The Canterbury Tales*, Vol. I (Cambridge, UK: D. S. Brewer, 2002), 404 [321–408].
21. *Ira* as defined in the "Parson's Tale" is remarkably expansive. Its manifestations include swearing, desecration of the host, faith in prognosticators, lying, flattery, backbiting, chiding, scorning, wicked counsel, and idle words, including "japery" and "janglerie"—that is, the very act of tale-telling "for they maken folk to laughe at hire japerie as folk doon at the gawdes of an ape" (*CT*, X, 651). Accidental killings, infanticide or abortion, and even unintentional but lust-motivated miscarriages, are designated manslaughter.
22. Jones, *Terry Jones's War*, 102.
23. John Barnie, *War in Medieval Society: Social Values and the Hundred Years' War, 1377–99* (London: Weidenfield and Nicolson, 1974), 131.
24. Jones, *Chaucer's Knight*, 153.
25. See Hans Kurath and S. M. Kuhn, eds. *Middle English Dictionary* (Ann Arbor: University of Michigan Press, 1952–) [*MED*] s.v. "fers," adj., defs 1(a) and 2(a).
26. See John A. Simpson and Edmund S.C. Weiner, eds., *The Oxford English Dictionary*, 2nd ed. (Oxford: Clarendon Press, 1989) [*OED*] s.v. "fierce," adj., def 1. "Of formidably violent and intractable temper, like a wild beast; vehement and merciless in anger or hostility. Less emphatic, and less associated with the notion of wanton cruelty, than ferocious adj., which was never used, like this word, in a good sense."
27. See Charlton T. Lewis and Charles Short, *A Latin Dictionary Founded on* [Ethan A.] *Andrews' Edition of Freund's Latin Dictionary* (Oxford: Clarendon Press, 1993 [1879]) *s.vv.* "ferus" and "ferox." The adjective "ferox" is defined first "In a good sense" to mean "courageously, valorously, bravely," but also "In a bad sense" to mean "fiercely, savagely, insolently." However, the adjective"ferus," meaning "wild, untamed," applies literally to animals and plants and tropologically to "wild, rude, uncultivated; savage, barbarous, fierce, cruel" humans.

28. See *OED* s.v. "fierce," adj., def. †3. "proud, haughty. Obs. Cf. French *fier*."
29. In *A Concordance to the Complete Works of Geoffrey Chaucer and to the Romaunt of the Rose* (Washington, DC: Carnegie Institution of Washington, 1927), John S. P. Tatlock cites 16 uses of "fierce" as an adjective and once as an adverb, "fiersly." For Chaucer, *fierceness* is associated with a lion (*CT* VIII, 198), and Cyclops (*Boece* Bk IV, m. 7, 20), and Achilles (*T&C* V, 1806), and "dangerous" Narcissus (*Romaunt*, 1482), and Daunger itself (*Romaunt*, 3372), and Love's assault troops (*Romaunt*, 7340) and proud Troilus when initially a scorner of Love (*T&C* I, 225), and the Flood restrained by Love (*T&C*, III 1760).
30. Knapp, *Chaucerian Aesthetics*, 147.
31. Alan T. Gaylord, "Chaucer's Dainty 'Doggerel': The 'Elvyssh' Prosody of *Sir Thopas*," *Studies in the Age of Chaucer*, I (1979): 83–104.
32. John M. Manly, "Sir Thopas, a Satire" in *Essays and Studies by Members of the English Association*, Vol. 113 (Oxford, 1928), 52–73. See too William Askins, "All That Glisters: The Historical Setting of the Tale of Sir Thopas" in *Reading Medieval Culture: Essays in Honor of Robert W. Hanning,* ed. Robert M. Stein and Sandra Pierson Prior (Notre Dame, IN: University of Notre Dame Press, 2005), 271–89.
33. See Caroline Strong, "Sir Thopas and Sir Guy," *Modern Language Notes* 23 (1908): 73–77 and 102–06; Laura Hibbard Loomis, "Chaucer and the Auchinleck MS: 'Thopas' and 'Guy of Warwick,'" in [no ed.], *Essays and Studies in Honor of Carleton Brown* (New York: New York University Press, 1940), 111–28; and Laura Hibbard Loomis, "Sir Thopas" in *Sources and Analogues of Chaucer's Canterbury Tales*, ed. William F. Bryan and Germaine Dempster (Chicago: University of Chicago Press, 1941), 486–559; John Finlayson, "Definitions of Middle English Romance: Part I," *Chaucer Review* 15 (1980): 44–62; John A. Burrow, "'Listeth, Lordes': Sir Thopas, 712 and 833," *Notes and Queries* 15 (1968): 326–27, and "Chaucer's Sir Thopas and La Prise de Nuevile," in *English Satire and the Satiric Tradition*, ed. Claude Rawson and Alvin Kernan (Oxford: Blackwell, 1984), 44–55; Nancy Mason Bradbury, "Chaucerian Minstrelsy: 'Sir Thopas,' *Troilus and Criseyde* and English Metrical Romance," in *Tradition and Transformation in Medieval Romance,* ed. Rosalind Field (Cambridge, UK: D. S. Brewer, 1999), 115–24.
34. The comic excess of "Sir Thopas" was evidently not evident to all postmedieval readers. See Joseph A. Dane, "Genre and Authority: The Eighteenth-Century Creation of Chaucerian Burlesque," *Huntington Library Quarterly* 48 (1985): 345–62; John A. Burrow, "Sir Thopas in the Sixteenth Century," in *Middle English Studies Presented to Norman Davis in Honour of His Seventieth Birthday*, ed. Douglas Gray and Eric G. Stanley (Oxford: Clarendon; 1983), 69–91; and Judith H. Anderson, "'A Gentle Knight Was Pricking on the Plaine': The Chaucerian Connection," *English Literary Renaissance* 15 (1985): 166–74. However, manuscript evidence suggests that Chaucer's drasty rhyming was evident to his earliest readers; see Judith Tschann, "The Layout of 'Sir Thopas' in the Ellesmere, Hengwrt, Cambridge Dd.4.24, and Cambridge Gg.4.27 Manuscripts," *Chaucer Review* 20 (1985): 1–13, and Rhiannon Purdie, "The Implications of Manuscript Layout in Chaucer's 'Tale of Sir Thopas," *Forum* 41 (2005): 263–74.
35. Joanne A. Charbonneau, "Sir Thopas" in *Sources and Analogues of The Canterbury Tales*, Vol. II, ed, Robert M. Correale and Mary Hamel (Cambridge, UK: D. S. Brewer, 2005), 649-50 [649–714].
36. John A. Burrow, "'Worly Under Wede' in Sir Thopas," *Chaucer Review* 3 (1969): 170–173.

37. The military future of the Squire promises to be even worse than the Knight's past because the insouciant son has already participated in a "chyvachie" within Christendom "In hope to stonden in his lady grace" (*CT* I, 85–88).
38. Paying obvious homage to *Monty Python*, Mary Hamel detailed the parodic parallels of Thopas's *amour de loin* (love at a distance) to the Prioress's (dangerously violent) Marian devotion in "'And Now for Something Different': 'The Relationship between the 'Prioress's Tale' and the 'Rime of Sir Thopas,'" *Chaucer Review* 14 (1980): 251–59.
39. See Derek Brewer, "The Arming of the Warrior in European Literature and in Chaucer" in Edward Vasta and Zacharias P. Thundy, ed., *Chaucerian Problems and Perspectives: Essays Presented to Paul E. Beichner, C. S. C.* (Notre Dame, IN: University of Notre Dame Press, 1979), 221–43;T. L. Burton, "Chaucer's 'Tale of Sir Thopas,'" *Explicator* 40 (1982): 4; Mark DiCicco, "The Arming of Sir Thopas Reconsidered.," *Notes and Queries* 244 (1999): 14–16.
40. See Lee Patterson, "'What Man Artow?' Authorial Self-Definition in 'The Tale of Sir Thopas" and "The Tale of Melibee," *Studies in the Age of Chaucer* 11 (1989): 117–75, and Ruth Waterhouse, "'Sweete Wordes' of Nonsense: The Deconstruction of the Moral 'Melibee,'" *Chaucer Review* 23 (1989): 53–63.
41. V. J. Scattergood, "Chaucer and the French War: 'Sir Thopas' and 'Melibee,'" in Glyn S. Burgess et al., ed., *Court and Poet* (Liverpool: Cairns, 1981), 287–96.
42. Yeager, "*Pax Poetica*," 116.
43. Dana M. Symons compares and contrasts the "Miller's Tale" and "Sir Thopas" in "Comic Pleasures: Chaucer and Popular Romance," in *Medieval English Comedy*, ed. Sandra M. Hordis and Paul Hardwick (Turnhout: Brepols, 2007), 83–109.
44. Christopher E. Crane,"Superior Incongruity: Derisive and Sympathetic Comedy in Middle English Drama and Homiletic Exempla" in *Medieval English Comedy*, ed. Hordis and Hardwick, [31]–60 at 68.
45. Crane, "Superiority," 59.
46. Knapp, *Chaucerian Aesthetics*, 129.
47. Bowden, *Commentary*, 50, and Charles Moorman, *A Knyght There Was: The Evolution of the Knight in Literature* (Lexington: University of Kentucky Press, 1967), 82. Jones, however, attributes the Knight's apparent poverty to the fortunes of war (*Chaucer's Knight*, 27).
48. Jones, *Chaucer's Knight*, 161.
49. Jones, *Chaucer's Knight*, 223. See too Jones's "The Monk's Tale" for a Colloquium in *Studies in the Age of Chaucer* 22 (2000): 387–97.
50. See *MED* s.v. "seli," adj., def. 1 (a).

CHAPTER 14

LEGS AND THE MAN: THE HISTORY OF A MEDIEVAL MOTIF

Richard Firth Green

The nineteenth-century valetudinarian Thomas Hood is little read today, but he made one significant contribution to the tradition of English letters; he effectively put an end to a venerable literary motif—that of the bellicose amputee.[1] Hood's poem "Faithless Nellie Gray," published in 1826,[2] opens in dramatic style:

> Ben Battle was a soldier bold,
> And used to war's alarms;
> But a cannon-ball took off his legs,
> So he laid down his arms!

Earlier champions had treated such setbacks as mere scratches, but Ben is clearly cast from lesser mettle. Things go from bad to worse for our noble hero who returns to his sweetheart Nellie Gray, only to find his affections no longer returned:

> Said she, "I loved a soldier once,
> For he was blithe and brave;
> But I will never have a man
> With both legs in the grave!"

Such female inconstancy proves too much for Ben who, having resolved to hang himself, perishes in a welter of bad puns. It would not be quite true to say that the tradition of heroic amputation comes to an end with Hood's verses for it continues much diminished down to our own day—in John Crowe Ransom's "Captain Carpenter," for example:

But God's deep curses follow after those
That shore him of his goodly nose and ears
His legs and strong arms at the two elbows
And eyes that had not watered seventy years.[3]

And in the folklore of twentieth-century British cinema, of course, it holds an honored position. But for serious literature, at least, "Ben Battle" effectively puts a stop to this honorable motif. In this, as in other things, the pasty-faced Victorians were unable to match the feats of their intrepid forebears.

The *locus classicus* for this motif is the sixteenth-century broadside, *Chevy Chase* or *The Hunting of the Cheviot,*[4] a ballad that inexplicably made Sir Philip Sidney's heart beat faster, aroused professional envy in Ben Jonson, and reminded Joseph Addison of the *Aeneid. Chevy Chase* is a somewhat fanciful account of a minor battle fought on August 19, 1388, at Otterburn on the Scots border between James, Earl of Douglas, and Henry "Hotspur" Percy, son of the Earl of Northumberland. The ballad has Percy killing Douglas and being himself killed in turn by one of Douglas's knights (Sir Hugh Montgomery), with the English finally emerging as victors, though in reality, Douglas was killed, Percy captured, and the Scots won the field.[5] After a description of the deaths of the two leaders, we are given a list of the fallen on each side, and conspicuous among the English dead is a knight (otherwise unknown to history) called Witherington:

For Witherington needs must I wayle
    as one in dolefull dumpes,
For when his leggs were smitten of,
    he fought vpon his stumpes.[6]

The rhyme *dumpes / stumpes* is perhaps not the most happily chosen, and when the minstrel Richard Sheale adapted a copy of *Chevy Chase* for his commonplace book around 1550 he very sensibly changed it :

For Wetharryngton my harte was wo,
    that euer he slayne shulde be;
For when both his leggis wear hewyne in to,
    yet he knyled and fought on his kny.[7]

Unfortunately, whatever improvements Sheale managed to make to the rhyme scheme must be set against his rather obvious metrical deficiencies. A somewhat later border conflict, the Battle of Ancrum Moor (1545),[8] provides us with another instance of the motif, though one that is almost certainly derived from *Chevy Chase.* An eighteenth-century minister of Melrose reported the former existence of a gravestone on the battle site with the inscription:

Fair maiden Lilliard lies under this stane
Little was her stature but great her fame.
On the English lads she laid many thumps,
And when her legs were off, she fought upon her stumps [9]

Thumps seems only a marginally better rhyme for *stumps* in the circumstances. Unfortunately, the minister's suggestion that a nearby ridge called Lilliards Edge was named after this formidable figure proves to be a folk etymology, since the name existed centuries before the battle, and the whole incident must reluctantly be consigned to local folklore. However, one indubitably historical sixteenth-century Scots hero, William Meldrum (d. ca. 1550), was said to have fought on his stumps. According to Sir David Lindsay, Meldrum was ambushed in 1517 by enemies who disapproved of his liaison with a lady called the widow of Gleneagles, but held out manfully until three men,

> come behind him cowartlie,
> And hackit on his hochis and theis
> Till that he fell vpon his kneis.
> Ȝit quhen his schankis wer schorne in sunder,
> Upon his kneis he wrocht greit wounder,
> Sweipand his sword round about,
> Not haifand of the deith na dout.[10]

Shortly after this he faints from loss of blood and his enemies leave him for dead, but remarkably he is nursed back to health and survives a further three decades. Lindsay does not say anything about prostheses, though it is clear that this episode effectively put an end to the squire's swashbuckling days.

Where did the sixteenth-century ballad makers find this motif? There are three possible routes. The first, and least likely, leads from the classical world. Addison points out many Virgilian echoes in *Chevy Chase*, but Witherington's amputation is not among them. However, Seneca the Younger does offer a possible source. The author of *Thyestes* clearly relished a good dismemberment (though admittedly not in this case on the battlefield), but in one of his essays, *De Providentia*, the stoic writes: "Unblemished happiness tolerates no shock, but where there has been an incessant striving against misfortunes, one becomes hardened to injury and surrenders to no affliction; even if he should fall, he fights on his knees" (*Non fert ullum ictum illaesa felicitas, at ubi assidua fuit cum incommodis suis rixa, callum per iniurias ducit, nec ulli malo cedit; sed etiamsi ceciderit, de genu pugnat*).[11] Granted, the fallen warrior here is not specifically said to be an amputee, but in one of his *Moral Letters* (64), Seneca supplies more detail: illustrating the point that it is a greater accomplishment to triumph over difficulties that to restrain one's joy, he writes of "the man who, cut through the hams, got to his knees and kept hold of his weapons" (*qui succisis poplitibus in genua se excepit nec arma dimisit*).[12] An early nineteenth-century editor of Seneca claims that this often happened in gladiatorial contests and cites surviving classical statues as evidence (*in certamine gladiatorum hoc saepe accidisse... et statuae hodieque existantes docent*).[13] He seems, however, to have been misled by the tendency of ancient statuary (the Venus de Milo, for instance) to shed limbs rather more readily than most of its animate models. In any event, this single, and far from unambiguous, Senecan instance seems an improbable source for the motif in sixteenth-century English broadsides.

A second possible source is the medieval popular romance. Combatants who fight on after losing limbs are pretty common in the later Middle English romances, but they present one major difficulty for our investigation—almost all the ones I have been able to find are villains rather than heroes. The giant Agolafre in *Sir Ferumbras* is typical. Charlemagne, hastening to relieve his besieged knights, Roland, Oliver, and Guy, must cross a bridge before the city of Mantrible that is defended by this "voule gome" described at length as "hudous" and "lodly," and wielding a huge axe.[14] After a prolonged battle with Charlemagne's knights, he is finally felled by Rayner, who, abandoning his sword, picks up an iron bar, "& gerd hym þer-Wyþ on þe molde, / þat ys legges gunne to volde, / & bursten euene atwo."[15] Charles's forces push on to the gates of the city itself, only to become aware of a noise behind them:

What yt was he wolde y-se,
& þyderward he gan take,
Þan was Agolafre noȝt ded þe ȝet,
Ac on his knes he hadde him set,
For his legges nere noȝt sonde,
& had wyþ ys axe a-slawe
An hep of frenschemen þat leye arawe,
Afforn hym on þe gronde.[16]

The emperor himself is forced to go back and dispatch him, and Agolafre's body is finally dumped unceremoniously into the river.[17] Another giant, Marras in *Sir Eglamour of Artois,* survives even longer—though in his case it is his right arm not his leg that is amputated:

Nerhand þe geant gan he ga:
His righte arme he strake hym fra
Fast by þe schuldir bane.
The geant wyth þe toþir hande
Alle þe daye he stode feghtande
Till þe sonne to ryste es gane.
Now may he no lengare dry:
He es so febill, wittirly,
Þat lyfe es lefte hym nane.[18]

Like the nightmarish monsters in some modern horror films, these medieval giants just keep coming back for more.

Less a sign of unyielding courage, then, the stubborn refusal of such figures to lie down and die ("þan was Agolafre noȝt ded þe ȝet") is more a mark of their sinister supernatural power. Greysteel, the opponent of both the brothers-in-arms Eger and Grime, exemplifies this quality. Not specifically said to be a giant (though beside his great mount, Eger's horse seems a mere foal),[19] Greysteel mutilates his victims by cutting off their little fingers, and when he finally meets his match, he dies very hard indeed. Grime, an expert swordsman, cuts through his leg with a backhanded blow:

With an arkward stroke ffull slee
He hitt Sir Gray-steele on the knee;
If he were neuer soe wight of hand
On the one foote he might but stand.[20]

Thus incapacitated, Greysteel fights on for another 56 lines. Grime, his back to the wall, stabs Greysteel through the body, but all this does is make him "boiling mad":

With an arkeward stroke full sore
Through liuer and longs Gray-steele he bore.
Gray-steele went walling woode.[21]

Grime is cracked over the head with a sword so fiercely that "his eares brushed out of blood" (1075), and only after "they fought together fell and sore / The space of a mile and somthing more" (1079–80), does he finally wrestle Greysteel to the ground and stab him through the heart.[22] In an act of retributive mutilation, Grime then cuts off his hand to take back as a trophy.[23] There is more than a hint here that the source of Greysteel's potency is sexual—"his speare that was both greate and long"—,[24] and this is made quite explicit in another instance of such gigantic endurance, the death of the Giant of St. Michael's Mount in the *Alliterative Morte Arture*. Here the giant's obscene lust is stressed,[25] and the amputation that Arthur inflicts on him involves physical emasculation:

He follows in fersly and fastenes a dint
High up on the haunch with his hard wepen
That he heled the sword half a foot large;
The hot blood of the hulk unto the hilt runnes;
Even into the in-mete the giaunt he hittes
Just to the genitals and jagged them in sonder![26]

Despite having had his genitals "jagged" and a sword buried in his innards ("in-mete"), this giant too fights on gamely: he narrowly fails to smash Arthur with his club and then resorts to wrestling with him:

On the crest of the crag he caught him in armes,
And encloses him clenly to crushen his ribbes;
So hard holdes he that hende that ner his herte bristes![27] (1133–35)

At the end of this distinctly unchivalric mode of combat—"Whilom Arthur over and other while under"—, the king manages, like Grime, to stab his opponent to death; he has the corpse decapitated and then takes the giant's club away with him as a trophy.[28] It seems that a taste for such bellicose amputees may have increased as the Middle Ages wore on: in Laȝamon's much earlier account of Arthur's battle with the Giant of Saint Michael's Mount, while there is indeed an amputation (Arthur cuts off one of the giant's legs—"and þat þih him of-smat"), it merely results in the giant doing the decent thing and surrendering.[29]

Another indication that the motif does not have the same heroic connotations in the Middle English romance that it does in *Chevy Chase* is the tendency for it to be associated with puns reminiscent of Thomas Hood. In the Percy Folio Manuscript version of *Sir Aldingar,* for instance, a steward who has falsely accused his queen is challenged to a judicial duel by a child who seems to be no more than four years old.[30] God, however, favors the innocent, so that when "the litle one . . . stroke the first stroke att Aldingar, / He stroke away his leggs by his knee."[31] The challenger's next speech underscores the point that Sir Aldingar is literally being cut down to size:

Sayes, Stand vp, stand vp, thou false traitor,
And fight vpon thy feete;
For and thou thriue as thou begins,
Of a height wee shalbe meete.[32]

Aldingar, however, declines this opportunity to be undercut further and calls for a priest, effectively putting an end to the contest. In *Syr Tryamowre,* where the hero fights a giant called Burlond, the pun is rather cleverer. In the course of the fight, Burlond slips and falls, and Tryamour "smote Burlond of be the kneys, / And hewe hys leggys all in pecys, / Ryght as he schulde ryse."[33] The triumphant Tryamour then puns cleverly on the words *size* and *assize* ("trial"):

"A lytull lower, syr," seyde hee,
"And let vs small go wyth thee,
Now are we bothe at oon assyse!"[34]

Burlond, however (made of sterner stuff than Aldingar), manages to carry on the fight a while longer:

Burlonde on hys stompus stode,
Wyte hym not yf he were wode,
Then faght he wondur faste![35]

In *Octavian*, the young, untried knight Florian takes on a giant outside the walls of Paris, and manages to remove an arm—"To the gyaunt he smote so sore / That hys ryghte arme flye of thore."[36] This, of course, only makes the giant worse, and we are told, "To the gyaunt there he stode: / There was no chyldys play."[37] The pun on the word *child,* "a boy or girl (usually to the age of puberty)," and "a youth of noble birth, esp. an aspirant to knighthood," scarcely needs explaining.[38] Finally, the author of *Sir Percyvell of Gales* indulges a similar taste for punning: the hero cuts off a giant's hand and foot, but his adversary, true to type, continues the fight until first his other hand, and finally his head are removed:

He strikes off the hande als clene
Als ther hadde never none bene.

(That other was awaye).
Sythen his hede gan he off hafe.

The narrator then adds, "He was ane unhende knave / A geant berde so to schafe,"[39] punning on the root meaning of *hende* ("courteous") as "handy": Percyvell, in other words, is "discourteous" to have shaved the giant's beard in this way, but only ironically "unhandy," having cut off his opponent's hands.

As these last examples show, legs are not the only limbs to be lost under such circumstances. Another amputated hand occurs in *Sir Tristrem* when the hero fights a giant called Urgan: "And of the geauntes hand / Tristrem smot that day."[40] Somewhat bizarrely, Tristrem then retrieves the hand and runs off with it:

Tristrem trad in the blod
And fond the hond that was his.
Away Sir Tristrem yode.[41]

The giant, having returned home for some hand medication—"Salves hadde he brought"—, catches up with him on a bridge, and they proceed to fight to the death (the giant's, of course).[42] The sequence is slightly clearer in the French original where it is implied that Urgan has the uncanny ability to reattach severed limbs. The only non-bipedal instance of this motif I know of is a dragon in *Sir Eglamour of Artois:* this gallant beast loses half his tail but continues to fight on, using the stump itself as a weapon:

Sir Eglamour, als I ȝow saye,
Halfe his tayle he smate awaye:
Þat fende bygan to ȝelle;
And with þe stompe þat hym was leuede
He strak þe knyght in þe heuede,
A wykkid wonde and a felle.[43]

The *palme d'or,* however, must go to one of Alexander's opponents in *Kyng Alisaunder*—Nygosar, king of Nineva. Fighting two knights called Philotas and Clitoun, Nygosar loses his sword arm to Philotas—"He smoot to hym and dude hym harme, / For of he carf his riȝth arme"—,[44] and then, after warding off a blow from Clitoun's axe (which remains stuck in his shield), he loses his shield arm too: "Philot hym ȝaf anoþere dabbe, / Þat [in] þe shelde þe gysarme / Bilaft þoo, and ek þe arme."[45] Armless, but undeterred, Nygosar then proceeds to butt two knights out of their saddles before Philotas finally dispatches him:

Negussar so from hym sterte.
Wiþ two kniȝttes ȝut he mette,
Myd his heued and myd his cors,
Ȝut he feld hem of her hors,
Ac Philotas was at his regge,

And smoot hym wiþ þe suerdes egge,
Þat þe heued fel a-doun.[46]

With the exception of Aldingar, and possibly Greysteel, this is the only example I know of in Middle English romance where the bellicose amputee is not a giant, and the only one where he is not clearly a villain. There is, however, one genre where fighting on one's stumps is an almost routine battlefield experience, and one that was clearly admired—the Norse Saga.

Let us begin with the climactic scene in the *Saga of Gunnlaug Serpent-Tongue*—the final confrontation between Gunnlaug and Hrafn, his bitter rival for the hand of a woman called Helga. It is worth quoting in full:

> At last [Gunnlaug] struck a great blow at Hrafn with the sword, and cut his leg off.
>
> Even then Hrafn did not altogether fall, but drew back to a tree stump, and propped the stump of his limb on it.
>
> "Now you're unfit for battle," said Gunnlaug then, "and I'll no longer fight with you, a maimed man."
>
> "It's true that things have gone heavily against me," answered Hrafn. "Yet I'd still do well enough if I could get something to drink."
>
> "No trickery, then," replied Gunnlaug, "if I bring you water in my helmet."
>
> "I shan't trick you," answered Hrafn.
>
> Then Gunnlaug went to a stream, fetched some water in his helmet, and brought it to him. But as Hrafn reached out for it with his left hand, he struck at Gunnlaug's head with the sword in his right hand, and it made a terrible wound.
>
> "Now you've been foully treacherous to me," said Gunnlaug, "and it was unmanly to act so when I trusted you."
>
> "That's true," said Hrafn, "but this was the reason for it, that I grudge you the embrace of Helga the Fair.'
>
> At that they fought again hotly, but it ended at last with Gunnlaug overcoming Hrafn, and Hrafn lost his life there.[47]

Gunnlaug, too, later dies of his wounds and, this being a saga, Hrafn's trickery only gives the family an excuse to prolong the feud, but there is no suggestion that Hrafn's last stand is seen as anything other than heroic.

This point is made even more clearly in the description of a battle between the Norwegian hero Hrolf and Eirik, king of Russia, in *Hrolf the Tramper's Saga*. Eirik's following is liberally sprinkled with dwarves, trolls, berserkers, and other such uncanny folk, but when one of them fights on after losing a leg, the saga writer is still happy to give him his due: "[Hrolf] sprang to his feet quickly and struck at Har, slicing through his leg at the knee.... Har had got up onto one leg and began hitting out with the club at anything near him. He killed eleven men before Stefnir dealt him his deathblow, and there, with all honour, his life came to an end."[48] A similar accolade is given to one of Hrolf's followers who refuses to let the loss of both hands hold him back: "Solvi rushed up to one of the enemy and, smashing his head into the man's chest, burst his ribs and killed him. Another man he first knocked flat, then bit out his throat, but afterwards they ran Solvi through with a spear; and so he died like a hero."[49] Admittedly, *Hrolf the Tramper's Saga* is a legendary romance that delights in tall tales—at one point earlier on, Hrolf himself had had both feet cut off but managed to get them reattached by a clever dwarf—[50] yet the motif turns up in perfectly sober family sagas as well. In *Gold Thorir's Saga,* for example, a man called Ketilbjorn is the victim of a quite routine family feud: "[Ketilbjorn] jumped back over the river, and in that instant Steinolf arrived and swung at his foot, taking it off at the ankle. Ketilbjorn did not die from the blow but turned toward them, killing two men before he fell."[51] Gnup in *The Saga of the People of Reykjadal and of Killer Skuta* suffers a similar fate: "Both of them had a shield and they fought for a long time. At length Vemund took off Gnup's lower leg so he stood on his knees and wanted to fight on, but Vemund said they would stop for the time."[52] Comparison of the wording of this passage with the passing remark in *The Saga of Án Bow-Bender,* that "one man fought on his knees" shows that there too we have an instance of the bellicose amputee.[53] Finally, the motif is given a comic twist (well, comic as the saga writers construe comedy) in *Grettir's Saga,* where the hero's grandfather, Onund Treefoot, having lost a leg in an earlier battle, settles his stump on a log of wood in preparation for a shipboard confrontation with some Vikings; one Viking takes a swing at him but only manages to get his sword stuck in the log, whereupon Onund promptly dispatches him.[54] Prominent in the Icelandic sagas, this heroic version of the bellicose amputee is probably part of a wider Germanic tradition (it occurs, for instance, at the end of the *Waltharius,* where Hagen cuts the hero's right hand off, and Walther calmly switches sword hands and goes on fighting),[55] but at all events the mostly likely route by which it reached *Chevy Chase* would seem to have been via an Old Norse tale.

Long before Thomas Hood, the gloss was beginning to wear off Witherington's heroic end. In the first part of Samuel Butler's mock-epic *Hudibras* (ca. 1660), the puritanical hero tries to break up a bear baiting and is promptly set upon by the mob:

> Enrag'd thus some in the rear
> Attacked him, and some ev'ry where;
> Till down he fell, yet falling fought,
> And, being down, still laid about;
> As *Widdrington,* in doleful Dumps,
> Is said to light upon his stumps.[56]

So neat is Butler's enjambment here that we may forgive him his misconstrual of *Chevy Chase* (where it is the poet, not Witherington, who falls in *dolefull dumpes*), but in any case the phrase "is said" speaks volumes. From 1716 to 1734, a man called Nathaniel Mist published a Tory response to papers like *The Spectator* called *The Weekly Journal,* and among other things he pilloried Addison's admiration for *Chevy Chase* by printing a mock-scholarly critique of the poem. Witherington's exploits draw his particular scorn: "Now I adjure you, tell me, oh *Physicians, Chirurgeons,* and ye maimed Inhabitants of a Thousand Hospitals, is it probable, said I, is it possible for a Man being mowed two Foot shorter, to run away upon his opened Veins, splintring Bones, and unstrung Sinews? No, nor could you with an Ox-goad force him to move a Step."[57] Mist had served in the Royal Navy, and no doubt he knew what he was talking about, but if anyone could have emulated Witherington in real life, it was surely Henry William Paget, Earl of Uxbridge (later Marquis of Anglesey). Lord Uxbridge, commander of the British cavalry at the Battle of Waterloo (1815), brings us to the last leg of our quest. Unfortunately, Uxbridge was struck in the right leg by grapeshot at the very end of the battle ("during the last attack, almost by the last shot"),[58] otherwise his lordship might well have gone on fighting (he had already had at least eight horses shot from under him that day). As it was, he is said to have remarked to the Duke of Wellington, "By God, sir, I've lost my leg!" (to which his commander responded laconically, "By God, sir, so you have!"),[59] after which he returned to headquarters to write a letter to his wife and discuss the battle with his staff. When the surgeons eventually removed his shattered leg, "he never moved or complained: no one even held his hand. He said once perfectly calmly that he thought the instrument was not very sharp." Only eight days later he was up and about, and he wore a patented prosthesis (known as the "Anglesey leg") for the rest of his long life (he died aged 85). But this is not quite the end of the story. The amputated leg was buried in the garden of the house where the operation took place, and the spot was marked with a commemorative plaque: "Ci est enterré la Jambe de l'illustre et vaillant Comte Uxbridge ...." (Here is buried the leg of the illustrious and valiant Earl of Uxbridge). For many years this shrine was regularly visited by English tourists to Belgium (among them Uxbridge himself, who "found the very table on which he had lain for the amputation of the limb, and...had dinner spread upon it").[60] In 1821, not long after its interment, the leg inspired an epitaph by the minor English novelist Thomas Gaspey, very much in the style of his younger contemporary Thomas Hood. Here is one of its slightly less excruciating puns:

A leg and foot to speak more plain
Lie here, of one commanding;
Who, though his wits he might retain,
Lost half his understanding.

And there, in all decency, we should probably let it rest.[61]

Notes

1. Stith Thompson, *Motif-index of Folk-Literature: A Classification of Narrative Elements in Folktales, Ballads, Myths, Fables, Mediaeval Romances, Exempla, Fabliaux, Jest-books, and Local Legends*, 6 vols. (Bloomington: Indiana University Press, 1955–58), 5:S162.1.
2. Thomas Hood, *Whims and Oddities in Prose and Verse* (London: Lupton Relfe, 1826), 139–42.

3. John Crowe Ransom, *Selected Poems*, rev. ed. (New York: Alfred A. Knopf, 1964), 43.
4. *The English and Scottish Popular Ballads*, ed. F. J. Child, 5 vols. (Boston: Houghton Mifflin, 1882–1898), 3: 303–15 (no. 162).
5. See Anthony Goodman and Anthony Tuck, eds., *War and Border Societies in the Middle Ages* (London and New York : Routledge, 1992).
6. Child, *ESPB*, 3:313 (162B, st. 50).
7. Child, *ESPB*, 3:310 (162A, st. 54). The relationship between the two versions of *Chevy Chase* has caused much debate; my assumption here is based on Andrew Taylor's "Bodleian MS Ashmole 48 and the Ballad Press," *English Manuscript Studies, 1100–1700* 14 (2008): 219–43.
8. For a description of the battle, see George MacDonald Fraser, *The Steel Bonnets: The Story of the Anglo-Scottish Border Reivers* (London: Barrie and Jenkins, 1971), 257–58.
9. [Andrew Milne], *A Description of the Parish of Melrose* (Kelso: James Palmer, [1743]), 21.
10. Sir David Lindsay, *Squyre Meldrum*, ed. James Kinsley (London and Edinburgh: Thomas Nelson, 1959), 58 (ll. 1346–52).
11. Seneca, *Ad Lucilium Epistulae Morales*, ed. Richard M. Gummere, 3 vols. (Cambridge, MA: Harvard University Press, 1967–1972), 2: 10 (my translation).
12. Seneca, *Moral Essays*, ed. William Basore, 3 vols. (Cambridge, MA: Harvard University Press, 1958), 32 [my translation]; Basore translates, "holds himself up on his knees," but *in genua se excepit* is modelled on *se in pedes excipere*, "to get to one's feet" (Lewis and Short, s.v. *excipio*, II.A.1).
13. Marie Nicolas Bouillet, ed., *L. Annaei Senecae omnia opera*, 6 vols. (Paris: Lemaire, 1827–31), 2: 12.
14. *Sir Ferumbras*, ed. Sidney J. Herrtage, EETS, e.s., 34 (London: Trübner, 1879), 137–38 (ll. 4427–46).
15. *Ferumbras*, p. 142 (ll. 4566–68).
16. *Ferumbras*, p.143 (ll. 4601–06).
17. *Ferumbras*, p.143 (ll. 4616–18).
18. *Sir Eglamour of Artois*, ed. Frances E. Richardson, EETS, o.s., 256 (London: Oxford University Press, 1965), 42 (ll. 689–97).
19. *Eger and Grime* in *Middle English Metrical Romances*, ed. Walter Hoyt French and Charles Brockway Hale, 2 vols. bound as one (1930; New York: Russell & Russell, 1964), 676 (l. 120).
20. *Eger and Grime*, 704 (ll. 1029–32).
21. *Eger and Grime*, 704–05 (ll. 1055–57).
22. *Eger and Grime*, 705 (ll. 1066–88).
23. *Eger and Grime*, 706 (ll. 1106–08).
24. *Eger and Grime*, 676 (l. 121).
25. *Alliterative Morte Arthure* in *King Arthur's Death: The Middle English Stanzaic Morte Arthur and Alliterative Morte Arthure*, ed. Larry D. Benson, rev. Edward E. Foster (Kalamazoo, MI: Medieval Institute Publications, 1994), 163 (ll. 1029–32).
26. *Alliterative Morte*, 166 (ll. 1118–23).
27. *Alliterative Morte*, 166 (ll. 1133–35).
28. *Alliterative Morte*, 168 (l. 1191).
29. Laȝamon, *Brut*, ed. G.L. Brook and R. F. Leslie, 2 vols., EETS, o.s., 250 & 277 (Oxford: Oxford University Press, 1963 and 1978): 2: 680 and 682 (ll. 12987–13030).

30. Child, *ESPB*, 2: 45 (59A, st. 28).
31. Child, *ESPB*, 2: 46 (59A, sts. 43–44).
32. Child, *ESPB*, 2: 46 (st. 45).
33. *Syr Tryamowre: A Metrical Romance*, ed. A. J. Erdman Schmidt (Utrecht: Broekhoff, 1937), 83 (ll. 1552–54).
34. *Tryamowre*, 83 (ll. 1555–57).
35. *Tryamowre*, 83 (ll. 1561–63).
36. *Octavian*, in *Six Middle English Romances*, ed. Maldwyn Mills (London: J. M. Dent, 1973), 101 (ll. 946–47).
37. *Octavian*, 101 (ll. 965–66).
38. *Middle English Dictionary*, s.v. *chīld*, 2a.a, and 6a.
39. *Sir Percyvell of Gales*, in *Ywain and Gawain, Sir Percyvell of Gales, and The Anturs of Arther*, ed. Maldwyn Mills (London, J. M.Dent, 1992), 155 (ll. 2090–95).
40. *Sir Tristrem*, in *Lancelot of the Laik and Sir Tristrem*, ed. Alan Lupack (Kalamazoo, MI: Medieval Institute Publications, 1994), 222 (ll. 2340–41).
41. *Tristrem*, 223 (ll. 2359–61).
42. *Tristrem*, 223–24 (ll. (2365–96).
43. *Eglamour*, 52 (ll. 738–44).
44. *Kyng Alisaunder*, ed. G.V. Smithers, 2 vols., EETS, o.s., 227 and 237 (London: Oxford University Press, 1952–57), 1: 129 (ll. 2289–90).
45. *Alisaunder*, 129–31 (ll. 2302–04).
46. *Alisaunder*, 131 (ll. 2305–11).
47. *Gunlaugs saga Ormstungu; The Saga of Gunnlaug Serpent-Tongue*, ed. P. G. Foote, trans. R. Quirk (London: Thomas Nelson, 1957), 36 (ch.12).
48. *Göngu-Hrolfs Saga*, trans. Hermann Pálsson and Paul Edwards (Edinburgh: Canongate, 1980), 100 (ch. 31).
49. *Göngu-Hrolfs Saga*, 101 (ch. 31).
50. *Göngu-Hrolfs Saga*, 82–85 (ch. 25).
51. *Gull-þoris Saga*, in *The Complete Sagas of Icelanders*, gen. ed. Viðar Hreinsson, 5 vols. (Reykjavík: Leifur Eiríksson, 1997), 3: 356 (ch. 18).
52. *Reykdæla Saga og Víga-Skútu*, in *The Complete Sagas of Icelanders*, gen. ed. Viðar Hreinsson, 5 vols. (Reykjavík: Leifur Eiríksson, 1997), 4: 275 (ch. 13).
53. *Áns Saga Bogsveigis*, trans. Shaun E. D. Hughes, in *Medieval Outlaws: Ten Tales in Modern English*, ed. Thomas H. Ohlgren (Stroud: Sutton, 1998), 211, (ch, 6); cf. "stóð hann á knjám og bauð enn bardagann," with "einn maðr barðist á knjánum."
54. *Grettir's Saga*, trans. Denton Fox and Hermann Pálsson (Toronto: University of Toronto Press, 1974), 8 (ch.4).
55. *Waltharius and Ruodlieb*, ed. and trans. Dennis M. Krantz (New York: Garland Publishing, 1984), 66–67 (ll. 1381–92).
56. Samuel Butler, *Hudibras*, ed. John Wilders (Oxford: Clarendon Press, 1967), 64 (Pt.1, Canto 3, ll. 91–95).
57. A. Sandford Limouze, "Burlesque Criticism of the Ballad in *Mist's Weekly Journal*," *Studies in Philology* 47 (1950): 614 [607–18].
58. [Henry Paget, [7]th] Marquess of Anglesey, *One-Leg: The Life and Letters of Henry William Paget, First Marquess of Anglesey* (London: Jonathan Cape, 1961), 149 (except where noted, the account of the amputation and the later history of the leg are taken from this source, pp. 148–52).
59. For a slightly different version see Charles C.F. Greville, *The Greville Memoirs (Second Part)*, 3 vols. (London: Longmans, Green, 1885), 1: 135.

60. Philip Henry [Stanhope], 5th Earl Stanhope *Notes of Conversations with the Duke of Wellington, 1831–1851* (New York: Longmans, Green, 1888), 183–84.
61. Hunting for examples of a motif, particularly one as bizarre as this, quickly turns into a communal quest. I should like particularly to thank my colleagues Andrew Hudgins, Drew Jones, Lisa Kiser, and Kevin Richards for supplying me with especially fine specimens.

CHAPTER 15

CHAUCER, LANGLAND, AND THE HUNDRED YEARS' WAR

David Wallace

It was not the inspiring vision of Chivalry taking to the field that his new eyes saw, but Destruction on the move.

Terry Jones, *The Knight and the Squire*

The first three pilgrim portraits of Geoffrey Chaucer's *Canterbury Tales* summarize English fighting capabilities during the Hundred Years' War, the conflict between England and France and allied powers that dragged on from 1337 to 1453. Chaucer's Knight carries himself with the meekness of a virgin (GP 1.69). His thoughts are not of Calais and Laon, but of fabulously distant locales at or beyond the far edge of Christendom: Alexandria, Morocco, al-Andalus, Turkey, Lithuania, Russia. The air of dreamy exoticism enveloping him seems to protect Chaucer's Knight from association with the bloody, sharp end of war: except that, as Terry Jones has definitively shown, those distant locales witnessed some of the greatest bloodbaths of fourteenth-century Europe.[1] Chaucer's "verray, parfit, gentil knight" (GP 1.72) might thus be imagined as the English military machine's super ego: if so, his Yeoman (GP 1.101-117) provides its id. At first glance, the Yeoman riding with the Knight and his son, the Squire, seems no more than a woodsman, a protector of the lordly domain. But although he knows woodcraft (GP 1.110), he is armed to the teeth. He carries a sword and a small shield ("bokeler"), "a gay dagere," sharpened like a spear, and "a gay bracer" (GP 1.111-14). The *bracer* is an arm guard, worn by an archer; fully five lines attest to his proficiency in preparing and firing arrows from his "mighty bow" (GP 1.108). The great English chivalric pretense of the Hundred Years' War is that key battles were won through English knightly valor and the will of God; the hidden truth is that they were chiefly won by the longbow, and by the yeomen who stringed and fired them. Agincourt, the most celebrated of all victories, owed little to chivalric prowess and almost everything to longbowmen; England's most distinguished historian of warfare has termed it a technological slaughter.[2]

The third member of Chaucer's Hundred Years' War troika is the Squire. His pilgrim description begins and ends with reference to his father, the Knight (GP 1.79, 100); his chief function is to uphold and perpetuate his father's name. He has curly hair, carves meat, plays the flute and wears clothes with flowery embroidery. He is a knight with training wheels, doing just enough to impress the ladies:

> And he hadde been somtyme in chyvachie
> In Flaundres, in Artoys, and Pycardie,
> And born hym wel, as of so litel space,
> In hope to stonden in his lady grace.
>
> (GP 1. 85-8)

All this seems innocuous: but there is blood and misery here, too. It will be noted that Chaucer's Squire has engaged not in *chivalrie,* but in "chyvachie," *chevauchée;* more on this crucial term anon. And he has campaigned in lands immediately abutting the recently conquered, recently Englished town of Calais, and its marches. Jones has written of this form of warfare, too: not in his scholarly monograph on Chaucer's Knight, but rather (and most appropriately) in his books for children about a young English squire.[3] This young man, too, seeks *aventure* by heading for an English troop muster at Calais, bent on *chevauchée.* But as our epigraph indicates, the scales of romance fall from his eyes as he sees how English armies actually fight in France.

Calais held out for almost a year before falling to Edward III in 1347; Edward was incensed by the delay, since it had enabled the Scots to invade England from the north. Once the famous scene of the burghers exiting Calais has been acted out, however, Edward, according to chronicler Jean Froissart, announces a new diktat: all men, women, and children must leave the town, "car je voeil la ville repeupler de purs Englès": in Lord Berner's translation, "for I wolde repeople agayne the towne with pure Englysshmen."[4] What can *purs Englès* possibly mean here? The notion of purity might refer to those born on English soil: but the sons of Edward III (and the sons of his sons) were often born on campaign, at places like Antwerp, Ghent, and Bordeaux, and his queen, heavily pregnant, is about to give birth again. Can Edward be invoking an inchoate sense of English nationhood? Perhaps, although the only use of the term *nation* in this narrative is applied to Calais itself: "ceuls de la nation de Calais," Edward declares, "on fera morir, car bien il l'ont deserve."[5] *Nation* here evokes, according to standard medieval usage, close bonds of kinship and family rather than our own more abstract sense of political entity. Whatever the case, Edward is determined to "repeople" Calais, and on getting back to London (Froissart and Berners tell us), he sets the wheels in motion: 36 prosperous English burghers are sent out with their wives and children, plus more than 400 others of lower estate.[6] Numbers increase daily, we are told, "for the kynge graunted there suche lyberties and franchysses, that men were gladde to go and dwelle there."[7] And Froissart is right: within days of entering Calais, Edward had proclamations read in the north and east of England promising liberties and commercial privileges to would-be Calais residents. All chronicles agree that most citizens were forced to leave; traces of refugee Calaisien communities have been found as far afield as Carcassone.[8]

The English victory at Poitiers in 1356, featuring the capture of the French King John, and the treaties of Brétigny and Calais in 1360 effectively transformed English presence in those parts from de facto occupation to consolidated juridical suzerainty. Much that R. R. Davies and other historians have to say about English infiltration of Scotland, Ireland, and (especially, in this period) Wales bears fruitful comparison with the experience of Calais and its hinterland, stretching out into Flanders, Artois, and Picardy. Calais and its marches thus join the list of "border communities" studied as constituent parts of the British Isles; the kinds of literature favored and produced here might be read as "history on the edge," joining and refining long-established traditions of British "border writing."[9]

Calais first appeared in the twelfth century as a little fishing village in the territory of Marck; by the early thirteenth century it was designated subject to the Duke of Burgundy, Count of Artois. The aging Guillaume de Machaut, pressed into military service to defend the sacred and royal city of Reims against the English in the winter of 1359–60, contemptuously refuses to name this two-bit village full of foreigners in his *Fonteinne amoureuse.*[10] Following the 1360 treaty of Brétigny, John, Duke of Berry (third son of King John of France and Machaut's patron) has been forced to accept exile in England in order to release his captive father. As they approach Calais, with the young duke resigned to captivity, Machaut evokes the strange spectacle of this English enclave on French soil:

En cest estat nous chevauchames
Tant que sus la mer nous trouvames
En une ville petiote,
De barat pleinne et de riote.
Or la nommez se vous volez,
Car il y a moult d'avolez.

(2807–12)

In this way we rode along
Until we found ourselves near the sea
In a very small village,
A place full of uproar and license.
Now you name the town if you like,
For the town is full of strangers.

In 1363, however, the Wool Staple was transferred to Calais, thus enhancing its reputation for "uproar and license" while decisively transforming its international significance. Calais became what Bruges and Anvers once had been: the principal seat of English merchants in continental Europe. And it thereby attracted a great deal of capital to itself. The large military garrison needed to be fed and provided for: most provisions were imported from England, and the cost of maintaining the garrison was always high. In 1371–72, a particularly quiet period, no fewer than 1,112 regular men of arms were in English service in the Calaisien enclave.[11] A mint was established in the town—still remembered in John Skelton's time—which led to complex, mutually dependent arrangements between mercantile entrepreneurs, soldiery, townspeople, town authorities, and customs officials.[12]

Chaucer (England's most famous customs official) was intensively involved with Calais in all phases of his many careers as soldier, squire, letter carrier, and controller of customs; he did business at Calais, worked with merchants from Calais, and set off from Calais to fight or negotiate. Yet he mentions Calais not at all. Perhaps for Chaucer, as for some of us, Calais was equivalent to Heathrow (Terminal Three): familiar, but not loved. While neglecting to mention Calais, however, Chaucer does map its space, as it were, in silhouette. His youthful Squire's war service, we have noted, was performed "in chyvachie / In Flaundres, in Artoys, and Pycardie" (*GP* 1.85-86): that is, in those regions immediately surrounding Calais and its marches. Chaucer's recurring historical presence at Calais suggests knowledge of the costs of war comparable to that confined by his *Knight's Tale* to the temple of Mars: burning ships bobbing on the sea, stables aflame, bodies in the woods, slit throats, crushed torsos, and much demand for the skills of "the barbour, and the bocher, and the smyth."[13] "Costs" here is the operative word, for *chevauchées* of the kind essayed by the young squire Chaucer before his capture and ransoming early in 1360 were primarily a tactic of economic warfare:[14] "the defenders' means of production (crops, fishponds, mills, barns) were among the prime targets for destruction," Christopher T. Allmand writes, "so that their economic capability was seriously undermined."[15] The typical radius of destruction for an English army on the march was about twenty kilometers (five leagues) either side of the main advancing body.[16] Later in 1360, Chaucer carried letters from Calais to Westminster, thus playing a minor role in the process that led to Brétigny, the treaty that decisively enlarged English holdings in France. He was back in Calais again for ceremonies attending formal ratification of the Treaty of Brétigny on October 24, 1360.

As the ink dried at Calais, thousands of English soldiers were suddenly found to be surplus to requirements; they were not shipped home, but cut loose. Landless and penniless, these English troops (along with Welsh, Irish, Scots, French, Gascon, Breton, and Flemish fighting men) ravaged their way southwards through France, looking for fresh employ. Large numbers of them, including Sir John Hawkwood (a close relative of Terry Jones's Sir John Hawkley) favored papal Avignon with a visit.[17] Having received plenary indulgences and large amounts of money from Innocent VI, they moved on to fresh wars in the Rhineland, Spain, and especially Italy (where they, and their descendants, would destabilize political life for the next two hundred years). Chaucer was to meet up with these English men of war, now *condottieri*, during his two trips to Italy in the 1370s. In 1372–73 he went on the king's "secret business" to Genoa, and then Florence, perhaps seeking finance for the procurement of seagoing vessels for Edward III, soon to launch a new invasion of France. And in 1378 he traveled to Lombardy with Sir Edward de Berkeley, briefed to negotiate English war needs with Milanese despot Bernabò Visconti, and with "our dear and faithful John Hawkwood."[18]

Italy might have been spared much unpleasantness had Edward III heeded Langland's Lady Meed: for a king *should* give "mede to men" who serve him, including "aliens."[19] A and B texts of *Piers Plowman* address events before and after the 1360 treaties of Brétigny and Calais as matters of considerable topical urgency.[20] On the Sunday after Easter, 1360, an English army approaching ten thousand stood arrayed for battle outside Paris. On the following day, April 13, there was a terrifying (and historically well-attested) hailstorm. When it seemed, as Froissart tells it, that the end of the world was nigh, Conscience (according to Langland's Meed) "crope into a cabane for cold of thi nayles" (crept into a military tent to warm your fingernails).[21] Interpreting such natural signs as divine command, the royal conscience was moved to the treaty table: and all, Meed says, through fear of a downpour (and dreddest to be ded for a dym cloude).[22]

Meed immediately goes on to condemn "pilours" who rob poor men of their brass utensils and hurry off to Calais to sell them (hence opening the possibility of buying passage back to England):

> Withouten pite, pilour, povere men thou robbedest
> And bere hire [their] bras at thi bak to Caleis to selle.
>
> (B 3.195-6)

Meed, *au contraire*, stays in the field to protect her lord ("I lafte with my lord his lyf for to save," B 3.197).[23] And she, Meed, cheers up these men in the field, slapping their backs, giving them hope, making them dance. "Hadde I ben marchal of his men," Meed continues,

> He sholde have be lord of that lond in lengthe and in brede.
>
> (B 3.201-3)

Meed is not making a precocious demand here for a standing, regularly paid army. She is attempting, rather, suggestively to nudge the *chevauchée* system into the nexus of gift-giving and payment that oils civil society and that she goes on to describe at considerable length. It behooves a king wishing to hold down a kingdom, Meed tells Conscience, to make gifts "to aliens and to alle men" (B 3.211); emperors and earls, after all, have "yomen" to do their bidding (B 3.214; "yemen," C 270). "Attendants" is underpowered as a gloss for "yomen" here; "yeomen" at least keeps in view the yeomen bowmen and archers of lower ranks who proved most efficacious at fighting.[24]

Meed, in a neat reversal, actually berates Conscience for being excessively money-minded: for "a litel silver" (some three million écus), Edward was persuaded "to leven his lordship" (B 3.207), that is—such was the provision of the treaty of Brétigny—renounce his claim to the French throne.[25] Such renunciation was retracted long before Langland undertook the last major revision of his poem.[26] It is fascinating to note, however, that while C-text drops some of the topical 1360s references, it actually expands meditation on the rights and constraints governing kings in disposing of conquered territory. For that which has been won through common enterprise, "thorw a comun helpe," involving the efforts of fighting men under royal direction, cannot just be sold off for profit; the humblest soldier in the retinue expects some reward "Whereby he may as a man for eueremore lyue aftur" (C 3.245, 250). The conquering king is naturally obliged "to help out *all* his host," or to allow them to keep their winnings, spending them however they like:

> To helpe heyliche alle his oste or elles graunte
> Al that his men may wynne, do ther-mid here beste.
>
> (C 3.252-3)

Such appeal to the rights of common soldiers as in some sense co-inheritors of conquered land brings us far from Froissart, but does suggest that Langland's imagining of debates in and around Westminster—of which Froissart formed part through the 1360s—opens out to Calais. In each of these intense and pressurized localities, Calais and Westminster, we find commercial and royal calculation, profiteering, merchandizing, war mongering, merchant business, and the minting of coin (in the Tower as at Calais); such a heady mixture suggests a whiff of the sexual opportunism memorably embodied by the Dutch wife of Calais, Mrs. Richard Fery, and by Lady Meed.[27] There is no evidence that Langland ever went to Calais, but (I am suggesting) he had a feel for what went on there. At the very least, we know (from all three versions of his poem) that he treated news from the French front, as purveyed by "mynstrales and messagers," with extreme skepticism. "Mynstrales and messagers," it is said, once met up with Lyere "And [with]helden hym half an yeer and ellevene days" (B 2.229: here I accept Schmidt's emendation of "helden" to "withhelden," since the term *withholden* can imply the joining of a household and the taking of a livery).[28] Half a year and 11 days, J. A. W. Bennett argued in 1943, measures the exact duration of Edward III's French campaign, from his landing on October 28, 1359, to the signing at Brétigny on May 8, 1360.[29]

The debate over the ethics and opportunities of continental warfare staged between Conscience and Meed is remarkable, especially when the king's kinswoman seems to be winning the debate ("By Crist," the king exclaims in all versions, "Mede is worthi the maistrie to have!").[30] Conscience's counterarguments, at least on the subject of how returning soldiers might be reintegrated into the rural economy, seem so hopelessly utopian—so unhistorical—that the king, one concludes, is right: "Alle that beren baselard," Conscience says,

> ...brood swerd or launce,
> Ax outher hachet or any wepen ellis, *or hatchet other weapon*
> Shal be demed to the deeth but if he do it smythye *unless he have it hammered*

Into sikel or to sithe, to shaar or to kultour— *scythe ploughshare cultour*
Conflabunt gladios suos in vomeres . . .
Ech man to pleye with a plow, pykoise or spade, *pickaxe*
Spynne, or spredde donge . . .

(B 3.305-10)[31]

I conclude by considering, very briefly, how these scenes of happy dung spreading by reformed soldiers might play in the 1360s, addressing *Piers Plowman* as the greatest English poem of the countryside, the rural economy, and (perhaps) of pardoning.

In the autumn of 1360 and in 1361, according to the Calendars of Patent Rolls, over 260 charters of pardon were granted to men who had served in the wars; more than three-quarters of these were murderers. In 1370, Sir Robert Knolles (himself the recipient of a pardon for past felonies) marched out from Calais with 55 named criminals, all granted royal pardons: 43 were murderers and the rest rapists and thieves. In the pas-de-Calais, as in Vietnam, there were complex systems of tunnels that allowed the peasantry, quite literally, to sink below the earth. A stairway leading from one church tower in the pas-de-Calais, for example, leads to a vast complex of some three hundred subterranean cells. Use of such underground complexes increased after 1356; fires were sometimes set to smoke out troglodyte peasantry.[32] The effect of all this is vividly recorded by poet Eustache Deschamps, himself twice burned out by English and Burgundian *chevauchées*. Deschamps in fact insists that his very name bears the impress of this endless Anglo-French conflict: "Now I am burned," he says in ballade 835, "so my name is changed: / from now on I'll have the name Burned-out[33] of the Fields":

Or sui tous ars, s'est mon nom remué:
J'aray desor a nom Brulé des Champs.

(835.7–8)

Elsewhere, in a remarkable poem, Deschamps writes from the viewpoint of peasants, men and women, who are gathering in the harvest some 40 miles south of Calais. Fat Margot swears by her distaff that there will never be peace until the English give up Calais (344.10). Berthelot is so frightened that he hardly dares get out of bed in the morning, "pour les Anglois qui nous sont destruisans" (on account of the English, who go about destroying us). Such powerful lines (and Deschamps has plenty more to offer) prompt us to ponder further on Langland's attitude toward those aspects of continental campaigns ignored by contemporary historians: "of the men at work, ransacking farm buildings and other stores," says H. J. Hewitt, "no chronicler gives any description nor have I found any pictorial illustration."[34] Even if, as a poet finely attuned to the delicate mechanisms of the rural economy, Langland knew or cared little about English ruination of French and Flemish countrysides, he certainly knew of the wide-ranging royal agents raising money and supplies in the English countryside, and of the demobilized troops perpetuating the habits of violence and pillage they had lived by on active service beyond the Calais pale.[35]

In 1347, the Commons had petitioned that no charters of pardon be given to murderers or notorious criminals, arguing that such charters actually increased incidences of murder, robbery, and rape. In 1353, it was pointed out that many pardoned criminals make quick trips overseas, return quickly home, and then carry on as before.[36] And in 1360, as things got dramatically worse, a rapid memo was sent from Westminster to Justices of the Peace (potentially spelling bad news for anyone given to Langlandian-like wanderings). The justices are

> to inform themselves and to inquire touching all those who have been plunderers and robbers beyond the sea and are now returned and go wandering ("et vont vagantz") and will not work as they were used to do before this time, and to take and arrest all those whom they are able to find by indictment or by suspicion, and to put them in prison.... to the end that the people be not by such rioters troubled or damaged, nor the peace broken, nor merchants or others passing on the high roads of the realm disturbed or put in fear of the peril which may arise from such evil-doers.[37]

Descendants of the English mercenaries who headed south after 1360 were still effectively holding Italy to ransom at the time of Machiavelli. Figures such as Sir John Hawkwood, who helped massacre five thousand people at Cesena in 1377, assumed legendary status.[38] The impact of those returning to the rural locales of Langlandian England from the French campaigns has been less well studied; Langland's poem might form part of this project. As for Chaucer: the Hundred Years' War infiltrates his *Canterbury Tales* with his very first trio of portraits. His "yemanly" Yeoman, with his well-dressed arrows and "myghty bowe" (*GP* 1.106–08), is given no tale to tell. The young, fictional Squire of the *General Prologue* has proved himself on the same terrain as the young, historical Chaucer; an older Chaucer was to revisit this former self and these French locales from a witness stand in 1386.[39] These same territories were well known to many of the poets whom Chaucer most admired, and from whom he learned most: Jean Froissart, Eustache Deschamps, Oton de Grandson, and above all Guillaume de Machaut. They, like Chaucer, served the Anglo-French conflict while counting its costs, its perennial fomenting of violence within peaceful locales: "Destruction on the move."[40]

Notes

1. See *Chaucer's Knight: The Portrait of a Medieval Mercenary*, rev. ed. (London: Methuen, 1985).
2. See John Keegan, *The Face of Battle* (London: Jonathan Cape, 1976). Archers are celebrated in a broadside entitled "Agincourt, or the English Bowman's Glory," but this dates from 1665, a much later phase of the complex afterlife of the 1415 battle. See Anne Curry, *The Battle of Agincourt: Sources and Interpretations* (Woodbridge, Suff.: The Boydell Press, 2000), 302–04. In his *History of the Battle of Agincourt* (London: Johnson and Co., 1832), Sir Harris Nicholas, K. H , includes extensive listing of retinues, 331–404.

3. Terry Jones, *The Knight and the Squire* (London: Puffin, 1999); *The Lady and the Squire* (London: Puffin, 2002).
4. Jean Froissart, *Chroniques. Livre I (première partie, 1325–1350) et Livre II. Rédaction du manuscrit de New York Pierpont Morgan Library M. 804,* ed. Peter F. Ainsworth and George T. Diller (Paris: Le Livre de Poche, 2001), 646; *The Chronicle of Froissart. Translated out of the French by Sir John Bourchier, Lord Berners*, ed. William Paton Ker, 6 vols. (London: David Nutt, 1901–03), I, 332.
5. Jean Froissart, *Chroniques. Début du premier livre. Édition du manuscrit de Rome Reg. lat. 869*, ed. George T. Diller (Geneva: Droz, 1972), 840; see further Peter Ainsworth, *Jean Froissart and the Fabric of History: Truth, Myth, and Fiction in the Chroniques* (Oxford: Clarendon Press, 1990), 298.
6. Froissart, *Chroniques. Livre I (première partie, 1325–1350) et Livre II. Rédaction du manuscrit de New York Pierpont Morgan Library M. 804,* 649.
7. *The Chronicle of Froissart*, I, 333; Froissart, *Chroniques. Livre I (première partie, 1325–1350) et Livre II. Rédaction du manuscrit de New York Pierpont Morgan Library M. 804,* 649.
8. See John Le Patourel, "L'occupation anglaise de Calais au XIVe siècle," *Revue du Nord*, 33 (1951): 228–41 (228-30); Dorothy Greaves, "Calais under Edward III," in *Finance and Trade under Edward III* (Manchester: Manchester University Press, 1918): 313–50 (314–15, 337); Henri Platelle and Denis Clauzel, *Histoire des Provinces Françaises du Nord, II: Des Principautés à l'Empire de Charles-Quint* (Dunkirk: Westhoek-Editions, 1989), 150–54.
9. Michelle Warren, *History on the Edge: Excalibur and the Borders of Britain* (Minneapolis: University of Minnesota Press, 2000), 3. For brief but cogent comparison of events in Calais with impositions of English communities in Wales and southern Scotland, see Christopher T. Allmand, *Lancastrian Normandy: The History of a Medieval Occupation* (Oxford: Clarendon Press, 1983), 50–51.
10. Text and translation follow Machaut, *The Fountain of Love (La fonteinne amoureuse)*, ed. and trans. R. Barton Palmer (New York: Garland, 1993); on the *Fonteinne Amoureuse* as "a poem of war," see Ardis Butterfield, *The Familiar Enemy: Chaucer, Language, and Nation in the Hundred Years War* (Oxford: Oxford University Press, 2009), 276–77.
11. Platelle and Clauzel, *Histoire*, 151. The head count includes Calais and its satellite towns: some 320 men at Ardres and others at places such as Guines, Marck, and Sangatte. Such numbers "font de Calais un phénomène presque unique de concentration des troupes en Europe" (151).
12. See the remarkable collection of essays in *Les champs relationnels en Europe du Nord et du Nord-Ouest des origines à la fin du Premier Empire. 1er Colloque Européen de Calais*, ed. Stéphane Curveiller (Calais: la Municipalité de Calais, 1994). In "The Bowge of Court," Ryote swears [by] "The arms of Calyce, I have no coyne nor crosse!" (John Skelton, *Poems*, ed. Robert S. Kinsman [Oxford: Clarendon Press, 1969], line 398). Fifteenth-century English coins, Kinsman notes, were often marked with a cross on the reverse side (142). Countenance swears "By the arms of Calais" in *Magnificence*, line 675 (ed. Paula Neuss [Baltimore: Johns Hopkins University Press, 1980]).
13. "the barber, and the butcher, and the smith" (1.2025). The third of these "forges sharp weapons on his anvil" (1.2026); the first deals with the injurious effects of such weapons, and it is best not to ponder what "the bocher" does. See further, for the full panoramic vision of war and its misadventures, *Knight's Tale*, 1.1995–2050.

14. Somewhere, he recalled in 1386, in the vicinity of Réthel: see Martin M. Crow and Clair C. Olson, ed., *Chaucer Life-Records* (Oxford: Clarendon Press, 1966), 23–28; Butterfield, *Familiar Enemy*, 173–74.
15. Christopher Allmand, *The Hundred Years War: England and France at War c. 1300–c. 1450* (Cambridge: Cambridge University Press, 1988), 56; Crow and Olson, *Chaucer Life-Records*, 27. See further the excellent account of Nicholas Wright, *Knights and Peasants: The Hundred Years War in the French Countryside* (Woodbridge, Suff.: Boydell Press, 1998), 68–69.
16. See Allmand, *Hundred Years War*, 69; Herbert Hewitt, *The Organization of War Under Edward III, 1338–1362* (Manchester, UK: Manchester University Press, 1966).
17. See Jones, *The Knight and the Squire*; Jones, "The Image of Chaucer's Knight," in *Speaking Images: Essays in Honor of V. A. Kolve*, ed. Robert F. Yeager and Charlotte C. Morse (Asheville, NC: Pegasus Press, 2001), 205–36 (219–33 and plates 5–6, 14–15); David Wallace, *Chaucerian Polity: Absolutist Lineages and Associational Forms in England and Italy* (Stanford, CA: Stanford University Press, 1997), 33–40.
18. See Crow and Olson, *Chaucer Life-Records*, 32–40, 54; Wallace, *Chaucerian Polity*, 13.
19. William Langland, *The Vision of Piers Plowman: A Critical Edition of the B-Text based on Trinity College Cambridge MS B.15.17*, ed. A. V. C. Schmidt, second ed. (London: Everyman, 1995), B 3.210–11. I here prefer the reading "mede to men" to Schmidt's "[men mede]"; the former reading appears in all B MSS. For texts of A and C, I follow *Piers Plowman: The A Version. Will's Vision of Piers Plowman and Do-Well. An Edition in the Form of Trinity College Cambridge MS R.3.14 Corrected from Other Manuscripts, With Variant Readings*, ed. George Kane, rev. ed. (London: The Athlone Press, 1988); William Langland, *Piers Plowman: A New Annotated Edition of the C-text*, ed. Derek Pearsall (Exeter: University of Exeter Press, 2008).
20. W. M. Ormrod, "The Domestic Response to the Hundred Years War," in *Arms, Armies and Fortifications in the Hundred Years War*, ed. Anne Curry and Michael Hughes (Woodbridge, Suff.: Boydell Press, 1984), 83–101 (86).
21. See Froissart, *Chronycle*, tran. Berners, II, 59 ("such a tempest of thonder, lyghtnyng, rayne, and hayle, in the kinges oost, that it semed that the worlde shulde have ended," a translation very close to the wording of French sources); *Piers Plowman* B 3.191; see also A 3.178. By all contemporary accounts (Jonathan Sumption cites seven), this was a spectacular storm: the English army was caught in open country; many men and horses died (*The Hundred Years War*, 3 vols. [Philadelphia: University of Pennsylvania Press, 1990–2009]), II, 443, 623 n73; see further Andrew Ayrton, "English Armies in the Fourteenth Century," in *Arms, Armies*, ed. Curry and Hughes, 21–38 (21–22).
22. B 3.193; see also A 3.180. Andrew Galloway notes that the "'dym cloude' surely evokes the name 'black Monday' that chroniclers call the day" (*The Penn Commentary on Piers Plowman, vol. 1: C-Prologue- Passus 4; B Prologue-Passus 4; A Prologue-Passus 4* (Philadelphia: University of Pennsylvania Press, 2006), 319.
23. These lines are not present in A. Bennett surmises that B 3.194–202, referring to a later phase of continental pillaging, was inserted during revision. See Langland, *Piers Plowman: The Prologue and Passus I-VII of the B text as found in Bodleian MS. Laud Misc. 581*, ed. Jack Arthur Walter Bennett (Oxford: Clarendon Press, 1972), 139.
24. Schmidt glosses "yomen" at B 3.214 as "attendants"; Pearsall at C 270 prefers "yeomen," with a reference to his glossary definition for this line as "freeholders under the rank of gentleman."

25. King John II of France, imprisoned in London, signed the treaty at a banquet in the Tower on June 14, 1360. He was transferred to Calais on July 8, but was only released—following slow French fund-raising efforts—on October 24 (when the Treaty of Brétigny, with amendments, was ratified by kings Edward and John). See John Palmer, "The War Aims of the Protagonists and the Negotiations for Peace," in *The Hundred Years' War*, ed. Kenneth Fowler (London: Macmillan, 1971), 59–60; Sumption, *Hundred Years War*, II, 445–54.
26. Hostilities broke out again in 1369. Derek Pearsall sees A text as a product of the 1360s, likely still being revised and written in 1369–70; B as largely a product of the 1370s, with "much allusion to the events of 1376-9"; and C as probably post-dating 1381 and not finished until soon after 1388 (*New Annotated Version of the C-Text*, 1). But see now Lawrence Warner, *The Lost History of Piers Plowman: The Earliest Transmission of Langland's Work* (Philadelphia: University of Pennsylvania Press, 2011).
27. On this Calais-based tale from the Burgundian *Cent nouvelles nouvelles,* featuring one John Stotton (squire and carver) and Thomas Brampton (cupbearer to the cardinal of Winchester), see David Wallace, *Premodern Places: Calais to Surinam, Chaucer to Aphra Behn* (Oxford: Blackwell, 2004), 44–45.
28. See further A 2.185-90 ("And withheld him"); Pearsall has "of-helden" at C 2.240-1, glossed as "detained."
29. See Jack Arthur Walter Bennett, "The Date of the A-text of *Piers Plowman*," *PMLA*, 58 (1943): 566–72.
30. B 3.228–29; see also A 3.215–16; C 3.284–85. For acute questions posed of issues arising, see Anna P. Baldwin, *The Theme of Government in Piers Plowman* (Cambridge, UK: D. S. Brewer, 1981), 25.
31. The Latin is from Isaiah 2.4: "they shall beat their swords into ploughshares."
32. See Hewitt, *Organization of War*, 30; Adrien Blanchet, *Les souterrains-refuges de la France* (Paris: Picard, 1923), 76, 186; Nicholas Wright, *Knights and Peasants*, 69, 101.
33. Thomas Kelly suggests that Deschamps here riffs on his name "Eustache Morel," "Eustache the Moor," a name accorded to him "on account of his dark complexion": "Deschamps, Eustache," *Dictionary of the Middle Ages*, ed. Joseph R. Strayer, 12 vols. (New York: Scribner's, 1982-89), 4.163–64 (163).
34. Hewitt, *Organization of War*, 102.
35. W. M. Ormrod, "The Domestic Response to the Hundred Years' War," in *Arms, Armies*, ed. Curry and Hughes, 83–101 (86).
36. See Hewitt, *Organization of War*, 174.
37. PRO Statute Roll (Chancery), no. 1, m. 10; text and translation follow Charles G. Crump and Charles Johnson, "The Powers of Justices of the Peace," *English Historical Review* 27 (1912): 226–38.
38. Lionel, Duke of Clarence, son of Edward III, and Chaucer's first master, married a daughter of the Milanese despot Bernabò Visconti in 1368 and mysteriously died soon after. Sir John Hawkwood too married a daughter of Bernabò: in 1377, some months after Cesena and a year before Chaucer was briefed to meet with him. Forty years after Hawkwood's death in 1394, Uccello painted the equestrian portrait of him that still hangs in the Duomo at Florence: but his bones lie in Sible Hedingham, Essex, expatriated following a special appeal from Richard II. See Jones, "Image of Chaucer's Knight'; Wallace, *Chaucerian Polity*, 34–40 and plate 1.
39. On the contexts of Chaucer's deposition at the Scrope-Grosvenor trial, as recorded in law French, see now Butterfield, *Familiar Enemy*, 173–75.
40. Jones, *The Knight and the Squire*, 240.

CHAPTER 16

JACK AND JOHN: THE PLOWMAN'S TALE

Priscilla Martin

I hate just being in the Prologue. I have a beginning and then nothing. Never mentioned again. I don't tell a story. Nothing comes after that description of the Plowman. But something comes before me. My brother. I'm just introduced as his brother. What does Master Geoffrey say about him? Learned. Poor but rich in holy thought and work. And do you know what's the first thing he deigns to notice about me? Shit. That I've led many a cart of dung. Frozen hands and feet. Back and forth along the furrow. Loads of dung. That's my life.

Its prologue was well enough. Till he came along. They'd lost two before me in the pestilence, only girls but they grieved. They prayed for another, they prayed for a boy. When they had only one coin Mother gave it for a mass penny, she offered it up for a boy. She begged Our Lady to help her because she had a son of her own, and the statue in the church, holding up her child so tenderly, inclined towards her in the draughty candlelight and smiled. So God sent me to them. I was born only two days after Our Lord, on the feast of St. John the Evangelist. I don't remember that, of course, but it comforts me in the dark cold time of the year, if I lie awake listening to the wind and the rain and the breathing of the cow, to think of the baby in the stable with the ox and the ass who was born to poor people like us. The priest says the poor are very dear to Jesus. I was very dear to my parents at first. My mother sang me to sleep at night before the fire. Lullay, lullay. Then I toddled after my father through the seasons, learning to do what he did. Or doing what I could. Weeding and clearing and planting and gleaning after the mowers. Pruning when I grew old enough to use a knife. Plowing would come later. Heavy work. Man's work. My father said I would be big and strong and make a good plowman. He was proud of me. They thought me the best child in the village. Mother said my little sisters were happy in heaven and she could be happy on earth again now because she had me. Soon I was older than my sisters were when they died. The longer a child lives, the better your chances of keeping it. Then I fell sick. They were afraid when I ailed, feared the worst and gave the new baby the same name, John. I was called Jack, he was called John. Sir John, they can call him, now he's a priest. And he has a special devotion to my saint, St. John the Evangelist, because he can read.

I had outlived and outgrown my sisters and I thought John could never catch up. He was younger than me and always smaller, mother said, than I had been. He trailed after me, whining to play and do the same things. But I had work to do and he could not keep up. "He's a pest," I told my father. "He's little yet," he said, "you must be patient with him, he's your brother. He'll grow up and help you." But even as he grew bigger John was not much help. He was slight, not strong but not nimble either. He was clumsy, forgetting and dropping and bumping into everything, not to be trusted with sharp tools. I've seen him walk into a tree. He said he was praying. I thumped him when Father wasn't looking. He seldom hit back. He said Jesus told us not to but I knew it was because he was feeble and didn't stand a chance against me. It was canny to forgive. Mother, Father and the priest said he had a gentle nature. I thought a gentle nature doesn't get the work done.

The windows in our church were bright with pictures of men working. Adam digging. Shepherds with their sheep. A plowman with his team toiling straight up the side of the glass. There were two brothers and when I was a boy I thought they looked like us. One was older, sturdy and dark. The other was slender and fair and had a silly face. I said they were a picture of us until the priest told me the story of Cain and Abel. It seemed unfair to me. Why should the Lord prefer Abel's offering? Why wasn't Cain's as good? And it wasn't like us because John didn't offer anything, compared with me.

At first I thought everyone favored him because he was younger. I couldn't be younger than him but I strove to be better. I was up before dawn without grudging. I could handle the heavy plow sooner than any other boy my size. I stayed late in the fields, helping my neighbor when my own work was done as the Bible bids us. My parents praised me. But they praised John too. It seemed they praised him more. For less. The priest singled him out and began to teach him letters. "A is for Adam, A is for Abel," the little knave muttered raptly. Over and over. Later he would chant to himself, "J is for Jesus, J is for John." What is for Jack? I wondered.

The priest told me we were all different, made with sundry gifts to serve God with in sundry ways. It was like dishes. The king in his court needed gold and silver ewers and basins and goblets for his honor and worship and courtesy. Lord Roger of the manor needed fine things but not as many as the king. He was below the king but above us. We only had a few earthenware pots and wooden bowls, which were all we needed and did just as well. Because God was the king of everyone we wanted to honor him with gold and silver, like the chalice in the cathedral and the crucifix with its shining gems, and with all the beautiful works we could build and carve and paint. But God was so courteous he loved everything we gave him, if it was the best we could give. He was so courteous that he came down from heaven and lived with humble folk who used wooden bowls. Our gifts, what God gave us and what we could give God, were various. I was one of the wooden bowls, humble and serviceable to God and man. John was like silver, or perhaps even like gold.

Later, when John went to school at the monastery the priest seemed to think I might miss him. So he explained to me the different ways of serving God. You could work or fight or pray. Most people had to work because we all needed food. So plowmen and yeomen and butchers and bakers were pleasing to our Lord. Our betters had to fight and protect us or win back God's holy places and sometimes we could go and fight under them in the king's service. When I was a boy Lord Roger went to France with some young men from the manor. I wished I could go but Mother was glad I was too young. Especially when some came back scarred and maimed and some never came back. Lord Roger was taken prisoner and we had to help pay for his ransom. It was a hard year. When he came home we lit bonfires and had a great feast. There was all the meat and all the ale anyone could want. We ate and drank and sang and danced. I danced with Alice. I would have been completely happy if I hadn't felt vexed with John. He was loath to dance, stiff and strange when we pulled him into the circle. He was paler than the other lads who spent all day in the fields. He looked distant, as if he would rather be with the monks and their books, and he ate sparingly and neatly, as if he were better than us. The priest said the better part was to pray, like Mary in the gospel who talked with Jesus while her sister labored in the kitchen. It was a sin for Martha to complain, because prayer was the most important work of all. But work was prayer too, for folk like me.

At least if John was going to be a monk and call prayer work, I would not have to see him. I would pay my tithes and he would pray for me and that would be all we owed each other. I would be rid of him. But, while I was walking out—and more—with Alice, I felt a little kinder to John. He would not have this. Perhaps it was more perfect to be a maiden, like Our Lord and St. John, but I didn't want to be perfect. The world had to be served this way too, I thought, by men and beasts. And lying out in the grass on a warm summer evening, there was that moment of pure and timeless joy, like they say we'll have in heaven. I was a wooden vessel running over.

John, silver or gold, was willing to forgo it. He was the same as other boys but he never grew interested in the girls. He didn't go into the monastery, though. The monks had another idea for him. They sent him to study more in Oxford. What else was there to learn? He knew his letters. He could read and write in Latin, like the priest, and he could talk in French, like Lord Roger. So he knew almost everything you could get from schools. But he said the more you learned the more you found to learn. It was like the work on the farm, there was always more to do.

But the work on the farm was the same every year, unless God sent some drought or tempest to punish us. The seasons circled round and we plowed and sowed and harvested in due season. And like the animals we were born and grew and mated and died. And a man's life was much like his father's and his son's was much like his. And I would tell my sons what my father told me. Red sky at night, shepherd's delight. Many words will not fill a bushel. If wishes were horses, beggars would ride. And Alice would tell our daughters what her mother told her. A stitch in time saves nine. A watched kettle never boils. You can't eat your cake and have it.

My life was like my father's but John's was not. He could read and write. He could study the Bible in Latin, as it was written, and tell poor people stories from it. As a young lad he knew more stories than his father. We said the same things again and again because they were good and true and the children should know them. And because we had not much else to say. But John had more words than us, more sayings and more stories. He would see more sights than us. My father never went beyond the manor and the market town. But when John was a spotty youth he traveled to the far country of Oxford, forty miles off. Father borrowed a horse and took him all the way to the market and came back with tears in his eyes. But John went on gladly on foot and did not weep at leaving.

He came back in the vacation to help with the harvest. As best he could. More hindrance than help, I often thought. But he would fetch and carry and was very willing. I should not have been annoyed. The story of the prodigal son was a reproach to me. When the younger son came back and everyone made much of him, his elder brother was angry and jealous and that was a sin. But I was more sinful yet. The prodigal's brother should have been kind and generous and forgiving but you could see his grudge. The story seemed even more unjust than Cain and Abel. The prodigal had acted worse and was being cherished more. But I disliked my brother because he had been better. John hadn't been prodigal. He had been given a little money and some oats and salt fish and he made it last and did some work as a scribe to pay for the rest and studied long hours and came back thin and wan and tired.

But he also seemed happy. He talked about his student friends. He talked about how they talked. It wasn't all reading and listening to the masters. The clerks drank and disputed together and told the tales and sang the songs of their towns and villages. They watched late, like idle folk. They argued about what the Bible said, though I thought it plain enough that you should love God and your neighbor. They made jokes in Latin. He reveled in it. He stayed on and on for years. I hoped he would stay forever. Or, when he was ordained, I thought that he might go to London. The priest told me that there was work for clerks in Chancery and the Exchequer. I was not sure what these were but they sounded important. Or they could earn good money praying and singing in chantries. Perhaps, I thought, as John would have no children of his own, he might help mine. God had taken two and spared four. But I did not much want money so long as I could work and keep my family and raise my sons to work well in their turn. I wanted John to stay away from home. I told myself that I wanted what was best for him.

But he had different ideas. Better ideas about best. He said Chancery and the Exchequer were worldly. He came back at last, to be parson of the next parish. At least it wasn't our parish. It wasn't so fair and fertile. The villages were scattered and struggling. Some have been deserted now. The people were poor and their tithes were meager. I sometimes had to help him. But he never complained. He worked hard for his flock. I have to admit that it was work. He was out in all weathers, walking long miles in rain and snow if someone was sick or in trouble. He suffered with them, in his mind as well as his body. He lost that joy he learned at Oxford and grew sad and solemn again. He looked like a scarecrow.

I was hale and strong. My work kept me strong. I never thought reading was healthy and now John was praying for hours on end in a damp church and watching with the sick, I expected him to fall sick himself and die. But I was the one who fell sick and might have died. I lay sweating and shivering and seeing strange phantoms. I dreamed that God had set a mark upon me and outlawed me to the heath beyond John's barren parish. I told the priest and he comforted me. He said that not all dreams came from God; the devil might take advantage of our weakness when we were sick and tempt us to despair. John came and prayed and failed to comfort me. In the end I was healed not by parsons or leeches but by St. Thomas. The miller went on pilgrimage to Canterbury and there he begged the blessed martyr to cure me and brought back a vial of holy water from the shrine. I thought John would be pleased by such devotion but he was strangely cool. He snubbed the good miller, who only wished to help his neighbor and told him God heard prayers from every place on earth. He even said something rude about the water. But I was healed by prayers and water from Canterbury and I knew I must journey there and thank St. Thomas, whatever John said against it.

It was the first time I had crossed him since we were boys. John said there was no good in pilgrimage. You could pray and amend your life at home. Often there was bad in it, envy, anger, gluttony and lechery, when pilgrims did things they could not do at home where everyone would know it. There was avarice at these shrines and deceit when poor people were sold worthless baubles and tempted into idolatry. Folk wandered out of idle curiosity, the sin that made Eve eat the apple and cause all our suffering. And they did not come back better but puffed with pride at knowing more than their neighbors. I thought, but did not say, that John had been eager to know more than his neighbors.

There was some justice in what he said. I wanted to thank St. Thomas and give him his due, as was right. But now I was well again and spring was near I felt a sharp longing to be up and away and see new places and people. I even thought that if I went alone I would know things John did not. So if that was sinful he had better come with me. In truth, I was afraid to go alone. I had no fear of work or weather but I feared leaving home and going among strangers. That was the only thing that held me back. Not John's opposition. Not the expense. We had had a good harvest and saved a little. Not care for the plowing. My eldest boy was a good worker. Like father, like son. And my father had never been anywhere.

So at last I prevailed and, although John would never admit it, he must be grateful to me. For this became a famous pilgrimage, they said, when Master Geoffrey made the book of the tales of Canterbury. Lord Richard, old Lord Roger's son, bought a handsome copy. He had learned to read, as many nobles do now, though I cannot see why they need it. Others can do it for them. Lord Richard had rather listen to a clerk than trouble his own eyes, so he asked John to read it to him. And John, despite his disapproval, read it all and copied some and remembered the rest and rehearsed most of it to me. Though he said it went against the grain. And it was like the pilgrimage and unlike the pilgrimage. Most of the stories were Geoffrey's own idea though tales were told in the evening. Not along the way, of course, as he makes out. How could 30 people on horse have heard each other? Or talked in rhyme? Geoffrey made it all sound better than it was.

We started off from London. I had never seen so many churches. Or so many people. John said hundreds dwelt in the city. I wondered how you could love your neighbor there. We walked all round it but did not stay within the walls. We lay across the river among the whorehouses in Southwark at the Tabard Inn. The Tabard was not cheap and was no whorehouse but where pilgrims gathered to ride together for safety. Some were Londoners and some from distant places. There were a few others from the West Country. A woman from Bath called Alice who had been married five times and talked more than any man. She must have talked her husbands to death. As different from my Alice as Jack from John. And a miller from Oxford, loud and rough, not like our kindhearted miller who rode to Canterbury the year before. And a clerk from Oxford. John was pleased to see him and wanted to hear all the news of the schools but the clerk was too shy and quiet to tell him much and his curiosity (as I thought it) was disappointed. Instead the miller offended him with lewd stories of lecherous clerks at Oxford. The clerk looked as if he hadn't heard any of it but John told the miller not to swear. Harry, the bossy Host of the Tabard, who went with us, said something about Lollards and I wished John would hold his peace. Most people were good–natured about each other's stories. A choleric reeve took offense at the miller's, a friar and a summoner said ill of each other, all the clergy disapproved of Alice. I did not care for the clerk's tale of a stupid patient wife who never gainsaid her husband, even when he pretended to have their children killed. I thought you would have to be childless and celibate to tell that story. Harry riled the Cook with talk of flies in his shop buzzing round the twice–cooked pasties. And he shouted at a perverted pardoner who boasted openly about how he conned humble people into buying false relics they couldn't afford. Harry said he might as well cut off the Pardoner's balls and treat them as relics. But most people were courteous, as you would expect of a great knight, a liberal franklin, a lovely prioress, and merchants and manciples and guildsmen and lawyers and doctors. I was the only pilgrim who worked the land, though that is what most folk do.

And I think I was the only one who worried about telling a story. Harry suggested we should have a competition and all tell tales so we wouldn't get bored, and the winner should be stood a dinner at the Tabard by all the rest when we got back to Southwark. No flies on Harry, whatever the Cook's shop was like. Of course, I knew I couldn't win the contest, a poor plowman among all these lettered folk, but I wondered if I could tell a tale at all. I knew some rude tales, worse than the miller's, but they wouldn't do on a pilgrimage. And I had many memories of my children but they were not saints and didn't warrant stories. I knew some tales from the Bible, like Cain and Abel and the Prodigal Son, but I couldn't tell them and risk getting them wrong or seem to sermonize with so many clerics present. The friar sniped at Alice for preaching and a plowman preaching would be almost as bad as a woman. Even if I could think of a tale I wasn't sure I could put it into proper words. I was afraid of telling a tale. Yet I minded not being asked.

It was pride to want to put myself forward or to fear to show my ignorance. So I tried to forget about myself and enjoy the other stories. There were so many.

Long and short, plain and fancy, sacred and shocking. "I wish I could tell tales," I said to Geoffrey. "I'm not very good at it myself," he said. So I knew he wouldn't win the prize and I wondered who would. I thought it might be John. And I hoped he would and I hoped he wouldn't. Could he match the noble tales of love and war, the tragedies, the lives of saints and martyrs? I waited and waited and worried and worried about what I would do if I were asked and about what John would do when he was asked.

Harry didn't summon John till the very end. "Come on, sir priest," said Harry, "Everyone's told a tale but you." I hadn't. "Wrap it all up now," said Harry, "It's getting late. Tell us something that will do us good but don't take too long about it. Let's have your story." But John wouldn't play. He said it was wrong to tell stories. St. Paul said so. He wasn't good at telling stories and he didn't want to. They were lies and we should live in the truth. He would gladly tell us God's truth, so he talked for a long time about repentance because that was the best theme for our purpose. Some pilgrims fell asleep.

So neither of us told a tale. John talked but did not tell a story. He knew many but would not. And I knew some but could not. The stories from the Bible seemed too big and the stories from my own life seemed too small. But I didn't see that all stories were wrong, when there were plenty in the Bible and Our Lord told stories himself. Perhaps John was wrong about this. Or perhaps stories were wrong for him and right for me, because God had made us different and him better. I always remembered the stories on the pilgrimage as I remembered the churches in London. I thought the tellers were offering their different gifts to God, like the masons and glaziers and goldsmiths. Like plowmen with their plow—alms. Wooden vessels. Gold and silver stories.

I think the pilgrimage was God's gift back to me. In sundry ways. I loved it all, the good and the bad, even though I was anxious about telling a story. I came back feeling better for it and more content. I dared not buy a drop of holy water and face John's scorn. But I said my prayers at the shrine and gave the saint the miller's greetings and asked him to help Alice's backache. And when the weather grew warmer he did and our love grew warm again. I have never grown to love John as I should but I am more in charity with him. I know that in some ways my life is happier than his. He did not enjoy the pilgrimage as I did. He was anxious about everyone else as well as himself and saddened by all their sinfulness and suffered with them. Whereas I only care for Alice and my children and my neighbors in the village and they are mainly a joy to me, though sometimes they are not. His work never ends but when I went on the pilgrimage I was almost carefree. He could not even take pleasure in the stories because he grieved over pride, envy, anger, emulation and of course there was plenty. There always will be while we are on this sinful earth. But God bids us love the sinners. And the saints too, which sinners may find harder. Why else was the blessed martyr murdered? But God made good come out of it. Pilgrims take their sins and their sickness to him, their ills of mind and body, their stories, and they ride from Canterbury with clearer faces. St. Thomas helped my sickness. In sundry ways.

CHAPTER 17

A PRAYER ROLL FIT FOR A TUDOR PRINCE

John J. Thompson

In *An Apology for Poetry*, Sir Philip Sidney describes the historian as "loaden with old mouse-eaten records, authorizing himself (for the most part) upon other histories, whose greatest authorities are built upon the notable foundation of hearsay; having much ado to accord differing writers, and to pick truth out of partiality."[1] In mocking the scholarly enterprise upon which the academic careers of so many contributors to this volume have been based, Sidney quotes from Cicero before him who had insisted that it is only when time itself has somehow been transcended that history can boast its disciplinary utility as *testis temporum, lux veritatis, vita memoriae, magistra vitae, nuncio vetustatis* (the witness of the ages, the light of truth, the life of memory, the governess of life, the herald of antiquity).[2] In its new context in *An Apology for Poetry*, the repurposed borrowing implies the solipsism and pedantry of the historical commentator rather than the science of the Ciceronian discipline. And Sidney's words still hold their sting for modern historians of the early book where much of our understanding of real, and not simply imagined, medieval readers and reading practices is reconstructed from the surviving material remnants of a bygone age and earlier attempts to deal with them as scientifically as possible, building upon whatever "notable foundation of hearsay" one can comfortably link to the surviving texts through the associated evidence of provenance and ownership, often deduced from later inscriptions or in casually added marginalia and underlinings or other readerly attempts to mark the text.[3]

As the recipient of this festschrift volume knows well, our ability to resort to anecdote and hearsay remains an important tool for teaching and studying the Middle Ages in the twenty-first century. It basically provides us with a key to understanding, on our own terms, the material survivals of a remote historical period—the extant buildings, archives, books, texts and other artifacts that represent a world and culture otherwise completely lost in time and alterity. By his many scholarly contributions, Terry Jones stylishly demonstrates that the historian's tools of the trade are not simply "old mouse-eaten records" or forgotten ruins. The acts of scholarly retrieval underlying the contemporary anecdotes from the Middle Ages inspired by such artifacts—the stories of Geoffrey Chaucer or Thomas Malory's knights, John Gower's priest-confessor and his lover, William Langland's plowman and other workers in the field, or, in Jones's case, the real human lives ordered by and caught up in the social hierarchies of their age—can often surprise the poetry critic or give the historian pause for thought. On occasion, a few critical hackles may be raised by the manner of the retelling of these stories and the hearsay surrounding them. But anecdotal evidence is perhaps at its most useful when this happens since it is always good to force a rethink or qualification of what we think we already know by asking further microhistorical questions and contributing more "mouse-eaten records" to "the notable foundation of hearsay" upon which Sidney believes that the discipline of history is built.

It is in this spirit that I want to both celebrate and test the validity of such an approach to history through anecdote and hearsay by examining the evidence for the ownership and reading of a Tudor artifact that has only recently been rediscovered by modern scholarship. The artifact in question is a late-fifteenth-century "bede" or prayer roll that was inscribed by Henry VIII when he was Prince of Wales but was probably written by a single copyist in the late 1480s. It is now London, British Library, MS Additional 88929.[4] The first thing to note is that this artifact is a roll and not a codex and that it has nothing written on its dorse. It consists of four attached membranes sewn together lengthwise with silken thread, the sections all uneven and ranging in width from 102–118 mm and in length from 700–938 mm. The written space used on the roll is just 59 mm wide, and it extends in total to about 3.5 meters when fully displayed. In its current state the decorative details and illustrations preserved in the first and last sections of the roll are in poorer condition than the material preserved in the middle two membranes, the result apparently of greater wear and tear, or perhaps exposure to the elements at some stage in its history. One can only guess what caused this damage since the roll's immediate post-Reformation whereabouts is largely unknown and will have to be reconstructed below from a foundation of hearsay rather than from anything more definitive. It is said that the roll was found in Liverpool in the 1850s, and it was then presented in 1862 to Ushaw College, near Durham. It remained at Ushaw until 2009 when it was loaned for the British Library exhibition (April 23—September 6, 2009) celebrating the five-hundredth anniversary of Henry VIII's accession. It was then sold to the British Library at auction in Sotheby's (June 2010).

The roll has earned a significant place in history because it provides one of just three surviving examples of Henry's handwriting prior to his accession to the throne in 1509. Because of his association with such a document, there is obviously much at stake here. Yet its survival poses a major problem for scholars of book history interested in reading and reception issues. The original circumstances of its production, particularly the decision to produce it in a roll format rather than as a small book, are unknown, and we do not know precisely how the roll would have been used, or even who would have used it and under what circumstances. Was it intended for public display rather than private reading or for a mixture of both? If Henry owned the roll as a young prince, then what might its survival tell us about the true nature of his reading and religious practices and devotional attitudes before his break with Rome?

This last question is perhaps the most tantalizing of all because of the close relationship between text and image on the roll itself. It contains a series of thirteen pictures, each followed by accompanying Latin prayers and prompts consisting of the opening phrases of other psalms and anthems, plus rubrics, in English, explaining the efficacy of performing the prescribed devotions and offering a generous estimate of the remission from sin that one might expect for so doing. The first picture on the first membrane, now damaged by exposure, shows details of the Trinity, with Christ depicted as bleeding and uncrowned on God's right, and a kneeling cleric or bishop with an angel as armiger bearing his (now sadly, unidentifiable) heraldic shield, below (1); next there is a crucifixion scene with Christ, centered, and flanked by the two thieves, all on Tau-shaped crosses (2).[5] This is followed on the second membrane by images of Christ standing in the sepulcher displaying his wounds, with the two crucified thieves in the background (3);[6] then the viewer is offered another image of Christ on the Tau-shaped cross, flanked by two angels, each holding scrolls, the inscription in the one on the left in Latin, while that in the scroll on the right is rubricated and in English (4); next is an image of two angels supporting a radiance enclosing the wound of Christ's side, with, below, the nails, pierced feet, hands and heart, and crown of thorns, flanked by a rubricated notice in English (5); this is followed by an image of the Virgin and Child, with a town in the distance, watched over by the heavenly host (6).[7]

There then follows in the latter half of the roll a set of seven illustrated memorials to specific saints: St. Michael conquering a hydra-like dragon (7); St. George slaying the dragon (8); then, on the fourth and final membrane (again damaged by exposure), St. Erasmus (also known as St. Elmo), wearing a bishop's miter, extended naked on the rack while two executioners torture him by winding his entrails round a windlass (9); St. Christopher as colossus bearing the Christ child (10); a discolored St. Anthony in black drapery, wearing two Tau-shaped crosses, one blue and one white (11); St. Pantaleon in a green cope being beheaded with a sword (12), and finally, St. Armagil, or Armyl, of Brittany, praying before a crucifix while calmly holding by its neckband the dragon he had earlier vanquished (13).

At the head of the roll, badly faded, there is a paler square, 45 × 50 mm, that may once have had the original illumination scrubbed out and another parchment patch inserted over it. This patch has now disappeared and the washed-out image underneath is almost completely lost. But the small square, now forming a largely blank space, is flanked, on the left, by two Tudor roses, each in a radiance and surmounted by crowns, out of one of which springs the feather of the Prince of Wales. On the right, now damaged and badly faded, is another Tudor rose and crown, beneath which is a barely visible representation resembling a flight of arrows, possibly either quivered or passing through a tower.

In terms of its original production, therefore, rather than its later utility, the roll is an example of an attempt to awaken in pious late-medieval lay English audiences a sentimental awareness of the nature and purpose of Christ's Passion. Such awareness was expected to be based on biblical details derived ultimately from the Gospels and liturgical motifs emphasizing Christ's pain and suffering. At the intellectual core of the literary tradition of such thinking in England, one finds works like Richard Rolle's hugely influential *Meditations on the Passion*, or, perhaps, even more emphatically—at least in terms of its widespread copying, translation, and adaptation—the Latin pseudo-Bonaventuran *Meditationes Vitae Christi* and its main derivative version known as the *Meditationes de Passione Domini*. Both these latter items spawned a series of Middle English renderings including, preeminently, Nicholas Love's *Mirror of the Blessed Life of Jesus Christ*, a prose item now extant in over 60 manuscripts that also circulated in no fewer than nine early printings between 1484 and 1530.[8] Such works projected the idea—perhaps even the imaginative necessity among a variety of educated pious readers and hearers with the leisure time available to do so—of immersing oneself, enthusiastically and sentimentally, in the lived experience of key biblical episodes and liturgical motifs inspired by the figure of Christ and the events of Holy Week. The texts and images in the first half of the prayer roll seem to capitalize on such interests.

On the other hand, the Tudor origins of the roll are unmistakable.[9] One indication is the rubric accompanying the prayer to St. Armagil and the final memorial image on the roll:

> He that prayth hartely to god and to Seint Armyl shalbe delyuerd fro all these sekenes vndre written. That is to sey of all Gowtis Aches Agwis Axces Feuers and Pockes and many other ynfirmytes as it aperith in his life and legend the which was brought oute of Britayne at the ynstans off the kyng owre souereyne lord harry the vijth.

Henry VII is referred to as the current king and the person who has brought the "Life and Legend of St. Armyl" to England. English devotion to Breton saints was not common before Henry VII, nor, indeed, for much after his death in 1509. Nevertheless, his particular interest in St. Armyl before he became king was presumably prompted by the period of long exile in southern Brittany, among a local aristocratic community where the saint was revered. As Duke of Richmond, Henry had fled there with his uncle and guardian in October 1471 and was resident in Brittany, and later France, along with a growing number of his English supporters in exile, until his eventual return and victory at the Battle of Bosworth Field in August 1485. The Tudor journey to Bosworth had begun with a previous abortive attempt to return to England and join Buckingham's failed uprising in October 1483, when St. Armyl's intervention was credited with saving Henry's fleet from disaster in stormy seas and preserving his life before his victory at Bosworth.

Tudor devotion to St. Armyl rapidly became part of the early consolidation of the dynastic myth during Henry VII's reign. Evidence is ample: in contemporary memorials to the saint and the Bosworth victory found in stained glass at Merevale Abbey, near the battle site, in several Tudor Books of Hours; in the funeral ornaments commissioned by Henry VII more than a decade before his death that he intended to adorn his eventual place of burial in the Lady Chapel at Westminster Abbey; St. Armyl also figures in the design at Canterbury Cathedral of the tomb for Henry VII's Archbishop and Lord Chancellor, Cardinal John Morton (d. 1500).[10]

The head of the prayer roll deploys images of the Tudor rose *en soleil* alongside the Prince of Wales feather, together with a representation of a sheaf of arrows (or, possibly, arrows passing through a tower), which is the livery badge of Katherine of Aragon. Katherine is another figure associated with the consolidation of the Tudor regime in its earliest days. She came to England in 1501, and in November of that year married Arthur, Prince of Wales, in St. Paul's Cathedral. Arthur was Henry VII's eldest son and heir to the throne, born in September 1486. His marriage to Katherine had been suggested as early as 1488, as part of the diplomatic negotiations with Aragon and Castile to achieve recognition in continental Europe of the legitimacy and stability of the Tudor monarchy. That diplomatic campaign led to the signing of the Treaty of Medina del Campo in March 1489.[11] A year later, some further attempt to establish the Tudor dynasty and free it from any remaining Yorkist threat resulted in four-year-old Arthur being invested as Prince of Wales in December 1490.

Yet despite all Tudor hopes to the contrary, Arthur's marriage to Katherine was cut short after less than six months by his sudden death from the "sweating sickness" at Ludlow Castle in April 1502.[12] He was buried amid great grief in the chantry chapel on the south side of the high altar in Worcester Cathedral, where his tomb was surrounded by a dazzling display of heraldic symbols proclaiming his exalted place in Tudor genealogy. That display included representations in stone of the same heraldic badges that are now damaged and faded but were once proudly and colorfully displayed at the head of the prayer roll.

On Arthur's death, Prince Henry quickly became his father's rightful heir, the next Prince of Wales, and the widowed Katherine's future husband. One suspects that this situation arose largely because of the dynastic problems that would otherwise have faced the crown. Thus Henry VII waited until he could be absolutely sure that the brief union of Arthur and Katherine had not produced a future Prince of Wales before bestowing the title on his second surviving son, who was already Duke of York. The new Prince of Wales became Henry VIII in due course and for the first time in recent history ascended to the English throne by right of inheritance on his father's death, rather than as a result of conquest or usurpation. For many, that state of affairs must have seemed inevitable, and most certainly preferable to what had gone before. But, as the summary of events outlined above has shown, it came about largely as the consequence of ever-vigilant attempts to ward off the threat of disaster in the face of misfortune and catastrophe. The Crown's promoting at every opportunity the symbols that reflected the legitimacy and stability of the early Tudor dynasty played a significant part in achieving this end.

BL MS Additional 88929 emerges, then, as an important Tudor relic from this fraught period in English history. Its decorative details suggest that the roll can hardly be dated much before 1490, when Arthur was made Prince of Wales.

Moreover, its Tudor royal associations were secured through Prince Henry's apparent ownership of it, presumably between 1502, when he was made Prince of Wales on Arthur's death, and 1509, when he became king. The key piece of evidence that links the prayer roll to Henry in this manner is his signed inscription in the space following the prayers associated with the first crucifixion scene (2) in the first membrane, and immediately preceding the image of the risen Christ displaying his wounds (3) with which the second membrane opens. The inscription reads, "Willyam Thomas, I pray yow pray for me your lovyng master: Prynce Henry."

Since the roll's first public display in modern times, during the major British Library exhibition "Henry VIII, Man and Monarch," the inscription has acquired weighty significance for many, who take it as settling "beyond doubt" what has been described as "the real nature of Henry's religious beliefs." According to this logic, the inscription makes it certain that the young Prince and his servant probably prayed together using the roll, suggesting that the future Henry VIII "practised the devotions characteristic of the late medieval popular piety that, with the Reformation, he would later come to reject."[13]

There are, however, a number of problems with this interpretation of the evidence, largely caused by a five-hundred-year vacuum that can only be filled imaginatively by hearsay. We cannot know how such "bedes" or prayer rolls were used or functioned in public and private household spaces, devotional practices, religious beliefs, and reading habits. Relying on the roll to estimate the nature of Prince Henry's private devotional reading practices effectively highlights this particular problem. We do not know the actual circumstances in which the roll was given to Henry, how or where it was stored and displayed, and whether it was ever used as part of Henry's private devotions or those of other members of his household. Many years ago, in his analysis of the so-called "arma Christi" rolls, Rossell Hope Robbins argued that these accounts of the instruments of Christ's Passion preserved in scroll form were not originally designed for use as private meditations, or even for private reading, but, rather, that they satisfied a demand for visual display, perhaps simply offering something to gaze upon adoringly or respectfully as other associated activities were taking place in a congregational setting.[14] Indeed, the promised remission of sins often recorded for the "arma Christi" usually stipulated looking at or beholding the image rather than reading the text. The roll format was designed for display rather than for private reading, so it would seem to have been well suited to this general purpose.

Although the Tudor credentials of the roll are clearly displayed at its head, there are also questions to be asked about the absence of specific references to a royal prince in the selected Latin prayers and memorials and the accompanying English rubrics where the instructions given to the intended audience are always anonymous and broadly conceived. For example, the accompanying rubric for the Latin prayers following the first crucifixion image (2), preceding Henry's inscription for William Thomas, instructs a target audience, here imagined "in sin or tribulation," to kneel down before the Cross. Most probably, the cross intended here is the one in the illustration on display at this point, but there is also a second illustration of the Crucifixion (4) later in the same roll, and one cannot entirely rule out the possibility that other suitable images of the crucified Christ might have been deployed imitatively for this exercise if more than one person was intended to follow the instructions. According to the accompanying rubric on the roll, readers and hearers are then expected to complete a visual scan of the Five Wounds, progressively beholding the image of the crucified Christ from the feet up, and to respond to the series of mnemonic prompts below the image urging repetition of the recommended psalms, prayers, anthems, and petitions, ending with a recitation of the Creed.

The intended audience addressed by the English rubrication on the roll is anonymous, occasionally assumed to be plural, yet the narrow width of the roll suggests that the Latin and English text accompanying the Crucifixion illustration was probably only available for one person to read at a time. Reading the Latin and English text on the roll was clearly an individual activity, up to a point. It is under this prayer sequence that Henry wrote his personal inscription for William Thomas. However, even with a trusted servant at hand to help with the progressive rolling and unrolling of the scroll that may have been necessary to make the recommended form of paraliturgical worship an inward private act, it is difficult to imagine how the recommended devotions could have been completed all at once. The supplicant was meant to kneel down, gaze at a Crucifixion image in the recommended manner, while, simultaneously, reading and reciting from memory the written prayers listed beneath the image on the scroll, all to be done in proper order and with due reverence and dignity. The anonymity of the target audience may also support the view that the recommended devotional activity was not necessarily intended for just one person to perform. The rubric was perhaps written to encourage several different members of some anonymous early Tudor household to engage in the same recommended public procedures for adoring the Cross and the details of Christ's Passion, both as individuals within a larger community and also congregationally.[15] Therefore, it is easy to speculate that the tiny roll may well have been displayed on occasion in a chantry setting or in some other convenient domestic space within an aristocratic Tudor household.

The image-conscious rubric below the picture of the wounded and bloody Christ in the sepulcher that follows Henry's words to William promises indulgence, "to all them that before this ymage of pyty deuawtely sey v. Pater Noster, v. Ave Maria and .i. Credo, shall haue lii.m.vii.c.xii. yeris and xl days of pardon graunted be St. Gregory and other holy men." As always, the instruction is anonymous and impersonal, and one would like to know more about how the indulgenced prayer actually worked in the multipurpose context provided by this particular scroll.[16] A premium is placed on encouraging everyone who gazes adoringly on the image to recite the familiar prayers. The texts do not have to be read from the roll, but they do have to be remembered and recited. Once again, the emphasis is on the possibility of an intense type of repetitive and imitative communal or congregational activity requiring actions as well as words, rather than on the forms of intimate and inward-looking private behavior a twenty-first-century audience is not used to seeing set out for display in a roll format. If only the artifact associated with Prince Henry had been produced as a small codex, one might all the more readily have identified his potential ownership of it with a personal commitment to the kinds of silent penitential reading book historians often like to associate (again often by some version of hearsay) with a prayer book source.[17]

There is also the question of how the prayer roll's talismanic properties might once have been regarded when it was not on display. Rolled up, it is certainly small enough to have been carried around in a pouch or pocket or some other enclosure as a general good luck charm to protect any man or woman and not specifically a Tudor prince from harm.[18] The lengthy rubric accompanying the second image of the Crucifixion (4) says as much, on the painted scroll unfurled by the angel on Christ's right in this image. The rubric states how the accompanying text "shal breke your enemys and encres your worldly goodes and if a woman be in trauell off childe ley this on her body and she shal be delyuered without parel the childe cristendin and the moder purificacyon." Meanwhile, the angel on the left of Christ offers up a Latin prayer to St. Cyricus and St. Julitta on that scroll, a pair of saints often named in English textual amulets intended to assist women in labor.[19] Other examples of such prayers survive, occasionally with text written on the dorse of the scroll (not the case with BL MS Additional 88929), perhaps so that the writing could make direct physical contact with the woman's body while the other material on the roll remained visible to those assembled for the birth, piously anxious, perhaps, but not actually experiencing directly the agonies of labor. The fact that the information on Henry's roll is contained not on the dorse but in two scrolls-within-a-scroll in the illustration of the Crucifixion gives the birthing advice a more remote and stylized quality. Its inclusion simply confirms the multipurpose character of this roll as a textual amulet. Little is revealed concerning the private devotional practices of individual princes but much about the general late medieval and Tudor obsession with wombs and tombs.

A chain of unfortunate mishaps associated with Katherine of Aragon's arrival and lengthy stay in England offers one possible way of explaining both the circumstances of the Tudor prayer roll's original production and also how it briefly fell into Henry's hands before 1509. Katherine was renowned for her cleverness and piety in early Tudor court circles, and the fortunate early survival of the roll seems linked to her doomed first marriage to Prince Arthur and also the diplomatic uncertainties surrounding her subsequent betrothal to Henry as Prince of Wales. The story is a familiar one, and its basic details have been reported many times. However, puzzles remain about two minor episodes, both of which may be relevant to the present discussion. The first concerns an astonishing error in a register of briefs in the Vatican archives. Dated October 20, 1505, the entry notes Pope Julius II's response to Arthur, Prince of Wales (who, by the date of the register entry, had been dead for over three years). The letter itself has not survived, so we have no way of checking whether it was ever sent or to whom it was addressed. Perhaps the papal secretary responsible for adding the archive detail in 1505 simply did not realize that Arthur was dead and that the English title had passed to Henry.[20] The letter apparently granted papal authority to the Prince to restrain his wife from continuing to engage in excessive religious observances injurious to her health since these would imperil the *maritalis consuetudo* (marital custom) of Roman law and endanger her ability to bear children. Rather too late in the day, Julius authorized the Prince of Wales (Arthur?) to insist his pious wife conduct less strenuous religious exercises, these to be determined on the advice of her confessor.

The second episode is much better known to modern historians, but any direct relevance it may once have had to the production of the Vatican document that was the basis of the papal brief described above is not at all clear. Following the death of Prince Arthur, a treaty for marriage between his widow Katherine and Prince Henry, now the new Prince of Wales, was signed on June 23, 1503. The couple was formally betrothed on June 25. Henry was 12 years old, Katherine 17, and the marriage was to be solemnized when the Prince reached his fifteenth year. Two years later, on June 27, 1505, Henry appeared before Richard Fox, Bishop of Winchester, and Lord Privy Seal (the churchman who had baptized him at Greenwich). Now that he had reached the years of maturity, the 14-year-old Prince said he wanted to put it on the record that he formally disowned his part of the marriage contract with Katherine. As a result of this move, Katherine was trapped in the 1503 agreement and forced to bide her time in England as a widow, still of marriageable age, patiently awaiting the pleasure of her once (and future?) father-in-law, Henry VII.

Prince Henry's apparent change of heart with regard to marrying Katherine was announced at the end of June 1505. Some four months later, the evidence suggesting that a papal letter had been sent to Arthur as Prince of Wales regarding the extreme religious enthusiasm of his wife was added, very late in the day, to the formal Vatican record of such documents. It is difficult to know what to make of all this with any certainty, but the impression lingers that both episodes were related in some way to the diplomatic intrigues surrounding Tudor ambitions on the continent regarding the most important European ruling dynasties. Katherine's father, Ferdinand II of Aragon, had already entered a difficult political period even before the diplomatic wrangling that had left his daughter living as a young English widow in much reduced circumstances.[21] He had been Ferdinand V of Castile *jure uxoris* (in right of his wife), but Queen Isabella I had died in 1504 and the Castilian crown had passed to their daughter Joanna and her husband, Philip, Archduke in the Hapsburg empire. Despite Ferdinand's best efforts, his son-in-law became Philip I of Castile and was recognized as such by the Tudors in a secret treaty agreed at Windsor, a situation that pertained until 1506 when Philip's unexpected death removed the impediment that had prevented Ferdinand from earlier becoming regent in Castile. It took Henry VII's death in 1509 to resolve finally the diplomatic impasse that had so delayed Katherine's second marriage to an English Tudor prince on her way to becoming Queen of England.

How might the two episodes outlined above throw light on the history of Prince Henry's association with the early Tudor prayer roll? The answer would seem to be linked to the early life and career in the royal princely households of William Thomas, groom of the privy chamber for both Arthur and Henry when they were Princes of Wales.[22] At some point between 1504 and 1509,

Prince Henry's signed inscription as "loving master" invites William Thomas to pray for him. Henry was born in 1491, while in a 1529 deposition taken as part of the legatine trial set up to establish the validity of Henry's marriage to Katherine, William Thomas is said to have been about 50 years old and to have lived in Carmarthen and Shropshire for about 25 years.[23] He was, therefore, little more than twelve years older than Henry and only, perhaps, about six or seven years older than Arthur, and he had probably spent most his early manhood in Tudor royal service. William Thomas was the son of Thomas ap Rhydderch of Aberglasney in the parish of Llangathen, Carmarthenshire. He was probably born around 1479, and, prior to entering Prince Arthur's service, he may have already demonstrated his youthful prowess and loyalty to the emerging Tudor cause on the battlefield; he is probably to be identified as the esquire of the same name who was rewarded by Henry VII after the Battle of Blackheath in 1497 for his part in the capture of Lord Audley's brother (an episode recorded in London, British Library, MS Stowe 440, fol. 82v).[24] As Arthur's groom, he presumably traveled with the Prince, but mostly, perhaps, he was based closer to his Welsh roots, at Ludlow Castle in Shropshire, where the Prince's council in Wales was based. Ludlow was considered a suitable training ground for future Tudor monarchs. Moreover, Arthur's residence there had major symbolic value since it represented an important and developing aspect of the early Tudor system of local and regional governance and control.[25] During Arthur's final sickness and death at Ludlow in 1503, William Thomas is likely to have been close by, presumably stationed at his prince's side. He may then have remained in Shropshire, or possibly returned to his home in Carmarthenshire, until he was recalled to London in 1504 to serve the new Prince of Wales.

As a groom of the privy chamber, William Thomas could certainly have acted, on occasion, as the personal escort for the two Princes of Wales under whom he served. As Henry's words on the roll suggest, he was possibly even the intimate and friend of both royal brothers. Quite what that might have meant in terms of whether or not he shared the same devotional interests and reading tastes as either or both princes is less certain. Nevertheless, he was rewarded for playing his part in the royal household. With hundreds of other royal servants and supporters, William Thomas is known to have attended Henry VII's funeral in London in May 1509. Among the first cluster of grants authorized by the new king in the same month, Thomas was made keeper for life of Ockeley Park, Salop, and, simultaneously, on the same terms, he became "troner and peser" in the port of London, Greenwich.[26] His title was presumably related in some way to the task of keeping a record of weights and measures at the port, but one cannot readily ascertain the nature of any responsibilities the new role may have brought with it, or even whether it required frequent physical presence at Greenwich. Rather more significantly, his 1529 deposition reveals that William Thomas was present at the marriage ceremony for Arthur and Katherine and that he was one of the few members of the royal household known to have been present when Henry and Katherine's nuptials were finally celebrated in Greenwich on June 11, 1509. This was followed on June 24 by their coronation at Westminster Abbey, at which Thomas was also present. On June 23, 1510, at about the age of 30, he received a royal grant of an annuity to be collected from the Principality of South Wales, which may mark the end of his period of formal service as groom to the new king.[27] He then seems to have settled into life as a property holder and Tudor family man in Shropshire and Carmarthenshire; he was knighted in 1513 and remained prominent locally as a member of the Council in the Marches and Justice of the Peace until his death in 1543.

In the latter half of Sir William Thomas's life, he presumably had to negotiate some aspects of the complicated and protracted issue of Henry VIII's "Great Matter."[28] The king's plans to divorce Katherine and marry Anne Boleyn certainly drew much public opprobrium. Questions were debated openly in England and on the continent regarding the legitimacy or otherwise of Henry's first marriage, particularly the validity of the papal dispensation that had licensed the union when it had eventually taken place. An important issue raised time and again was whether Henry's union with Katherine could or should have been permitted on grounds of affinity—Henry had married his dead brother's wife, but had Katherine's earlier marriage to Arthur been consummated? If it had, did the pope have the authority to issue a dispensation? It is perhaps worth noting in this context that, although now a justice of the peace in Wales and not an expert in canon law, William Thomas was probably one of only a handful of trusted persons who might have untied the Gordian knot that Henry's pangs of conscience, and his legal team, had so laboriously created and elaborately sustained. As Arthur's groom of the privy chamber, Thomas's experience of the intimate details of court life in both London and Ludlow would have enabled him to clear up the "Great Matter" in an instant simply by telling the truth, at least "the truth" as far as he had understood it at the time. In 1529, that may have been exactly what he did. When William Thomas was called upon to testify formally before John Tayler, Archdeacon of Buckingham, and the notaries appointed by the legatine court in England to take his deposition, his statement as a loyal royal servant records, with little elaboration and no scurrilous anecdote, that Arthur and Katherine had lived together normally as man and wife, as far as he was able to tell. According to the archive record, this statement was repeated on June 30 in the Parliament Chamber.

The "Great Matter" was still some time in the future when Prince Henry wrote the note on the prayer roll for William Thomas. Far from having originally been made for Henry, the roll may well have been an important relic from an earlier period in Tudor history, a gift of some kind that was designed to commemorate the union of the House of Tudor and the House of Castile on the occasion of the marriage of Arthur, Prince of Wales, and Katherine in November 1501. Henry knew well how to recycle gifts for which he may have no longer had much use. On New Year's Day 1506, for example, when his betrothal was back on track after his formal withdrawal from it, Henry presented to Katherine "a ring with an emerald"; on the same date in 1508 she was presented with "a fair ring of rubies set in a rose white and green." Both were gifts Henry had earlier received from others. Henry was just as unsentimental with Katherine's presents to him, giving away no fewer than three as New Year gifts to his father, in 1507, 1508, and 1509. [29] Books too were passed around at New Year, and often came into Henry's hands and passed out again by a number of different routes.[30] Clothes from the Great Wardrobe and other household coverings were periodically culled and repurposed.[31] It is hardly much of a stretch of the imagination, then, to read Prince Henry's autograph inscription to William Thomas in the prayer roll as an indication that he was now simply recycling another object that had originally belonged to someone in his late brother Arthur's household.

If this were the case, then the roll's transfer was part of the Tudor culture of gift-giving, reward, and exchange from which William Thomas had presumably often prospered and to which Henry and other members of his royal household had always so enthusiastically subscribed. Henry's generosity on this occasion may well have been prompted as much by sentimental reasons as by the roll's talismanic properties or monetary value. The gift was perhaps linked through its decoration to some memory of his father's investment in an early marriage attempt to secure the House of Tudor's future. The act of giving it may even have signaled Henry's formal recognition of his groom's former loyal service to his late brother. The important point is that Henry's eventual ownership of the prayer roll and the likelihood that he passed the scroll on to William Thomas need not necessarily have had much to do with his own religious interests or devotional enthusiasms. The gift-giving may rather have marked some significant milestone for both master and groom, perhaps the liminal moment when the groom who had formerly been Prince Arthur's man was now retiring from his post in Prince Henry's household. In other words, it seems likely that Henry had probably inherited the roll on the death of his brother when he took up the title of Prince of Wales and gave it up to William Thomas shortly before his coronation as King of England.

There is little doubt that the Tudor prayer roll at the heart of this historical anecdote has great significance and might be read in ways that would prove a more successful means of bringing us closer to the practicalities of Tudor devotional practices than have been demonstrated in this essay. BL MS Additional 88929 provides us with an unusual opportunity to observe the processes by which Latin and English devotional material of a liturgical character was taken through the congregational arena into the domestic sphere in the early Tudor period. The now faded and largely indecipherable heraldry reproduced on the shield in the opening image on the roll hints that this was perhaps through some early process of episcopal gift-giving during the early part of Henry VII's reign. Other decorative features on the roll suggest that members of Prince Arthur's household in either London or Ludlow were perhaps most likely to have been the obvious beneficiaries. Such processes are "medieval" in the sense that they repeat behaviors that are evident for a long time prior to the Tudor scroll's copying and decoration. From at least the time of Wyclif, the question of lay religious attitudes had exercised the imaginations of many writers and visual artists, but the real or imagined threat of Lollardy ensured that a concern with the spread of lay literacy, and what has recently come to be known as "vernacular theology," had greatly stirred anxieties in the minds of English kings and archbishops. This was long before the Tudors left their mark on English religious history. The regimen of repetitive devotional exercises inspired by the roll may even offer us a Tudor update on this royal and archepiscopal anxiety, if it is seen as a model, of sorts, for the kinds of piety and religious enthusiasm that the papal brief in the Vatican archive would have us believe Prince Arthur once complained about to the higher authority of the Holy See in Rome. Allegedly, this was in relation to his new wife's overzealous religious exertions, presumably at Ludlow. After Arthur's death and Henry's marriage to Katherine, the royal panic may have subsided for a time, until Henry's prosecution of the "Great Matter" encouraged him to believe that Katherine would be better off in a nunnery. By then, the roll had come into William Thomas's possession in Wales, where it may well have remained in the possession of his successors until its journey to Liverpool (not a great distance) in the nineteenth century. After 1509, the roll had become another recycled Tudor artifact for which Henry VIII probably had very little personal attachment, either as the late Prince Arthur's younger teenage brother, or as a literate—possibly even conventionally devout—lay reader.

Notes

1. *An Apology for Poetry: or, The Defence of Poesy, by Sir Philip Sidney*, ed. Geoffrey Shepherd, rev. third ed., ed. Robert Maslen (Manchester, UK: Manchester University Press, 2002), 89, ll. 8–18.
2. Cicero, *De oratore* 2.9.36, in *Cicero Rhetorica*, vol. I, ed. Arthur Wilkins (Oxford: Clarendon Press, 1963).
3. This general point is well illustrated by numerous recent essays on late-medieval audiences and reading by scholars of the early book; see for example, the relevant essays in *Design and Distribution of Late Medieval Manuscripts in England*, ed. Margaret Connolly and Linne Mooney (Woodbridge, Suff.: York Medieval Press, 2008).
4. See the recent description in Neil Ripley Ker and Alan John Piper, *Medieval Manuscripts in British Libraries, IV Paisley-York* (Oxford: Clarendon Press, 1992), 538–40; also Edward Charlton, "Roll of Prayers Formerly Belonging to Henry VIII When Prince," *Archaeologia Aeliana* n.s. 2 (1858): 41–45. For the purchase of the roll by the British Library, see the newsletter of the Association for Manuscripts and Archives in Research Collections, *AMARC Newsletter* 55 (October 2010) ["New Arrivals" section]; http://www.amarc.org.uk (accessed April 23, 2011).
5. See color reproduction posted on the British Library Medieval and Earlier Manuscripts Blog; http://britishlibrary.typepad.co.uk/digitisedmanuscripts/ (accessed April 23, 2011).
6. Color reproduction in *Henry VIII, Man and Monarch*, ed. Susan Doran (London: British Library, 2009), 46 [plate 35].
7. Illustrations 4, 5, 6 reproduced in color in David Starkey, *Henry, Virtuous Prince* (London: Harper Press, 2008), 208–09.
8. Full listing in Michael Sargent, ed. *Nicholas Love: The Mirror of the Blessed Life of Jesus Christ, A Full Critical Edition* (Exeter: University of Exeter Press, 2005), xvi-xviii.
9. For debate over just how indiscriminately and widely the symbolism underlying such ubiquitous markers of Tudor kingship and authority was exploited and understood, see Kevin Sharpe, *Selling the Tudor Monarchy: Authority and Image in Sixteenth-Century England* (New Haven, CT: Yale University Press, 2009).
10. Sean Cunningham, *Henry VII* (Abingdon: Routledge, 2007), 117–19; see also Margaret Condon, "God Save the King! Piety, Propaganda and the Perpetual

Memorial," in *Westminster Abbey: The Lady Chapel of Henry VII* (Woodbridge, Suff.: Boydell & Brewer, 2003), 59–97.

11. Cunningham, *Henry VII*, 60, 100–01.
12. See *Arthur Tudor, Prince of Wales: Life, Death and Commemoration*, ed. Steven Gunn and Linda Monckton (Woodbridge, Suff.: Boydell & Brewer, 2009).
13. *Henry VIII, Man and Monarch*, ed. Doran, 46; see also Starkey, *Henry, Virtuous Prince*, 201–05.
14. Rossell Hope Robbins, "The 'Arma Christi' Rolls," *Modern Language Review* 34 (1939): 415–21.
15. See the interesting comments on the cross-fertilization between individual and congregational aspects of devotional experience of this kind in Eamonn Duffy, *The Stripping of the Altars: Traditional Religion in England, 1400–1580* (New Haven , CT: Yale University Press, 1992), 103–109.
16. See also Robert Swanson, *Indulgences in Late Medieval England: Passports to Paradise?* (Cambridge, UK: Cambridge University Press, 2007), 278–348.
17. For the problems of writing a convincing history of intimacy for the later Middle Ages, see also Eamon Duffy, *Marking the Hours: English People and Their Prayers 1240–1570* (New Haven, CT: Yale University Press, 2006), esp. 3–64.
18. Don Skemer, *Binding Words: Textual Amulets in the Middle Ages* (University Park, PA: Pennsylvania State University Press, 1986), 156–62.
19. Skemer, *Binding Words*, 235–78 [Henry's prayer roll is discussed at 264–67].
20. This is the explanation preferred by John Scarisbrick, *Henry VIII* (Berkeley and Los Angeles: University of California Press, 1968), 9.
21. Frank Arthur Mumby, *The Youth of Henry VIII: A Narrative in Contemporary Letters* (Boston and New York: Houghton Mifflin Company, 1913).
22. Ralph Griffiths, *The Principality of Wales: The Structure and Personnel of Government, I South Wales, 1277–1536* (Cardiff: University of Wales Press, 1972), 205–06.
23. *Letters and Papers, Foreign and Domestic of the Reign of Henry VIII*, 4.3, arranged and cataloged by John Brewer (London: Longman , 1876), 2578–81 [5774.5.ii, 5774.17].
24. William Robinson, "Henry VIII's Household in the Fifteen-Twenties: The Welsh Connection," *Historical Research* 68 (1995): 178–79 [173–190].
25. Griffiths, *The Principality of Wales*; William Robinson, "The Tudor Revolution in Welsh Government 1536–1543: Its Effects on Gentry Participation," *The English Historical Review* 406 (1988): 1–20.
26. *Letters and Papers, Foreign and Domestic of the Reign of Henry VIII*, 1.1, cataloged by John Brewer, revised by Robert Brodie (London: His Majesty's Stationery Office, 1920), 29 [54.18, 19].
27. Robinson, "Henry VIII's Household," 179, n.23 and ref.
28. Henry Ansgar Kelly, *The Matrimonial Trials of Henry VIII* (Stanford, CA: Stanford University Press, 1976).
29. Starkey, *Henry, Virtuous Prince*, 278 and refs.
30. James Carley, *The Libraries of King Henry VIII* (London: The British Library in association with the British Academy, 2000), xlvi-lv.
31. Maria Hayward, *Dress at the Court of King Henry VIII* (Leeds: Maney and Son, 2007); Lisa Evans, "'The Same Counterpoincte Beinge Olde and Worene': The Mystery of Henry VIII's Green Quilt," in *Medieval Clothing and Textiles, 4*, ed. Robert Netherton and Gail Owen Crocker (Woodbridge, Suff: Boydell & Brewer, 2008), 193–208.

CHAPTER 18

MACBETH AND MALORY IN THE 1625 EDITION OF PETER HEYLYN'S *MICROCOSMUS*: A NEARLY UNFORTUNATE TALE

Toshiyuki Takamiya

Peter Heylyn, MA, DD (1599–1662), known chiefly nowadays for his Laudian polemic and staunch support for Charles I, was a most prolific controversialist in the seventeenth century.[1] Throughout his life he found himself criticized as authoritarian, polemical, or choleric by his enemies (his rival, John Hackett, called him a "bluster-master," for example); nonetheless, he was justly famous among his contemporaries as England's foremost geographer.[2] I strongly suspect Terry Jones—no stranger to prolific controversy—would have loved to portray this extraordinary man in one of the *Monty Python* episodes, especially since, on one occasion at least, Heylyn seems to have teetered, tragic-comically enough, on the brink of disaster.

Heylyn's *Microcosmus, or a Little Description of the Great World, A treatise historicall, geographicall, politicall, theologicall*, based on the very popular lectures he began delivering at Oxford soon after obtaining his BA at Magdalen College in 1617, was heralded at its publication in 1621 as an epoch-making achievement.[3] In no small part this was because it offered one of the earliest descriptions in English of the New World. As Nicolas Barker remarks:

> In 1621 two remarkable best-sellers made their first appearance, both printed in Oxford: Burton's *Anatomy of Melancholy,* and the first modern geography to be printed in English, Peter Heylyn's *Microcosmus*. The latter...in its time it was even more successful: eight Oxford editions in quarto in 1639 were followed before the end of the century by another eight in folio, printed at London under the title of *Cosmographie*.[4]

O. F. G. Sitwell, who has classified the geographical works published in English for the last four centuries, regards the *Microcosmus* as one of the earliest and most important works of "special geography."[5] It well deserves, therefore, to be better known—and as I shall argue, by scholars of literature, as well as history and geography.

The first (1621) edition of the *Microcosmus*, of about 420 pages in small quarto, appeared from Oxford University Press, dedicated to then-Prince Charles.[6] Heylyn evidently took the title from Samuel Purchas's work, *Microcosmus, or the Historie of Man* (1619) and modified the subtitle from George Abbot's work, *A Briefe Description of the Whole World* (1599), both best-selling volumes in the period, while adding *A treatise historicall, geographicall, politicall, theologicall*, thereby indicating his intention to make the work encyclopedic.[7]

Heylyn does not conceal his contrivance to draw on earlier works as heavily as possible. In the preface he makes it clear that "the matter I deriue from others, the words for the most part are mine owne, the method totallie." This "method" was of Heylyn's own devising. Robert Mayhew calls special attention to what he deems Heylyn's "binary method," in which each subject is divided into two. First comes the "real" world, such as continents and nations, later adding islands, and the "imaginary world" denoted by latitude and longitude. In describing Europe, for example, Heylyn starts with Spain in the west, moves on eastward to Greece, and then discusses the four islands, including Britain. Mayhew also identifies what he calls "commonplacing": Heylyn lists in the margin of the *Microcosmus* the sources on which he depended for information. This would have been intended as a guide for students attending his Oxford lectures. Most of these references are names of authors, rather than titles of their works, and they range widely from classical writers such as Aristotle and Plutarch to more modern, even contemporary, figures such as Abraham Ortelius, William Camden, and Samuel Purchas. This "commonplacing" reveals Heylyn's extensive reading—amazing by any standard. In his preface he enumerates his sources by nation. Generally speaking, he is scathing in his commentaries, particularly to earlier historians.[8]

As Heylyn's interest turned in the direction of theology and religion, he took to revising the *Microcosmus*. In his new preface to the second edition of 1625 (as well as in the enlarged *Cosmographie* in 1652), he had moreover to admit, to his shame, that he had not paid due attention to the authenticity of the works he quoted in the first edition, often depending on sources of secondary quality. The "revised and augmented" edition of 1625 was almost twice the size of the first. It is this second edition of 1625 that is, I believe, of special interest for scholars of William Shakespeare and Thomas Malory. Here Heylyn introduces material with direct bearing upon the wider audiences of *Macbeth* and *Le Morte d'Arthur*.

Undoubtedly the most outstanding augmentation in the revised *Microcosmus* is Heylyn's lengthy and elaborate insertion, into the section of Scottish kings, of a 678-word episode on the rise and fall of Macbeth, which in the second edition runs to two full pages.[9] As it has never been reprinted in any modern version, it follows in full:

> Now before I come vnto *Kenneth*, I will in this place relate the story of *Machbed*, one of his successours: a history then which for variety of action, or strangenesse of euent, I neuer met with any more pleasing. The story in briefe is thus[.] *Duncan*

King of *Scotland*, had two principall men whom he employed in all matters of importance; *Machbed* and *Banquho*. These two travelling together through a forrest were mette by three Fairies, or Witches (*Weirds* the *Scots* call them) whereof the first making obeisance vnto *Machbed*, saluted him *Thane* (a title vnto which that of Earle afterward succeeded) of *Glammis*, the second, *Thane* of *Cawder*. and the third, King of *Scotland*. This is vnequall dealing said *Banquho*, to giue my friend all the honors and none vnto me: to whom one of the *Weirds* made answere, that he indeed should not be King, but out of his loynes should come a race of kings that should for euer rule *Scotland*. And having thus said they all suddenly vanished. Vpon their arriuall to the Court, *Machbed* was immediatly created *Thane* of *Glammis*; and not long after, some new seruice of his requiring new recompence, he was honoured with the title of *Thane* of *Cawder*. Seeing then how happily the prediction of the three *Weirds* fell out in the two former; hee resolued not to bee wanting to himselfe in fulfilling the third; and therefore first hee killed the King, and after by reason of his command among the Souldiers and common people, he succeeded in his throne. Being scarce warme in his seat, he called to minde the prediction giuen to his companion *Banquho*, whom herevpon suspecting as his supplanter he caused to be killed, together with his whole kindred, *Fleance* his son onely with much difficulty escaping into *Wales*. Freed now from this feare, he built *Dunsinane* Castle making it his ordinary seat: and afterward on new feares consulting with certaine wizards about his future estate; was by one told that he should neuer bee ouercome till *Bernane* wood (which was some few miles distant) did come to *Dunsinane* Castle: and by the other that he neuer should be slaine by any man borne of a woman. Secure then as he thought, he omitted no kinde of libidinousnesse or cruelty for the space of 18 yeares, for so long he raigned, or to say better, tyrannized. *Mackduffe* gouernour of *Fife*, ioyning to himselfe some fewe Patriots, which had not yet felt the tyrants sword; priuily met one night at *Bernane* wood, and early in the morning marched, euery man bearing a bough in his hand the better to keepe them from discouery; toward *Dunsinane* Castle; which they presently tooke by scaladoe. *Machbed* escaping, was pursued, ouertaken, and vrged to fight by *Mackduffe*; to whom the tyrant halfe in scorne replied, that in vaine he attempted his death: for it was his destinie neuer to be slaine by any man borne of a woman. Now then is thy fatall houre come, said *Mackduffe*, for I was neuer borne of a woman, but violently cut out of my mothers belly, she dying before her deliuery: which words so danted the tyrant, though otherwise a man of good performance, that he was easily slaine; and *Malcolme Conmor* the true heire of the Crowne, seated in the throne. In the meane time *Fleance* so thriued in *Wales* that he fell in loue with the *Welch* Princes daughter, and on her begat a sonne named *Walter*. This *Walter* flying *Wales* for a murther, was entertained in *Scotland*, and his descent once knowne, he was preferred to be *Steward* vnto King *Edgar*, from which office the name of *Steward* became as the sir-name of all his posterity. From this *Walter* descended that *Robert Steward*, who was after in right of his wife, King of *Scotland*; since which time there haue been successiuely nine Soueraignes of this name in *Scotland*. But it is now high time (the prophecies being fulfilled, and my story finished) to attend King *Kenneth*, & his successours.

(Heylyn 1625: 508–10; no counterpart in Heylyn 1621)

Heylyn introduces the Macbeth episode immediately after he refers to Kenneth, skipping a few kings who followed him, including Duncan and his son Malcolm.

This suggests that Heylyn was aware of the importance of Kenneth, as the king with whom hereditary rule began in Scotland. Macbeth's usurpation, and the subsequent recovery of the crown by Malcolm, might suggest that the Scottish line was unstable—an issue likely to offend King James I, who emphasized royal absolutism. Presumably Heylyn, who clearly had the king in mind as an important reader of his book, tried to avoid foregrounding this problem. Thus, Malcolm is removed from his text, and the kinship between Macbeth and Duncan is ignored.[10]

Despite notice by some few Shakespeareans, scant critical attention has been paid to Heylyn's account of the Macbeth story.[11] His source has yet to be identified. Strong possibilities are Shakespeare's *Macbeth*, first published in the First Folio (1623), its sources, that is, the Scottish chronicles of Raphael Holinshed and John Bellenden, or even perhaps the latter's source, Hector Boece and George Buchanan. (Heylyn, however, was highly critical of Buchanan's Latin chronicles.) But Heylyn's version is not identical with any of these.[12]

A cursory comparison of spellings of proper names for major characters between Heylyn's and Holinshed's Macbeth narratives reveals the uniqueness of Heylyn's spelling "Machbed," which he uses five times, with no variants. This is a mildly striking phenomenon, because proper names in the *Microcosmos* generally show variants of one kind and another. Heylyn must have found reason to have written, inserted, and proofread the episode on his own, implying that "Machbed" was introduced on purpose. Graham Caie has suggested that the spelling seems of Gaelic origin.[13] This opens the possibility of a Scottish chronicle, now lost, as Heylyn's source. But more likely (despite the contrary view of William Carroll, who maintains that Shakespeare's tragedy was unknown to him), Heylyn's idiosyncratic spelling results from his memory of *Macbeth* on stage.[14] Certainly the memorandum of one Simon Forman (1552–1611), astrologer, alchemist, and physician, who witnessed the play in 1611, stands as an example of an audience member relying on his memory for his spellings "Mackbeth," "Bancko," and "King of Codon."[15] Interestingly, Heylyn's anecdote was reprinted verbatim in his enlarged *Cosmographie* (1652), with the exception of the spelling "Machbed," which was changed in the latter edition to the more Shakespearean "Machbeth" (II, 302).

Heylyn's source is worthy of pursuit, however, because it might help explain why Heylyn, who had not touched on Macbeth at all in the first edition, took the trouble in the revised second edition to add two full pages dealing with Macbeth. The decision seems the more curious in light of his claim in his preface that he would emphasize the truth and reject the fabulous in his account of old Scottish kings. One thus naturally wonders how he could justify the addition of an account of Macbeth with the Weird Sisters in it.

A possible answer has been offered by Willard Farnham, who argues that Heylyn did so hoping to rectify what may have been a conflict between King James and himself.[16] In the first edition of the *Microcosmus* (1621), Heylyn got slightly carried away with his pen about an early custom of the Scottish society, which reads as follows.

> The people haue one barbarous custome yet continuing, if any two be displeased they expect no law, but bang it out brauely, one and his kindred against the other and his: and thinke the king much in their common, if they grant him at a certaine day to keepe the peace. This fighting they call their *Feides*, a word so barbarous, that were it to be expressed in *Latine* or *French*, it must be by circumlocution.[17]

In the margin, Heylyn mentions as a source the *Basilicon Doron* (1599), the manual for the princely education that James wrote for his son Henry, before the Crown Prince's premature death. In the second edition of the *Microcosmus*, Heylyn has moved this note into the main text, with telling additions:

> The people had not long since one barbarous custome: which was, if any two were displeased, they expected no law; but bang't out brauely, one & his kindred, against the other and his, and thought the King much in their common, if they granted him at a certaine day to keepe the peace. This fighting they call their *Feides*, a word so barbarous, that were it to bee expressed in *Latine* or *French*, it must be by circumlocution. These deadly feids, his Maiestie in his most excellent *Basilicon Doron*, aduiseth his sonne to redresse with all care possible; but God hath giuen him a long life, to see it in his owne daies remedied; wherein he hath gotten a greater victory ouer that people, then euer any sorraigne Prince, or any of his predecessours: an act indeed truely royall, and worthy himselfe. . . .[18]

Farnham's conjecture must remain only that, then—conjecture—for we have no positive evidence to support it. Nothing indicates that Heylyn had met James before 1625, the year both of the publication of the *Microcosmus* second edition, and the king's death. Nevertheless, as Farnham points out, several more instances of what appear to be peace offerings to the king can be found in the revised edition.[19] One is the placement of the Macbeth story between Heylyn's rejection of fabulous kings and his inclusion of the historical kings of Scotland. Another is suggested by Heylyn's knowledge of James' work, *Daemonologie* (1597), in which the king discusses witch hunting and witch trials. This may have implied a royal interest that Heylyn sought to turn to his advantage.

Still, the most substantial clues, as yet unnoticed, of Heylyn's attempt to use literary references to propitiate the king may in fact forge a closer link with Shakespeare's play. In the beginning of his retelling of the Macbeth story, Heylyn mentions three "Fairies, or Witches (*Weirds* the *Scots* call them)" (Heylyn 1625: 509). The use of "Weirds" in this context certainly seems to imply direct knowledge of *Macbeth*, and one may wonder whether Heylyn had in mind using this play to mollify the allegedly disgruntled king with a convoluted form of flattery. At IV. iii. 141–161, Shakespeare presents a famous scene on the "king's evil" (or scrofula), which is usually interpreted as the Bard's own paean to James.

> DOCTOR: Ay, sir: there are a crew of wretched souls
> That stay his cure; their malady convinces
> The great assay of art, but at his touch,
> Such sanctity hath heaven given his hand,
> They presently amend.

MALCOLM: I thank you, doctor.
MACDUFF: What's the disease he means?
MALCOLM:'Tis called the Evil.
A most miraculous work in this good king,
Which often since my here-remain in England
I have seen him do. How he solicits heaven
Himself best knows, but strangely visited people
All swoll'n and ulcerous, pitiful to the eye,
The mere despair of surgery, he cures,
Hanging a golden stamp about their necks
Put on with holy prayers, and 'tis spoken
To the succeeding royalty he leaves
The healing benediction. With this strange virtue,
He hath a heavenly gift of prophecy,
And sundry blessings hang about his throne
That speak him full of grace.[20]

The "he" in the passage is Edward the Confessor, respected as a special saint by English monarchs from Richard II forward. The "King's Evil" was named in the belief, then widely held, that along with the crown a rightful monarch alone inherited the ability to cure the disease with a touch. Edward the Confessor was thought to have gained this gift initially, and most interestingly, Heylyn includes in his second edition of the *Microcosmus* a reference also to the Confessor's healing touch:

> [Edward the Confessor] was in his life of that holinesse, that he receaued power from aboue to cure many diseases; amongst others the swelling of the throat, called by vs the *Kings evill*: a prerogatiue that continueth hereditary to his successours of England. Finally after his death he was canonized for a Saint: & died hauing raigned 24 yeares.[21]

Two major conciliatory messages to King James may underlie Heylyn's strategy here. James clearly believed in his healing power, practicing cures using the "touch piece" and the "Angel coin."[22] A John Ernest from Weimar witnessed and recorded one instance on September 19, 1613:

> When [the service] was concluded, his Majesty stood up . . . immediately the Royal Physician brought [the sufferers] who were afflicted . . . and bade them kneel down . . . and as the Physician had already examined the disease (which he is always obliged to do, in order that no deception may be practiced), he then pointed out the afflicted part . . . to his Majesty, who thereupon touched it, pronouncing these words: *Le Roy vous touche, Dieu vous guery* (The King touches, may God heal thee!) and then hung a rose-noble round the neck [of the sufferer] . . . with a white silk ribbon . . . .[23]

It may have seemed to Heylyn, no less than it is surmised it did to Shakespeare, that the king would take as a compliment such a reference to his power to cure the King's Evil—the more so because, as a mystical gift from rightful king to rightful king from Edward the Confessor on, James's ability to cure sufferers with a touch could only enhance public recognition of his legitimacy to rule. The divine right of kings, moreover, was a long-standing point-at-issue for James, beginning with his defense of it in the *True Law of Free Monarchie* (1598). He stated to the English parliament in 1609 his strongly held belief that a monarch derived the right to rule directly from the will of God and was subject to no earthly authority. The view guided his relations with parliament thereafter. Any supportive allusion to it must only have been interpreted by James as conciliatory.

A second possible clue that perhaps literature was seen by Heylyn as a suitable bridge to the king's better side is present in what he may have excerpted from Malory's *Morte d'Arthur.*[24] Again, a veiled reference to the King's Evil seems to underlie Heylyn's singling out Malory's original story of Lancelot's healing of the wounded Sir Urry by touching in book 19, chapters 10–12.[25] Sir Urry, a Hungarian knight, although he defeated an opponent in a battle in Spain, was subject to seven wounds by the magic of his mother, which were curable only by the best knight in the world. For seven years he traveled far and wide in search of such a knight, but to no avail. When finally Sir Urry came to visit King Arthur's court at Carlile, all of the 110 knights then assembled, along with Arthur himself, tried to cure him, but in vain.[26] When Sir Lancelot came back to the court, he healed Urry miraculously:

> And than syr Launcelot prayed syr Urre for to let him see his head. And tha*n* deuoutly kneelynge, hee ransaked the three woundes, that they bledde a littel. And forthwyth the three woundes faire healed, and seemed as though they had bene hole a seuen yere tofore. And in lykewise he serched his body of three other woundes, and they healed in likewise. And tha*n* the last of all he serched, the which was in his hand and anon it healed faire. Than kinge Arthur and all the other kynges and knightes kneeled downe, and gaue thanckes and prayse unto god and to his blessed mother, and euer syr Launcelot wept as he had ben a chyld that had ben beaten.[27]

Worthy of attention here is the fact that Heylyn deals with no other episode from Malory in the second edition of the *Microcosmus* except the "Healing of Sir Urry." This suggests that Heylyn found important the potential of this story as a means to reference once again King James's curing of the King's Evil. A further compliment to the king could be paid because Sir Urry was healed by the touch of Sir Lancelot, the best knight of the world. Although he was not King Arthur, his knightly perfection could only have been taken as a high compliment by James. Heylyn might well have felt that these two literary inclusions into the second edition of his major work would win, or restore, the king's favor.

Unfortunately for Heylyn, he was undermined in his attempts (if attempts they were) to flatter the king with references taken from English literature by circumstances beyond his control—events that have substantial importance for the bibliophilic history of the *Microcosmus* and explain why the second edition went into a second issue. Despite Heylyn's best intentions, a colossal mistake was revealed as the first copies of the revised edition arrived, one of which was delivered to King James by the kind offices of John Young, Dean of Winchester, Heylyn's acquaintance.[28] At the top of page 491, the same page in which the "Healing of Sir Urry" appears, the king's eye fell upon an unflattering description in connection with England's royal coat of arms: "France is the larger & more famous [than England]." The king was reportedly so displeased that he ordered the Lord Keeper to call in the book. Young, who played the role of go-between, suggested to Heylyn that he should immediately go to the royal court, but Heylyn obstinately declined, staying on at Oxford and writing a lengthy letter of apologies. He maintained that his account was of the period of Edward III, and "is" a misprint for "was." The compositor, Heylyn affirmed, should have been responsible for the error. (In the third and subsequent editions of the *Microcosmus*, "is" is corrected to "was," but the description otherwise remains unchanged.) The passage concerned has survived, finding its place in the enlarged *Cosmographie* (1652), as "France, at the time of the first quartering of them, was the larger and more famous kingdom" (I, 286).

The incident makes an interesting case in the history of the book and helps bring the story of the nearly unfortunate Peter Heylyn to a close. Details have been in confusion and published accounts have been vague, if not altogether misleading. Anthony Milton, for example, makes no mention of the incident in his entry for the *Oxford DNB*, and is vague in his article of 2002, using the expression "reportedly."[29] Barker's account contains serious misinformation:

> [Heylyn] annoyed James I by saying in *Microcosmos* that "France is the greater and more famous Kingdom than England"; "is" was a misprint for "was," he replied, and the passage referred to the time of Edward III, *but he wisely suppressed it in later editions.*[30]

Our investigation, however, betrayed the existence of as many as five extant copies of the second edition in which "& more famous" was deleted with pen and ink.[31] These copies carry errata in the last printed page, and are clearly a second issue. Probably they were not examined by either Milton or Mayhew. The British Library, the Bodleian Library, the Cambridge University Library (all major libraries that English scholars would surely visit as a first choice) have each got a copy of the *Microcosmus*, second edition, first issue, in which one cannot detect on page 491 any sign of deletion or obliteration. The five extant copies, which bear the sign of deletion, are all second edition, second issue.

A variety of inferences can be drawn from the copies showing deletions: 1) Heylyn himself may have effected the deletions in copies of the second edition, second issue, which were still in stock at the Oxford University Press; 2) the deletions were made by contemporary owners who understood the situation from hearsay coming from the court; 3) the deletions were the work of later owners. Although certainty about the hands behind the individual deletions may never be ours, nevertheless the fact that the same passage was deleted in several copies in the similar way as we see, makes it is not unreasonable to surmise that royal displeasure at this passage actually occurred as reported. It must, therefore, have been a narrow escape from punishment for Heylyn, presumably thanks to the go-between's kind intervention—although the death of the king on March 25, 1625, might also have been a factor. In the end, the "unfortunate" Heylyn was, perhaps, quite fortunate indeed.

Notes

1. The section on Heylyn's Macbeth episode in the present article is partly based on the unpublished BA thesis of Ms. Junko Furukawa, "Peter Heylyn and the Stuarts in the 1620s: A Study of the First Two Editions of the *Microcosmus*," Keio University, 2011. Her research was done under my supervision, and I gratefully acknowledge her kind permission to draw upon it here. I am grateful also for invaluable assistance I have received in the preparation of the article from Professor Graham Caie, Mr. Christopher Edwards, Ms. Junko Furukawa, Dr. Linda Gowans, Mr. Robert Harding, Dr. Ryoko Harikae, Dr. Simon Horobin, Professor Arata Ide, and Dr. Daniel Wakelin. I am also indebted to the members of the following libraries for information and service: the Chetham Library, the Duke University Library, and the Huntington Library.
2. It is perhaps relevant here to mention my sources for Heylyn's biographical information, given the scarcity of his extant autograph manuscripts and letters, the understandable result of his unsettled life as a refugee, moving in England from one place to another when the political conflicts became extreme after the 1640s. I have drawn variously on the following: Peter Heylyn, "Heylyn's Own Memoranda," in *Memorial of Bishop Waynflete*, ed. John Rouse Bloxam (London: Caxton Club, 1851; New York: Franklin, 1967) x-xxiv; [George Vernon], "The Life of the Most Learned and Reverend Dr. Peter Heylyn," in *The historical and Miscellaneous Tracts of the Reverend and Learned Peter Heylyn, D.D.* (London: Harper, 1681), pp. i-xxviii; George Vernon, *The Life of the Learned and Reverend Dr. Peter Heylyn* (London: Harper, 1682); John Barnard, *Ecclesia Restaurata: Or, the History of the Reformation of the Church*, by Peter Heylyn (London, 1683; ed. James Craigie Robertson, Cambridge, UK: Cambridge University Press, 1849); Michael Creighton's anonymous article in the *DNB*; Anthony Milton's in the *Oxford DNB*; and the latter's seminal monograph, *Laudian and Royalist Polemic in Seventeenth-Century England: The Career and Writings of Peter Heylyn* (Manchester: Manchester University Press, 2007).
3. Peter Heylyn, *Microcosmus, or a little description of the great world* (Oxford: printed by John Lichfield and James Short, printers to the famous University, 1621).
4. Nicolas Barker, *The Oxford University Press and the Spread of Learning: An Illustrated History* (Oxford: Clarendon, 1978), 9; Peter Heylyn, *Cosmographie* (London: Henry Seile, 1652); ed. and introd. Robert Mayhew (Bristol: Thoemmes, 2003).
5. O. F. G. Sitwell, *Four Centuries of Special Geography* (Vancouver: University of British Columbia Press, 1993).
6. For detailed bibliographical descriptions of editions of the *Microcosmus*, see John Huber Walker, "A Descriptive Bibliography of the Early Printed Works of Peter Heylyn," Unpublished PhD Dissertation, the Shakespeare Institute, the University of Birmingham, 1978.
7. Samuel Purchas, *Microcosmvs, or the Historie of Man* (London: William Stansby, 1619; Amsterdam: Theatrum Orbis Terrarum, 1969); George Abbot, *A Briefe Description of the Whole Worlde* (London: T. Judson, 1599; Amsterdam: Theatrum Orbis Terrarum, 1970).
8. Robert J. Mayhew. "Peter Heylyn." *Geographers: Biobiblio- graphical Studies* 28 (2009): 1–16.
9. Heylyn, *Microcosmus* (1625) 508–10; no counterpart in the 1621 edition.
10. I am grateful to Dr. Ryoko Harikae for this view, which she expressed at the annual general meeting of the English Literary Society of Japan, held at the City

University of Kita Kyushu on June 22, 2011, when I read a paper on the subject, on which the present article is based.

11. For example, Ingrid Benecke, "Simon Forman's Notes on *Macbeth*—The Alternative Reading," *Notes and Queries* 57.3 (2010): 389–93; Willard Farnham, *Shakespeare's Tragic Frontier: The World of His Final Tragedies* (Oxford: Blackwell, 1973); S. Schoenbaum, *William Shakespeare: Records and Images* (London: Scolar, 1981); Leah Scragg, "Macbeth on Horseback," *Shakespeare Survey* 26 (1973): 81–88.
12. Raphael Holinshed, *Holinshed's Chronicle*, 1st ed. (London: H. Bynneman for John Harrison, 1577); 2nd ed. (London: J. Hooker and Vowell Gent, 1587); John Bellenden, *Hystory and Croniklis of Scotland* (Edinburgh: Thomas Davidson, c. 1537); Hector Boece, *Scotorum Historiae* (Paris: Badius Ascensius, 1527); George Buchanan, *Rerum Scoticarum historia* (Edinburgh: A. Arbuthnot, 1582).
13. I am grateful to Professor Graham D. Caie of the University of Glasgow for this view, which he mentioned in our conversation in Tokyo in January 2011.
14. William C. Carroll, "'Two Truths are Told': Afterlives and Histories of Macbeths," *Shakespeare Survey* 57 (2004): 69–80. Carroll argues that Heylyn did not know Shakespeare's tragedy, because he did not mention either Lady Macbeth or Macbeth's good governance for well over ten years. J. P. Hudson suggests some possible connections between Heylyn and Shakespeare in "Peter Heylyn's Poetry Notebook," *British Museum Quarterly* 34 (1969): 19–27.
15. Forman, *Boeke of Plaies*, Bodleian Library MS Ashmole 208, ff. 207r-v; quoted in William Shakespeare, *Macbeth*, ed. A. R. Braunmuller (Cambridge, UK: Cambridge University Press, 1997), 57–58. See further, Benecke, Farnham, and Scragg in note 10 above, and Carroll in note 13; Lauren Kassell, *Medicine and Magic in Elizabethan London: Simon Forman, Astrologer, Alchemist, and Physician* (Oxford: Oxford University Press, 2005); J. M. Nosworthy, "'Macbeth' at the Globe," *The Library*, S5.11 (1947): 108–18; A. L. Rowse, *Simon Forman: Sex and Society in Shakespeare's Age* (London: Weidenfeld & Nicolson, 1974); Barbara Howard Traister, *The Notorious Astrological Physician of London: Works and Days of Simon Forman* (Chicago: University of Chicago Press., 2001); John Dover Wilson and R. W. Hunt, "The Authenticity of Simon Forman's *Bocke of Plaies*," *Review of English Studies* 23 (1947): 193–200.
16. Farnham, *Shakespeare's Tragic Frontier*, 87.
17. Heylyn, *Microcosmus* (1621), 266.
18. Heylyn, *Microcosmus* (1625), 503–04.
19. Farnham, *Shakespeare's Tragic Frontier*, 87.
20. William Shakespeare, *Macbeth*, ed. Braunmuller.
21. Heylyn, *Microcosmus* (1625), 463.
22. For discussions of the king's evil, see Marc Bloch, *Les rois thaumaturges* (Paris: Colin, 1961) and Raymond Crawfurd, *The King's Evil* (New York: AMS, 1977).W. R. Rye, *England as Seen by Foreigners* (1865), 151: quoted by Braunmuller, William Shakespeare, *Macbeth* 244.
23. Rye, *England as Seen*, 151: quoted by Braunmuller, *Macbeth*, 244.
24. If one agrees that the episode that Heylyn introduces is derived from Malory's *Morte*, this presence in Heylyn's *Microcosmus* would represent only the earliest reference to the *Morte* in the seventeenth century, the others being William Stansby's edition of the *Morte* in 1634 and William Nicolson's *Historical Library* in 1696. See Marylyn Jackson Parins, ed., *Malory: The Critical Heritage*, (London: Routledge, 1988), and further Linda Gowans, "Three Malory Notes," *BBIAS*, 58 (2006):

425–34, and Raluca L. Radulescu, "Malory's Lancelot and the Key to Salvation," *Arthurian Literature*, 25 ( ): 93–118, especially 106.

25. No source has been found for this episode. See, for a summary of the possible sources and analogues, Ralph Norris, *Malory's Library: The Sources of the Morte Darthur* (Cambridge, UK: D. S. Brewer, 2008), and the following note.
26. Heylyn seems particularly interested in the Round Table, which originally seated 150 knights, as he stresses in his version of "Sir Urry" that only 110 were present, the rest being absent on missions. In the *Microcosmus*, 1625 edition, Heylyn makes a brief account of "The Healing of Sir Urry" in terms of the order of knighthood of the Round Table, listing major orders of knighthood in England: "The principal orders of knighthood are, 1 of the Round Table, instituted by Arthur King of the Brittaines, and one of the Worlds nine Worthies. It consisted of 150 knights, whose names are recorded in the history of K. Arthur, there where Sir Vr a wounded knight, came to be cured of his hurts, it being his fate, that only the best Knight of the whole order could be his Chirurgion. The principall of them were Sir Lancelot, Sir Tristrum, Sir Lambrocke, Sir Gawaine, &c. They were all placed at one Round Table, to auoide quarrels about priority and place. The Round Table hanging in the great hall at Winchester, is falsely called Arthurs Round Table; it being not of sufficient antiquity, and containing but 24 seats. Of these knights there are reported many fabulous stories" (Heylyn 1625: 491). It is worthy to note, first of all, that, despite extensive research done in the past, no specific source has been identified of the "Healing of Sir Urry," and so it has been generally regarded as original to Malory. Heylyn's *The History of King Arthur* must therefore be drawn from Malory's *Morte*, particularly the fifth blackletter edition published by Thomas East about 1578, when it was entitled *The Story of King Arthur.* Arthur is mentioned as one of the Nine Worthies by William Caxton in his preface to the *Morte*, which is included in East's edition. The number of the Arthurian knights of the Round Table, which began with Wace's Anglo-Norman chronicle, *Le Roman de Brut*, in the late twelfth century, differs from one work to another, but Malory in book 3 mentions Guinevere bringing to Arthur's court as a bridal gift a round table seating 150 knights, which was once presented by Uther Pendragon, Arthur's father, to her own father. Like Malory, Heylyn refers to the Round Table as consisting of 150 knights, criticizing the Winchester Round Table with 24 seats as a false one.
27. Malory, *The Story of King Arthur*, ed. Thomas East, c.1578: sig. Ll5v; book 19, chapter 12.
28. For an account of this incident, see Michael Creighton's anonymous account of Heylyn in the *DNB*, which is based on Wood's *Athenae Oxonienses* (London: R. Knaplock, 1721), II, 275–90; rev. Philip Bliss (London: n.p., 1817; rpt. Hildesheim: Olms, 1969).
29. Anthony Milton, "The Creation of Laudianism: A New Approach," in *Religion and Popularity in Early Stuart Britain: Essays in Honour of Conrad Russell*, ed. Thomas Cogswell, Richard Cust and Pater Lake (Cambridge, UK: Cambridge University Press, 2002), 162–84.
30. Barker, *Oxford University Press and the Spread of Learning*, 9. (Italics mine.)
31. These are in the Chetham Library, the Duke University Library, the Huntington Library, the Keio University Library, and the present author's collection. I shall publish elsewhere a bibliographical note on this intriguing phenomenon.

CONTRIBUTORS

Michael Bennett is Professor of History at the University of Tasmania. He is the author of four books on late-medieval and early Tudor history, and has written a range of articles on the history of Middle English literature. In addition to continuing his work on late-medieval England, he is currently writing a global history of the early spread of vaccination.

John M. Bowers is an internationally known scholar of medieval English literature with books on Chaucer, Langland, and the *Pearl* Poet. His dozens of articles span the tradition from St. Augustine to Shakespeare. Educated at Duke University, the University of Virginia, and the University of Oxford, where he was a Rhodes Scholar, he taught at the California Institute of Technology and Princeton University before settling at the University of Nevada, Las Vegas. His work has been supported by fellowships from the National Endowment for the Humanities and the John Simon Guggenheim Foundation. His "Great Courses" lectures, "The Western Literary Canon in Context," were released as CDs/DVDs by the Teaching Company. He recently published *End of Story*, his first novel. His latest scholarly volume is *An Introduction to the "Gawain" Poet.*

Martha Driver is Distinguished Professor of English and Women's and Gender Studies at Pace University in New York City. A co-founder of the Early Book Society for the study of manuscripts and printing history, she has edited or published 21 books and journals, including *The Image in Print: Book Illustration in Late Medieval England* and the *Journal of the Early Book Society*. She is a co-editor of the Texts and Transitions book series published by Brepols.

Chris Given-Wilson is Professor of Late Medieval History at the University of St. Andrews, Scotland. His research interests focus on the political and social history and historiography of the fourteenth and fifteenth centuries, mainly in England. He is the author or editor of eight books, including *The Royal Household and the King's Affinity*, *The English Nobility in the Late Middle Ages,* and *Chronicles: The Writing of History in Late Medieval England.* He is also the general editor of *The Parliament Rolls of Medieval England*. He is currently writing a biography of Henry IV of England.

Richard Firth Green is a Professor of English and Director of the Center for Medieval and Renaissance Studies at The Ohio State University. He is the author of *A Crisis of Truth: Literature and Law in Ricardian England*, *Poets and Princepleasers: Literature and the English Court in the Late Middle Ages*, and of numerous articles in such journals as *Speculum*, *Medium Aevum*, *Chaucer Review*, and *Studies in the Age of Chaucer*. He is a former John Simon Guggenheim Memorial Foundation fellow (1989–90), and is a past president of the New Chaucer Society (2008–2010).

Sanae Ikeda is a PhD candidate at Keio University. She is working on the library of Dr. Philip Gaskell, a British bibliographer, now part of the Keio University Library. She has read papers in bibliography and the history of the book at the international congresses of the Early Book Society, and has published "Caxton's Printing of Christine de Pisan's *Fayttes of Armes and of Chyualrye*" in the *Journal of the Early Book Society*.

V. A. Kolve, BA, University of Wisconsin; BA, the University of Oxford (Jesus College, as a Rhodes Scholar); D.Phil, the University of Oxford, where he taught as a Junior Fellow for four years, at St. Edmund Hall. He is the author of *The Play Called Corpus Christi*, *Chaucer and the Imagery of Narrative*, and *Telling Images: Chaucer and the Imagery of Narrative II*, and co-edited, with Glending Olson, the *Norton Critical Edition of Chaucer's Canterbury Tales*. In a long career distinguished by gifted students who became medievalists, he taught at the University of Oxford, Stanford University, the University of Virginia, and University of California, Los Angeles, from which he retired in 2001.

Priscilla Martin teaches English Literature and Classics at the University of Oxford. She has also taught at the universities of Edinburgh, London, Colorado, Washington, and California. Her publications include *Piers Plowman: the Field and the Tower*, *Chaucer's Women: Nuns, Wives and Amazons*, *Iris Murdoch: A Literary Life* and introductions and articles on Tyndale, the *Gawain*-poet, Shakespeare, and twentieth-century novelists.

Peter Nicholson is Professor of English at the University of Hawai`i at Manoa, where he has taught since 1974. He is the author of *An Annotated Index to the Commentary on John Gower's Confessio Amantis*, *Love and Ethics in Gower's Confessio Amantis*, and numerous articles on medieval literature, English and continental.

W. Mark Ormrod is Professor of History at the University of York and a specialist in the political and cultural history of later medieval England. The author of *Political Life in Medieval England, 1300–1450* and (with Anthony Musson) *The Evolution of English Justice: Law, Politics and Society in the Fourteenth Century*, he is co-editor of *The Parliament Rolls of Medieval England* and of *A Social History of England, 1200–1500*. His *Edward III* is published in the Yale University Press "English Monarchs" series. He has led a series of major projects resulting in the cataloguing and indexing of record series at the National Archives (London) and the Borthwick Institute for Archives (York). He is a fellow of the Royal Historical Society and of the Society of Antiquaries, a trustee of the Richard III and Yorkist History Trust, and a councillor of the Pipe Roll Society.

Michael Palin was born in Sheffield in Yorkshire in 1943. He met Terry Jones at the University of Oxford and teamed with him to write for BBC's *The Frost Report* in 1966, and later on the Monty Python TV shows and films as well as the BBC series *Ripping Yarns*. He appeared in films like *A Fish Called Wanda* and *The*

Missionary, and cowrote *Time Bandits* with Terry Gilliam. In 1989, his documentary travel series *Around the World in Eighty Days* was aired on the BBC. He has since made six more, including *Pole to Pole* and *Himalaya*. He has published two volumes of diaries and a novel, *Hemingway's Chair*. He is currently working on a book and series about Brazil.

Derek Pearsall became Gurney Professor of English at Harvard University in 1985 after teaching for twenty years at the University of York, where he helped found the Centre for Medieval Studies. He retired from Harvard in 2000 and returned to live in York. Published work includes a biography of John Lydgate, *Old English and Middle English Poetry*, a critical study of the *Canterbury Tales*, *Geoffrey Chaucer: a Critical Biography*, *Arthurian Literature: An Introduction*, *Gothic Europe*, and, most recently, a fully annotated edition, newly revised, of the C-Text of Langland's *Piers Plowman*. There are also many essays and articles on medieval romance, on fifteenth-century literature, on *Sir Gawain and the Green Knight*, on Gower, as well as on Chaucer, Lydgate, and Langland.

William A. Quinn is Professor of English and the Director of the Medieval and Renaissance Studies program at the University of Arkansas. His recent research interests have been the history of poetic form in England, the implications of authorial recital for interpretations of Chaucer's early narratives, and a consideration of subsequent scribal translations of those recital intentions.

Nigel Saul is Professor of Medieval History at Royal Holloway, University of London, and author of *Richard II*. His most recent book is *For Honour and Fame: Chivalry in England, 1066–1500*.

Toshiyuki Takamiya, now emeritus, studied and taught at Keio Univerisity, and worked at Cambridge University under the guidance of Derek Brewer and Ian Doyle. A medievalist in English literature, he published books and articles on Malory and Hilton. He is well known as a collector of medieval manuscripts and a pioneer in the digitization of rare books. He is an FSA, Hon.LittD (Sheffield) and Hon.DLitt (Glasgow). In July 2011, the international conference of the Early Book Society was held in his honor in York.

John J. Thompson is Professor of English Textual Cultures at Queen's University Belfast. He has published widely on vernacular production and reception issues in late-medieval Britain and has been the director of two large collaborative research projects funded by the UK Arts and Humanities Research Council: "Imagining History" (a cultural mapping exercise for manuscripts of the Middle English prose *Brut*, a text known to later readers of the printed versions as "the Chronicles of England"), and "Geographies of Orthodoxy" (a profile of the English texts and afterlives of the Latin affective tradition of remembering the life of Christ, epitomized by the *Meditationes vitae Christi*). He is now working on other neglected aspects of English vernacular biblical and historical understanding in the pre-Enlightenment period and their wider European impact.

David Wallace studied at York, Perugia, and Cambridge and has been Judith Rodin Professor, University of Pennsylvania, since 1996, with visiting spells at London,

Princeton, Melbourne, and Jerusalem. His work situates English culture within and as part of a greater European milieu. Documentary features for BBC Radio 3 include *Bede*, *Margery Kempe*, *Malory*, and *John Leland*, with actors taking the main speaking roles. President of the New Chaucer Society (2004–06), his teaching pays particular attention to performativity. Most recent books are *Premodern Places* and *Strong Women*, and he is currently editing the first literary history of Europe, 1348–1418, to be published in 82 chapters and two volumes by Oxford University Press.

R. F. Yeager is Professor of English and Foreign Languages and chair of the department at the University of West Florida. He is President of the International John Gower Society, editor of *JGN (The John Gower Newsletter)*, and has published widely on medieval English and European literatures. His special interests are Old English literature and language, the French of England, and the poetry of Chaucer and Gower. He has written and edited more than seventeen books and collections of essays, including *John Gower's Poetic: The Search for a New Arion*; *A Concordance to the French Poetry and Prose of John Gower*; and *Who Murdered Chaucer? A Medieval Mystery*, with Terry Jones, Terry Dolan, Alan Fletcher and Juliette Dor, and he has edited and translated *John Gower: The Minor Latin Works*, and a companion volume, *John Gower: The French Balades* and, with Brian W. Gastle, has coedited *Approaches to Teaching John Gower's Poetry*, for the Modern Language Association.

WORKS CITED

Aberth, John. *A Knight at the Movies: Medieval History on Film*. New York: Routledge, 2003.

Ainsworth, Peter. *Jean Froissart and the Fabric of History: Truth, Myth, and Fiction in the Chroniques*. Oxford: Clarendon Press, 1990.

Alexander, J. J. G. "Painting and Manuscript Illuminations for Royal Patrons in the Later Middle Ages." In *English Court Culture in the Later Middle Ages*, edited by V. J. Scattergood and J. W. Sherborne, 141–62. London: Duckworth, 1983.

Allmand, Christopher T. *Lancastrian Normandy: The History of a Medieval Occupation*. Oxford: Clarendon Press, 1983.

Almon, John. *The Peerage of Scotland: A Genealogical and Historical Account of All the Peers of that Ancient Kingdom*. London, 1767.

Amours, F. J., ed. *The Original Chronicle of Andrew of Wyntoun*. 6 vols. Edinburgh: The Scottish Text Society, 1903–14.

Anderson, Judith H. "'A Gentle Knight Was Pricking on the Plaine': The Chaucerian Connection." *English Literary Renaissance* 15 (1985): 166–74.

Archer, Rowena E. "Rich Old Ladies: The Problem of Late Medieval Dowagers." In *Property and Politics: Essays in Later Medieval English History*, edited by Anthony J. Pollard, 15–35. Stroud, Glos.: Alan Sutton, 1984.

Aristotle. *Nichomachean Ethics*. Translated by Martin Ostwald. VI.x.1143a. Indianapolis, IN: Bobbs-Merrill, 1962.

———. *Rhetoric*. Translated by W. Rhys Roberts. II.14, 1390^{b}. New York: Random House, 1954.

———. *The Politics*. Translated by T. A. Sinclair and revised by Trevor J. Saunders VII. xiv.1332b32. Harmondsworth: Penguin, 1981.

Aronstein, Susan. "When Civilization Was Less Civilized: *Erik the Viking*." In *The Vikings on Film: Essays on Depictions of the Nordic Middle Ages*, edited by Kevin J. Harty, 72–82. Jefferson, NC: McFarland, 2011.

———. *Hollywood Knights: Arthurian Cinema and the Politics of Nostalgia*. New York: Palgrave Macmillan, 2005.

Askins, William R. "The Tale of Melibee." In *Sources and Analogues of The Canterbury Tales*, edited by Robert M. Correale and Mary Hamel, vol. 1, 321–408. Cambridge, UK: D. S. Brewer, 2002.

———. "All That Glisters: The Historical Setting of the Tale of Sir Thopas." In *Reading Medieval Culture: Essays in Honor of Robert W. Hanning*, edited by Robert M. Stein and Sandra Pierson Prior, 271–89. Notre Dame, IN: University of Notre Dame Press, 2005.

Aston, Margaret. *Thomas Arundel: A Study of Church Life in the Reign of Richard II*. Oxford: Clarendon Press, 1967.

Ayrton, Andrew. "English Armies in the Fourteenth Century." In *Arms, Armies and Fortifications in the Hundred Years War,* edited by Anne Curry and Michael Hughes, 21–38. Woodbridge, Suff.: Boydell Press, 1999.

Baldwin, Anna P. *The Theme of Government in Piers Plowman*. Cambridge, UK: D. S. Brewer, 1981.

Barber, Richard. "Joan, *suo jure* Countess of Kent, and Princess of Wales and of Aquitaine." In *Oxford Dictionary of National Biography*. Oxford: Oxford University Press, 2004.

Barker, Juliet R. V. *The Tournament in England 1100–1400*. Woodbridge, Suff.: Boydell & Brewer, 1986.

Barney, Stephen A. *The Penn Commentary on Piers Plowman*. Vol. 1, *C-Prologue-Passus 4; B Prologue-Passus 4*; A Prologue-Passus 4. Philadelphia: University of Pennsylvania Press, 2006.

Barr, Helen. "Chaucer's Knight : A Christian Killer?" *English Review* 12.2 (2001): 2–3.

Barron, Caroline M. "The Quarrel of Richard II with London." In *The Reign of Richard II: Essays in Honor of May McKisack*, edited by Caroline M. Barron and F. R. H. Du Boulay, 179–80. London: Athlone, 1971.

———. "The Tyranny of Richard II." *Bulletin of the Institute of Historical Research* 41 (1968): 1–18.

———. *London in the Later Middle Ages: Government and People, 1200–1500*. Oxford: Oxford University Press, 2004.

Beaven, Alfred P. The *Aldermen of the City of London*. 2 vols. London: Eden Fisher, 1908–13.

Beichner, Paul E. "Gower's Use of the *Aurora* in the *Vox Clamantis*." *Speculum* 30 (1955): 582–95.

Bell, Adrian R. "Medieval Chroniclers as War Correspondents during the Hundred Years War: The Earl of Arundel's Naval Campaign of 1387." *Fourteenth Century England* 6 (2010): 171–84.

———. "The Fourteenth-Century Soldier: More Chaucer's Knight or Medieval Career." In *Mercenaries and Paid Men: The Mercenary Identity in the Middle Ages*, edited by John France. Leiden: Brill, 2008, 146–60.

Bennett, J. A. W. "The Date of the A-text of *Piers Plowman*." *PMLA*, 58 (1943): 566–72.

Bennett, J. A. W., and G. V. Smithers, eds. *Early Middle English Verse and Prose*. Oxford: Oxford University Press, 1982.

Bennett, Michael. "The Court of Richard II and the Promotion of Literature." In *Chaucer's England: Literature in Historical Context*, edited by Barbara Hanawalt, 3–20. Minneapolis: University of Minnesota Press, 1992.

———. "Edward III's Entail and the Succession to the Crown, 1376–1471." *The English Historical Review* 113 (1998): 580–609.

———. "Isabelle of France, Anglo-French Diplomacy and Cultural Exchange in the late 1350s." In *The Age of Edward III*, edited by James S. Bothwell, 215–25. Woodbridge, Suff.: Boydell & Brewer for York Medieval Press, 2001.

———. *Richard II and the Revolution of 1399*. Stroud, Glos.: Sutton, 1999.

Benson, Larry D., ed. *Alliterative Morte Arthure*. In *King Arthur's Death: The Middle English Stanzaic Morte Arthur and Alliterative Morte Arthure*, revised by Edward E. Foster. Kalamazoo, MI: Medieval Institute Publications, 1994.

———. "The 'Love-Tydynges' in Chaucer's *House of Fame*." In *Chaucer in the Eighties*, edited by Julian N. Wasserman and Robert J. Blanch, 3–22. Syracuse, NY: Syracuse University Press, 1986.

———, ed. *The Riverside Chaucer*. Boston: Houghton Mifflin, 1987.

Bergen, Henry, ed. *Lydgate's Troy Book*. 4 vols. EETS e.s. 97 (1906).

Berthelette, Thomas. *Jo. Gower de Confessione Amantis*. London, 1532.

Bloch, R. Howard. *Etymologies and Genealogies: A Literary Anthropology of the French Middle Ages*. Chicago: University of Chicago Press, 1983.

———. *Medieval French Literature and Law*. Berkeley and Los Angeles: University of California Press, 1977.

Bloomfield, Morton W. "Reflections of a Medievalist: America, Medievalism, and the Middle Ages." In *Medievalism in American Culture*, edited by Bernard Rosenthal and Paul E. Szarmach, 13–29. Binghamton, NY: Center for Medieval and Early Renaissance Studies, 1989.

Boffey, Julia, and A. S. G. Edwards. "The *Legend of Good Women*." In *The Cambridge Companion to Chaucer*, 2nd ed., edited by Piero Boitani and Jill Mann, 112–26. Cambridge, UK: Cambridge University Press, 2003.

Bond, Edward A., ed. *Chronica Monasterii de Melsa*. 3 vols. London: Rolls Series, 1868.

Bouillet, Marie Nicolas, ed. *L. Annaei Senecae omnia opera*. 6 vols. Paris: Lemaire, 1827–31.

Bowden, Muriel. *A Commentary on the "General Prologue" to The Canterbury Tales*. 2nd ed. London: Macmillan, 1969.

Bowers, John M. "'Beautiful as Troilus': Richard II, Chaucer's Troilus, and Figures of (Un)Masculinity." In *Men and Masculinities in Chaucer's "Troilus and Criseyde,"* edited by Tison Pugh and Marcia Smith Marzec, 9–27. Cambridge, UK: D. S. Brewer, 2008.

———. "Chaucer after Retters: The Wartime Origins of English Literature." In *Inscribing the Hundred Years' War in French and English Cultures*, edited by Denise N. Baker, 91–125. Albany, NY: State University of New York Press, 2000.

———. "Chaucer after Smithfield: From Postcolonial Writer to Imperialist Author." In *The Postcolonial Middle Ages*, edited by Jeffrey Cohen, 53–66. New York: St. Martin's Press, 2000.

———. "Rival Poets: Gower's *Confessio* and Chaucer's *Legend of Good Women*." In *John Gower, Trilingual Poet: Language, Translation, and Tradition*, edited by Elisabeth Dutton, John Hines, and Robert F. Yeager; 276–287. Cambridge, UK: D. S. Brewer, 2010.

———. "Three Readings of *The Knight's Tale*: Sir John Clanvowe, Geoffrey Chaucer, and James I of Scotland." *Journal of Medieval and Early Modern Studies* 34 (2004): 279–307.

Bradbury, Nancy Mason. "Chaucerian Minstrelsy: 'Sir Thopas,' *Troilus and Criseyde* and English Metrical Romance." In *Tradition and Transformation in Medieval Romance*, edited by Rosalind Field, 115–24. Cambridge, UK: D. S. Brewer, 1999.

Bressie, Ramona. "The Date of Thomas Usk's *Testament of Love*." *Modern Philology* 26 (1928): 17–29.

Brewer, Derek. "The Arming of the Warrior in European Literature and in Chaucer." In *Chaucerian Problems and Perspectives: Essays Presented to Paul E. Beichner*, edited by Edward Vasta and Zacharias P. Thundy, 221–43. Notre Dame, IN: University of Notre Dame Press, 1979.

Brink, Bernhard Ten. *History of English Literature*. Translated by Clarke Robinson. New York: Henry Holt and Company, 1893.

Brown, Carleton, ed. *English Lyrics of the Thirteenth Century*. Oxford: Clarendon Press, 1932.

Brown, David Herlihy. "Age, Property and Career in Medieval Society." In *Aging and the Aged in Medieval Europe*, edited by Michael M. Sheehan, 143–158. Toronto: Pontifical Institute of Mediaeval Studies, 1990.

Brown, Elizabeth A. "Diplomacy, Adultery and Domestic Politics at the Court of Philip the Fair: Queen Isabelle's Mission to France in 1314." In *Documenting the Past: Essays in Medieval History presented to George Peddy Cuttino*, edited by Jeffrey S. Hamilton and P. J. Bradley, 53–83. Woodbridge, Suff.: Boydell & Brewer, 1989.

Brown, Sanford, Brown Meech, and Hope Emily Allen, eds. *The Book of Margery Kempe*. EETS, o.s. 212 (1940).

Brusendorff, Aage. *The Chaucer Tradition*. Oxford: Clarendon Press, 1925.

Bullón-Fernández, María. *Fathers and Daughters in Gower's Confessio Amantis: Authority, Family, State and Writing*. Cambridge, UK: D. S. Brewer, 2000.

Bullough, Vern, and Cameron Campbell. "Female Longevity and Diet in the Middle Ages." *Speculum* 55 (1980): 317–25.

Burde, Mark. "Monty Python's Medieval Masterpiece." *The Arthurian Yearbook* 3 (1993): 3–20.

Burlin, Robert B. *Chaucerian Fiction*. Princeton, NJ: Princeton University Press, 1977.

Burrow, John A. *The Ages of Man: A Study in Medieval Writing and Thought*. Oxford: Clarendon Press, 1986.

———. "Chaucer's Sir Thopas and La Prise de Nuevile." In *English Satire and the Satiric Tradition*, edited by Claude Rawson and Alvin Kernan, 44–55, Oxford: Blackwell, 1984.

———. "'Listeth, Lordes': Sir Thopas, 712 and 833." *Notes and Queries* 15 (1968): 326–327.

———. "The Portrayal of Amans in *Confessio Amantis*." In *Responses and Reassessments*, edited by A. J. Minnis, 5–24. Cambridge, UK: D. S. Brewer, 1983.

———. "Sir Thopas in the Sixteenth Century." In *Middle English Studies Presented to Norman Davis in Honour of His Seventieth Birthday*, edited by Douglas Gray and E. G. Stanley, 69–91. Oxford: Clarendon, 1983.

———. "'Worly Under Wede' in Sir Thopas." *Chaucer Review* 3 (1969): 170–173.

Burt, Richard. *Medieval and Early Modern Film and Media*. New York: Palgrave Macmillan, 2008.

Burton, T. L. "Chaucer's 'Tale of Sir Thopas.'" *Explicator* 40 (1982): 4.

Butler, Samuel. *Hudibras*. Edited by John Wilders. Oxford: Clarendon Press, 1967.

Butterfield, Ardis. *The Familiar Enemy: Chaucer, Language, and Nation in the Hundred Years War*. Oxford: Oxford University Press, 2009.

Calendar of Inquisitions Post Mortem, Edward I–Henry VI. 26 vols. London: Her/His Majesty's Stationery Office/TNA, 1904–2009.

Calendar of the Close Rolls Preserved in the Public Record Office. Edward III. vol. 13, *1369–1374*. London: His Majesty's Stationery Office, 1911.

Calendar of the Close Rolls Preserved in the Public Record Office. Richard II. vol. 2, *1381–1385*. London: His Majesty's Stationery Office, 1920.

Calendar of the Close Rolls Preserved in the Public Record Office, Edward II–Richard II. 24 vols. London: Her/His Majesty's Stationery Office, 1892–1927.

Calendar of the Fine Rolls Preserved in the Public Record Office, Edward II–Richard II. 10 vols. London: His Majesty's Stationery Office, 1912–29.

Calendar of the Patent Rolls Preserved in the Public Record Office, Edward II–Richard II. 27 vols. London: Her/His Majesty's Stationery Office, 1894–1916.

Cannon, Christopher. "Raptus in the Chaumpaigne Release and a Newly Discovered Document Concerning the Life of Geoffrey Chaucer." *Speculum* 68 (1993): 74–94.

Carley, James. *The Libraries of King Henry VIII*. London: The British Library in association with the British Academy, 2000.

Carlin, Martha. *Medieval Southwark*. London: Hambledon Press, 1996.

Carlson, David R. "English Poetry, July–October 1399, and Lancastrian Crime." *Studies in the Age of Chaucer* 29 (2007): 375–418.

———. "Gower on Henry IV's Rule: The Endings of the *Cronica Tripertita* and Its Texts." *Traditio* 62 (2007): 207–36.

———. "Gower's Early Latin Poetry: Text-Genetic Hypotheses of an Epistola ad regem (ca. 1377–1380) from the Evidence of John Bale." *Mediaeval Studies* 65 (2003): 293–317.

———. "The Invention of the Anglo-Latin Public Poetry (circa 1367–1402) and Its Prosody, esp. in John Gower." *Mittellateinisches Jahrbuch* 39 (2004): 389–406.

———. "The Parliamentary Source of Gower's *Cronica Tripertita* and Incommensurable Styles." In *John Gower, Trilingual Poet: Language, Translation and Tradition*, edited by Elisabeth Dutton, John Hines, and Robert F. Yeager, 98–111. Cambridge, UK: D. S. Brewer, 2010.

———. "A Rhyme Distribution Chronology of John Gower's Latin Poetry." *Studies in Philology* 104 (2007): 15–55.

Chamberlayne, Joanna. "Joan of Kent's Tale: Adultery and Rape in the Age of Chivalry." *Medieval Life* 5 (1996): 7–9.

Chapman, Graham, John Cleese, Eric Idle, Terry Jones, Terry Gilliam, and Michael Palin, *The Pythons' Autobiography by the Pythons* (London: Orion, 2003), 49.

Charbonneau, Joanne A. "Sir Thopas." In *Sources and Analogues of The Canterbury Tales*, edited by Robert M. Correale and Mary Hamel, vol. 2, 649–714. Cambridge, UK: D. S. Brewer, 2005.

Charlton, Edward. "Roll of Prayers Formerly Belonging to Henry VIII When Prince." *Archaeologia Aeliana* 2 (1858): 41–45.

Chaucer, Geoffrey. *Dream Visions and Other Poems*. Edited by Kathryn L. Lynch. New York: W. W. Norton, 2007.

Chew, Samuel C., *The Pilgrimage of Life* (New Haven, CT: Yale University Press, 1962), especially 153–73.

Child, Francis James, ed. *The English and Scottish Popular Ballads*. 5 vols. Boston: Houghton Mifflin, 1882–1898.

Cicero. *De oratore* 2.9.36. In *Cicero Rhetorica*, edited by Arthur Wilkins. Oxford: Clarendon Press, 1963.

Clarke, M. V. *Fourteenth Century Studies*. Edited by L. S. Sutherland and M. McKisack. Oxford, 1968.

Classen, Albrecht. "Anger and Anger Management in the Middle Ages: Mental Historical Perspective." *Mediaevistik* 19 (2006): 21–50.

Coffman, George R. "John Gower in His Most Significant Role." In *Elizabethan Studies and Other Essays in Honor of George F. Reynolds*, 52–61. Boulder: University of Colorado Studies, 1945.

———. "John Gower, Mentor for Royalty: Richard II." *PMLA* 69 (1954): 953–64.

Cohn, Norman. *The Pursuit of the Millennium: Revolutionary Millenarians and Mystical Anarchists of the Middle Ages*. Rev. ed. London: Maurice Temple Smith, 1970.

Cokayne, George Edward. *The Complete Peerage of England, Scotland, Ireland, Great Britainand the United Kingdom*. 13 vols. London: St. Catherine Press, 1910–59.

Cole, Charles Augustus, ed. *Memorials of Henry V King of England*. London: Rolls Series, 1858.

Coleman, Joyce. "Philippa of Lancaster, Queen of Portugal—and Patron of the Gower Translations?" In *England and Iberia in the Middle Ages, 12th-15th Century: Cultural, Literary, and Political Changes*, edited by María Bullón Fernández, 135–65. New York: Palgrave Macmillan, 2007.

———. "The Flower, the Leaf, and Philippa of Lancaster." In *The Legend of Good Women: Context and Reception,* edited by Carolyn P. Collette, 35–58. Cambridge, UK: D. S. Brewer, 2006.

Condon, Margaret. "God Save the King! Piety, Propaganda and the Perpetual Memorial." In *Westminster Abbey: The Lady Chapel of Henry VII,* edited by Tim Tatton-Brown and Richard Mortimer. Woodbridge, Suff.: Boydell Press, 2003, 92–117.

Connolly, Margaret, and Linne Mooney, eds. *Design and Distribution of Late Medieval Manuscripts in England.* Woodbridge, Suff.: Boydell & Brewer for York Medieval Press, 2008.

Cooper, Helen. "Welcome to the House of Fame: 600 Years Dead: Chaucer's Deserved Reputation as 'the Father of English Poetry'." *TLS* 5091 (October 2000): 3–4.

Crane, Christopher E. "Superior Incongruity: Derisive and Sympathetic Comedy in Middle English Drama and Homiletic Exempla." In *Medieval English Comedy,* edited by Sandra M. Hordis and Paul Hardwick, 31–60. Turnhout: Brepols, 2007.

Crow, Martin M., and Clair C. Olson, eds. *Chaucer Life-Records.* Oxford: Clarendon Press, 1966.

Crump C. G., and C. Johnson. "The Powers of Justices of the Peace." *English Historical Review* 27 (1912): 226–38.

Cunningham, Sean. *Henry VII.* Abingdon: Routledge, 2007.

Curry, Anne. *The Battle of Agincourt: Sources and Interpretations.* Woodbridge, Suff.: Boydell & Brewer, 2000.

Curtius, Ernst Robert. *European Literature and the Latin Middle Ages.* Translated by Willard R. Trask. New York: Pantheon, 1953.

Curveiller, Stéphane, ed. *Les champs relationnels en Europe du Nord et du Nord-Ouest des origines à la fin du Premier Empire. 1er Colloque Européen de Calais.* Calais: la Municipalité de Calais, 1994.

Dane, Joseph A. "Genre and Authority: The Eighteenth-Century Creation of Chaucerian Burlesque." *Huntington Library Quarterly* 48 (1985): 345–62.

Darling, Sir James, "Tutorial," *American Oxonian* 97 (2010): 328.

Darnton, Robert. *The Great Cat Massacre and Other Episodes in French Cultural History.* New York: Basic Books, 1984.

David Starkey. *Henry, Virtuous Prince.* London: Harper Press, 2008.

Davis, Norman ed. *The Paston Letters.* 2 vols. Oxford: Clarendon Press, 1976.

Day, David D. "*Monty Python and the Holy Grail*: Madness with a Definite Method." In *Cinema Arthuriana,* rev. ed., edited by Kevin J. Harty, 127–35. Jefferson, NC: McFarland, 2002.

de Beauvoir, Simone. *La Vieillesse.* Paris: Gallimard, 1970.

de Pizan, Christine. *Lavision-Christine.* Edited by Sister Mary Towner. Washington, DC: Catholic University of America Studies in Romance Languages and Literatures, 1932.

Devon, Frederick, ed. *Issues of the Exchequer, Henry III–Henry VI.* London: Record Commission, 1847.

DiCicco, Mark. "The Arming of Sir Thopas Reconsidered." *Notes and Queries* 244 (1999): 14–16.

Diggelmann, Lindsay. "Hewing the Ancient Elm: Anger, Arboricide, and Medieval Kingship." *Journal of Medieval and Early Modern Studies* 40, no. 2 (2010): 249–71.

Dinshaw, Carolyn. "Rivalry, Rape, and Manhood: Gower and Chaucer." In *Violence Against Women in Medieval Texts,* edited by Anna Roberts, 137–60. Gainsville: University Press of Florida, 1998.

Dobson, R. B. *The Peasants' Revolt of 1381.* 2nd ed. London: Macmillan: 1983.

Dobson, R. B., and J. Taylor. *Rymes of Robyn Hood: An Introduction to the English Outlaw*. Book Club Associates, 1976.

Dodd, Gwilym. *Justice and Grace: Private Petitioning and the English Parliament in the Late Middle Ages*. Oxford: Oxford University Press, 2007.

Don Skemer. *Binding Words: Textual Amulets in the Middle Ages*. University Park: Pennsylvania State University Press, 1986.

Doran, Susan, ed. *Henry VIII: Man and Monarch*. London: British Library, 2009.

Doyle, A. I., and M. B. Parkes. "The Production of Copies of the *Canterbury Tales* and the *Confessio Amantis* in the early fifteenth century." In *Medieval Scribes, Manuscripts & Libraries: Essays presented to N. R. Ker*, edited by Malcolm B. Parkes and Andrew G. Watson, 163–203. London: Scolar Press, 1978.

Driver, Martha W., and Jonathan Rosenbaum. "'Stond and Delyver': Teaching the Medieval Movie." In *The Medieval Hero On Screen: Representations from Beowulf to Buffy*, edited by Martha W. Driver and Sid Ray, 212–15. Jefferson, NC: McFarland, 2004.

Duby, Georges, "Dans la France du Nord-Ouest, au XIIe siècle: Les jeunes dans la société aristocratique." *Annales. Economies—Sociétés—Civilisations* 19 (1964): 835–46.

———. *L'histoire de Guillaume de Maréchal ou le meilleur chevalier du monde: William Marshal the Flower of Chivalry*. Translated by Richard Howard. New York: Pantheon, 1985.

Duffy, Eamon. *Marking the Hours: English People and Their Prayers 1240–1570*. New Haven and London: Yale University Press, 2006.

———. *The Stripping of the Altars: Traditional Religion in England 1400–1580*. New Haven and London: Yale University Press, 1992.

Eadie, John. "The Author at Work: The Two Versions of the Prologue to the *Legend of Good Women*." *Neuphilologische Mitteilungen* 93 (1992): 135–43.

Eberle, Patricia J. "Richard II and the Literary Arts." In *Richard II: The Art of Kingship*, edited by Anthony Goodman and James Gillespie, 231–53. Oxford: Clarendon, 1999.

Edward, Second Duke of York. *The Master of Game*. Edited by W. A. and F. Baillie-Grohman, with an introduction by Theodore Roosevelt. London: Ballantyne, Hanson & Co., 1904.

Edwards, Robert R. "Ricardian Dreamwork: Chaucer, Cupid, and Loyal Lovers." In "*The Legend of Good Women*": *Context and Reception*, edited by Carolyn P. Collette, 59–82. Cambridge, UK: D. S. Brewer, 2006.

Edwards, Suzanne. "The Rhetoric of Rape and the Politics of Gender in the *Wife of Bath's Tale* and the 1382 Statute of Rapes." *Exemplaria* 23 (2011): 3–26.

Elvin, Charles R. S. *Records of Walmer*. London: H. Gray, 1890.

Emmerson, Richard K. "Reading Gower in a Manuscript Culture: Latin and English in Illustrated Manuscripts of the *Confessio Amantis*." *Studies in the Age of Chaucer* 21 (1999): 143–86.

Evans, Lisa. "'The Same Counterpoincte Beinge Olde and Worene': The Mystery of Henry VIII's Green Quilt." In *Medieval Clothing and Textiles*, edited by Robert Netherton and Gail R. Owen Crocker, vol. 4, 193–208. Woodbridge, Suff.: Boydell & Brewer, 2008.

Everett, Dorothy. "Some Reflections on Chaucer's 'Art Poetical'." In *Essays on Middle English Literature*, edited by Patricia Kean, 149–74. 1950. Rpt. Oxford: Clarendon, 1955.

Federico, Sylvia. "The Imaginary Society: Women in 1381." *Journal of British Studies* 40 (2001): 159–83.

Fein, Susanna. *John the Blind Audelay: Poems and Carols*. TEAMS, Middle English Texts Series. Kalamazoo: Western Michigan University, 2009.

Ferster, Judith. "O Political Gower." In *Fictions of Advice: The Literature and Politics of Counsel in Late Medieval England,* 108–36. Philadelphia: University of Pennsylvania Press, 1996.

Finlayson, John. "Definitions of Middle English Romance: Part I." *Chaucer Review* 15 (1980): 44–62.

Fisher, John H. "The Revision of the Prologue to the *Legend of Good Women*: An Occasional Explanation." *South Atlantic Bulletin* 43 (1978): 75–84.

———. *John Gower: Moral Philosopher and Friend of Chaucer.* London: Methuen, 1965.

Fletcher, Christopher. *Richard II: Manhood, Youth, and Politics, 1377–99.* Oxford: Oxford University Press, 2008.

———. "Manhood and Politics in the Reign of Richard II." *Past and Present* 189 (2005): 3–39.

Foljambe, Cecil G. S., Earl of Liverpool, and Compton Reade. *The House of Cornewall.* Hereford: privately printed, 1908.

Folts Jr., James D. "Senescence and Renascence: Petrarch's Thoughts on Growing Old." *Journal of Medieval and Renaissance Studies* 10 (1980): 207–37.

Foote, P. G., ed. "Gunlaugs saga Ormstungu." In *The Saga of Gunnlaug Serpent-Tongue,* translated by R. Quirk. London: Thomas Nelson, 1957.

Forhan, Kate L. "Poets and Politics: Just War in Geoffrey Chaucer and Christine de Pizan." In *Ethics, Nationalism, and Just War: Medieval and Contemporary Perspectives,* edited by Henrik Syse and Gregory M. Reichberg, 99–116. Washington, DC: Catholic University Press, 2007.

Fortescue, Sir John. *The Governance of England.* Edited by C. Plummer. Oxford: Clarendon, 1885.

Fowler, Kenneth. *Medieval Mercenaries.* vol. 1, *The Great Companies.* Oxford: Blackwell, 2001.

Fox, Denton. *Grettir's Saga.* Translated by Hermann Pálsson. Toronto: University of Toronto Press, 1974.

Frank Jr., Robert W. "The Legend of the *Legend of Good Women.*" *Chaucer Review* 1 (1966): 110–33.

Frank, Roberta. "The Invention of the Viking Horned Helmet." In *International Scandinavian and Medieval Studies in Memory of Gerd Wolfgang Weber,* edited by Michael Dallapiazza, 199–208. Trieste, Italy: Edizione Parnaso, 2001.

Fraser, George MacDonald. *The Steel Bonnets: the Story of the Anglo-Scottish Border Reivers.* London: Barrie and Jenkins, 1971.

Fredell, Joel. "Reading the Dream Miniature in the *Confessio Amantis,*" *Medievalia et Humanistica,* n.s., 22 (1995): 61–93.

Froissart, Jean. *Chronicles.* Translated and edited by Geoffrey Brereton. London: Penguin Books, 1968.

———. *Chroniques. Début du premier livre. Édition du manuscrit de Rome Reg. lat. 869.* Edited by George T. Diller. Geneva: Droz, 1972.

———. *Le joli buisson de Jonece.* Anthime Fourrier edition. Geneva: Librarie Droz, 1975.

Galbraith, V. H., ed. *The Anonimalle Chronicle, 1333–1381.* Manchester: Manchester University Press, 1927.

Galway, Margaret. "Joan of Kent and the Order of the Garter." *University of Birmingham Historical Journal* 1 (1947–48): 13–50.

Gambier-Parry, T. R. "Alice Perrers and Her Husband's Relatives." *English Historical Review* 47 (1932): 272–6.

Ganim, John M. "The Hero in the Classroom" In *The Medieval Hero Onscreen: Representations from Beowulf to Buffy,* edited by Martha W. Driver and Sid Ray, 237–49. Jefferson, NC: McFarland, 2004.

Garbáty, Thomas J. "A Description of the Confession Miniatures for Gower's *Confessio Amantis*, with Special Reference to the Illustrator's Role as Reader and Critic." *Mediaevalia* 19 (1996), 319–43.

Gaylord, Alan T. "Chaucer's Dainty 'Doggerel': The 'Elvyssh' Prosody of *Sir Thopas*." *Studies in the Age of Chaucer* 1 (1979): 83–104.

Gillespie, James L. "Richard II: Chivalry and Kingship." In *The Age of Richard II*, edited by James L. Gillespie, 115–38. Stroud, Glos.: Sutton, 1997.

Gilmour-Bryson, Anne. "Age-Related Data from the Templar Trials." In *Aging and the Aged in Medieval Europe*, edited by Michael M. Sheehan, 143–158. Toronto: Pontifical Institute of Mediaeval Studies, 1990.

Given-Wilson, Chris, ed. *The Chronicle of Adam Usk 1377–1421*. Oxford: Clarendon Press, 1997.

———, ed. *Chronicles of the Revolution 1397–1400*. Manchester, UK: Manchester University Press, 1993.

———, ed. "The Earl of Arundel's Naval Campaign of 1387." *Fourteenth Century England* 6 (2010): 171–84.

———, ed. *The Parliament Rolls of Medieval England 1275–1504*. vol. 7, *Richard II 1385–1397*. Woodbridge, Suff.: Boydell & Brewer, 2005.

———. "Richard (II) Fitzalan, Third Earl of Arundel and Eighth Earl of Surrey." In *Oxford Dictionary of National Biography*. Oxford: Oxford University Press, 2004–2011.

———, ed. "Richard II: Parliament of January 1395, Text and Translation" In *The Parliament Rolls of Medieval England*. Scholarly Digital Edition. http://www.sdeditions.com/PROME.

———, ed. "Richard II: Parliament of September 1397, Text and Translation" In *The Parliament Rolls of Medieval England*. Scholarly Digital Edition. http://www.sdeditions.com/PROME.

———. "Wealth and Credit, Public and Private: The Earls of Arundel, 1306–1397." *English Historical Review* 106 (1991): 1–26.

Given-Wilson, Chris, and Alice Curteis. *The Royal Bastards of Medieval England*. London: Routledge, 1984.

Goddard, H. C. "Chaucer's *Legend of Good Women*." *Journal of English and Germanic Philology* 7 (1907): 87–129 and 8 (1909): 47–111.

Goldberg, Jeremy. *Communal Discord, Child Abduction, and Rape in the Later Middle Ages*. Basingstoke, UK: Palgrave Macmillan, 2008.

Goodman, Anthony. "Anglo-Scottish Relations in the Later Fourteenth Century: Alienation or Acculturation." In *England and Scotland in the Fourteenth Century: New Perspectives*, edited by Andy King and Michael A. Penman, 236–53. Woodbridge, Suff.: The Boydell Press, 2007.

———. *John of Gaunt: The Exercise of Princely Power in Fourteenth-Century Europe*. London: Longman, 1992.

Goodman, Anthony, and Anthony Tuck, eds. *War and Border Societies in the Middle Ages*. London and New York: Routledge, 1992.

Gower, John. *The Major Latin Works of John Gower*, trans. Eric W. Stockton. Seattle: University of Washington Press, 1962.

Grady, Frank. "Chaucer Reading Langland: *The House of Fame*." *Studies in the Age of Chaucer* 18 (1996): 3–23.

———. "Gower's Boat, Richard's Barge, and the True Story of the *Confessio Amantis*: Text and Gloss." *Texas Studies in Literature and Language* 44 (2002): 1–15.

Gransden, Antonia. "The Alleged Rape by Edward III of the Countess of Salisbury." *The English Historical Review* 87 (1972): 333–44.

Greaves, Dorothy. "Calais under Edward III." In *Finance and Trade under Edward III,* edited by George Unwin, 313–50. Manchester, UK: Manchester University Press, 1918.

Greville, Charles C. F. *The Greville Memoirs.* 3 vols. London: Longmans, Green, 1885.

Griffiths, Jeremy. "*Confessio Amantis*: The Poem and its Pictures." In *Gower's Confessio Amantis: Responses and Reassessments*, edited by A. J. Minnis, 163–78. Cambridge, UK: D. S. Brewer, 1983.

Griffiths, Ralph. *The Principality of Wales: The Structure and Personnel of Government.* vol. 1, *Wales, 1277–1536.* Cardiff: University of Wales Press, 1972.

Gundy, Allison. "The Earl of Warwick and the Royal Affinity in the Politics of the West Midlands 1389–1399." In *Revolution and Consumption in Late Medieval England*, edited by Michael Hicks, 57–70. Woodbridge, Suff.: Boydell Press 2001.

Gunn, Steven, and Linda Monckton, eds. *Arthur Tudor, Prince of Wales: Life, Death and Commemoration.* Woodbridge, Suff.: Boydell & Brewer, 2009.

Hamel Mary. "'And Now for Something Different': 'The Relationship between the 'Prioress's Tale' and the 'Rime of Sir Thopas.'" *Chaucer Review* 14 (1980): 251–59.

Hammond, Eleanor Prescott. *Chaucer: A Bibliographical Manual.* New York: Macmillan, 1908.

Hanawalt, Barbara A. "The Widow's Mite: Provisions for Medieval London Widows." In *Upon My Husband's Death: Widows in the Literature and Histories of Medieval Europe*, edited by Louise Mirrer, 21–45. Ann Arbor: University of Michigan Press, 1992.

Harris, William V. *Restraining Rage: The Ideology of Anger Control in Classical Antiquity.* Cambridge, MA: Harvard University Press, 2001.

Hartley, L. P., *The Go-Between* (London: Hamish Hamilton, 1953).

Haydock, Nickolas. *Movie Medievalism: The Imaginary Middle Ages.* Jefferson, NC: McFarland, 2008.

Hayward, Maria. *Dress at the Court of King Henry VIII.* Leeds: Maney and Son, 2007.

Hector, L. C., and Barbara F. Harvey, eds. *The Westminster Chronicle.* Vol. 1, *1381–1394.* Oxford: Clarendon Press, 1982.

Helgeland, Brian. *A Knight's Tale: The Shooting Script.* New York: Newmarket Press, 2001.

Herlihy, David. "The Generation in Medieval History." *Viator* 5 (1974): 347–64.

"Hermentrude." *Notes and Queries.* 7th ser., 7. London: Bell & Daldy, 1889.

Herrtage, Sidney John, ed. *Sir Ferumbras.* EETS e.s., 34. London: Trübner, 1879.

Hewitt, Herbert. *The Organization of War Under Edward III, 1338–1362.* Manchester, UK: Manchester University Press, 1966.

Heyworth, P. L., ed. *Jack Upland, Friar Daw's Reply and Upland's Rejoinder.* London: Oxford University Press, 1968.

Hines, John, Nathalie Cohen, and Simon Roffey. "*Johannes Gower, Armiger, Poeta*: Records and Memorials of His Life and Death." In *A Companion to Gower,* edited by Siân Echard, 36–41. Cambridge, UK: D. S. Brewer, 2004.

Hoccleve, Thomas. *The Regiment of Princes.* Edited by Charles Blyth. TEAMS, Middle English Texts Series. Kalamazoo: Western Michigan University, 1999.

Hofstadter. Douglas. *Le Ton Beau de Marot.* New York: Basic Books, 1997.

Hood, Thomas. *Whims and Oddities in Prose and Verse.* London: Lupton Relfe, 1826.

Housley, Norman. *Fighting for the Cross: Crusading to the Holy Land.* New Haven, CT: Yale University Press, 2008.

Hoyt, Walter French, and Charles Brockway Hale, eds. *Eger and Grime* in *Middle English Metrical Romances.* 2 vols. New York: Russell & Russell, 1964.

Hreinsson, Viðar, ed. *Gull-þoris Saga.* In *The Complete Sagas of Icelanders.* vol. 3, chap. 18. Reykjavík: Leifur Eiríksson, 1997.

———. *Reykdæla Saga og Víga-Skútu*. In *The Complete Sagas of Icelanders*. vol. 4, chap. 13. Reykjavík: Leifur Eiríksson, 1997.

Hudson, Anne. *The Premature Reformation: Wycliffite Texts and Lollard History*. Oxford: Clarendon Press, 1988.

Hulbert, J. R. "Chaucer and the Earl of Oxford." *Modern Philology* 10 (1912/13): 433–37.

Hyams, Paul. "What Did Henry III of England Think in Bed and in French about Kingship and Anger?" In *Anger's Past: The Social Uses of an Emotion in the Middle Ages*, edited by Barbara H. Rosenwein, 92–126. Ithaca, NY: Cornell University Press, 1998.

Ingledew, Francis. *Sir Gawain and the Green Knight and the Order of the Garter*. Notre Dame: University of Notre Dame Press, 2006.

Isidore of Seville. *Etymologiarum sive originum*. Edited by W. M. Lindsay. 2 vols. Oxford: Clarendon Press, 1911.

James I. *The Chronicle of James I: King of Aragon, Surnamed the Conqueror*. Edited by Pascual de Gayangos. Translated by John Forster. London: Chapman and Hall, 1883.

Jolliffe, John Edward Austin. "*Ira et Malevolentia*." In *Angevin Kingship*, 87–109. London: Adam and Charles Black, 1955.

Jones, Michael. *Ducal Brittany, 1364–1399*. Oxford: Oxford University Press, 1970.

Jones, Terry. *Chaucer's Knight: The Portrait of a Medieval Mercenary*. New York: Methuen, 1985.

———. *Douglas Adams' Starship Titanic: A Novel by Terry Jones*. New York: Ballantine, 1997.

———. "The Image of Chaucer's Knight." In *Speaking Images: Essays in Honor of V.A. Kolve*, edited by Robert F. Yeager and Charlotte C. Morse, 205–36. Asheville, NC: Pegasus Press, 2001.

———. Introduction to *Douglas Adams' Starship Titanic: A Novel by Terry Jones*. New York: Ballantine, 1997, 2.

———. *The Knight and the Squire*. London: Puffin, 1999.

———. *The Lady and the Squire*. London: Puffin, 2002.

———. "The Monk's Tale." *Studies in the Age of Chaucer* 22 (2000): 387–97.

———. "Richard II: Royal Villain or Victim of Spin?" *The Times of London*. October 4, 2008.

———. *Terry Jones's War on the War on Terror*. New York: Nation Books, 2005.

———. "Was Richard II a Tyrant? Richard's Use of the Books of Rules for Princes." *Fourteenth Century England* 5 (2008): 130–60.

———. *Terry Jones' Medieval Lives*. London: BBC Books, 2005.

Jones, Terry, and Alan Ereira. *Terry Jones' Barbarians*. London: BBC Books, 2007.

Jones, Terry, Robert F. Yeager, Terry Dolan, Alan Fletcher, and Juliette Dor. *Who Murdered Chaucer? A Medieval Mystery*. New York: St. Martin's Press, 2004.

Kane, George. "Outstanding Problems of Middle English Scholarship." In *Chaucer and Langland: Historical and Textual Approaches*. Berkeley: University of California Press, 1989, 228–41.

Kaufman, Lloyd, and Ashley Wren Collins. *Produce Your Own Damn Movie!* New York: Focal Press, 2009.

Keegan, John. *The Face of Battle*. London: Jonathan Cape, 1976.

Kelly, Henry Ansgar. "Statutes of Rapes and Alleged Ravishers of Wives: A Context for the Charges against Thomas Malory, Knight." *Viator* 28 (1997): 361–419.

———. *The Matrimonial Trials of Henry VIII*. Stanford, CA: Stanford University Press, 1976.

Kemp, Martin, ed. *The Oxford History of Western Art.* Oxford: Oxford University Press, 2000.

Ker, Neil Ripley, and Alan John Piper. *Medieval Manuscripts in British Libraries.* vol. 4, *Paisley-York.* Oxford: Clarendon Press, 1992.

Ker, William Paton. *The Chronicle of Froissart.* Translated by Sir John Bourchier, Lord Berners. 6 vols. London: David Nutt, 1901–03.

Kiser, Lisa. *Telling Classical Tales: Chaucer and the "Legend of Good Women."* Ithaca, NY: Cornell University Press, 1983.

Klapisch-Zuber, Christiane. *Tuscans and Their Families: A Study of the Florentine Catasto of 1427.* New Haven, CT: Yale University Press, 1985.

Knapp, Peggy A. *Chaucerian Aesthetics.* New York: Palgrave Macmillan, 2008.

Knighton, Henry. *Knighton's Chronicle 1337–1396.* Translated and edited by G. H. Martin. Oxford: Clarendon Press, 1995.

Knowles, Dom David. *The Monastic Order in England 940–1216.* 2nd ed. Cambridge, UK: Cambridge University Press, 1963.

———. *The Religious Orders in England.* 3 vols. Cambridge, UK: Cambridge University Press, 1963.

Krantz, Dennis M., ed. and trans. *Waltharius and Ruodlieb.* New York: Garland Publishing, 1984.

Kurath, Hans, and Sherman M. Kuhn, eds. *Middle English Dictionary.* Ann Arbor: University of Michigan Press, 1952.

Lacey, Helen. *The Royal Pardon: Access to Mercy in Fourteenth-Century England.* York: York Medieval Press, 2009.

Langland, William. *Piers Plowman: A New Annotated Edition of the C-text.* Edited by Derek Pearsall. Exeter: University of Exeter Press, 2008.

———. *Piers Plowman. The Prologue and Passus I-VII of the B text as found in Bodleian MS. Laud Misc. 581.* Edited by J. A. W. Bennett. Oxford: Clarendon Press, 1972.

———. *The Vision of Piers Plowman. A Critical Edition of the B-Text based on Trinity College Cambridge MS B.15.17.* Edited by A. V. C. Schmidt. 2nd ed. London: Everyman, 1995.

Laȝamon. *Brut.* Edited by G. L. Brook and R. F. Leslie. 2 vols. EETS, e.s., 250 & 277 (Oxford: Oxford University Press, 1963 & 1978): 2: 680 & 682 (ll. 12987–13030).

Legge, Mary Dominica, ed. *Anglo-Norman Letters and Petitions.* Oxford: Anglo-Norman Text Society, 1941.

Letters and Papers, Foreign and Domestic, of the Reign of Henry VIII. Arranged and catalogued by John Brewer. London: Longman, 1876.

Letters and Papers, Foreign and Domestic, of the Reign of Henry VIII. Catalogued by John Brewer, revised by Robert Brodie. London: His Majesty's Stationery Office, 1920.

Levy, Brian, and Lesley Coote. "The Subversion of Medievalism in *Lancelot du Lac* and *Monty Python and the Holy Grail.*" *Studies in Medievalism* 13 (2004): 99–126.

Lewis, Andrew W. *Royal Succession in Capetian France: Studies on Familial Order and the State.* Cambridge, MA: Harvard University Press, 1981.

Lewis, C. S. *The Allegory of Love.* Oxford: Oxford University Press, 1930.

Lewis, Charlton T., and Charles Short. *A Latin Dictionary Founded on Andrews' Edition of Freund's Latin Dictionary.* Oxford: Clarendon Press, 1993.

Limouze, A. Sandford. "Burlesque Criticism of the Ballad in *Mist's Weekly Journal.*" *Studies in Philology* 47 (1950): 607–18.

Lindenbaum, Sheila. "The Smithfield Tournament of 1390." *Journal of Medieval and Renaissance Studies,* 20 (1990): 1–20.

Lindsay, Sir David. *Squyre Meldrum.* Edited by James Kinsley. London and Edinburgh: Thomas Nelson, 1959.

Loomis, Laura Hibbard. "Chaucer and the Auchinleck MS: 'Thopas' and 'Guy of Warwick.'" In *Essays and Studies in Honor of Carleton Brown*, 111–28. New York: New York University Press, 1940.

——— "Sir Thopas" In *Sources and Analogues of Chaucer's Canterbury Tales*, edited by William F. Bryan and Germaine Dempster, 486–559. Chicago: University of Chicago Press, 1941.

Loomis, Roger Sherman. "The Allegorical Siege in the Art of the Middle Ages." *American Journal of Archaeology* 23 (1919): 255–69.

Lossing, Marian. "The Prologue to the *Legend of Good Women* and the *Lai de Franchise*." *Studies in Philology* 39 (1942): 15–35.

Love, Nicholas. *The Mirror of the Blessed Life of Jesus Christ: A Full Critical Edition*. Edited by Michael Sargent. Exeter: University of Exeter Press, 2005.

Lowes, John Livingston. "The Prologue to the *Legend of Good Women* Considered in Its Chronological Relations." *PMLA* 20 (1905): 749–864.

Luce, Siméon, ed. *Chronique des Quatres Premiers Valois (1327–1393)*. Paris: Renouard, 1862.

Lupack, Alan. *The Oxford Guide to Arthurian Literature and Legend*. Oxford: Oxford University Press, 2005.

———, ed. "Sir Tristrem." In *Lancelot of the Laik and Sir Tristrem*. Kalamazoo, MI: TEAMS Medieval Institute Publications, 1994.

Lynch, Kathryn L. "Dating Chaucer." *Chaucer Review* 42 (2007): 1–22.

Lyon, Mary, Bryce Lyon, Henry S. Lucas, and Jean de Sturler. *The Wardrobe Book of William de Norwell*. Brussels: Académie Royale de Belgique, 1983.

Macaulay, G. C., ed. *The Complete Works of John Gower*. 4 vols. Oxford: Clarendon Press, 1899–1902.

———. *The English Works of John Gower*. London: Oxford University Press, 1900–01.

Machaut, Guillaume de. *The Fountain of Love*. Edited and translated by R. Barton Palmer. New York: Garland, 1993.

Macpherson, D., ed. *Rotuli Scotiæ in turri Londinensi et in domo capitulari Westmonasteriensi asservati*. 2 vols. London: Record Commission, 1814–19.

Maddern, Philippa C. *Violence and Social Order: East Anglia, 1422–1442*. Oxford: Clarendon Press, 1992.

Mah, Harold. "Suppressing the Text: The Metaphysics of Ethnographic History in Darnton's Great Cat Massacre." *History Workshop Journal* 31 (1991): 1–20.

Maidstone, Richard. *Concordia (The Reconciliation of Richard II with London)*. Edited by David R. Carlson. Translated by A. G. Rigg. Kalamazoo, MI: TEAMS Medieval Institute Publications, 2003.

Manly, John. M. "Sir Thopas, a Satire." In *Essays and Studies by Members of the English Association*, vol. 113, 52–73. Oxford: Clarendon Press, 1928.

Mann, Jill. *Chaucer and Medieval Estates Satire*. Cambridge, UK: Cambridge University Press, 1973.

Marquess of Anglesey. *One-Leg: The Life and Letters of Henry William Paget, First Marquess of Anglesey 1768–1854*. London: Jonathan Cape, 1961.

Marshall, G. W. "The Barons of Burford, I." *Genealogist* 3 (1879): 225–30.

Martellotti, Guido, Pier Gorgio Ricci, Enrico Carrara, and Enrico Bianchi, eds. *Petrarch*. Milan Naples: Ricciardi Editore, 1955.

Maslen, Robert, ed. *An Apology for Poetry, or, The Defence of Poesy / Sir Philip Sydney*. Rev. 3rd ed. Manchester: Manchester University Press, 2002.

Mathew, Gervase. *The Court of Richard II*. New York: Norton, 1968.

McCracken, Peggy. *The Romance of Adultery: Queenship and Sexual Transgression in Old French Literature*. Philadelphia: University of Pennsylvaina Press, 1998.

McFarlane, K. B. *Lancastrian Kings and Lollard Knights*. Oxford: Clarendon Press, 1972.

McGavin, John J. "Robert III's 'Rough Music': Charivari and Diplomacy in a Medieval Scottish Court." *The Scottish Historical Review* 75 (1995): 144–58.

McHardy, Alison K., ed. *The Church in London, 1375–1392*. London: London Record Society, 1977.

McNiven, Peter. *Heresy and Politics in the Reign of Henry IV: The Burning of John Badby*. Woodbridge, Suff.: Boydell & Brewer, 1987.

Meiss, Millard. *French Painting in the Time of Jean de Berry*. 2 vols. London: Phaidon, 2nd ed., 1969.

Mills, Maldwyn, ed. *Octavian*. In *Six Middle English Romances*. London: J. M. Dent, 1973.

———. *Sir Percyvell of Gales*. In *Ywain and Gawain, Sir Percyvell of Gales, and The Anturs of Arther*, London: J. M. Dent, 1992.

Milne, Andrew. *A Description of the Parish of Melrose*. Kelso: James Palmer, 1743.

Minnis, Alastair J., Vincent J. Scattergood, and Jeremy J. Smith. *Oxford Guides to Chaucer: The Shorter Poems*. Oxford: Clarendon, 1995.

Mitchell, Linda E. *Portraits of Medieval Women: Family, Marriage, and Politics in England, 1225–1350*. Basingstoke: Palgrave, 2003.

Mitchell, Sabrina. *Medieval Manuscript Painting*. New York: Viking Press, 1964.

Moller, Herbert. "The Social Causation of the Courtly Love Complex." *Comparative Studies in Society and History* 1 (1958–59): 137–63.

Mooney, Linne R. "Chaucer's Interest in Astronomy at the Court of Richard II." In *Chaucer in Perspective: Middle English Essays in Honour of Norman Blake*, edited by Geoffrey Lester, 139–60. Sheffield: Sheffield Academic Press, 1999.

Moorman, Charles. *A Knyght There Was: The Evolution of the Knight in Literature*. Lexington: University of Kentucky Press, 1967.

Mortimer, Ian. *The Greatest Traitor. The Life of Sir Roger Mortimer, 1st Earl of March, Ruler of England, 1327–1330*. London: Jonathan Cape, 2003.

———. *The Perfect King. The Life of Edward III, Father of the English Nation*. London: Jonathan Cape, 2006.

Mumby, Frank Arthur. *The Youth of Henry VIII: A Narrative in Contemporary Letters*. Boston and New York: Houghton Mifflin Company, 1913.

Mutzenbecher, Almut, ed. *Corpus Christianorum*. Latina ser., 44A. Turnhout: Brepols, 1975.

Myers, A. R. *English Historical Documents*. vol. 4, *1327–1485*. London, 1969. Scholarly Digital Editions, Leicester, 2005; *Rotuli Parliamentorum* (6 vols., London, 1767–77), 3: 301.

Myers, A. R., ed. *English Historical Documents*. vol. 4, *1327–1485*. London, 1969.

Myers, A. R. *London in the Age of Chaucer*. Norman: University of Oklahoma Press, 1972.

Neufeld, Christine M. "Coconuts in Camelot: *Monty Python and the Holy Grail* in the Arthurian Literature Course." *Florilegium* 19 (2002): 127–48.

Neuss, Paula ed. *Magnificence*. Baltimore, MD: Johns Hopkins University Press, 1980.

Nicholas, Sir Harris. *History of the Battle of Agincourt*. London: Johnson and Co., 1832.

Nichols, J. *A Collection of All the Wills, Now Known to be Extant, of the Kings and Queens of England, Princes and Princes of Wales, and Every Branch of the Blood Royal*. London: Printed by John Nichols, sold by H. Peyene, 1780.

Nicholson, Peter. *Love and Ethics in Gower's Confessio Amantis*. Ann Arbor: University of Michigan Press, 2005.

———. "Poet and Scribe in the Manuscripts of Gower's *Confessio Amantis*." In *Manuscripts and Texts: Editorial Problems in Later Middle English Literature*, edited by Derek Pearsall, 130–142. Cambridge, UK: D. S. Brewer, 1987.

Norton-Smith, John. *Geoffrey Chaucer*. London: Routledge and Kegan Paul, 1974.

Ohlgren, Thomas H., ed. *Áns Saga Bogsveigis*. In *Medieval Outlaws: Ten Tales in Modern English*, translated by Shaun F. D. Hughes. Stroud, Glos.: Sutton, 1998.

Ormrod, W. Mark. "The Domestic Response to the Hundred Years War." In *Arms, Armies and Fortifications in the Hundred Years War*, edited by Anne Curry and Michael Hughes, 83–101. Woodbridge, Suff.: Boydell & Brewer, 1984.

———. "In Bed with Joan of Kent: The King's Mother and the Peasants' Revolt." In *Medieval Women: Texts and Contexts in Late Medieval Britain: Essays for Felicity Riddy*, edited by Jocelyn Wogan-Browne, Rosalynn Voaden, Arlyn Diamond, Ann Hutchinson, Carol M. Meale, and Lesley Johnson, 277–92. Turnhout: Brepols, 2000.

———. "Richard II's Sense of English History." In *The Reign of Richard II*, edited by Gwilym Dodd, 97–110. Stroud, Glos.: Sutton, 2000.

———. "The Sexualities of Edward II." In *The Reign of Edward II: New Perspectives*, edited by Gwilym Dodd and Anthony Musson, 22–47. Woodbridge, Suff.: Boydell & Brewer for York Medieval Press, 2008.

———. "The Trials of Alice Perres." *Speculum* 83 (2008): 366–96.

O'Sullivan, Carol. "A Time of Translation: Linguistic Difference and Cinematic Medievalism." In *Medieval Film*, edited by Anke Bernau and Bettina Bildhauer, 60–85. Manchester: Manchester University Press, 2009.

Packe, Michael. *King Edward III*. Edited by L. C. B. Seaman. London: Routledge & Kegan Paul, 1983.

Palmer, John. "The War Aims of the Protagonists and the Negotiations for Peace." In *The Hundred Years' War*, edited by Kenneth Fowler. London: Macmillan, 1971.

Palmer, John Joseph Norman. *England, France and Christendom 1377–1399*. London: Routledge and Kegan Paul, 1972.

Palmer, R. Barton, ed. *Guillaume de Machaut: Le Livre dou Voir Dit (The Book of the True Poem)*. Translated by Daniel Leech-Wilkinson. New York: Garland Publishing, 1998.

Pálsson, Hermann, and Paul Edwards, trans. *Göngu-Hrolfs Saga*. Edinburgh: Canongate, 1980.

Patourel, John Le. "L'occupation anglaise de Calais au XIVe siècle." *Revue du Nord* 33 (1951): 228–41 (228–30).

Patterson, Lee. "'What Man Artow?' Authorial Self-Definition in 'The Tale of Sir Thopas' and 'The Tale of Melibee.'" *Studies in the Age of Chaucer* 11 (1989): 117–75.

———. *Negotiating the Past: The Historical Understanding of Medieval Literature*. Madison: University of Wisconsin Press, 1987.

Payling, Simon J. "Social Mobility, Demographic Change, and Landed Society in Late Medieval England." *Economic History Review* 2nd ser. 45 (1992): 51–73.

Payne, Robert O. "Making His Own Myth: The Prologue to Chaucer's *Legend of Good Women*." *Chaucer Review* 9 (1975): 197–211.

Pearsall, Derek. "Chaucer's Tomb: The Politics of Reburial." *Medium Aevum* 64 (1995), 51–73.

———. *John Lydgate (1371–1449): A Bio-Bibliography*. English Literary Studies, Monograph Series No. 71. Victoria, BC: University of Victoria.

———. *Life of Geoffrey Chaucer: A Critical Biography*. Oxford: Blackwell, 1992.

———. "The Manuscripts and Illustrations of Gower's Works." In *A Companion to Gower*, edited by Siân Echard, 73–97. Cambridge, UK: D. S. Brewer, 2004.

———. "The Organisation of the Latin Apparatus in Gower's *Confessio Amantis*: The Scribes and Their Problems." In *The Medieval Book and a Modern Collector: Essays in Honour of Toshiyuki Takamiya*, edited by Takami Matsuda, Richard Linenthal, and John Scahill, 99–112. Cambridge, UK: D. S. Brewer, 2004.

Peck, Russell A. "Governance in Gower." In *A Companion to Gower*, edited by Siân Echard, 36–41. Cambridge, UK: D. S. Brewer, 2004.

———. *Kingship and Common Profit in Gower's Confessio Amantis*. Carbondale and Edwardsville, IL: Southern Illinois University Press, 1978.

Pegg, Mark. *The Corruption of Angels: The Great Inquisition of 1245–1246*. Princeton, NJ: Princeton University Press, 2001.

Philip Morgan. *War and Society in Medieval Cheshire, 1277–1403*. Chetham Society, 3rd ser., vol. 34. Manchester: Chetham Society, 1987.

Philips, Seymour. *Edward II*. New Haven CT: Yale University Press, 2010.

Platelle, Henri, and Denis Clauzel. *Histoire des Provinces Françaises du Nord, II: Des Principautés à l'Empire de Charles-Quint*. Dunkirk: Westhoek-Editions, 1989.

Post, John B. "Sir Thomas West and the Statute of Rapes, 1382." *Bulletin of the Institute of Historical Research* 53 (1980): 24–30.

Powell, J. Enoch, and Keith Wallis. *The House of Lords in the Middle Ages*. London: Weidenfeld & Nicolson, 1968.

Pratt, John H. *Chaucer and War*. Lanham, MD: University Press of America, 2000.

———. "Was Chaucer's Knight Really a Mercenary?" *Chaucer Review* 22, no. 1 (1987): 8–27.

Prestwich, Michael. *The Three Edwards: War and State in England, 1272–1377*. 2nd ed. London: Routledge, 2003.

Price, Reynolds, *Ardent Spirits: Leaving Home, Coming Back* (New York: Scribner's, 2003), 130.

Purdie, Rhiannon. "The Implications of Manuscript Layout in Chaucer's 'Tale of Sir Thopas'." *Forum* 41 (2005): 263–74.

Ransom, John Crowe. *Selected Poems*. Rev. ed. New York: Alfred A. Knopf, 1964.

Reeves, A. Compton. *Lancastrian Englishmen*. Washington, DC: University Press of America, 1981.

Register of Edward the Black Prince. 4 vols. London: His Majesty's Stationery Office, 1930–33.

Reinecke, George F. "F. N. Robinson (1872–1967)." In *Editing Chaucer: The Great Tradition*, edited by Paul G. Ruggiers, 231–51. Norman, OK: Pilgrim Books, 1984.

Riley, Henry Thomas, ed. *Annales Ricardi Secundi et Henrici Quarti*. In *Johannes de Trokelowe et Anon. Chronica et Annales*. Rolls Series, 1866.

———. *Memorials of London and London Life in the XIIIth, XIVth, and XVth Centuries A.D. 1276–1419*. London: HMSO, 1868.

Robbins, Rossell Hope. "The 'Arma Christi' Rolls." *Modern Language Review* 34 (1939): 415–21.

Robertson, Kellie. "Laboring in the God of Love's Garden: Chaucer's Prologue to *The Legend of Good Women*." *Studies in the Age of Chaucer* 24 (2002): 115–47.

Robinson, F. N., ed. *The Poetical Works of Chaucer*. Boston: Houghton Mifflin, 1933.

———. *The Works of Geoffrey Chaucer*. 2nd ed. Boston: Houghton Mifflin, 1957.

Robinson, William. "Henry VIII's Household in the Fifteen-Twenties: The Welsh Connection." *Historical Research* 68 (1995): 173–190.

———. "The Tudor Revolution in Welsh Government 1536–1543: Its Effects on Gentry Participation." *The English Historical Review* 406 (1988): 1–20.

Robinson, William Clarke. *History of English Literature*. vol. 2, *Wyclif, Chaucer, Earliest Drama, Renaissance*. London: George Bell & Sons, 1893.

Rodger, N. A. M. *The Safeguard of the Sea: A Naval History of Britain*. Vol. 1, *660–1649*. London: Harper Collins, 1997.

Root, Robert K. "Chaucer's Legend of Medea." *PMLA* 24 (1909): 124–53.

Rosenstone, Robert A., ed. *Revisioning History: Film and the Construction of a New Past.* Princeton, NJ: Princeton University Press, 1995.

Rosenthal, "Medieval Longevity: and The Secular Peerage, 1350–1500." *Population Studies* 27 (1973): 287–325.

Roskell, John S., Linda Clark, and Carole Rawcliffe. *The House of Commons, 1386–1421.* 4 vols. Stroud, Glos.: Alan Sutton, 1993.

Rossi, Vittorio, and Umberto Bosco, eds. *Petrarca: Le Familiari.* Florence: Sansoni, 1933–42.

Rothwell, Harry, *The Chronicle of Walter of Guisborough.* London: Camden Series, 1957.

———, ed. *English Historical Documents.* Vol. 3, *1189–1327.* London: Eyre and Spottiswoode, 1975.

Rymer, Thomas, ed. *Foedera, conventions, litterae, et cujuscunque generic acta publica.* 3 vols. London: Record Commission, 1816–30.

Salih, Sarah. "Cinematic Authenticity-Effects and Medieval Art: A Paradox." In *Medieval Film*, edited by Anke Bernau and Bettina Bildhauer, 20–39. Manchester: Manchester University Press, 2009.

Salisbury, Eve. "Promiscuous Contexts: Gower's Wife, Prostitution, and the *Confessio Amantis.*" In *John Gower: Manuscripts, Readers, Contexts*, edited by Malte Urban, 219–40. Turnhout: Brepols, 2009.

Samuels, Michael L., and Jeremy J. Smith. "The Language of Gower" In *The English of Chaucer and His Contemporaries*, edited by Jeremy J. Smith, 13–22. Aberdeen: University Press, 1988.

Saul, Nigel. "A Farewell to Arms? Criticism of Warfare in Late Fourteenth-Century England." *Fourteenth Century England* 2 (2002): 131–45.

———. *Knights and Esquires: The Gloucestershire Gentry in the Fourteenth Century.* Oxford: Oxford University Press: 1981.

———. *Richard II.* New Haven, CT: Yale University Press, 1997.

Scarisbrick, John. *Henry VIII.* Berkeley and Los Angeles: University of California Press, 1968.

Scase, Wendy. *Piers Plowman and the New Anticlericalism.* Cambridge, UK: Cambridge University Press, 1989.

Scattergood, Vincent J. "Chaucer and the French War: 'Sir Thopas' and 'Melibee'." In *Court and Poet*, edited by Glyn S. Burgess, 287–96. Liverpool: Cairns, 1981.

———. "Literary Culture at the Court of Richard II." In *English Court Culture in the Later Middle Ages*, edited by Vincent J. Scattergood and James W. Sherborne, 29–41. London: Duckworth, 1983.

———. *Politics and Poetry in the Fifteenth Century.* London: Blandford Press, 1971.

Schueler, Donald. "The Age of the Lover in Gower's *Confessio Amantis.*" *Medium Aevum* 36 (1967), 152–58.

Schmidt, Anna Johanna Erdman, ed. *Syr Tryamowre: A Metrical Romance.* Utrecht: Broekhoff, 1937.

Scudder, Bernard, trans. "Egil's Saga." In *The Sagas of the Icelanders: A Selection.* With a preface by Jane Smiley and an introduction by Robert Kellogg, 157–158. New York: Penguin, 2000.

Searle, Eleanor, and Robert Burghart. "The Defense of England and the Peasants' Revolt." *Viator* 3 (1972): 365–88.

Sears, Elizabeth. *The Ages of Man: Medieval Interpretations of the Life Cycle.* Princeton, NJ: Princeton University Press, 1986.

Seneca, Lucius Annaeus. *Ad Lucilium Epistulae Morales.* Edited by Richard M. Gummere. 3 vols. Cambridge, MA: Harvard University Press, 1967–1972.

———. *Moral Essays.* Edited by William Basore. 3 vols. Cambridge, MA: Harvard University Press, 1958.

Seymour, M. C. *A Catalogue of Chaucer Manuscripts.* Vol. 1, *Works before "The Canterbury Tales."* Aldershot: Scolar Press, 1995.

Sharpe, Kevin. *Selling the Tudor Monarchy: Authority and Image in Sixteenth-Century England.* New Haven and London: Yale University Press, 2009.

Sharpe, Reginald, R., ed. *Calendar of Letter Books of the City of London.* 11 vols. London: Corporation of the City of London, 1899–1912.

———. *Calendar of Wills Proved and Enrolled in the Court of Husting, London.* 2 vols. London: Corporation of the City of London, 1889–90.

Shears, F. S. *Froissart: Chronicler and Poet.* London: Routledge, 1930.

Sheehan, Michael M., ed. *Aging and the Aged in Medieval Europe.* Toronto: Pontifical Institute of Mediaeval Studies, 1990.

Sherborne, James. "The English Navy: Shipping and Manpower, 1369–1389." In *War, Politics and Culture in Fourteenth-Century England*, edited by Anthony Tuck, 29–39. London: Hambledon Press, 1994.

Shook, Laurence K. "*The House of Fame.*" In *Companion to Chaucer Studies*, edited by Beryl Rowland, 341–54. Oxford: Oxford University Press, 1968.

Sir Ferumbras, ed. Sidney J. Herrtage, EETS, e.s., 34. London: Trübner, 1879. 137–38.

Skeat, Walter W. *The Chaucer Canon.* Oxford: Clarendon, 1900.

———. *Complete Works of Geoffrey Chaucer.* 6 vols. Oxford: Clarendon, 1894.

———, ed. *Pierce the Ploughmans Crede.* EETS, o.s. 30 (1867).

Skelton, John. *Poems.* Edited by Robert S. Kinsman. Oxford: Clarendon Press, 1969.

Skemer, Don C. *Binding Words: Textual Amulets in the Middle Ages.* University Park: Pennsylvania State Press, 1986.

Smith, Jeremy J. "Spelling and Tradition in Fifteenth-Century Copies of Gower's *Confessio Amantis*," In *The English of Chaucer and His Contemporaries*, edited by Michael L. Samuels and Jeremy J. Smith. 96–113. Aberdeen: University Press, 1988.

Smithers, G. V., ed. *Kyng Alisaunder.* 2 vols. EETS, e.s., 227 and 237. London: Oxford University Press, 1952–57.

Spriggs, Gareth M. "Unnoticed Bodleian Manuscripts, Illuminated by Herman Scheerre and His School." *Bodleian Library Record* 7 (1962–67): 193–203.

Staley, Lynn. "Gower, Richard II, and Henry of Derby, and the Business of Making Culture." *Speculum* 75:1 (2000): 68–96.

Standhope, Earl Philip Henry. *Notes of Conversations with the Duke of Wellington, 1831–1851.* New York: Longmans, Green, 1888.

Stearns, Peter N., ed. *Old Age in Preindustrial Society.* New York: Holmes and Meier, 1982.

Stone, Lawrence. *Sculpture in Britain in the Middle Ages.* Harmondsworth: Penguin, 1955.

Storey, R. L. "Liveries and Commissions of the Peace, 1388–90" In *The Reign of Richard II: Essays in Honour of May Mckisăck*, edited by F. R. H. Du Boulay and Caroline M. Barron, 131–52. London: Athlone Press, 1971.

Stow, George B, ed. *Historia Vitae et Regni Ricardi Secundi.* Philadelphia: University of Pennsylvania Press, 1977.

———. "Richard II in the *Continuatio Eulogii*: Yet Another Alleged Historical Incident?" In *Fourteenth Century England*, 5, edited by Nigel Saul, 116–29. Woodbridge, Suff.: Boydell & Brewer, 2008.

Stow, John. *Annales, or, A General Chronicle of England.* London: A.M. for R. Meigher, 1631.

Strayer Joseph R., ed. *Dictionary of the Middle Ages.* 12 vols. New York: Scribner's, 1982–89.

Strohm, Paul. *England's Empty Throne: Usurpation and the Language of Legitimation, 1399–1422*. New Haven, CT: Yale University Press, 1998.

———. *Huchon's Arrow: The Social Imagination of Fourteenth-Century Texts*, 145–60. Princeton, NJ: Princeton University Press, 1992.

Strong, Caroline. "Sir Thopas and Sir Guy." *Modern Language Notes* 23 (1908): 73–77 and 102–06.

Sumption, Jonathan. *The Hundred Years War*. Vol. 3, *Divided Houses*. London: Faber and Faber, 2009.

Swanson, Robert. *Indulgences in Late Medieval England: Passports to Paradise?* Cambridge, UK: Cambridge University Press, 2007.

Symons, Dana M. *Chaucerian Dream Visions and Complaints*. Kalamazoo, MI: TEAMS Medieval Institute Publications, 2004.

———. "Comic Pleasures: Chaucer and Popular Romance." In *Medieval English Comedy*, edited by Sandra M. Hordis and Paul Hardwick, 83–109. Turnhout: Brepols, 2007.

Szittya, Penn R. *The Antifraternal Tradition in Medieval Literature*. Princeton, NJ: Princeton University Press, 1986.

Tangherlini, Timothy R. "'How Do You Know She's a Witch?': Witches, Cunning Folk, and Competition in Denmark." *Western Folklore* 59, no. 3/4 (Summer–Autumn 2000): 279–303.

Tatlock, John S. P. *A Concordance to the Complete Works of Geoffrey Chaucer and to the Romaunt of the Rose*. Washington, DC: Carnegie Institution of Washington, 1927.

———. *The Development and Chronology of Chaucer's Works*. 2nd ser., issue 37. London: Chaucer Society, 1907.

———. *The Mind and Art of Chaucer*. Syracuse, NY: Syracuse University Press, 1950.

Taylor, Andrew. "Bodleian MS Ashmole 48 and the Ballad Press." *English Manuscript Studies, 1100–1700* 14 (2008): 219–43.

Taylor, John, Wendy Childs, and L. Watkiss, eds. *The St Albans Chronicle: the Chronica Maiora of Thomas Walsingham*. Vol. 1, *1376–1394*. Oxford: Clarendon Press, 2003.

Theilmann, John. "Political Canonization and Political Symbolism in Medieval England." *Journal of British Studies* 29 (1990): 241–66.

Thomas, Keith. *Religion and the Decline of Magic*. London: Weidenfeld and Nicolson, 1971.

Thompson, E. M., ed. *Chronicon Angliae*. London: Rolls Series, 1874.

Thompson, Raymond H. "The Ironic Tradition in Arthurian Films Since 1960." In *Cinema Arthuriana*, rev. ed., edited by Kevin J. Harty, 110–17. Jefferson, NC: McFarland, 2002.

Thompson, Stith. *Motif-index of Folk-Literature: A Classification of Narrative Elements in Folktales, Ballads, Myths, Fables, Mediaeval Romances, Exempla, Fabliaux, Jest-books, and Local Legends*. 6 vols. Bloomington: Indiana University Press, 1955–58.

Tschann, Judith. "The Layout of 'Sir Thopas' in the Ellesmere, Hengwrt, Cambridge Dd.4.24, and Cambridge Gg.4.27 Manuscripts." *Chaucer Review* 20 (1985): 1–13.

Tuck, Anthony. "Nobles, Commons and the Great Revolt of 1381." In *The English Rising of 1381*, edited by R. H. Hilton and T. H. Aston, 194–212. Cambridge, UK: Past and Present Society, 1984.

———. *Richard II and the English Nobility*. London: Edward Arnold, 1973.

Underhill, Frances A. *For Her Good Estate: The Life of Elizabeth de Burgh*. New York: St Martin's Press, 1999.

Ursins, Jean Juvenal des. "Histoire de Charles VI." In *Nouvelle collection de memoires relatives à l'histoire de France*, edited by Joseph François Michaud and Jean Joseph François Poujoula, 1st ser. 2., 335–569. Paris: Adolphe Everat, 1857.

Vasari, Giorgio. *The Lives of the Painters, Sculptor and Architects.* Edited by William Gaunt and translated by A. B. Hinds. 4 vols. New York: Dutton, 1963.

Wallace, David. "Absent City." In *Chaucerian Polity: Absolutist Lineages and Associational Forms in England and Italy,* 156–181. Stanford, CA: Stanford University Press, 1997.

———. *Chaucerian Polity: Absolutist Lineages and Associational Forms in England and Italy.* Stanford, CA: Stanford University Press, 1997.

———. "'If That Thou Live': Legends and Lives of Good Women," In *Chaucerian Polity:Absolutist Lineages and Associational Forms in England and Italy,* 156–181. Stanford, CA: Stanford University Press, 1997.

———. *Premodern Places: Calais to Surinam, Chaucer to Aphra Behn.* Oxford: Blackwell, 2004.

Walsingham, Thomas. *The St. Albans Chronicle.* Vol. 1, *1376–1394.* Edited by John Taylor, Wendy R. Childs, and Leslie Watkiss. Oxford: Clarendon Press, 2003.

Warner, Lawrence. *The Lost History of Piers Plowman: The Earliest Transmission of Langland's Work.* Philadelphia: University of Pennsylvania Press, 2011.

Warren, Florence, and Beatrice White, eds. *The Dance of Death.* EETS, o.s. 181 (1931).

Warren, Michelle. *History on the Edge: Excalibur and the Borders of Britain.* Minneapolis: University of Minnesota Press, 2000.

Waterhouse, Ruth. "'Sweete Wordes' of Nonsense: The Deconstruction of the Moral 'Melibee'." *Chaucer Review* 23 (1989): 53–63.

Watt, D. E. R., ed. *Scotichronicon by Walter Bower in Latin and English.* 9 vols. Aberdeen: Aberdeen University Press, 1987–1998.

Webster, Bruce. "The County Community of Kent in the Reign of Richard II." *Archaeologia Cantiana* 100 (1984): 219–20.

Wentersdorf, K. P. "The Clandestine Marriages of the Fair Maid of Kent." *Journal of Medieval History* 5 (1979): 203–31.

White, Stephen D. "The Politics of Anger." In *Anger's Past: The Social Uses of an Emotion in the Middle Ages,* edited by Barbara H. Rosenwein, 127–52. Ithaca, NY: Cornell University Press, 1998.

Whiteford, Peter, ed. *The Myracles of Oure Lady.* Wynkyn de Worde's edition. Heidelberg: Carl Winter, 1990.

Whiting, Ella Keats. *The Poems of John Audelay.* EETS, o.s 184, 1931 for 1930.

Whittingham, Selby. "The Chronology of the Portraits of Richard II." *Burlington Magazine* 113 (1971): 12–21.

Wickert, Maria. *Studien zu Gower.* Cologne: University Press of Cologne, 1953.

———. *Studies in John Gower.* Translated by Robert J. Meindl. Washington, DC: University Press of America, 1981.

Williams, Arnold. "Chaucer and the Friars." *Speculum* 28 (1953): 499–513.

Williams, Deanne. "The Dream Visions." In *The Yale Companion to Chaucer,* edited by Seth Lerer, 147–78. New Haven, CT: Yale University Press, 2006.

Willson, Thomas B. *History of the Church and State in Norway from the Tenth to Sixteenth Centuries.* Westminster: Archibald Constable, 1903.

Wood, Charles T. *Joan of Arc and Richard III. Sex, Saints, and Government in the Middle Ages.* Oxford: Oxford University Press, 1988.

Wright, Nicholas. *Knights and Peasants: The Hundred Years War in the French Countryside.* Woodbridge, Suff.: Boydell & Brewer, 1998.

Wright, Sylvia. "The Author Portraits in the Bedford Psalter-Hours: Gower, Chaucer and Hoccleve." *British Library Journal* 18 (1992): 190–201.

Wrottesley, George. "Crécy and Calais, AD 1346–1347, from the Rolls in the Public Record Office." *Collections for a History of Staffordshire.* new ser. 18. 1896.

Yeager, Isabella Neale. "Did Gower Love His Wife? And What Does It Have to Do with the Poetry?" *Poetica* (Japan) 73 (2010): 67–86.

Yeager, Robert F. "Chaucer's 'To His Purse': Begging, or Begging Off?" *Viator* 36 (2005): 373–414.

———. "Did Gower Write *Cento*?" In *John Gower: Recent Readings*, edited by Robert F. Yeager, 113–32. Kalamazoo, MI: Medieval Institute Press, 1988.

———. "Gower's Lancastrian Affinity: The Iberian Connection." *Viator* 35 (2004): 483–515.

———. *Who Murdered Chaucer? A Medieval Mystery* with Terry Jones, Terry Dolan, Alan Fletcher and Juliette Dor. London: Methuen, 2003.